GUIDE TO SEA FISHES OF AUSTRALIA

RUDIE H. KUITER

NEW
HOLLAND

Published in Australia by
New Holland Publishers (Australia) Pty Ltd
Sydney • Auckland • London • Cape Town

14 Aquatic Drive Frenchs Forest NSW 2086 Australia
218 Lake Road Northcote Auckland New Zealand
24 Nutford Place London W1H 6DQ United Kingdom
80 McKenzie Street Cape Town 8001 South Africa

First published in 1996
Reprinted with amendments in 1997 and 1999
Reprinted in 2000 (twice) by New Holland Publishers (Australia) Pty Ltd

National Library of Australia Cataloguing-in-Publication Data:

Kuiter, R. H.
Guide to sea fishes of Australia.

Reprinted with amendments.
Includes index.
ISBN 1 86436 091 7

1. Marine fishes—Australia—Identification—Handbooks, manuals, etc.
2. Marine fishes—Australia—Classification—Handbooks, manuals, etc. I. Title.

597.0994

Publishing General Manager: Jane Hazell
Publisher: Averill Chase
Editors: Barbara McKenzie and Robyn Flemming
Editorial Assistant: Jacquie Brown
Indexer: Alan Walker
Typesetting: Asset Typesetting Pty Ltd
Cover Design: Arne Falkenmire
Reproduction: cmyk pre-press Cape Town
Printed and bound by: Kyodo Printing Co (S'pore) Pte Ltd

CONTENTS

ACKNOWLEDGMENTS

Writing on a specialised subject and taking the large number of photographs required for a book such as this would not have been possible without the guidance and contributions of many friends, colleagues and my family who generously shared their knowledge and time.

In the early 1970s the staff at the Australian Museum were very helpful, giving me access to scientific works and introducing me to scientists from various institutions, such as the CSIRO and the departments of fisheries of New South Wales, Victoria, South Australia and Tasmania. I would like to thank the numerous taxonomists who have assisted me over the years and I am very grateful for the help and encouragement I have received from many others, including scientists overseas.

I would also like to thank my many dive buddies, and to apologise to those I kept waiting while trying to photograph something. Listing all the people who have helped me would fill many pages, but I would especially like to mention Lew Reynolds, who has taken me out on his boat to many great places; John Meredith, my regular Sydney buddy; Jerry Allen and Roger Steene, the tropical diving pair; Helmut Debelius, who will dive anywhere there are colourful fishes; and my Japanese friend, Toshi Kozawa, who provided me with the best underwater camera housing by far. Helen Larson, as always, helped out with the little gobies and Dr Senou from Japan gave general comments on many fish families. Thanks to Martin Gomon for his technical support and to the many other scientists who have contributed to the identification of Australian fishes.

Of course, special thanks to my best buddies of all: my wife Alison, and my sons Steven and Hendrik, for taking great interest in my work and finding many goodies — keep it up, guys.

HOW TO USE THIS GUIDE

This book describes the features that distinguish species from other similar ones. It does not attempt to fully describe each species. The 1000 fish species covered in this guide are listed in the widely accepted scientific order as explained on pages 3–4. A complete list of the fish families (with common and scientific names), and their main features are found on pages vi–xvii. The external features of fishes are annotated on pages 4–5.

The main section of this book consists of the species account (pages 7–423). On these pages each species' entry is listed under family order. The family write-up in this section often deals with the relationship to other closely related families and provides some general information about behaviour, occurrence or habitat. Individual species may deviate from the norm in some areas.

Each species entry, as with the family write-up, provides general information about behaviour and habitat. Each entry is accompanied by a distribution map on the left. The coastal areas shaded in blue broadly indicate where each species can be found. For identification purposes, each species is also accompanied by one or more photographs. With few exceptions, the fishes were photographed in their natural habitat. Colour variations between sexes or in juveniles are often shown by additional photographs or are referred to in the text, and very similar or sibling species are either shown or described. In many cases a fish has a sibling species distributed on the east and/or west coasts, often showing only minor differences. Rather than using an extra photograph I have described the differences in the text.

Length measurements

Each entry usually finishes with a length measurement of the fish. The method used to measure the length of a fish needs to be explained because measurements quoted in the literature vary according to the method used. In this book the measurement used is the measurement for the total length: from the tip of the snout to the end of the caudal fin or tail, without distorting the body by stretching it. It also includes all the rigid or semi-rigid parts of fins, thus not extended filamentous rays.

For rays, the width of the disc is given instead of length, because tail-length is highly variable and the tail is often damaged. Standard length is commonly used in scientific papers and excludes the caudal fin. Fork length, where the length is measured to the centre of the caudal fin, is often used for sport fish. Maximum size given in this guide relates to Australian populations only. Some species reach a much greater size in other parts of the world — for example, *Pseudanthias squamipinnis* in Australia reaches only 10 centimetres in length, whereas in the cooler Japanese waters it reaches almost double this length. In some cases, such lengths are given in this book and comments made on overseas populations, especially when such lengths are used in other Australian works. If a particular species grows to a common adult size but occasionally reaches an unusually large size, both a maximum length and a common (or usual) length are given.

FISH FAMILIES

Fish families are the framework for genera and species, and are part of the higher classification for fishes (for further information on classification please see page 3). Families are listed in scientific order, an internationally accepted order that has been devised by scientists and taxonomists to logically group families which have similar features or are closely related to each other in some way. With the discovery of new species, this scientific order is continually under review and thus constantly changing.

The scientific order begins with sharks and rays. These are considered the most primitive families as they have remained virtually unchanged from their original ancestors. The order ends with the most highly evolved, the Pufferfishes and Porcupine fish families. Below is a list of the fish families found in this book, followed by a brief description of their main features.

Horn Sharks — HETERODONTIDAE (page 8)
Blunt head with a crest above each eye. Identically shaped dorsal fins (second fin is slightly smaller than first), each headed by a usually venomous spine. Small mouth positioned low and anteriorly.

Collared Catsharks — PARASCYLLIIDAE (page 8)
Slender shaped with small head, distinct nasal barbels with a groove joining nostrils to mouth and mouth not reaching to below eyes. Ventral, dorsal and anal fins alternate in position along body.

Catsharks — SCYLIORHINIDAE (page 10)
Snout pointed, sometimes very elongate. Mouth positioned underneath head, below eyes. First dorsal fin positioned just behind ventral fin and second dorsal fin just behind anal fin. In some species, all fins placed over posterior half of body.

Blindsharks — BRACHAELURIDAE (page 10)
Long nasal barbels. Both dorsal fins positioned between origins of ventral and anal fins. Usually black or dark brown coloured.

Zebra Sharks — STEGOSTOMATIDAE (page 12)
Small nasal barbels, very long tail and distinct ridges along upper sides. Juveniles have a distinct zebra-like black and white banding, becoming spotted in adults.

Wobbegongs — ORECTOLOBIDAE (page 12)
Long barbels on snout. Head features numerous dermal flaps. Flattened body shape and marbled dorsal patterns results in them sometimes being called carpetsharks.

Angelsharks — SQUATINIDAE (page 12)
Flattened body, laterally expanded fins, and lacks anal fin. Angelsharks superficially resemble rays except that fins are not attached to head as with rays.

Whaler Sharks — CARCHARHINIDAE (page 14)
Streamlined body, thickest below first dorsal fin.

Shovelnose Rays — RHINOBATIDAE (page 16)

Thick and elongated body, head greatly depressed with pectoral fins united to head and not greatly expanded. Snout varies from rounded to pointed, sometimes elongated.

Sharkfin Guitarfishes — RHYNCHOBATIDAE (page 16)

Front part similar to those of shovelnose rays (they were only recently separated from that family). Posterior part of the body more shark-like.

Skates — RAJIDAE (page 18)

Body and head greatly flattened, extending laterally with pectoral fins forming a large disk. Eyes raised dorsally. Small, ventrally positioned mouth with nostrils in front of its corners. Five pairs of gill slits.

Electric Rays — TORPEDINIDAE (page 18)

Round, soft and flabby disc, thick at body. Head often blunt with pair of large kidney-shaped electric organs on sides of head. Tail variously sized with one or two dorsal fins. Colour varies from sandy grey and yellow to almost black.

Stingarees — UROLOPHIDAE (page 20)

Disc greatly flattened and usually rounded, with width similar to length. Small caudal fin. Tail is not whip-like as in many other similar rays and carries one or two venomous spines. Eyes raised to view laterally, with large spiracles just behind.

Stingrays — DASYATIDIDAE (page 22)

Tail usually long and whip-like, often longer than disc. The disc is at least as long as it is wide. Head only slightly raised with eyes viewing laterally.

Eagle Rays — MYLIOBATIDIDAE (page 24)

Disc very angular with large snout protruding from it. Head raised with eyes on sides, mouth in pavement-like arrangements with strong crushing teeth, followed by five pairs of gill slits. Slender whip-like tail, at least twice as long as disc. Prominent dorsal fin followed by single spine.

Elephant Fishes — CALLORHINCHIDAE (page 24)

Shark-like body and fins, but the head is peculiar with snout produced in a trunk-like fleshy proboscis. Single pair of gill slits, lacking spiracle.

Snake Eels & Worm Eels — OPHICHTHIDAE (page 26)

Long tubular bodies. Head and tail are usually sharply pointed.

Moray Eels — MURAENIDAE (page 28)

Body muscular, with tough thick skin, and posteriorly compressed. Single median fin, originating anteriorly above small gill opening and continuing around the tail to the anus. Mouth often large with long jaws.

Herrings — CLUPEIDAE (page 32)

Silvery fishes with weakly attached scales. A single, centrally placed dorsal fin, large distensible jaws with tiny teeth and numerous elongated gill rakers. Fins are short-based and entirely soft-rayed.

Anchovies — ENGRAULIDAE (page 34)

Elongate, silvery and blunt protruding snout.Weakly attached scales and entirely soft-rayed fins. Australian species has a blue coloured snout.

Eeltail Catfishes — PLOTOSIDAE (page 34)

Australian species have five pairs of barbels around the mouth and possess prominent venomous spines heading the dorsal and pectoral fins.

Sergeant Bakers — AULOPIDAE (page 36)

Salmon-like with large head and jaws with several rows of fine teeth. Eyes positioned dorsally above end of mouth. Fins entirely soft rayed.

Lizardfishes — SYNODONTIDAE (page 36)

Almost torpedo-shaped bodies, some tapering to caudal fin, covered with moderately-sized cycloid scales. Exceptionally large mouth and eyes dorso-laterally placed, centrally above mouth. Soft-rayed and short-based fins, and a tiny adipose fin placed above the anal fin. Large ventral fins have nine rays.

Sauries — HARPADONTIDAE (page 38)

Dull-coloured fish. Similar to lizardfishes but have numerous rows of needle-like, close-set teeth in jaws and ventral fin with a feeble spine and eight rays.

Handfishes — BRACHIONICHTHYIDAE (page 40)

Hand-like paired fins with pectoral fins extended like short arms with strange leaf-like appendage at elbow. Have luring apparatus above mouth.

Anglerfishes — ANTENNARIIDAE (page 40)

Have a greatly enlarged third dorsal spine and usually a modified first dorsal spine serving as a luring apparatus to attract prey.

Frogfishes — BATRACHOIDIDAE (page 46)

Have tough smooth skin, and a large round head with broad mouth. Jaws are set with bands of small sharp teeth, and body and head have fleshy papillae along the mouth and above the eyes.

Clingfishes — GOBIESOCIDAE (page 46)

Small to tiny fishes. The Australian genus *Alabes*, shore eels, differs considerably from the rest, with eel-like body and fins except the caudal fin degenerated or absent. Most clingfishes have united ventral fins forming a strong sucker disc.

Beardies — MORIDAE (page 50)
Features include a large head, elongated body with tiny cycloid scales, chin barbel, and ventral fins with extended rays as feelers.

Lings — OPHIDIIDAE (page 52)
Body slimy and long, eel-like, tapering posteriorly. Ventral fins reduced to feeler-like filaments, usually placed forward below head, in some situated below eye. Often barbels present around mouth.

Garfishes — HEMIRAMPHIDAE (page 52)
Shiny silvery, greenish above, with greatly extended beak-like lower jaw. Ventral fins abdominal, placed far back. Scales large and easily removed.

Long Toms — BELONIDAE (page 54)
Jaws extremely elongate with numerous needle-like teeth which are short in juveniles and lengthen with age.

Hardyheads — ATHERINIDAE (page 54)
Found in large schools. Slender body featuring a broad silvery lateral band. Large eyes, short-based fins with spaced dorsal fins, and ventral fins situated below first dorsal fin. Moderate-sized cycloid scales.

Surf Sardines — ISONIDAE (page 56)
Swim in small to large schools. Features a greatly compressed body and a deep keel-like convex abdomen. Silvery and highly reflective.

Pineapplefishes — MONOCENTRIDIDAE (page 56)
Prominent light organ on sides of the lower jaw used at night to locate prey.

Roughies — TRACHICHTHYIDAE (page 58)
Have a series of scutes (scales with a keel-like ridge) placed ventrally along the abdomen. Body is compressed and often deep. Some produce loud clicking or buzzing sounds. Small to medium-sized.

Squirrelfishes & Soldierfishes — HOLOCENTRIDAE (page 60)
Squirrelfishes have a prominent spine (venomous in some) on lower corner of gill cover. Soldierfishes have a small gill cover spine and blunter head.

Nannygais & Red Snapper — BERYCIDAE (page 64)
Predominantly red with moderately large ctenoid scales. Feature a large, deeply forked caudal fin and an anal fin usually with 4 spines. Most school in great numbers.

Dories — ZEIDAE (page 66)
Feature large oblique mouth with jaws that expand into a long suction tube used to target small fishes.

Flutemouths — FISTULARIIDAE (page 66)

Long tubular bodies with extremely long snout, but rather small mouth at end. Middle pair of rays in caudal fin have extremely long filaments with large connecting membrane in juveniles. Soft-rayed fins.

Trumpetfishes — AULOSTOMIDAE (page 68)

Dorsal fin has small separate spines, each followed by a triangular membrane, the soft part of which is large and situated near the tail. Have a similar anal fin opposite.

Shrimpfishes — CENTRISCIDAE (page 68)

Usually found in large synchronised schools. Species similar, but genera distinguished by either a rigid or hinged large dorsal spine.

Seamoths — PEGASIDAE (page 68)

Body encased in rigid plates and tail encircled with bony rings. Ventral fins reduced to pairs of slender structures used for crawling on substrate and pectoral fin wing-like. Snout has a produced rostrum.

Ghostpipefishes — SOLENOSTOMIDAE (page 70)

Head is pipefish-like with long tubular mouth. Body short and compressed, protected by bony plates. Two separate dorsal fins and large caudal, pectoral and ventral fins. Anal fin is opposite second dorsal fin.

Seahorses, Seadragons & Pipefishes — SYNGNATHIDAE (page 72)

Body protected by bony plates, arranged in rings. Long tubular snout with toothless small oblique mouth at end. No ventral fins and anal and caudal fins small or lacking.

Scorpionfishes — SCORPAENIDAE (page 82)

Most are extremely well camouflaged and have spiny ridges on head.

Prowfishes — PATAECIDAE (page 92)

Compressed with a long-based single dorsal fin which originates over front of head. Ventral fins absent and large pectoral fins placed low. Tough skin instead of scales.

Red Velvetfishes — GNATHANACANTHIDAE (page 94)

Well-developed ventral fins with membrane attached to abdomen. High dorsal fin with deep notch. Skin covered with fleshy projections, giving a velvety feel in adults.

Flying Gurnards — DACTYLOPTERIDAE (page 94)

Exceptionally large pectoral fins which reach the caudal fin and, when spread out, are almost circular in shape. Fins used for display or startling possible predators.

Gurnards — TRIGLIDAE (page 94)

Armoured head with bony plates. Pectoral fins usually very large. Rounded, lower rays free and thickened. Inside of fins often have yellow and iridescent blue markings.

Flatheads — PLATYCEPHALIDAE (page 98)

Head greatly depressed, bearing bony ridges and frequently armed with large pungent spines. Spines in fins strong and slender, except first in dorsal fin which is typically tiny, detached and partly embedded.

Rockcods, Groupers & Basslets — SERRANIDAE (page 100)

Most have tiny scales, indistinct lateral line, 24 vertebrae and strongly rounded to emarginate caudal fins.

Barramundi — CENTROPOMIDAE (page 124)

Head has a concave dorsal-profile and large mouth reaching to below eye. The dorsal fin is deeply notched and the anal fin is short-based. Features large scales and a distinct lateral-line.

Dottybacks — PSEUDOCHROMIDAE (page 124)

Body elongated, head long and eyes large with elongated pupil. Colour is diagnostic; in a few species it is highly variable and in some it differs between the sexes.

Spiny Basslets — ACANTHOCLINIDAE (page 128)

Closely related to Pseudochromidae, possessing more dorsal and anal fin spines, but ventral fins have only one or two rays.

Longfins — PLESIOPIDAE (page 128)

The large temperate species are known as blue devils, featuring iridescent blue spots or lines and large fins. The tropical species are small.

Pearlperches — GLAUCOSOMATIDAE (page 132)

Deep-bodied, and silvery coloured as adults, often with lines as juveniles. The western species has long filaments trailing from corners of median fins.

Trumpeters & Grunters — TERAPONTIDAE (page 132)

Feature small ctenoid scales, extended into sheaths along dorsal and anal-fin bases, a prominent spine on opercle, and strong spines in fins. Generally marked with longitudinal stripes or spots.

Bigeyes — PRIACANTHIDAE (page 136)

Very large eyes and mouth. Body somewhat elongated and compressed. Ventral fins are connected to the belly by a membrane. Usually reddish brown; blotched or banded patterns can change quickly.

Cardinalfishes — APOGONIDAE (page 136)

Separate angular dorsal fins, distinctive body shape and large mouth and eyes. There are two spines in the anal fin compared to three with most related families. Many form large schools around coral during the day.

Longfin Pikes — DINOLESTIDAE (page 150)
Features an elongate shape with body almost cylindrical and head pointed. Has a large number of soft rays in dorsal and anal fins, and only one spine in the anal fin.

Blanquillos & Tilefishes — MALACANTHIDAE (page 152)
Slender, flexible body with tiny scales. Small head with prominent spine at end of opercle. Long-based single dorsal and anal fins. Most species are distinctly coloured.

Tailors — POMATOMIDAE (page 152)
Body streamlined with smooth scales and large tail. Jaws with small compressed sharp teeth in single rows.

Remoras — ECHENEIDIDAE (page 154)
Features an unusual sucker disc on top of head, which is a modified dorsal fin.

Jacks & Trevallies — CARANGIDAE (page 154)
Compressed body oblong to elongate. Covered with small to tiny, often embedded smooth scales. Usually with enlarged spiny scutes along posterior part of lateral line.

Ponyfishes — LEIOGNATHIDAE (page 164)
Usually greatly compressed, deep-bodied with slimy skin. Shiny silvery sides, usually darker on back with mottled or banded patterns. Scales are tiny and embedded. Mouth very protractile. A series of small spines along the dorsal and anal-fin bases.

Silver Bellies — GERREIDAE (page 166)
Very similar in looks and behaviour to ponyfishes, but distinctly scaled. Usually shiny silver on sides, and dorsal fin elevated anteriorly, except in genus.

Whiptails & Spinecheeks — NEMIPTERIDAE (page 168)
Identification is best by colour. Spinecheeks have a prominent spine below the eye. Whiptails are more slender and adults often feature long filaments on caudal fin tips.

Emperors — LETHRINIDAE (page 172)
Distinctly scaled. Fins generally large with a strong spinous section. Eyes also large.

Snapper & Breams — SPARIDAE (page 176)
Oval-shaped and shiny silvery coloured. Has moderately large and slightly ctenoid scales. Mouth is positioned low and jaws have conical teeth and anterior canines.

Sweetlips — HAEMULIDAE (page 178)
Most go through elaborate colour changes during growth. Small juveniles are usually boldly spotted or striped. Adults are often plain with small spots or numerous thin lines. Juveniles have large tails.

Coral Snappers — LUTJANIDAE (page 182)

Perch-like with an elongated scaly body and a single slightly notched dorsal fin with strong spinous section. Identification is usually easy with diagnostic colour patterns. Juveniles may differ from adults.

Fusiliers — CAESIONIDAE (page 186)

Oval-elongated, compressed and streamlined. Have a small mouth and large forked tail.

Jewfishes — SCIAENIDAE (page 188)

Moderately elongate, somewhat compressed, and small, ctenoid scales. Dorsal fin is deeply notched with long-based soft section and anal-fin base is very short.

Goatfishes — MULLIDAE (page 190)

Elongate, slightly compressed with moderately large, finely-ctenoid scales. Have well-separated dorsal fins and a pair of strong barbels on chin. Caudal fin is deeply forked.

Bullseyes — PEMPHERIDIDAE (page 194)

Distinctly rounded head and dorsally straight body profile. Posterior tip of dorsal fin is above anterior tip of anal fin. Have large eyes positioned above oblique mouth and a very short snout.

Silver Batfishes — MONODACTYLIDAE (page 198)

Silvery fishes with small deciduous scales. Deep-bodied, compressed, with long-based dorsal and anal fins. Tips are slightly elevated. Fin spines are reduced and leading soft rays are longest.

Sweeps — SCORPIDIDAE (page 200)

Highly compressed, some elongating slightly as adults. Shiny silvery blue coloured with reduced fin spines. Dorsal soft rays are elevated anteriorly with a similarly shaped anal fin opposite.

Drummers — KYPHOSIDAE (page 200)

Closely related to the sweeps but have heavier, more elongate bodies and incisor-like teeth in a single row in each jaw.

Blackfishes — GIRELLIDAE (page 202)

Body is oval-shaped, slightly compressed and covered with small adherent ctenoid scales. Have a long-based spinous dorsal fin which originates anteriorly. Caudal fin is truncate to slightly concave.

Stripeys & Mado — MICROCANTHIDAE (page 204)

Have oblong shaped bodies, with strong spines in dorsal, anal and ventral fins. Teeth are close-set and brush-like.

Butterflyfishes — CHAETODONTIDAE (page 206)

Very deep compressed body and snout is usually pointed to very elongated. Teeth are typically brush-like, slender and close-set with recurving tips. Fin spines are large and solid. Most species very colourful.

Angelfishes — POMACANTHIDAE (page 226)

Have a prominent spine on lower corner of operculum. Slightly more elongate than butterflyfishes with moderately deep and compressed bodies. Usually ornamented with bright colours.

Batfishes — EPHIPPIDAE (page 236)

Bodies are disc-shaped. Juveniles have extremely tall fins above and below, which reduce in height progressively with age. Shapes of juveniles are rather unfish-like and often mimic various floating leaves.

Boarfishes — PENTACEROTIDAE (page 238)

Head is large and encased with rough, striated bony plates. Strong and large fin spine in most. Body deep, elongate to round, very compressed and covered with small ctenoid scales. Vertical fins often tall.

Old Wifes — ENOPLOSIDAE (page 240)

Easily identified by shape and black and silvery striped pattern. Usually observed in schools but often form pairs around a reef.

Morwongs — CHEILODACTYLIDAE (page 240)

Have thick rubbery lips, long elongated pectoral fin rays, a forked caudal fin and are usually distinctly coloured.

Trumpeters — LATRIDIDAE (page 244)

Similar to morwongs. Have a deeply notched dorsal fin and small rounded pectoral fins. Scales on body are small and numerous.

Seacarps — APLODACTYLIDAE (page 244)

Elongated with small cycloid scales, a deeply notched dorsal fin and a short-based anal fin. Are drab-coloured with large dusky blotched patterns and pale irregular spotting.

Kelpfishes — CHIRONEMIDAE (page 246)

Distinct head profile with large eyes. Tips of dorsal fin spines have variable number of short filaments, forming distinct tufts in some species. They are closely related to the tropical hawkfishes.

Hawkfishes — CIRRHITIDAE (page 246)

Easily recognised by shape and the small tufts on dorsal fin spine tips.

Damselfishes — POMACENTRIDAE (page 250)

Generally deep rounded with compressed bodies varying to almost elongate shapes. Mouth is small, jaws have one or a few rows of compressed teeth. Anal fin has two spines, the first being very short.

Wrasses — LABRIDAE (page 268)

Most have elongated bodies, a terminal mouth, thick lips, protruding canine teeth, and cycloid scales covering the body.

Cales & Weed Whitings — ODACIDAE (page 312)

Diverse group with mostly elongate to very elongate species. Differ mainly from labrids in dentition. Have only four rays in ventral fin or no ventral fin.

Parrotfishes — SCARIDAE (page 314)

Two subfamilies based on differences in dentition. The Scarinae have teeth fused into strong beak-like plates, giving rise to their common name.

Grubfishes — PINGUIPEDIDAE (page 320)

Small and slender featuring long-based dorsal fin with short spinous section of four or five spines. The anal fin is headed by a feeble spine. Eyes are large and bulging and positioned high on head.

Stargazers — URANOSCOPIDAE (page 324)

Features a large bulky head with dorsally placed eyes, a protrusible mouth, and a large backward-pointing spine dorsally above pectoral-fin base, which can be venomous.

Thornfishes — BOVICHTIDAE (page 324)

Slender with large, close-set, dorsally placed eyes and two dorsal fins. The first fin is spinous and short-based, the second soft-rayed and long-based.

Blennies — BLENNIIDAE (page 326)

Generally slender with slimy skin replacing scales. Teeth are in comb-like arrangements, often with greatly enlarged canines. Have a long-based single dorsal fin with flexible spines and soft rays.

Threefins — TRIPTERYGIIDAE (page 332)

Mostly tropical and a few centimetres long. Dorsal fin is in three parts and the sections are separated by a gap or joined at the base by membrane. Anal fin has its base longer than any dorsal fin section.

Weedfishes & Snake-Blennies — CLINIDAE (page 336)

Well-camouflaged and highly variable to suit habitat, ranging in colour from yellow to brown or green. Most have diagnostic patterns or morphological features.

Dragonets — CALLIONYMIDAE (page 340)

Have tough skin instead of scales. Eyes are placed high on head and mouth is small but greatly protrusible out and downwards. Dorsal fin is in two parts and pectoral and ventral fins are rather large.

Gobies — GOBIIDAE (page 342)

Most have ventral fins united into a single large cup-shaped fin. Dorsal fins are in two parts: the first with flexible spines and the second soft-rayed, usually headed by a single spine. Anal fin similar.

Dart Gobies & Worm Gobies — MICRODESMIDAE (page 360)

Worm gobies are long and slender with almost a tubular body and small head. Dart gobies often occur in large schools above reefs when feeding.

Surgeonfishes — ACANTHURIDAE (page 364)

Feature a movable spine on caudal peduncle. Generally medium-sized, ovate to oblong and usually with highly compressed bodies. Mouth rather small with numerous small teeth in jaws.

Moorish Idols — ZANCLIDAE (page 374)

Features a long white wimple-like dorsal fin filament. Strongly compressed, almost circular bodies. Snout is produced with small mouth at tip. Jaws have long bristle-like teeth covered by fleshy lips.

Rabbitfishes — SIGANIDAE (page 374)

Have a spine at each end of ventral fins with three rays between and seven spines in anal fin. Mouth is small and well in front of the eyes. The jaws have a single row of small close-set incisiform teeth.

Left-Eyed Flounders — BOTHIDAE (page 380)

Generally extremely compressed with eye on left side of head. Left side pigmented to match surroundings, right side unpigmented. Pectoral fins are present and caudal fin is free from dorsal and anal fins.

Large-Tooth Flounders — PARALICHTHYIDAE (page 382)

Ventral fins are short-based, clearly separate with length much greater than base width. Caudal fin bluntly pointed over middle rays. Both eyes on left pigmented side and blind underside usually unpigmented. Mouth moderately large with uniserial teeth in each jaw and often with enlarged canines.

Right-Eyed Flounders — PLEURONECTIDAE (page 382)

Elongate to very deep-bodied with both eyes on right side. Left side unpigmented. Lateral line distinct. Eyes small and close together, directly above each other. Fins entirely soft-rayed.

Soles — SOLEIDAE (page 384)

Usually elongate. Both eyes on right side, left side unpigmented and used as underside. Pigmented side often with distinct banded or spotted patterns. Head and eyes small, and snout elongated over mouth.

Triggerfishes — BALISTIDAE (page 386)

Ovate, compressed bodies. Dorsal fin in two parts. Pectoral fins small and paddle-like, and ventral fins rudimentary encased with small scales. Mouth is small but with large and very strong teeth in jaws.

Leatherjackets & Filefishes — MONACANTHIDAE (page 392)

Prominent, separate first dorsal-fin spine. Body covered with tiny prickly scales, forming a tough leathery or velvet-like skin. Head is large, eyes are set high and mouth is small.

Temperate Boxfishes — ARACANIDAE (page 404)

Have a hard-shelled carapace protecting the body, with holes for fins and slits for gills.

Tropical Boxfishes — OSTRACIIDAE (page 406)

Body is encased to a greater extent with a separate hole for each moving part. The mouth is set low and the lips are more tubed. Spines are usually on extremities of ridges, pointing forwards or backwards.

Pufferfishes — TETRAODONTIDAE (page 410)

Have small beak-like mouth with fused teeth, only divided in front. Fins are entirely soft-rayed. Have small paddle-like similar-sized dorsal, anal and pectoral fins.

Porcupinefishes — DIODONTIDAE (page 420)

Have large spines over most of the body, prominent eyes, large soft-rayed paddle-like rounded fins, and small slit-like gill opening just anterior to pectoral-fin base. The head points outwards when the body is inflated.

INTRODUCTION

I started off my interest in aquarium fishes as a hobby, but I soon became intrigued by the pretty fishes found in Sydney waters, most of which I couldn't identify. The purpose of this book is to provide a comprehensive guide for fish watchers, identifying about 1000 species variously distributed along the Australian coasts. Although this is less than one-third of all the known Australian fishes, it covers most of the shallow reef species seen by snorkellers, divers and coastal fishermen.

Taking care

Many fishes are toxic, posing a threat if consumed or handled, but harm can usually be avoided if care is taken, and all fishes should be treated with respect. Several species, including boxfishes, soles and roughies release a poison when under stress, and although it does not affect us air-breathers, it should be noted when collecting fishes for aquariums as it kills other fishes, and even themselves if confined.

An historical account

The earliest recorded accounts of Australian fishes, made by the Dutch, date back to the late 17th and early 18th century. Significant works published in museum memoirs began early this century with Alan R. McCulloch, and the prolific Gilbert P. Whitley who published several hundred scientific papers and some small popular books.

Major popular books appeared in 1962 when Edgar Wait's and T.D. Scott's work led to *The Marine and Freshwater Fishes of South Australia*, and in 1965 when Ernie Grant published the first book on Queensland fishes, *Guide to Fishes*. More recent publications on Australian fishes include a comprehensive guide to Tasmanian fishes by P.R. Last, E.O.G. Scott and F.H. Talbot, and field guides with paintings by B. Hutchins and R. Swainston on southern fishes and by G.R. Allen and R. Swainston on north-western marine fishes, depicting a large number of species. The CSIRO publication *Sharks and Rays of Australia* by P.R. Last and J.D. Stevens, is a definitive work on cartilaginous fishes. The first comprehensive fish books, covering all species in their designated regions and illustrated with colour photographs, were *The Fishes of Australia's South Coast* by M.F. Gomon, C.J.M. Glover and R.H. Kuiter, and *Coastal Fishes of South-Eastern Australia* by R.H. Kuiter.

Habitats

The geographical area covered in this guide includes the Australian mainland and Tasmania, a coastline nearly 37 000 kilometres long and encompassing several biogeographical regions (often referred to as provinces). These regions range from tropical in the north to temperate in the south. Fishes living in the depth range from intertidal to 30 metres are covered, including deep water dwellers that often enter shallow depths. Open-water pelagics such as tuna and many sharks are excluded.

Habitats vary greatly and include long sandy surf beaches, rocky shores, mangroves, estuaries, lagoons and harbours. Depth, type of substrate, light input are some factors influencing each type of habitat. For example, seagrasses may look similar, but creatures found there can differ greatly from one place to the next. All habitats are affected by currents, tides and weather to varying degrees. Fishes have adapted to every one of them, and inhabit rock pools and tidal rivers or travel along the shore in schools.

Australia's unique global location exposes its waters to Antarctic conditions in the south and the rich Indo-Malay region bordering the north. Consequently, the floras and faunas differ greatly between north and south, with corals dominating on shallow reefs in the north and weeds in the south. A mixture occurs over a relatively small area about midway along the east and west coasts, and here tropical and temperate species can be found together. Most tropical fishes have a pelagic larval stage and, since currents with a general southerly direction flow inshore on both sides of Australia, many of these are carried south well beyond their normal breeding areas and intermittently expand their geographical range. Sometimes conditions are favourable for a few years and some of the migrants may even breed in more southern areas. However, upwellings or eddies from cold areas eventually kill the tropical expatriates.

Changing species

The southern fishes are descendants from Gondwana times when Australia was part of the Antarctic region, and many are endemics with restricted distribution. During Australia's movement north the circumpolar current took hold and conditions changed many times, with ice ages and sea-level changes. Faunas shifted where possible or modified themselves to cope with the changes.

In areas where changes were rapid, species either adapted or became extinct. This is evident in southern waters, where species in a particular genus have changed mostly along the coastal areas facing south, where migration to warmer or cooler conditions was not possible. In contrast, those species in the eastern and western regions were able to stay in touch with their habitat without pressure to change. There are several examples among southern fishes where the most colourful and differing species within the genus are in southern waters and the least colourful, similar yet distinct species occur on the west and east coasts, thus furthest apart. This phenomenon, where a species changed completely in its place of origin over time, or died out, whilst at the same time the population migrated from the area in various directions, occurs worldwide. It often results in different populations forming a complex of species, with those migrating furthest changing the least.

Species populations separating in our southern waters have changed to varying degrees between east and west, becoming sibling species or subspecies. Some returned to their original areas, often by seasonal migration, and usually overlap in the Bass Strait region. The northern fishes are mostly arrivals from regions situated north of Australia, floating into range as larval fishes and settling. North-western species are an extension of the Asian mainland fauna, and many species range through the China seas as far as southern Japan. Great Barrier Reef fishes are an extension of those found in the eastern New Guinea region and coral seas, and the northern region is closely associated with the Indonesian fauna. Few species occur along both the east and west coasts, and those regarded as a single species usually show colour variations.

The popularity of scuba diving has resulted in the greatly accelerated discovery or recognition of new species. The sexes or various colour forms of many species which at some stage were thought to be different species have, in many cases, been linked by underwater observations. Although most species on the south coast are now known, many remain undescribed, despite specimens having been deposited in the Australian Museum well over 10 years ago.

CLASSIFYING FISHES

Fishes have common names and scientific names (see below), and are classified into families. Similar to the way species are placed in a genus, closely related genera belong in a family, a group of families belong in an order, and orders belong in classes. The highest classification used in this book is families and a complete list of the fish families, both commonly and scientifically named, can be found on pages vi–xvii.

Common names

There are no official common names for Australian fishes. Many species, especially those caught by recreational anglers or in commercial fishing, have local names. However, there are preferred common names that have been used in many publications. Most names used in early books are still current today — for example, those used in *The Edible Fishes of New South Wales* by David G. Stead (1908), which listed all the edible species known at the time.

For this book I have taken Australian authors into account first, especially those who published popular books, such as Ernie Grant, Ian S. Munro and Gilbert Whitley. I have disregarded American and South African common names used in recent publications on Australian fishes, such as *Fishes of the Great Barrier Reef and Coral Seas*, by Randall, Allen & Steene. Only when no common name is available should an author provide or adapt a name used in other parts of the world.

Names are often well established, even when there are actually two species with the same name as in the case of east and west coast species. In the case of the Blue Groper they are called Eastern and Western Blue Groper, but locally people use the name Blue Groper. Using scientific names as part of common names is preferred only when it is well established (e.g. Three-spot Dascyllus), but this is no reason to use it for other members of the genus. If no common name is available the new one should, if possible, reflect a particular feature or have some other relevance to the species.

Scientific names

These are always in two parts: the first part is the name of the genus, which may contain several species; the second is the actual species, of which there is only one. Scientific names have changed greatly in past decades and continue to do so on a regular basis. This is due to our relatively poor knowledge of fishes, compared to birds or reptiles. We have only recently penetrated the aquatic world, and with many similar species and new discoveries, names have often been wrongly applied. Also, many taxonomists still disagree on the use of names.

Some tropical species cannot be separated on the basis of morphological features; they may also lose colour after death. Goatfishes (Mullidae) are a good example, as they have very distinctive colour patterns and are easily identified underwater, whereas preserved material is difficult to identify to species level. Rabbitfishes (Siganidae) are divided into two subgenera and comprise about 30 species.

Scientific names used in this book are based on numerous scientific papers, including family revisions by specialists throughout the world, consultations with specialists, and my own research on Australian and Indo-Pacific fishes. I take full responsibility for the use of names, including those in conflict with some recent works on Australian fishes.

IDENTIFYING FISHES

Photographs are the main tool for identifying a species. Comparing photographs with a fish in hand is relatively easy, but identifying a fish from memory after a dive is difficult and requires training. When observing an unknown fish that one wants to identify, one should take mental notes of particular markings, such as spots or vertical or horizontal lines. Colour is not always the best means for identification as it changes with depth, unless an artificial light is used. Fishes with vivid colours, especially red, look very different with natural light when at depths of 6 metres or more. Species which are camouflaged can vary the most, usually matching their surrounding colours.

External Features

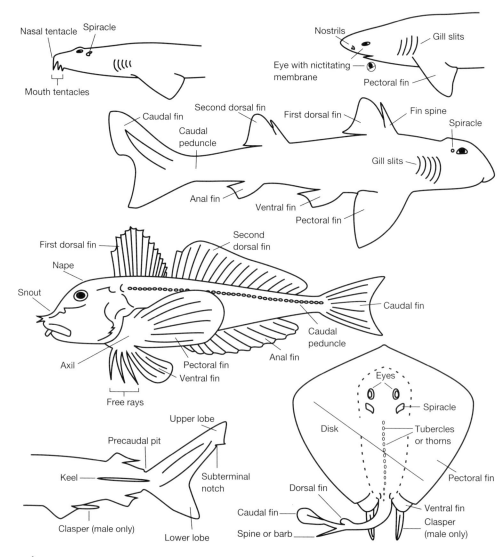

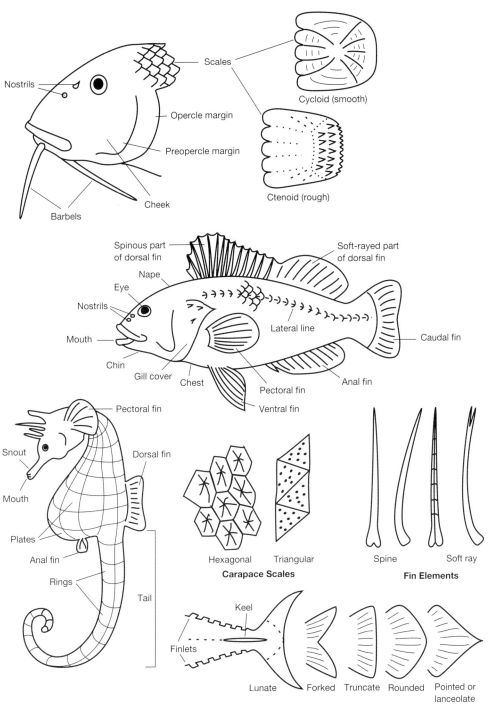

Nostrils
Scales
Opercle margin
Preopercle margin
Cheek
Barbels

Cycloid (smooth)

Ctenoid (rough)

Spinous part of dorsal fin
Soft-rayed part of dorsal fin
Nape
Eye
Nostrils
Mouth
Chin
Gill cover
Chest
Lateral line
Caudal fin
Anal fin
Pectoral fin
Ventral fin

Pectoral fin
Snout
Mouth
Dorsal fin
Plates
Anal fin
Rings
Tail

Hexagonal   Triangular
Carapace Scales

Spine   Soft ray
Fin Elements

Keel
Finlets
Lunate   Forked   Truncate   Rounded   Pointed or lanceolate
Caudal Fin Shapes

5

Photographing fishes

All of the photographs in this book are my own, some of them taken over 20 years ago. The photographs were all taken with a flash, thus showing colours as if the fishes were on the surface. It is impossible to show all colour variations within the scope of this book, but many species that occur in groups or mixed sexes are easily linked by observation, including those where males look completely different from females or juveniles; however, many examples of the latter are included. It doesn't take long to learn the most common species or groups — for example, leatherjackets or butterflyfishes — and this helps greatly when trying to identify a particular species.

Opportunities to photograph some of the elusive species can be rare, seasonal or change with time. Species that are usually rare may be common at a particular time, or may be found in different habitats where diving is not always possible. Many fishes are easily photographed, but to get great pictures it is a real advantage to know the species and their behaviour. I still see new fishes or other forms of marine life in places I've been diving in since 1964. It is important, when developing an interest in any aspect of the marine world, to record it on film. I concentrated on fishes, and even among my earliest material I find photographs which would be difficult to obtain or set up now. Being in the right place at the right time really does apply to underwater photography.

The serious fish photographer needs a single-lens reflex camera, so that what you see through the viewfinder is what you get. Underwater, the face-mask restricts the closeness to the camera, so a special action finder enables you to see the entire picture. The Nikon action finder is the best and can only be used on the Nikon F4. Canon discontinued their action finder on the current cameras, but hopefully this will become a feature in new underwater systems, combined with Nexus housings. All the photographs in this book were taken with Nikon cameras, ranging from F1 to F4, starting with Ikelite housings and then, in more recent photographs, Nexus housings. Most temperate fishes were photographed with 50 mm or 60 mm Macro lenses and tropical species with the 105 mm Macro lens. Some small pelagics (e.g. pilchard) were taken with the 105 mm Macro lens, combined with a 2x Tele Converter. For true colours and sharpness, Kodachrome 64 is the best film and was used for about 99 per cent of the pictures in this book. Some of the older photographs, and a few recent ones, were taken on Ektachromes.

Taking up underwater photography is expensive, and equipment must usually be chosen for a particular purpose; the more difficult the subject, the more expensive the equipment. Fish photography is the most demanding and is comparable to bird photography on land. Because of the poor visibility underwater, the length of lenses is limited, but the various accessories needed add to the expense. Using land cameras requires watertight housings, which are an additional cost. The market for underwater photographic equipment is small, and consequently prices are high. In addition, the lack of natural light makes it necessary to illuminate the subjects with powerful artificial lights. Recommending the right equipment is difficult and depends very much on one's budget. The best option is Nikon cameras combined with Nexus housings, but these also tend to be the most expensive.

SPECIES ACCOUNTS

HORN SHARKS — HETERODONTIDAE

Small Indo-Pacific family, consisting of a single genus with 8 species, of which 3 occur in Australian waters. Also known as bullhead sharks or generally as Port Jackson sharks; however, the latter name should be reserved for the common species in Sydney Harbour, which was originally called Port Jackson. Features blunt head with a crest above each eye; 2 identically shaped dorsal fins, each headed by a spine which is usually venomous, second fin slightly smaller than the first; and a small mouth which is low and anteriorly placed. Females produce distinctive spirally flanged egg cases which are usually laid in reef cracks; however, some have long tendrils for anchorage in weeds. Up to 15 eggs are produced, and young between 15 and 20 cm long hatch after about 8–10 months. Horn sharks are slow-moving fish, docile, often resting on the substrate or in ledges. They feed primarily on benthic invertebrates.

Crested Horn Shark *Heterodontus galeatus*

High crests above eyes; gill slits white; body without defined lines but diffused dark blotches. Dorsal fin more rounded on top compared to other species. Inhabits coastal and offshore reefs, occasionally entering harbours, but close to seaside. Usually on sand next to reef or rocks in depths of 20+ m. Egg cases with curly tendrils up to 2 m long. Maximum length 1.2 m.

Port Jackson Shark *Heterodontus portusjacksoni*

Dorsal fins pointed at tips; distinctive bands over interorbital, below eyes, mid-dorsally and, most noticeably, a harness-like band from nape to pectoral and ventral fins, dividing 3 ways as a small triangle above the pectoral fin. The third Australian species, the Zebra Horn Shark *H. zebra*, with its distinctive vertical banding, is only known from the north-west coast from trawls. Port Jackson Sharks often congregate in large open caves along shallow coastal reefs. Egg cases wedged among rocks and lack long tendrils. Maximum length 1.6 m, but usually less than 1 m.

COLLARED CATSHARKS — PARASCYLLIIDAE

West Pacific family with 2 genera, one of which is found in Australian waters with 4 endemic species. These benthic sharks resemble true catsharks (next family) but differ in having distinct nasal barbels, a groove joining nostrils to mouth, and mouth not reaching to below eyes. Slender fishes with small head. Ventral, dorsal and anal fins alternate in position along body. One species enters shallows, is nocturnal and hides under rocks or in reefs during the day, but others usually found in depths of 100+ m. Only 2 species observed by diving.

Varied Catshark *Parascyllium variolatum*

Variable pale grey to dark brown; distinctive broad black band with tiny white spots over head behind eyes. Body indistinctly dark-banded, paler interspaces with a series of variously placed white spots. Commonly enters shallow coastal bays in mixed rock and seagrass habitats. The Rusty Catshark *P. ferrugineum* is mainly offshore and rarely seen, but sometimes comes inshore at night. It differs in its paler colour with dusky saddles and small black spots over most of the body. Varied Catshark reported to 180 m depth. Maximum length 1 m.

Crested Horn Shark

Port Jackson Shark

Varied Catshark

9

CATSHARKS — SCYLIORHINIDAE

Large family of small sharks, recently estimated to comprise 17 genera and about 100 species worldwide, of which 8 genera and 32 species occur in Australian waters. Snout pointed, sometimes very elongate, and mouth underneath head, below eyes. First dorsal fin positioned just behind ventral fin, and second dorsal fin just behind anal fin; in some species, all fins placed over posterior half of body. Includes species called swellsharks, capable of increasing their size by inflating stomach to deter predators. The majority of species are poorly known, some from only a few specimens, occurring primarily in very deep water. A few are occasionally found at relatively shallow depths, less than 60 m, which from a diver's point of view is still deep.

Gulf Catshark   *Asymbolus vincenti*

Coloured with dusky blotches with patches of numerous close-set white spots, some forming a series along dark areas. Enters seagrass beds in Bass Strait and around islands in the Great Australian Bight. At night sometimes very shallow, but usually trawled in depths of 100+ m. Maximum length 60 cm.

Dark-spotted Catshark   *Asymbolus analis*

Dusky grey to brownish with large darker blotches over top, each with black spots along or near its margins. Fins without spots, or only a few near their bases. Inshore from about 10 m depth in boulder areas along reef margins to 60 m depth. Reports from very deep water are probably based on other species. Maximum length 90 cm.

Black-spotted Catshark   *Aulohalaelurus labiosus*

Pale with greyish dusky upper half of head, followed by several large saddles which decrease in size to small posteriorly. Evenly spaced black spots all over, and some white spots in darker upper parts. Clear coastal to deep offshore reefs. In heavily vegetated reefs when in shallows. Maximum length 70 cm.

BLINDSHARKS — BRACHAELURIDAE

Eastern Australian family, with a single genus and 2 species. Best recognised by presence of long nasal barbels and the position of both dorsal fins between origins of ventral and anal fins. One species commonly seen in coastal waters.

Blindshark   *Brachaelurus waddi*

Small juveniles almost black; adults brown with indistinct black saddles and a few pale spots sparsely distributed over body. Secretive in ledges during the day. Inhabits coastal reefs, often in shallows on algae reef, and juveniles occur in high-energy zones, feeding on invertebrates at night. Maximum length 1 m.

Gulf Catshark

Black-spotted Catshark

Dark-spotted Catshark

Blindshark

ZEBRA SHARKS — STEGOSTOMATIDAE

Monospecific. Very long tail and distinct ridges along upper sides and small nasal barbels.

Zebra Shark *Stegostoma fasciatum*

Juveniles with distinct zebra-like black and white banding, becoming spotted with age; adults mainly light brown with dark spots over body. Usually seen solitary but congregate in specific areas in large numbers to mate. Occasionally inshore, but usually on deep sandflats. Maximum length reported 3.5 m, usually 2 m.

WOBBEGONGS — ORECTOLOBIDAE

Small West Pacific family with 3 genera and 7 species, all genera and 6 species occurring in Australian waters. Wobbegongs are benthic sharks, and are known elsewhere as carpetsharks because of their flattened bodies and marbled patterns dorsally. Head features numerous dermal flaps and long barbels on snout. Seemingly sluggish, they are surprisingly fast and unpredictable, and should not be handled or speared. Wobbegongs are capable of biting their own tail. Extremely tough and muscular sharks which may attack large prey, screwing up their entire body to tear the prey apart. Overfishing in New South Wales has caused a decline in the 2 previously common species there.

Spotted Wobbegong *Orectolobus maculatus*

Greenish brown to grey brown with pale ring-like markings above, matching surroundings. The very similar Ornate Wobbegong *O. ornatus* differing slightly in colour by having more bluish grey spotting and lacking the pale ring-like markings. Spotted Wobbegong occurs inshore, entering estuaries, and the Ornate Wobbegong is usually offshore. Maximum length of both about 3 m.

Tasselled Wobbegong *Eucrossorhinus dasypogon*

Distinct species with numerous tassels around mouth, extremely well camouflaged eyes and general grey colouration. In caves or crevices during the day, hunting at night, favouring cephalopods and crustaceans. Clear coastal to inner reefs, often in lagoons, and commonly observed by divers in the tropics. Maximum length 1.3 m.

ANGELSHARKS — SQUATINIDAE

Small broadly distributed family, consisting of a single genus with 13 or 14 species worldwide, of which 4 occur in Australian waters. Only one species commonly encountered at shallow depths. Similar to wobbegongs with flattened body, but have laterally expanded fins and lack an anal fin. Angelsharks superficially resemble rays, but fins not attached to head, as in rays. They bury themselves in sand and, like many sandfishes, are white below and sandy coloured above for camouflage. Ovoviviparous, producing about 10 young per litter approximately 30 cm long. Diet comprises benthic invertebrates, and were seen taking octopus and squid at Montague Island, New South Wales, with ink pouring from the gills after swallowing prey.

Angelshark *Squatina australis*

Grey to brownish above, depending on colour of substrate; some white spotting, and young with white fin margins. Buries in sand, and only the most observant diver would notice the outline of the body or eyes and nostrils on the surface. Usually discovered by accident when disturbed and swims away. Shallow to deep coastal waters along reef fringes. Maximum length 1.5 m.

Zebra Shark

Spotted Wobbegong

Tasselled Wobbegong

Angelshark

WHALER SHARKS — CARCHARHINIDAE

Large family of small to large sharks with 12 genera and about 50 species, most of which can be encountered in Australian waters. Body streamlined, thickest below first dorsal fin. Fast sharks and long-distance travellers, which include the Tiger Shark and many other well-known pelagic species. Primarily open-water dwellers, but a few species regularly enter coastal waters and are probably responsible for most shark attacks around the world. Bronze Whalers are often blamed for attacks, but this well-known name is used for several closely related species. More likely to attack are Black Whalers, which grow larger and are more likely to enter estuaries, and could be responsible for some of the beach attacks; or Bull Sharks, which not only enter estuaries but travel far upstream into fresh water (they have been reported 4000 km from the sea in the Amazon). All members of this family should be treated with respect and not provoked.

Black Whaler *Carcharhinus obscurus*

Sleek grey-blue species when seen underwater, black from above. Often forms schools and enters shallow estuaries at certain times of the year. Mostly confined to continental coastlines, inshore in surf and deeper waters to 400 m. Often confused with Bronze Whaler *C. brachyurus* which prefers clearer offshore conditions. Maximum length 3.6 m.

Bull Shark *Carcharhinus leucas*

Rather stocky for genus and with broad mouth. Greyish dusky above and pale below. Large individuals dark and deep-bellied. Can be encountered just about anywhere, even in clear waters where it seems safe for divers, but this species is probably the champion in attacks on humans, dogs or other warm-blooded creatures which take to rivers or turbulent coastal waters to cool off. Two large females seen by author on separate occasions in Queensland, one at 20 m and the other at 30 m depth, both behaving identically: first cruising past at a distance, coming back a few minutes later but passing much closer, which was a good enough reason to leave the area. Maximum length 3.4 m.

Blacktip Reef Shark *Carcharhinus melanopterus*

Light below and grey above, with distinct black tip on first dorsal fin and lower lobe of caudal fins. Most commonly observed shark on shallow reef-flats, often entering subtidal zones, hunting parrotfish, even jumping between channels over exposed reef. Not dangerous, but could bite one's legs in shallows. Forms small groups or lives solitary in deeper water. Maximum length 1.4 m, usually 1 m.

Whitetip Reef Shark *Triaenodon obesus*

Easily recognised by slender body, and white tip on first dorsal fin and upper lobe of caudal fins. Other white-tipped species are deeper bodied and pelagic. This species typically cruises along reef wall and slopes, but is sometimes seen resting on deep sand patches in small groups. Harmless species which often can be approached at close range. Maximum length 2.1 m.

Black Whaler

Bull Shark

Blacktip Reef Shark

Whitetip Reef Shark

15

SHOVELNOSE RAYS — RHINOBATIDAE

Subtropical family with 4 genera and about 40 species, according to most recent estimates, of which 3 genera and 8 species are recognised in Australian waters (but one doubtful). Body thick and elongate; head greatly depressed; pectoral fins united to head and not greatly expanded. Snout varies from rounded to pointed and is sometimes elongated. Benthic fishes, often buried in substrate, some entering estuaries and commonly found around seagrass beds. Diet comprises benthic invertebrates. Ovoviviparous or viviparous, usually producing small litters with 2–8 embryos per egg capsule.

Eastern Shovelnose Ray *Aptychotrema rostrata*

Sandy coloured, with or without indistinct dark blotches; snout long and pointed; head greatly depressed and eyes slightly raised, viewing laterally. Until recently *A. bougainvilli* was thought to be different in having a shorter snout, but now regarded as the same species. Inhabits sandflats near reefs in depths of about 20 m or more. Maximum length 1.2 m.

Western Shovelnose Ray *Aptychotrema vincentiana*

Similar to eastern cousin above, but normally shows distinct large dusky blotches dorsally. Occurs on sandy flats near reefs or along seagrass bed margins in shallows to about 30 m depth. Commonly found in South Australia's gulfs. Maximum length 80 cm.

Eastern Fiddler Ray *Trygonorrhina fasciata*

Almost identical to the Southern Fiddler Ray (next species), the only obvious difference being in dorsal colouration. This species has a triangular pattern just behind the interorbital. Inshore, mainly on rocky reefs in coastal bays, but occasionally enters estuaries. Reported to depths of 120 m. Maximum length 1.2 m.

Southern Fiddler Ray *Trygonorrhina guaneria*

This species has stripes instead of a triangle behind the interorbital, and is more brownish grey compared to the greenish grey of the Eastern Fiddler Ray (previous species). Commonly enters estuaries in muddy substrate near seagrass beds. Offshore to depths of about 50 m. Maximum length 1.2 m.

SHARKFIN GUITARFISHES — RHYNCHOBATIDAE

Doubtful family with 2 genera and perhaps 5 species, with one species of each genus occurring in Australian waters. The front parts of these fish are similar to those of shovelnose rays and they were only recently separated from that family, but the posterior part of the body is more shark-like.

White-spotted Guitarfish *Rhynchobatus djiddensis*

Highly variable above, from pale sandy to almost totally black colour. The light forms have a distinct black round spot where the inner pectoral fin connects to the body. Sometimes small white spots over part of the body. Inhabits sandy open substrate, entering very shallow depths. The other Australian member in the family is only known from trawls. Maximum length 3 m.

Eastern Shovelnose Ray

Western Shovelnose Ray

Eastern Fiddler Ray

Southern Fiddler Ray

White-spotted Guitarfish

17

SKATES — RAJIDAE

Very large family with at least 15 genera and over 200 species worldwide, of which 5 genera and 38 species are recognised in Australian waters. Most species are restricted to deep water in excess of 100 m, and only 2 are commonly encountered in divable depths. Body and head greatly flattened, extending laterally with pectoral fins forming a large disk. Snout usually pointed, projecting considerably and firm in some. Dorsally: Eyes raised, facing laterally and followed closely by spiracles. Ventrally: A small straight mouth with nostrils in front of its corners, and 5 pairs of gill slits. Tail variable, from thin and feeble to thick and robust with lateral folds and usually 2 small dorsal fins, a series of thorns, and a pair of slender electric organs.

Thornback Skate *Raja lemprieri*

Grey to brown above with mixture of varying sized dark blotches or reticulations. Often a distinct white spot about mid-base of pectoral fin, and the underside of the snout tip black. Shore species, but recorded to 170 m depth, entering bays; adults are usually seen in sandy channels near seagrass beds. Feeds primarily on benthic crustaceans and fishes. Maximum length 52 cm.

Melbourne Skate *Raja whitleyi*

Dorsal surface plain light grey or brown to near black, often with irregularly placed white flecks. Inhabits coastal sandy bays on open substrate, often entering estuaries. Large almost black individuals are occasionally seen from the surface, swimming over seagrass beds during the daytime. Largest Australian skate, maximum length 1.7 m.

ELECTRIC RAYS — TORPEDINIDAE

Small family with 10 genera and about 40 species worldwide, of which 3 genera and 8 species occur in Australian waters. Rays with rounded, soft and flabby disc, thick at body, head often blunt. Tail variously sized, and one or two dorsal fins arranged differently between various genera. Pair of large kidney-shaped electric organs on sides of head, and discharge can produce powerful shock. Viviparous, producing small litters. Diverse group including smallest of all cartilaginous fishes at about 10 cm fully grown. Only one species commonly encountered in shallow depths.

Numbfish *Hypnos monopterygium*

Sandy grey to yellow or almost black. Dorsal fins close together and just in front of caudal fin. Eyes small and are raised when active. Numbfishes spend most of their time buried in mud or sand, with just open nostrils visible. Feeds on relatively large prey which are stunned and eaten whole. Commonly found in harbours. Maximum length 60 cm.

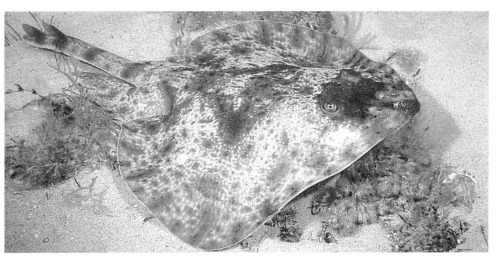

Thornback Skate

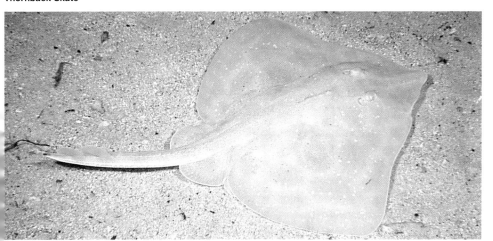

Melbourne Skate

Numbfish

STINGAREES — UROLOPHIDAE

Moderate-sized family with 3 genera and 40 species. All genera and 22 species occur in Australian waters. Differs from related families in possessing a small caudal fin, and the tail is not whip-like as in many other similar rays. Tail carries one or two venomous spines, and in addition a small dorsal fin is sometimes present (variable within species). Disc greatly flattened and usually rounded, with width similar to length. Eyes raised, viewing laterally, with large spiracles just behind. Mouth slightly arched with large nostrils in front of its corners, and 5 pairs of gill slits behind. Benthic, fast-moving species, buries to hide in sand when resting but active day and night. Feeds primarily on benthic invertebrates. Stingarees are potentially dangerous for waders and divers, and will attack if stepped on or provoked. Can strike at lightning speed from any direction, and can even swim as fast backwards as forwards. A stab from its spine is extremely painful, often causing a deep hole with venom taking immediate effect. Initial bleeding may be beneficial, and applied heat may give pain relief (immerse the affected part in hot water, or use a heat blower or even hot stones or sand).

Sparsely Spotted Stingaree *Urolophus paucimaculatus*

Sandy coloured, grey to brown, usually has several distinct dark-edged white spots on disc. Very common in south coast inlets, including muddy and sandy bays along reefs and seagrass beds. Often buried during the daytime and commonly out at night over shallow sandbanks. May attack with little provocation. Maximum length 40 cm.

Spotted Stingaree *Urolophus gigas*

Dark brown to black, usually whitish blotches in small groups variously arranged on disc, along its margin and on tail. Markings usually distinct in juveniles, but large adults are sometimes all black and the pattern may be obscured by mud on the back. Front of disc more rounded compared to other local species. Tail is short and the spine not always visible but gives a nasty sting. Common in coastal bays and estuaries, in mixed reef and seagrass areas. Maximum length 70 cm.

Banded Stingaree *Urolophus cruciatus*

Distinctly marked with black lines and spots along and across the back, and because of markings often called Cross-back Stingaree. Dorsal surface otherwise grey to brown. The striped variation of the Common Stingaree (next species) is also called Banded Stingaree and is often confused in New South Wales with this species, but the pattern is different and the tail longer. Inhabits sandflats near reefs and enters seagrass estuaries. Maximum length 50 cm.

Common Stingaree *Trygonoptera testacea*

Variable from uniform grey to brown, often with dusky shading below the eyes. Juveniles often with a dark stripe between eyes and mid-dorsally to tail, but some adults offshore retain the juvenile pattern which can lead to confusion with other species. Various habitats, from shallow coastal bays, in muddy as well as clean sand habitat to deep offshore; often congregates in small groups. Maximum length 45 cm.

Bight Stingaree *Trygonoptera ovalis*

Light to dark brown, broad black patch below the eyes and a pair of long patches just posterior to centre of disc. Coastal to offshore reefs, on sand along weedy reef margins and sponge reefs to moderate depths; trawled most commonly in about 45 m depth. Maximum length 60 cm.

Sparsely Spotted Stingaree

Spotted Stingaree

Banded Stingaree

Common Stingaree

Bight Stingaree

21

STINGRAYS — DASYATIDIDAE

Large family with at least 5 genera and probably 60 species worldwide, of which all genera and 22 species are recognised in Australian waters. Tail usually long and whip-like, and the disc at least as long as it is wide. Large species easily separated from other large rays in not having greatly raised or anteriorly protruding head. Head only slightly raised with eyes viewing laterally. Diverse family with disc width ranging from 30 cm to almost 3 m, and the tail often longer than the disc. Its largest species weighs up to 350 kg. Tail has one or two venomous spines which are potentially dangerous. Stingrays often show aggression by bending the tail up and pointing it forwards, and should not be approached at such times. Benthic feeders, exposing prey by blowing water jets from the mouth below, taken in through large spiracles from above, often digging large crater-like holes in the sand or mud. Usually they swim about slowly but can move very fast if necessary.

Blue-spotted Fantail Ray *Taeniura lymna*

Greenish to ochre above with bright blue spots over most of disc; eyes raised, with large spiracle behind. One or two stings near end of tail. Most commonly observed coral reef species, usually under coral plates or ledges during the daytime, moving out at dusk or at certain tides to feed on molluscs on shallow flats. Maximum width 30 cm.

Blotched Fantail Ray *Taeniura meyeni*

Variable light to dark grey with black blotches randomly scattered over disc, most distinct in juveniles and becoming more mottled with age to an almost uniformly dark colour with light scribbles all over. Usually feeds on sandflats near reefs, often very deep along bases of drop-offs. Large feeding individuals are sometimes followed by smaller stingray species. Maximum width 1.8 m.

Blue-spotted Stingray *Dasyatis kuhlii*

Swimming individuals are easily recognised by their long tail with white tip and banding over last one-third. Disc dusky brown with randomly placed light blue spots, and dark shading below eyes and on interorbital. Coastal, usually on silty mud and sand slopes well away from reefs, and often in groups distributed over an area, mostly buried during the day with just eyes exposed but quickly moving out of the way if approached. Small species, maximum width 40 cm.

Mangrove Ray *Himantura granulata*

Nearly always black, best recognised by the distinctive white colour on whip-like tail from spine on, as if dipped in white paint. Often has small white spots all over disc. Shallow sandy to muddy habitat in sheltered coastal bays and estuaries around mangroves, feeding on crustaceans dug from substrate. Maximum width 1 m.

Rough-back Stingray *Himantura jenkinsii*

Uniformly light yellowish brown with numerous close-set denticles over the back and partly tail to spine. The spine is white, which helps with identification. Shy species on open sandflats in moderate depths, usually in small groups. The similar Estuary Stingray *Dasyatis fluviorum* is darker brown and usually occurs in a silty habitat, ranging further south to Sydney. Maximum width 1 m.

Blue-spotted Fantail Ray

Blotched Fantail Ray

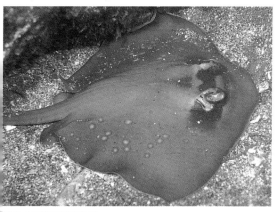

Blue-spotted Stingray

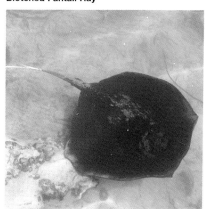

Mangrove Ray

Rough-back Stingray

Cowtail Stingray *Pastinachus sephen*

Easily recognised by the deep fin-like skinfold below the very long tail. Disc is light to dark grey-brown. Active during the day, visiting shallow flats and estuaries, large individuals often accompanied by piloting fish or remoras, and sometimes reef fishes on the lookout for escaping prey when ray digs in substrate. Maximum width 1.8 m.

EAGLE RAYS — MYLIOBATIDIDAE

Small family with 5 genera and about 25 species worldwide, of which 3 genera and 5 species are known from Australian waters. Disc very angular, head raised with eyes on sides, and snout largely protruding from disc. Mouth below with, in pavement-like arrangements, strong crushing teeth in jaws, followed by 5 pairs of gill slits. Tail slender and at least twice as long as the disc, whip-like, with at base a small but prominent dorsal fin followed by single spine. Benthic feeders, excavating prey by blowing water-jet from mouth, taken in through particularly large spiracles. Often swims near reefs at any level in the water column. Extremely fast swimmers and capable of leaping high into the air.

Southern Eagle Ray *Myliobatis australis*

Dark greenish grey above with pale bluish or greyish bands, bars, streaks or spots. Head blunt to rounded. Commonly occurs in southern coastal bays, often very shallow, ranging to deep offshore waters. Often seen feeding on sand near reefs in loose groups. Viviparous, producing litters of about 3–7 young. Maximum width 1.2 m.

White-spotted Eagle Ray *Aetobatus narinari*

Distinct species, dorsal surface greenish grey to almost black, with numerous white spots over most of disc and ventral fins, but intermittently over head and anterior part of disc. Underside white. Usually swims high above substrate and often in large groups, descending to sandy substrate to dig for various benthic invertebrates. Maximum width 3 m, but usually less than 2 m.

ELEPHANT FISHES — CALLORHINCHIDAE

Family comprises single genus with 4 described species, 3 recognised as valid, restricted to temperate seas of the Southern Hemisphere. Only one species known from Australian waters. Body and fins are shark-like in appearance, but the head is peculiar with snout produced in a trunk-like fleshy proboscis. Elephant fishes are related to ghost sharks, which also have a single pair of gill slits and no spiracle. Benthic feeders, probing sand for prey and entering shallow bays to deposit eggs. Egg capsules spindle-shaped with broad marginal flanges, about 20 cm long and gold in colour when fresh.

Elephant Fish *Callorhinchus milii*

Easily identified by shape and colour, shiny silvery with dark markings showing when viewed from above. Swims mainly with its large pectoral fin like a ray. Inhabits offshore on deep sandflats and banks. Females enter shallow bays in summer to deposit eggs in muddy channels and seagrass areas. Young hatch after about 8 months and move out to deeper water. Maximum length 1.2 m.

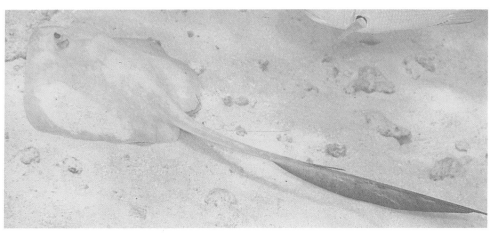

Cowtail Stingray

Southern Eagle Ray

White-spotted Eagle Ray

Elephant Fish (frontal view)

Elephant Fish (female)

SNAKE EELS & WORM EELS — OPHICHTHIDAE

Very large family of marine eels with more than 50 genera and 250 species globally distributed in tropical to temperate zones, of which 16 genera and 235 species are reported from Australian waters. Diverse in shape with long to extremely long tubular bodies, often snake- or worm-like, hence their common names. Head and tail usually sharply pointed. Most species bury themselves in substrate and move easily through sand, some exposing the head during the day and hunting in the open at night. A few tropical species hunt during the day in shallow water, mimicking seasnakes. Diet comprises fishes, cephalopods and crustaceans. Length varies from about 20 cm to 2.5 m.

Giant Snake Eel *Ophisurus serpens*

Large robust species; usually just head visible at burrow in substrate during the day. Becomes active on dusk and hunts at night. Adults greenish or brownish above, juveniles silvery. Common in shallow estuaries of New South Wales, such as Sydney Harbour and Botany Bay, in mud or soft sand. Very powerful jaws with sharp teeth, and large specimens should be left alone. Reported maximum length 2.5 m.

Short-head Worm Eel *Muraenichthys breviceps*

Body long, very robust, ending in strong pointed tip used to bury itself backwards in sand. Commonly occurs in southern sandy estuaries. Nocturnal but often seen during overcast days near rocks or weeds in search of prey, mostly shrimps. Several similar species in Australian waters, with about 20 in the genus worldwide. Maximum length 60 cm, but usually about 40 cm.

Banded Snake Eel *Myrichthys colubrinus*

Easily recognised by its banded pattern and very long body with pointed end. Some geographical variations with alternating bands and saddles. Commonly out during the day in shallow lagoons and reefs, often observed by snorkellers and usually mistaken for venomous seasnakes. Widespread in the tropical Indo-Pacific. Maximum length almost 1 m.

Spotted Snake Eel *Myrichthys maculosus*

Very elongate species with distinctive large blotches, closely but variably placed together. Nocturnal, often seen during night dives at varying depths from very shallow to over 30 m. Inhabits coastal reef-flats and slopes, often in silty habitat of mixed reef and sand. Widespread in the tropical Indo-Pacific. Maximum length almost 1 m.

Giant Snake Eel

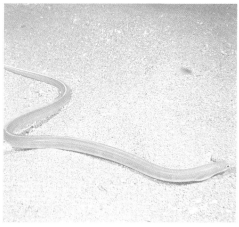

Short-head Worm Eel

Banded Snake Eel

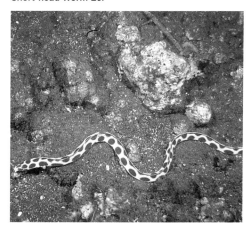

Spotted Snake Eel (out at night)

Spotted Snake Eel (close-up)

MORAY EELS — MURAENIDAE

Large family of marine eels comprising at least 10 genera and about 150 species (200 according to some authors), distributed worldwide in all tropical and subtropical seas. In Australia, 9 genera and 50 species are recognised. Body muscular, with thick tough skin, and posteriorly compressed. Single median fin, originating anteriorly above gill opening, continuing around the tail to the anus. Gill opening is a small hole, often tubed, behind the head. Mouth often large with long jaws. Teeth variable, from small pointed to large molariform, according to genus. Some have venomous fangs on roof of mouth. Largest genus is *Gymnothorax*, with about 120 species, many of which are found on coral reefs. Most species distinctly marked with spots or various patterns, but can change with habitat or size. Moray eels are usually nocturnal, often seen during the day with head looking out from crevice or hole in reef. Diet comprises a variety of fishes and invertebrates, depending on species which often are selective. Although not aggressive, the powerful jaws of large specimens can inflict serious wounds. Species range in maximum length from about 30 cm to 2 m.

Ribbon Eel *Rhinomuraena quaesita*

Monotypic genus, easily recognised by extremely long body, distinct features of head and colour, though several colour forms. Mainly inhabits coastal reef-flats and slopes in burrows near coral heads or in rubble. Usually solitary, but on occasion pairs share the same burrow. Sometimes leaves burrow for a short swim. Feeds on small fish, mainly hunting at dusk. Maximum length about 1.2 m with height about 4 cm.

Honeycomb Moray *Gymnothorax favagineus*

Distinctly coloured large species, spots proportionally reduce in size from juvenile to adult. Inhabits shallow, protected areas within coastal surge zones to deep slopes with isolated outcrops of rock or coral heads. Widespread in the tropical Indo-Pacific, west to Africa. Despite its large size, a non-aggressive, shy species. Reported maximum length 2 m.

White-mouth Moray *Gymnothorax meleagris*

Two very similar species which differ by colour in mouth and spotted pattern. This species white and other, *G. nudivomer*, with yellow mouth and spots closer, often joining to form short scribbles in adults. Also known as White-spotted Moray, its spots are more numerous with age. Found in corals and rocky reefs on shallow flats in sheltered clear coastal zones to depths of about 20 m. Large adults usually deepest. Reported maximum length 1 m, usually much smaller.

Undulate Moray *Gymnothorax undulatus*

Distinctive in colour with leopard pattern of large blotches which may break up into more spotted patterns with age. Head yellow when juvenile. Long snout characteristic of genus. Inhabits coastal reef crests and slopes. Nocturnal, actively hunting fishes sleeping in crevices or sponges. Can be aggressive if disturbed. Tropical Indo-Pacific. Confirmed maximum length 1 m, but reported to 1.5 m.

Yellow-edged Moray *Gymnothorax flavimarginatus*

Distinctive yellow edge on fins posteriorly. Juveniles yellow with dark brown mottling; adults become dark on head and blotches reduce proportionally with age and size. Dark spot around gill opening. Widespread in the Indo-Pacific, coral and rocky reefs from coastal to outer reefs. Participates in fish feeding and becomes used to divers, but large specimens should be treated with respect. Maximum length 1.2 m

Ribbon Eel (adult)

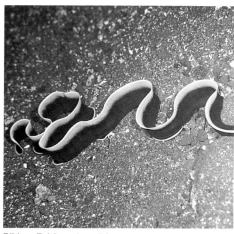

Ribbon Eel (large juvenile)

Honeycomb Moray

White-mouth Moray

Undulate Moray

Yellow-edged Moray

29

Giant Moray *Gymnothorax javanicus*

Probably the largest moray. Brown with dark spots dorsally on body and fin. Distinctive large dark blotch on gill opening. Lives in most reef habitats in a wide depth range from intertidal to about 50 m. Widespread in the tropical Indo-Pacific. Large individuals can inflict serious wounds and should not be interfered with. Reported maximum length 2.4 m, weight over 30 kg.

Sieve-patterned Moray *Gymnothorax cribroris*

Brown to yellowish with irregular but diagnostic spotting on head behind eye. Body pattern from mottled to mosaic. Coastal and in estuaries in rocky reef or under harbour debris. Common in Sydney Harbour, but secretive and usually observed at night. A small species, maximum length about 45 cm (doubtfully reported to 75 cm).

Green Moray *Gymnothorax prasinus*

Probably the best-known Australian moray. Very common in New South Wales. Also in New Zealand and very similar species in east Pacific. Brown to green often related to depth, as green pigment is caused by algae cells in skin tissue. Small juveniles pale brown. Various rocky and kelp habitats from silty harbours to clear offshore reefs. Often acts curious towards divers and may bite. Maximum length about 1 m.

Western Moray *Gymnothorax woodwardi*

Pale yellowish brown, distinct mosaic body pattern and head plain with slender shape. Body pattern more pronounced in juveniles. Endemic to Western Australia; fairly common on rocky reefs and under jetties in the hollows of pylons, in coastal bays of southern areas. A shy species, but may bite if provoked. Maximum length 75 cm.

Mosaic Moray *Enchelycore ramosa*

Typical of genus with long jaws and needle-like teeth. Pale yellow with strong mosaic pattern in juveniles, becoming more spotted and mottled with age. Subtropical south Pacific, east to Easter Island. Common on clear rocky reefs in central New South Wales and northern New Zealand. Feeds on fishes and crustaceans at night. May bite if provoked. Maximum length 1.5 m.

White-eyed Moray *Siderea thyrsoidea*

Easily identified by the bright white eyes. Head usually dark grey with pale snout, variable pale to mottled brown body. Coastal rocky reefs in ledges, often near urchins, in New South Wales. Silty habitats in tropics, often on coastal shipwrecks. Sometimes pairs, or shares places with other moray species. Widespread in the west to central Pacific. A small species, maximum length 40 cm (doubtfully reported to 65 cm).

Giant Moray

Sieve-patterned Moray

Green Moray (adult and close-up)

Western Moray

Mosaic Moray

White-eyed Moray

31

Peppered Moray *Siderea picta*

Very pale, almost white, to dark grey with small dark close-set spots. Silty coastal bays and reefs, often in rubble under jetties in tropical waters. Usually inhabits very shallow waters only a few metres deep, and may leap from the water at prey such as crabs, its main diet. Widespread in the Indo-Pacific. Maximum length at least 1 m.

Clouded Moray *Echidna nebulosa*

White snout, and distinctive body pattern with a series of yellow-centred dark blotches along its entire length. Intertidal and shallow coastal reefs. Often in tidal pools and lagoons, hunting out in open for crabs during the day, or hiding under rock and coral pieces. Widespread in the tropical Indo-Pacific. Also known as Snowflake Moray. Maximum length 70 cm.

HERRINGS — CLUPEIDAE

Large family of small fishes, with about 65 genera and 180 species, globally distributed in tropical to temperate waters, with 15 genera and 32 species in Australia. Comprises herrings, sardines and pilchards, and constitutes an important food source for predators such as tuna. Probably the largest single group exploited by commercial fisheries. Silvery fishes with weakly attached scales, a single centrally placed dorsal fin, large distensible jaws with tiny teeth, and numerous elongated gill rakers. Fins are short-based and entirely soft-rayed. Many small and similar species in tropical waters; largest but fewer species in temperate zones.

Pilchard *Sardinops neopilchardus*

A common temperate species, easily identified by a series of evenly spaced dark spots along the lateral line and below the dorsal fin. Migrates along the south coast and congregates in large numbers in bays. Juveniles in estuaries, usually in small schools or mixed in with closely related sprats. Commercially used as baitfish. Small genus with 4 other species elsewhere in temperate waters. Maximum length 25 cm.

Goldspot Herring *Herklotsichthys quadrimaculatus*

Silvery, greenish lateral line with yellow spot above and below, just behind gill opening. Eyes large. Schools densely in tropical waters, often along beaches, forming large dark patches that appear as a single entity. Several very similar species may masquerade under this name. Also known as Fourspot Herring. Maximum length 15 cm.

Southern Herring *Herklotsichthys castelnaui*

Deep-bodied, greenish grey above. Caudal fin deeply forked with dusky tips. Coastal, mainly estuarine, forming large loose schools in tidal channels to feed on zooplankton in the current. Southern occurrence intermittent, depending on temperature and currents. Enters brackish water. Maximum length 20 cm.

32

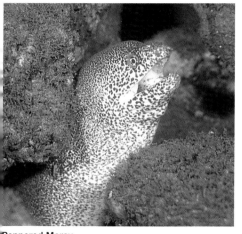

Peppered Moray

Clouded Moray

Pilchard (adult)

Pilchard (schooling)

Goldspot Herring

Southern Herring

33

ANCHOVIES — ENGRAULIDAE

Large family of small fishes with about 16 genera and 140 species, of which 4 genera and 19 species are recognised in Australian waters. Mostly tropical and a single temperate species. Elongate, silvery and blunt protruding snout. Scales weakly attached and fins entirely soft-rayed. Anchovies are typical planktivores, with numerous long and slender gill rakers, usually swimming fast with mouth fully extended to filter large volumes of water for food. Schools found in shallow coastal habitats, though reported to a depth of 200 m, and commonly entering large estuaries. Commercially important and preyed on by pelagics such as trevally, and also birds.

Australian Anchovy Engraulis australis

Only southern species, easily recognised by its typical snout and blue back. Found in coastal sandy bays in current-prone tidal areas feeding in spread-out schools, darting at prey. Also occurs in New Zealand. Maximum length 15 cm.

Little Priest Thryssa baelama

Several very similar tropical genera and species. This genus has a series of small scutes anterior to the ventral fins. Others differ in body depth and relation between fin origins, which can help with field identification. Found in the Indo-Pacific, west to the Red Sea. Forms large, dense schools in coastal waters, often near freshwater run-offs. Maximum length 15 cm.

EELTAIL CATFISHES — PLOTOSIDAE

One of about 25 catfish families, most are freshwater with forked caudal fins. This family has 8 genera and about 40 species, about half of which are confined to freshwater systems in Australia and New Guinea. Fishes have a tapering body, ending in an eel-like tail. Skin smooth and slimy, and lateral line consist of pores. Australian marine species have 5 pairs of barbels around the mouth, and possess prominent venomous spines, heading the dorsal and pectoral fins. Its sting is very painful and potentially dangerous. To relieve pain, apply heat to kill the venom as soon as possible, immerse in hottest bearable water, use hot air blower, or even sun-heated stones and sand. Coastal and estuarine habitats, and one species occurs on coral reefs. Diet consists of various bottom-dwelling invertebrates and fishes.

Estuary Catfish Cnidoglanis macrocephalus

Yellow to dark brown or grey with darker or black mottling, usually progressively darker towards the tail. Mouth very broad, head large and eyes small. Coastal and estuarine in protected, often silty, habitats. Solitary, usually in back of holes or ledges during the day and most of the night. Rarely seen out and about. The sting from its venomous spines is extremely painful, and repeat stabs can be fatal. Reputed to be good eating. Maximum length about 60 cm.

Striped Catfish Plotosus lineatus

Distinctly dark with two pale lines. Tiny juveniles are black; swim together extremely tightly as a single body, usually taking on shapes of objects in the area. Groups probably represent a single brood. Mainly in coastal bays, but also in island or reef lagoons. Larger juveniles school increasingly loosely, and adults can be found in small numbers together or sometimes solitary in the back of crevices. Benthic feeders when young, taking small invertebrates and algae; adults nocturnal, taking invertebrates and small fish. Maximum length 35 cm.

Australian Anchovy

Little Priest

Estuary Catfish (adult)

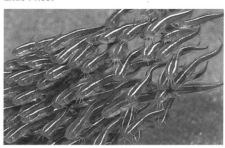

Striped Catfish (small juveniles)

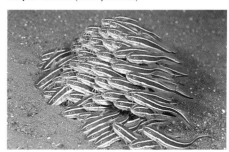

Striped Catfish (large juveniles)

Estuary Catfish (juvenile)

Striped Catfish (young adult)

35

SERGEANT BAKERS — AULOPIDAE

Small worldwide family with about 10 species in a single genus, 3 of which are known in Australian waters. Mostly live in very deep water, benthic on continental shelf, but an included species enters relatively shallow depths. Salmon-like with large head and jaws with several rows of fine teeth. Eyes dorsally above end of mouth, and males have elongated rays in dorsal fin. Fins entirely soft-rayed. Diet comprises swimming invertebrates and fishes, ambushed at great speed from a strategic position on substrate.

Sergeant Baker *Aulopus purpurissatus*

With a single species found in shallows, easily identified by shape and manner of resting on substrate, perching on ventral fins. Males have greatly extended anterior dorsal fin rays, often reaching the small adipose fin situated near the caudal fin. Coastal to very deep, on rocky reef with rich invertebrate growth such as sponges and gorgonian corals to depths of 250 m. Often hooked and reported as good eating. Maximum length 60 cm.

LIZARDFISHES — SYNODONTIDAE

Primarily tropical family with 2 genera, one monotypic and cosmopolitan, and the other with about 35 species, of which 14 recorded from Australian waters. Fishes with almost torpedo-shaped bodies, some tapering to caudal fin, covered with moderate-sized cycloid scales. Mouth exceptionally large with needle-like teeth along entire jaws. Eyes dorso-laterally placed, centrally above the mouth. Fins entirely soft-rayed and short-based, and a tiny adipose fin placed above the anal fin. Large ventral fins have 9 rays. Most species are variable and similarly marked, and are sometimes difficult to identify underwater. Some species bury themselves in the substrate with just their eyes exposed. Diet comprises primarily fishes, ambushed from a strategic position on or near reefs from sand.

Painted Lizardfish *Trachinocephalus myops*

Easily identified by blue lines or dashes along the body, although nearly always buried. When disturbed it swims quickly to another location and immediately buries itself again. Inhabits coastal bays and estuaries on open sandflats and slopes at depths from very shallow to 200 m. Usually in small spread-out groups sharing the same habitat. Tropical cosmopolitan. Maximum length 30 cm in some places, usually 25 cm in Australia.

Variegated Lizardfish *Synodus variegatus*

Variable from pale with dark blotches to reddish with bright red markings, and can change colour. The specimen in the photograph is typical, with reddish dashes midlaterally, almost forming a red stripe. Double bar below the eye is almost straight. Coastal to offshore, usually exposed on reef or rubble substrate. Widespread in the tropical Indo-Pacific. Maximum length about 25 cm.

Tail-blotch Lizardfish *Synodus jaculum*

Easily identified by the dark blotch on the caudal peduncle. The back has a green sheen. Found in reef and sand areas, where it often buries itself, and sometimes in small groups of 3 or 4 individuals close together. Shallow protected reef-flats to deep sandflats to 30 m. Sometimes swims high above the substrate. Maximum length 20 cm.

Sergeant Baker (adult)

Sergeant Baker (large male)

Painted Lizardfish

Variegated Lizardfish

Tail-blotch Lizardfish

Two-spot Lizardfish *Synodus dermatogenys*

Several similar species with a double spot on the snout, this one pale greyish with bluish grey streak along the body at eye level. Sand and mixed reef habitat, often partly buried and readily buries itself to escape danger. Coastal to offshore. Widespread in the tropical Indo-Pacific. Maximum length 22 cm.

Ear-spot Lizardfish *Synodus similis*

Slender species with a distinct ear-like spot on top of the gill cover. Bluish grey streak from earmark to upper caudal peduncle. Clear offshore habitat on deep sandflats or gentle slopes in 20 m depth or more. Typically sits on the bottom with its head raised, giving an arched-back profile. Maximum length 20 cm.

Red-marbled Lizardfish *Synodus rubromarginatus*

Small deep-water species with bright red markings (looks almost black in natural light) and short pointed head. Fairly common in west Pacific, but often goes unnoticed. Found near clear water drop-offs on adjacent sand and rubble patches but sometimes on corals, usually in depths of 15 m or more. Maximum length about 12 cm.

SAURIES — HARPADONTIDAE

Small circumtropical family with 2 genera and about 14 species, of which 9 are known from Australian waters. Very similar to lizardfishes but have numerous rows of needle-like, close-set teeth in jaws and ventral fin with a feeble spine and 8 rays. Dull-coloured fishes which live in silty coastal or deep offshore soft-bottom habitats. Genus *Harpadon*, the bombayducks, are restricted to deep water and are not included here. Sauries are also known as grinners and enter shallow depths. Usually buried in sand or mud. Mainly hunts fishes and swimming invertebrates, taking surprisingly large prey which are swallowed whole.

Blotched Saury *Saurida nebulosa*

Slender, marked with dusky blotches matching habitat. Usually buried, partly or entirely, in strategic places to capture prey swimming over the top, usually near rocky outcrops on sand or mud. Mostly occur in protected coastal bays or large estuaries near the sea. Widespread in the tropical Indo-Pacific. Maximum length about 16 cm.

Slender Saury *Saurida gracilis*

Similar to Blotched Saury (previous species), but usually with more defined dark areas and the head is often dark. Coastal rubble and dark sand or mud slopes in various depths from 0.5 to 100+ m. Enters estuaries and mangrove areas. Widespread in the tropical Indo-Pacific. Maximum length 16 cm.

Two-spot Lizardfish

Ear-spot Lizardfish

Red-marbled Lizardfish

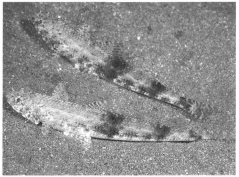

Blotched Saury

Slender Saury

HANDFISHES — BRACHIONICHTHYIDAE

Small family restricted to temperate Australian waters with species concentrated in Tasmania. Single genus with about 6 species, some undescribed, and 2 known from the mainland. Peculiar fishes related to anglerfishes, with hand-like paired fins. Pectoral fins extended like short arms with strange leaf-like appendage at elbow. Benthic fishes which move slowly, walking on paired fins, but can swim well. Have luring apparatus above mouth but its function unclear. Perhaps attracts prey with smell or has sensing capabilities. Most species live deep and are trawled, but a few are found in the shallows and are often seen at night. Their diet comprises primarily worms, molluscs and crustaceans.

Spotted Handfish *Brachionichthys hirsutus*

Identified by the numerous small distinct spots, sometimes with dark saddles and orange colour in the fins. Common Tasmanian species not known from the mainland, and restricted to sheltered bays on the south-east coast and Derwent Estuary. Once common, now an endangered species because of introduced starfish coveting habitat. Feeds on small shells and worms. Maximum length 12 cm.

Red Handfish *Brachionichthys politus*

Easily identified when coloured like the specimen in the photograph; however, the amount of red varies and sometimes has a blotchy pattern. Only known from few specimens found near Port Arthur on mixed sand and rocky reef in depths of 15–20 m. Feeds on worms and crustaceans. Maximum size 8 cm.

ANGLERFISHES — ANTENNARIIDAE

Family of specialised predatory fishes in 12 genera with 41 species worldwide, of which all genera and 23 species are found in Australian waters. Unique in having a greatly enlarged third dorsal spine and usually a modified first dorsal spine serving as a luring apparatus to attract prey. The lure consists of 2 parts: the illicium, the rod or stalk; and the esca, the bait. The latter varies between species and is highly specialised, mimicking worms, shrimp, fish, almost anything the anglerfish's prey would be fond of. Most species target particular prey, and their bait represents the food for this prey. Anglerfishes are among the most camouflaged and variable species; they copy various sponges and other fixed invertebrates in finest detail. Some juveniles exhibit bright colours, looking like poisonous nudibranchs. Anglerfishes feed primarily on other fishes, though some of our temperate species prefer crustaceans, and are capable of swallowing large prey. Tropical species produce pelagic eggs, while temperate Australian species show parental care by guarding the eggs.

Sargassum Anglerfish *Histrio histrio*

Coloured like the weed in which it floats, with from pale bleached colours to dark brown. Often has short leaf-like appendages over the body. Adapted to floating sargassum weed rafts where eggs and juveniles share the same habitat. Found in all tropical seas except the east Pacific, often carried by currents well beyond their breeding range. Has an interesting strategy for escaping from predators: it jumps on top of floating weeds, out of the water, and stays there for a considerable time before jumping back. Maximum length 15 cm.

Tasselled Anglerfish *Rhycherus filamentosus*

Two almost identical species, mainly differing in type of bait: worm-like in *R. filamentosus* and clump-like in *R. gloveri*. The latter occurs in south-western coastal areas. *R. filamentosus* is common in Port Phillip Bay, where it congregates in early summer on low rocky reefs, using crevices to breed. Often gravid females are surrounded by several males. Large egg-mass with about 5000 eggs guarded by female and covered with her body. Young hatch after about 30 days and sink to substrate, crawling to nearest crevice. Large species, maximum length 23 cm.

Spotted Handfish

Red Handfish

Sargassum Anglerfish (large adult)

Sargassum Anglerfish (showing hand-like fins)

Tasselled Anglerfish (large adult)

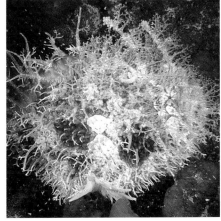

Tasselled Anglerfish (juvenile)

Smooth Anglerfish *Phyllophryne scortea*

Highly variable from black to bright yellow, orange and combinations with patches of grey. Esca mimics amphipod on which sand gobies (*Nesogobius* spp.) feed, and in turn anglerfish feeds on these gobies. Very common in the vicinity of Adelaide below jetties and in boulder reefs. Secretive under rocks or pieces of debris, usually hanging upside down. Small species to about 10 cm long.

Prickly Anglerfish *Echinophryne crassispina*

Orange to brick-red with prickly skin due to tiny close-set bifurcate spinules all over. Secretive among low rocky reefs on sand, usually found when turning over rocks. Feeds primarily on shrimps. Similar *E. reynoldsi* lives in sponges and is more yellow. Third species in genus *E. mitchelli* is only known from a few specimens from Bass Strait and Portsea Pier, Victoria. Small species, maximum length 7 cm.

Striped Anglerfish *Antennarius striatus*

Probably most frequently encountered species by divers in Australia, especially in New South Wales where it is common in Sydney Harbour. Although highly variable, usually a typical striped pattern is present; even black-looking specimens show stripes under good light. In Sydney Harbour there is a great variation in colour, from black to white, with yellow and orange most common, copying sponge colours there. Bait unfolds into a worm-like piece which is wriggled when in use. Common to widespread in the tropical Indo-Pacific. Maximum length at least 20 cm.

Shaggy Anglerfish *Antennarius hispidus*

Similar to the Striped Anglerfish (previous species) but bait like fluffy ball and striations are shorter and more spot-like. Sheltered shallow coastal bays in tropical waters, stragglers south to Sydney and usually in deep water. Tropical Indo-Pacific in depths from 3 to 90 m. Maximum length 20 cm.

Smooth Anglerfish

Smooth Anglerfish (variation)

Smooth Anglerfish (variation)

Striped Anglerfish

Striped Anglerfish (variation)

Prickly Anglerfish

Shaggy Anglerfish

43

Painted Anglerfish *Antennarius pictus*

One of the most variable species, with almost endless combinations of colours depending on area and geographical location. Sydney specimens from black to white, bright red or yellow, with spots or saddles. Beautiful yellow or orange-spotted black form on the Great Barrier Reef and in Indonesia. The hand-like pectoral fin usually has white 'fingers'. Found on coastal reefs and in estuaries in sponge areas in the Indo-Pacific. Depth range 3–50 m. Maximum length 16 cm.

Giant Anglerfish *Antennarius commersonii*

Highly variable, mimicking the colours of sponges on reefs in coastal areas and outer reef lagoons. Adults easily recognised by size, growing larger than other similar species. Often found very shallow on jetty pylons in island lagoons. Juveniles similar to other species, and luring apparatus needs to be examined for positive identification. Tropical Indo-Pacific, ranging to the Red Sea and Hawaii. Maximum length 30 cm.

Clown Anglerfish *Antennarius maculatus*

Similar to some juveniles of other species but has a 'clean' look, with few markings on the body except for strong banding. Juveniles have dark backgrounds with bright colours, mimicking nudibranchs. Tropical Indo-Pacific in protected coastal bays. Maximum length 10 cm.

Spotfin Anglerfish *Antennarius nummifer*

A large black blotch on the base of the soft dorsal fin. Body colour highly variable, often yellow, pink or red, depending on the area and local sponge colours. Has shrimp-like bait and feeds on small reef fishes. Tropical Indo-Pacific. Small species, maximum length 13 cm, usually 10 cm.

Painted Anglerfish

Painted Anglerfish (variation)

Painted Anglerfish (variation)

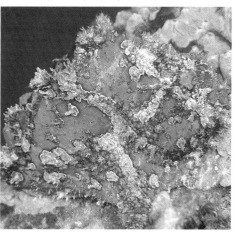

Giant Anglerfish

Clown Anglerfish

Spotfin Anglerfish

FROGFISHES — BATRACHOIDIDAE

Moderate-sized family with 18 genera and about 46 species, though poorly represented in Australia with 2 genera and 8 species. Feature tough smooth skin, and large round head with broad mouth. Jaws are set with bands of small sharp teeth, and body and head have fleshy papillae in various places, in particular along the mouth and above the eyes. Some fin spines are thought to be venomous. Various habitats, but mainly in estuaries in silty or muddy environment. Hides under objects, and eggs deposited on the ceilings of narrow or low overhangs. Diet comprises various invertebrates, swallowed whole. Capable of making loud croaking noises with its swim bladder. Stomach expandable to accommodate large prey.

Eastern Frogfish *Batrachomoeus dubius*

Small juveniles are pale with broad dark bands. Common in Sydney Harbour and regularly observed by divers. Mostly found under pieces of rubbish or rock slabs. Protected coastal bays and harbours in muddy to silty sand habitat from subtidal to depths of at least 150 m. Similar species *B. occidentalis* in western waters. One of the largest species, maximum length at least 30 cm.

Northern Frogfish *Halophryne diemensis*

This genus has more elaborate tentacles above the eyes than other Australian genus. Also, the gill slit is shorter and higher placed in relation to pectoral fin. Coastal silty bays and protected inner reef under rocks and coral slabs. Variable from spotted to irregular blotches forming a barred pattern over back and reticulations under head and ventral part of abdomen. Maximum length about 27 cm.

CLINGFISHES — GOBIESOCIDAE

Large family of small to tiny fishes with 33 described genera and over 100 species; many known which are still undescribed, and no doubt more will be discovered. Undetermined number in Australia, with several genera and many undescribed species in temperate waters. All very cryptic and secretive in weeds or on fixed invertebrates such as sponges and tunicates. Australian genus *Alabes*, shore eels, differs considerably from the rest, with eel-like body and fins except the caudal fin degenerated or absent; possibly warrants family status. Most clingfishes have united ventral fins forming a strong sucker disc. Many weed species similar and small, often difficult to identify; those on reefs more colourful and distinct. Diet comprises benthic invertebrates and zooplankton, and a few species specialise in removing parasites from other fishes.

Featherstar Clingfish *Discotrema* sp.

Associates with crinoids or featherstars of the genus *Oxycomanthus*. Similar species *D. crinophila* has an additional line mid-dorsally over the back to snout-tip; and *D. lineata* has a more pointed snout and several more lines, and associates with other crinoids in deeper water. All are widespread in the tropical Indo-Pacific in current-prone areas along drop-offs and slopes. *D. lineata* associates with dark hosts; *D.* sp. and *D. crinophila* matches colours of various hosts. Usually occur in pairs on the host. Maximum length 40 mm.

Long-snout Clingfish *Diademichthys lineatus*

Easily identified by colour pattern and very long snout. Protected rich coral reefs. Adults swim openly near coral-heads, often near long-spine urchins; juveniles seek protection among spines. Sometimes occurs in small groups. Also known as Striped Clingfish, but there are many striped species in the tropics. Maximum length to 50 mm.

Eastern Frogfish

Northern Frogfish

Featherstar Clingfish

Long-snout Clingfish

Grass Clingfish

One of several undescribed species and genera. Slender, on seagrasses and weeds, matching colours from green to brown and various fine spotting on the sides and top. Male with tall dorsal and anal fin used for display (folded down in the photograph). Shallow protected bays in seagrass beds and on young kelp. Very common in southern Victoria. The western population may represent another species. Maximum length 32 mm.

Tasmanian Clingfish *Aspasmogaster tasmaniensis*

One of several similar secretive species. This one is mostly encountered by divers who look under rocks. Pinkish to greenish with dusky bands. The similar *A. costatus* on the east coast has an irregular banded pattern. Found in shallow protected coastal bays and estuaries among rubble reef on sand, including tidal pools. Maximum length 8 cm.

Eastern Cleaner Clingfish *Cochleoceps orientalis*

Variable from yellow to orange with close-set small brown to red spots, and blue dashes or spots over the back. Lives on kelp or weeds in the shallows and on ascidians or sponges in deeper water. Actively cleans fishes, especially boxfish, porcupinefish, morwongs and seadragons, but many other reef fishes as well, depending on localised habits. Eggs are laid on the host and guarded by the parents. Maximum length 55 mm.

Western Cleaner Clingfish *Cochleoceps bicolor*

Very similar to its eastern cousin (previous species) and replaces it on the south coast. Blue lines more pronounced and often encircle the body. Primarily on ascidians and sponges, and visited by a variety of reef fish for cleaning services. Variable orange to red, often the posterior is half dark grey. Very similar species in Bass Strait and Tasmania, *C. bassensis*, which lacks the blue lines. Maximum length 70 mm.

Shore Eel *Alabes dorsalis*

Highly variable from green, brown and orange with or without large lateral spots or ocelli. Very common in southern waters in the intertidal zone under rocks, sometimes left almost dry with the low tide. Several other species in weeds, but although common, they are rarely observed because of their nearly translucent appearance and secretive nature. Maximum length 12 cm; other species much smaller, 50 mm.

Grass Clingfish

Tasmanian Clingfish

Eastern Cleaner Clingfish

Western Cleaner Clingfish (Port Phillip Bay)

Western Cleaner Clingfish
(Western Australia)

Shore Eel

49

BEARDIES — MORIDAE

Large family, including deepsea cods and rock cods, with about 15 genera and 70 species worldwide, of which 12 genera and 24 species are recorded in Australian waters. Mostly deep water, but a few inhabit shallow coastal reefs. Features include a large head, elongated body with tiny cycloid scales, chin barbel, and ventral fins with extended rays as feelers. Nocturnal fishes found in caves and in the back of large overhangs during the day, some very shy and completely hidden. Feed at night on a variety of fishes, crustaceans and cephalopods, sometimes out in the open and well away from reefs.

Largetooth Beardy *Lotella rhacina*

Best identified by distinctive white margins on fins. Colour variable from dark grey to reddish brown. Commonly observed in New South Wales from rocky estuaries to offshore reefs, usually in depths from 10 to 90 m. A second much smaller species *L. schuettea* is more slender but is very secretive and prefers more silty coastal and estuarine habitats. Reported maximum length 66 cm, rarely over 40 cm.

Finetooth Beardy *Eeyorius hutchinsi*

Moderate-sized chin barbel. Uniform dark brown, paler below with cream or pinkish lips and, in the south-west, sometimes yellow margins on fins. Secretive but common in sheltered shallow bays in rocky reefs or under jetties among debris Usually observed during night dives. Small species, maximum length 20 cm.

Bearded Rockcod *Pseudophycis barbata*

Small chin barbel. Plain pale grey to reddish, sometimes with a mottled pattern and a diffused dark area above the pectoral-fin base. Often confused with *P. bachus* (next species), which is reddish and has a more defined dark spot above the pectoral-fin base. Recorded between 1 and 300 m, but only small juveniles enter the shallows. Adults usually on deep reefs, in estuaries and offshore. Reported maximum length 80 cm, usually 50 cm.

Red Cod *Pseudophycis bachus*

Grey above and pinkish below when shallow, to brown-red in deep water. Caudal fin rounded with dusky margin in young becoming more truncate in large adults. Deep in mainland waters, but enters shallow depths in large rocky estuaries in Tasmania, often in caves. Type locality New Zealand; Australian population may be different, in which case the Australian population needs to be renamed. Maximum length 80 cm.

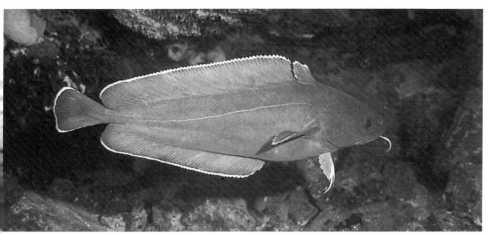

Largetooth Beardy

Finetooth Beardy

Bearded Rockcod

Red Cod

LINGS — OPHIDIIDAE

Large family with almost 50 genera and over 150 species worldwide, of which 8 genera and about 25 species reported from Australian waters. Body slimy and long, eel-like, tapering posteriorly. Ventral fins reduced to feeler-like filaments, usually placed forward below head, in some situated below eye. Often barbels present around mouth. Nocturnal reef fishes living far in back of crevices, and sometimes only the head is visible in dark areas of reefs or shipwrecks. Diet comprises fishes, cephalopods and crustaceans, which are hunted over reefs at night.

Bearded Rockling *Brotula multibarbata*

Arrangement of barbels and ventral fins identifies this species; only similar to catfish, which have small ventral fins placed near anus. Uniformly light brown to almost black, juveniles with white margin on median fins. Only seen at night swimming actively close to substrate to hunt prey. Retreat quickly under light to nearest hole, swimming either backwards or forwards. Maximum length 60 cm, usually 40 cm.

Rockling *Genypterus tigerinus*

Juveniles distinctly banded, changing gradually with growth to spotted pattern of adults. Shallow to deep protected reefs in rock piles, caves and often in shipwrecks. Juveniles in shallow seagrass areas with reef outcrops. Adults retreat to deeper water offshore. The larger cousin, *G. blacodes*, is mainly known from trawls on muddy bottoms offshore. Maximum length of *G. tigerinus* 1.2 m and weight 9 kg.

GARFISHES — HEMIRAMPHIDAE

Moderate-sized family with about 12 genera and 80 species, of which 7 genera and 18 species are recognised in Australian waters. Surface fishes, primarily tropical marine and a few species in subtropical or temperate zones. Some adapted to fresh water. Shiny silvery, greenish above, with greatly extended beak-like lower jaw. Ventral fins abdominal, placed far back. Scales large and easily removed. Despite generally small size, regarded as good food fish. Diet comprises a variety of algae, zooplankton and insects.

Eastern Garfish *Hyporhamphus australis*

Common New South Wales species, but overlaps in range with the closely related, almost indistinguishable Southern Garfish (next species) which has fewer scales and grows larger. Coastal bays and estuaries in tidal currents, feeding on surface algae and plankton. Commercially targeted, netted off beaches, and also often caught on lines around jetties. Maximum length 45 cm.

Southern Garfish *Hyporhamphus melanochir*

Coastal bays and seaward part of estuaries in tidal current areas. The only other species in southern waters, River Garfish *H. regularis*, occurs in upper reaches of estuaries and coastal lakes or rivers. Commercially important and popular with anglers, commonly hooked around bay jetties. One of the largest species, maximum length 50 cm, weight 0.6 kg.

Dussumier's Garfish *Hyporhamphus dussumieri*

Plain silvery with greenish back. Scales moderately large and easily visible underwater. Clear coastal waters and lagoons in small groups. Widespread tropical species commonly encountered. Another common tropical, *Hemiramphus far* is more estuarine and has a series of dark blotches laterally, barred in juveniles. Dussumier's Garfish, maximum length 25 cm.

Bearded Rockling

Rockling

Eastern Garfish

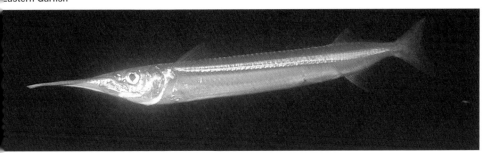

Southern Garfish

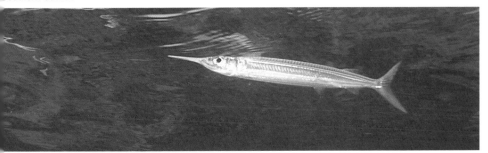

Dussumier's Garfish

53

LONG TOMS — BELONIDAE

Family of surface fishes with about 10 genera and 30 species worldwide, of which 4 genera and 11 species are recognised in Australian waters. Many similar shiny silvery species. Jaws extremely elongate with numerous needle-like teeth, short in juveniles, lengthening with age. Marine species reach a maximum length of 1.3 m and weight of 5.2 kg. Some freshwater species as small as 10 cm are fully grown. Coastal to outer reef habitat, hunting small surface fishes; in turn, hunted by large predators, including dolphins. Long Toms can leap well and 'run' along the surface on their tail. May be attracted by lights at night and leap high at source. Several known occasions of fatally injuring fishermen with spear-like beak. No accident reported with divers, apart from minor collisions.

Crocodile Longtom *Tylosurus crocodilus*

Probably the most frequently observed species in the tropics, the largest and most impressive. Other species very similar: some more slender, and others showing some difference in fin positions. Mostly seen solitary, sometimes in small loose groups, swimming just below the surface. Coastal to outer reefs and large individuals pelagic. Some species near mangroves and over seagrass beds. Tropical global distribution. Maximum length 1.3 m.

HARDYHEADS — ATHERINIDAE

Large family of small silvery fishes with about 29 genera and over 150 species worldwide, of which 11 genera and at least 30 species found in Australian waters. Also known as silversides, baitfish or greybacks. Features broad silvery lateral band; slender body with small to moderate-sized cycloid scales; large eyes; short-based fins with spaced dorsal fins, and ventral fins situated below first dorsal fin. Forms very large schools in coastal waters and estuaries. No commercial value, but important food source for pelagic fishes such as trevally and also birds. Some species move up rivers and into lakes; a few inhabit only fresh water.

Small-mouth Hardyhead *Atherinosoma microstoma*

Several similar southern species, this one very common in all coastal habitats ranging to freshwater and high-salinity lakes. The similar Silverfish *Lepatherina presbyteroides* has smaller scales and prefers clear coastal waters. The Pike-head Hardyhead *Kestratherina esox* lives in shallow seagrass areas and has a large head. The latter is largest, maximum length 15 cm; most others 10 cm.

Elongate Hardyhead *Atherinosoma elongata*

Very similar to Small-mouth Hardyhead (previous species) but more slender, fewer scales above midlateral line, eye large and white, and mouth reaching to just below eye. Clear coastal sandy bays, in schools over shallow flats, occasionally entering estuaries and river mouths. Maximum length 95 mm.

Small-scale Hardyhead *Atherinason hepsetoides*

Easily recognised by its small scales. Forms large schools at various depths, feeding on zooplankton, or in pursuit of mysids near the substrate to depths of about 30 m. A common Bass Strait species, seasonally entering bays. Maximum length 9 cm.

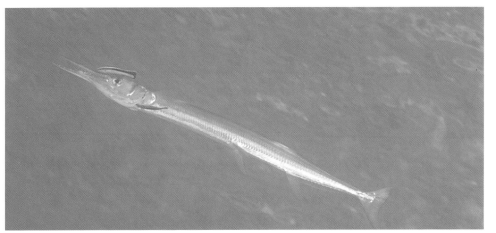

Crocodile Longtom

Small-mouth Hardyhead

Elongate Hardyhead

Small-scale Hardyhead

55

Robust Hardyhead *Atherinomorus lacunosus*

Body moderately deep and eye large. Coastal bays and estuaries, commonly sheltering in the shade of jetties in protected areas, hovering closely in large schools. Feeds on zooplankton during tidal currents. Widespread in the tropical Indo-Pacific. Maximum length 13 cm.

Ogilby's Hardyhead *Atherinomorus ogilbyi*

Sheltered inner reefs and coastal bays, entering estuaries in tidal currents. In small to moderate-sized schools, spreading out feeding in the current on zooplankton. Greenish silvery with pearly-edged scales on its back. Maximum length 12 cm.

SURF SARDINES — ISONIDAE

Indo-Pacific family with a single genus and about 5 species, of which one is found in Australian waters. Closely related to hardyheads (Atherinidae), featuring a greatly compressed body and a deep keel-like convex abdomen. Silvery and highly reflective, it causes a sparkling effect in the sun when feeding on plankton in surf or waves near the surface. Swims in small to large schools in turbulent high-energy zones.

Flower of the Waves *Iso rhothophilus*

Best recognised by its silvery reflective colour and deep keel. Schools usually observed near the surface along rocky outcrops or headlands in coastal waters or islands. Light flashes reflected from the sides during feeding can be seen from a great distance or from above the surface. Maximum length 75 mm.

PINEAPPLEFISHES — MONOCENTRIDIDAE

Small family with 2 genera and 3 species, of which one a common Australian endemic. The second, a widespread species, is known only from a few records in Australia. Prominent light organ on sides of the lower jaw used at night to locate prey. Light is produced by phosphorescent bacteria cultured on a patch of skin. Pineapplefishes hide in caves during the day, singly or in small groups. Move out at night over open sand to hunt shrimps. Found in shallow rocky estuaries to deep offshore, to a depth of at least 250 m.

Pineapplefish *Cleidopus gloriamaris*

Well known by divers in New South Wales and a popular aquarium fish. Easily recognised by its appearance. Colour variable from yellow to orange. Light organ looks blue–green in young and red in adults, but the light produced is greenish. Slight differences between eastern and western populations. Maximum length about 20 cm, reported to 25 cm.

Japanese Pineapplefish *Monocentris japonica*

Similar to Pineapplefish (previous species), but more rounded and a pointed snout. Reported from various Australian localities, sometimes trawled and one juvenile specimen collected in Botany Bay. Prefers a depth of 50 m or more in Australia. Maximum length 16 cm.

Robust Hardyhead

Ogilby's Hardyhead

Flower of the Waves

Pineapplefish

Japanese Pineapplefish

57

ROUGHIES — TRACHICHTHYIDAE

Global family with 7 genera and about 32 species, all the genera and about half the species found in Australian waters. Mostly very deep water, only a few in shallow depths. Often called sawbellies because of the series of scutes, scales with a keel-like ridge, placed ventrally along the abdomen. Body is compressed and often deep. Some produce loud clicking or buzzing sounds. Small to medium-sized fishes, some commercially trawled — for example, Orange Roughy. Inhabit rocky reefs, in ledges and caves during the day, feeding out in the open at night, mainly on shrimps. Shallow species form small aggregations from the seaward part of estuaries to moderate depths offshore. Deep-water species may form large schools.

Roughy *Trachichthys australis*

Small juveniles are black with 3 white patches, changing to brownish red when adult with a white bar on cheek and leading fin edges white. Deep-bodied, head and eyes large. Singly, pairs or small aggregations in large caves or overhangs. Clear coastal estuaries to offshore habitat, adults usually in depths of about 15 m or more. Maximum length 18 cm.

Sandpaperfish *Paratrachichthys* sp.

Greyish brown, pale greenish yellow over back and fins. Undescribed; until recently, confused with New Zealand species. Usually very deep, from 20 to 220 m; only in Tasmania is it common in the shallower part of the range, but one specimen observed at Montague Island, New South Wales, in 20 m. Rocky reefs, usually small aggregations in back of caves during daytime. Maximum length 25 cm.

Slender Roughy *Optivus elongatus*

Slender species, strongly oblique mouth and dark streaks to tips of caudal fin. Grey to light brown, sometimes with pale irregular blotches. Clear rocky estuary reefs to offshore in narrow ledges, often in large groups of mixed sizes. Described from New Zealand, but some slight differences. Also known as Violet Roughy. Maximum length 12 cm. Similar, undescribed species in south-western Australia.

Golden Roughy *Aulotrachichthys pulsator*

Golden-yellow sides. Only known from Topgallant Island in the Great Australian Bight which has a unique habitat with steep drop-offs to about 30 m with many seemingly endless caves at about 25 m depth. In the almost dark areas, these fishes are in small groups. Collected specimens produced loud clicking noises, similar to the sound made by rapidly hitting a cup with a spoon, for which this fish was named *pulsator*. Small species, maximum length 8 cm.

Roughy (adult)

Roughy (sub-adult)

Sandpaperfish

Slender Roughy

Golden Roughy

SQUIRRELFISHES & SOLDIERFISHES — HOLOCENTRIDAE

Large, globally distributed family with 2 distinct subfamilies: Holocentrinae with 3 genera, known as squirrelfishes, with a prominent spine (venomous in some) on lower corner of gill cover; and Myripristinae, the soldierfishes, with 5 genera in which the gill cover spine is small and the head blunter. About 70 species worldwide, of which 32 are recorded from Australian waters. Most Australian species are widespread in the tropical Indo-Pacific. Nocturnal fishes gather in caves and crevices during the day and some, extremely shy, are only seen at night; others swim boldly in front of caves or around coral heads, and sometimes show curiosity towards divers.

Redcoat Squirrelfish *Sargocentron rubrum*

Stripes light to dark red with dark blotches fused with lines at tail-base. Several similar striped species: In *S. cornutum* (next species), tail blotches are very distinct; and in *S. praslin,* stripes are very dark, almost black. Latter mainly on oceanic reefs. *S. rubrum* usually in small aggregations, but sometimes in large groups. At moderate depths on gentle slopes, reef-flats and lagoons with large coral bommies, or below overhangs and in caves. Maximum length 27 cm.

Red Striped Squirrelfish *Sargocentron cornutum*

Very similar to the Redcoat Squirrelfish (previous species), but stripes are darker red and the upper stripe over the caudal peduncle ends in a black blotch on fin base. Inhabits coastal reef slopes with rich coral growth. Secretive in corals or crevices during the day, singly or forms small groups, only coming out at night. Maximum length 18 cm.

Crown Squirrelfish *Sargocentron diadema*

Bright red at night, darker during the day. Thin white lines along body, one in dorsal fin which is sometimes divided into 2 sections. Singly or in small groups, often semi-exposed during the day but near a safe retreat. Protected clear, coastal and inner reefs along drop-offs and lagoons on rich coral reefs with large coral heads, or in ledges at various depths to about 30 m. Maximum length 17 cm.

Fine-lined Squirrelfish *Sargocentron microstoma*

Very similar to Crown Squirrelfish (previous species), best identified by more obvious white midlateral line and a second thick line posteriorly above, often as a distinct streak at a slight angle to horizontal lines. In shallow caves and crevices along outer reefs, common in oceanic locations. Maximum length 20 cm.

Pink Squirrelfish *Sargocentron tiereoides*

Stripes and interspaces subequal. Pinkish with red stripes. Fins pale red to mauve. Dorsal fin with red edges and tipped with white. Shy, usually only seen at night. Hunts close to substrate along rock faces at night, but hides in the back of deep caves during the day. Clear coastal rocky reefs and protected inner reefs on coarsely undulating substrates. Maximum length 16 cm.

Speckled Squirrelfish *Sargocentron punctatissimum*

Best recognised by red marginal band in the spinous dorsal fin when visible. Mostly red at night, pale during the day and with fine dark speckles. Secretive, and usually only seen at night swimming close to substrate in rich coral reefs, often very shallow in semi-exposed areas. Maximum length 20 cm.

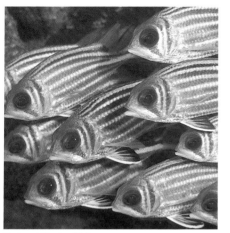

Redcoat Squirrelfish

Red Striped Squirrelfish

Crown Squirrelfish

Fine-lined Squirrelfish

Pink Squirrelfish

Speckled Squirrelfish

61

Violet Squirrelfish *Sargocentron violaceum*

Distinctive species, with red head, mauve body and white edges on large body scales. Appears blue in deep water with natural light. Nearly always solitary, shy during the day in small caves or crevices in clear coastal waters to protected inner reef slopes and walls with rich coral growth. Maximum length 25 cm.

White-tail Squirrelfish *Sargocentron caudimaculatum*

Distinctive white tail during the day, but completely red at night. Hunts solitary over open reef substrate, retreating to caves and overhangs during the day, often gathering in large numbers. Clear coastal to outer reef lagoons along drop-offs and steep slopes with long ledges and tunnel-like caves. Maximum length 25 cm.

Giant Squirrelfish *Sargocentron spiniferum*

Largest squirrelfish. Tall red dorsal fin and red-edged silvery scales, but variable to bright red almost all over. The spine on the head is very large, and for this it is known also as Sabre Squirrelfish. Solitary in some areas but may school in others. In caves or around large bommies in deep lagoons and along reef walls, sometimes under large plate corals. Maximum length 45 cm.

Crimson Soldierfish *Myripristis murdjan*

Strongly white-edged fins, offset by dark red to near black areas bordering. Spinous dorsal fin is red. Several very similar species with white-edged fins and a dark bar behind head: *M. berndti* differs in having a yellow spinous dorsal fin; and *M. hexagona*, most similar, has larger scales and prefers clearer inner to outer reef habitat, compared to *M. murdjan* which inhabits coastal, often silty habitat. All similar sized, maximum length 25 cm.

Epaulette Soldierfish *Myripristis kuntee*

Scales smaller than in other similar species, and the band behind the head is less defined. Variable from pinkish red above and silvery below to light red, but can look pale in natural light at depth. Rich coral reefs in lagoons and along slopes, often swimming above large plated coral heads, retreating between the plates for safety. Solitary or loose groups, often mixed with other species. Maximum length 20 cm.

Shadowfin Soldierfish *Myripristis adusta*

Largest soldierfish. Distinctive pale appearance underwater, outlined scales and large pale fins ending in very broad black borders, covering nearly half of the soft dorsal, anal and caudal fins. Usually in pairs in deep lagoons on outer reefs in front of caves or large overhangs, schooling in some oceanic locations. Maximum length 35 cm.

Violet Squirrelfish

White-tail Squirrelfish

Giant Squirrelfish

Crimson Soldierfish

Epaulette Soldierfish

Shadowfin Soldierfish

63

White-tipped Soldierfish *Myripristis vittata*

Spinous dorsal fin with distinct white tips. Pink-red to bright red, looks bluish in deep water. Pale reddish bar, sometimes indistinct, behind the head. Clear coastal and outer reef walls, often deep, 50+ m, usually in groups under large overhangs swimming against the ceiling, and often inverted. Small species, maximum length 20 cm.

Big-eyed Soldierfish *Myripristis pralinia*

Red all over, and a vertical pattern of scales shows on the sides. Very large eyes. Shy nocturnal species rarely seen during the daytime, but commonly appears throughout the Indo-Pacific on coastal to outer reef walls and rich coral areas in protected bays. Small species, maximum length 20 cm.

Spotfin Squirrelfish *Neoniphon sammara*

Body silvery with thin dark red lines along scale rows, thick over lateral line, showing prominent at night. Large dark spot anteriorly on the spinous dorsal fin, spine tips and bases white. Usually in small aggregations in large branching corals, in lagoons or clear coastal reefs. Scatter over reef at night, hunting crustaceans. Maximum length 24 cm.

Mouthfin Squirrelfish *Neoniphon opercularis*

Body plain, dorsal fin very distinct black with white tips and bases, patterned like a large mouth with teeth. Flashes its fin when approached, so is easily photographed with fins erected. Deep along walls in large caves and overhangs with black corals or other forms of semi-protection. Largest in genus, maximum length 35 cm.

NANNYGAIS & RED SNAPPER — BERYCIDAE

Small family with representatives worldwide, 2 genera and 9 species, of which both genera and 6 species occur in Australian waters. The deep-water genus *Beryx*, the alfonsinos, are only known from trawls, with 2 widespread temperate species. *Centroberyx* also lives at moderate depths, but some species enter shallow coastal bays, particularly when juvenile. Perch-like fishes, predominantly red with moderately large ctenoid scales. Feature a large deeply forked caudal fin and an anal fin usually with 4 spines (3 in most perch-like fishes). Most school in great numbers, feeding midwater on zooplankton. Some are of commercial value.

Eastern Nannygai *Centroberyx affinis*

Pink, silvery below to bright orange or red. No pale fin margins. Replaced west of its range by Western Nannygai, which has yellow eyes. Juveniles in estuaries and coastal reef under large overhangs and in caves, often forming large schools extending away from the reef until potential danger approaches. Adults offshore, usually schooling in depths of 25 m or more. Maximum length 40 cm.

White-tipped Soldierfish

Big-eyed Soldierfish

potfin Squirrelfish

outhfin Squirrelfish

Eastern Nannygai

Swallowtail *Centroberyx lineatus*

More slender than other species and the tail very long, deeply forked with pale margin. Pale spot behind the eye near origin of lateral line. Reddish above and pale below. Clear coastal waters to deep offshore. Only enters very shallow depths in the south-west, where often schooling under jetties, but deep elsewhere. In New South Wales on coastal reefs at 25 m or more, sharing habitat with nannygai but forming separate schools. Maximum length 36 cm.

Red Snapper *Centroberyx gerrardi*

Distinct white lateral line and white fin margins. Solitary on rocky reefs, shallow in South Australia to offshore, to at least 300 m depth. Nocturnal, behaviour like squirrelfish, moving about at night, probably taking shrimps. Often in shipwrecks, taking advantage of sheltering places. Large species, maximum length 46 cm.

DORIES — ZEIDAE

Small global family with 7 genera and 13 species, most widespread and one cosmopolitan in the Northern and Southern Hemispheres, of which 5 genera and 9 species are found in Australian waters. Most dories live in depths between 100 and 300 m, where they are commonly trawled. Only the well-known John Dory enters shallow depths and is regularly observed by divers. Feature large oblique mouth; jaws greatly expandable into a long suction tube used to target small fishes. Solitary hunters, cunningly approach prey.

John Dory *Zeus faber*

Easily recognised by its shape and the presence of large ocellus almost centrally on sides. Although most common between 60 and 400 m, it is regularly seen by divers, and in some areas as shallow as about 5 m. Temperate fish, a single species in both the Northern and Southern Hemispheres with global distribution. Juvenile dark with large vertically extended fins. Mostly protected coastal bays to deep offshore, but enters estuaries as well. Maximum length 66 cm.

FLUTEMOUTHS — FISTULARIIDAE

Family comprises single genus with only 4 species, of which 2 occur in Australian waters, one tropical and the other subtropical entering shallows. Long tubular bodies with extremely long snout, but rathe small mouth at end. Middle pair of rays in caudal fin greatly produced into extremely long filaments with large connecting membrane in juveniles. Fins entirely soft-rayed. Coastal to offshore reefs to continental shelf depths. Young commonly in estuaries. Hunt small fishes as main food source. Large fishes, maximum length 2 m.

Rough Flutemouth *Fistularia petimba*

Although widespread in the tropical Indo-Pacific, rarely observed as it occurs very deep, except in New South Wales where it is common in shallow coastal bays and juveniles commonly occur in estuaries. The more tropical Smooth Flutemouth *F. commersonii* is commonly seen on coral reefs in shallow depths. Adults feature thin blue lines or dashes dorsally. *F. petimba* the largest species, maximum length 2 m.

Swallowtail

Red Snapper

John Dory

Rough Flutemouth (adult)

Rough Flutemouth (juvenile)

67

TRUMPETFISHES — AULOSTOMIDAE

Family with a single genus and only 2 species, divided between the Atlantic and Pacific Oceans. Dorsal fin has small separate spines, each followed by a triangular membrane, the soft part large and situated near the tail, and a similar anal fin opposite. Pacific species wide-ranging, in tropical to subtropical waters.

Trumpetfish *Aulostomus chinensis*

Similar to flutemouth which has filaments on the tail, but otherwise easily identified by colour. Yellow form common in some areas. Juveniles have stripes or faint barring, colour highly variable and changes when retreating to resting places. Single widespread species in all protected reef habitats from silty inshore to clear outer reefs, but often with black coral or soft coral beds. Reported maximum length 90 cm, rarely exceeds 60 cm.

SHRIMPFISHES — CENTRISCIDAE

Small family of peculiar fishes with 2 genera and 4 species recognised in the Indo-Pacific, with one in each genus in Australian waters. Adapted to vertical position, but move horizontally for speedy retreat. Usually in large synchronised schools in seawhip areas or tall branching corals. Small juveniles float together with weeds on the surface and settle among spines of diademas (long-spined urchins), before joining the schooling adults. Species similar, but genera distinguished by either a rigid or hinged large dorsal spine. Diet comprises small swimming crustaceans or zooplankton.

Coral Shrimpfish *Aeoliscus strigatus*

Hinged dorsal fin spine. Clear coastal to outer reef lagoons. Forms large schools, usually staying close together even when threatened, taking horizontal position to make a fast get-away. Body stripe is usually blackish. Maximum length 14 cm.

Rigid Shrimpfish *Centriscus scutatus*

Fixed, rigid dorsal fin spine. Body stripe dark reddish. Coastal reef slopes, often in silty habitat. In pairs, small schools and sometimes in larger schools like the Coral Shrimpfish (previous species). Often overlooked because of similarity to other species. Maximum length 15 cm.

SEAMOTHS — PEGASIDAE

Indo-Pacific family with only 2 genera and 5 species; both genera and the 3 species found in Australian waters are included here. Peculiar fishes, snout with produced rostrum; small downward-protrusible mouth, inferior, below base of rostrum. Gill opening restricted to above wing-like pectoral fin. Body encased in rigid plates and tail encircled with bony rings. Ventral fins reduced to pairs of slender structures used for crawling on substrate. Susceptible to epibiotic growth of algae, hydroids and other organisms, and regularly sheds outer layer of skin. Diet comprises tiny benthic invertebrates

Slender Seamoth *Pegasus volitans*

Variable colour, matching sand with dark mottling, or light patches on rubble, young often all black. Widespread in the Indo-Pacific in sheltered bays along borders of seagrass beds, usually in tidal current zones. Juveniles often float near the surface in open water before finding a place to settle. Usually shallow, but reported to 75 m depth. Maximum length 14 cm.

Trumpetfish (yellow form)

Trumpetfish (normal form)

Coral Shrimpfish

Rigid Shrimpfish

Slender Seamoth

Sculptured Seamoth *Pegasus lancifer*

Variable from pale sandy to bony white or patchy brown. Body broad, tail long. South coast endemic. Males with ornamental patches on edge of pectoral fins, used for display to females. Sandy bays, usually in vicinity of seagrass beds or low rubble reef. Mostly buried during the day, active at dusk. Maximum length 12 cm.

Little Dragonfish *Eurypegasus draconis*

Extremely well camouflaged and can mimic local objects such as old shell pieces or rubble bits. Rostrum short in small juveniles, lengthening during growth. Males with broad bluish white margin on pectoral fins, used to startle predators and for display to females. Protected coastal bays on silty sandflats near slopes. Maximum length 8 cm.

GHOSTPIPEFISHES — SOLENOSTOMIDAE

Small tropical Indo-Pacific family, consisting of a single genus and probably 5 species. Recent revision inconclusive, failing to recognise some species. Superficially similar to pipefishes (Syngnathidae) but differ totally in fin arrangements; in addition the female, as opposed to the male, incubates eggs. Head is pipefish-like with long tubular mouth. Body short and compressed, protected by bony plates, and all typical fins present. Two separate dorsal fins, anal fin opposite second dorsal fin, large caudal, pectoral and ventral fins; latter in female hooked to the body, forming pouch for brood. Highly variable in colour, mimicking invertebrates, algae or weeds. Diet comprises small crustaceans, often mysids, along reef edges near sand. Hovers vertically with head down.

Ornate Ghostpipefish *Solenostomus paradoxus*

Variable from red, yellow to black, semitransparent with regular patterns of spots, blotches or scribbles. Slender, thin appendages over body and fins, particularly on head and snout. Usually regularly spaced and sometimes very long. Caudal peduncle long. Protected coastal reefs close against rock faces on sand and often with small reef outcrops on sand slopes with black corals or crinoids. Often in pairs, occasionally in small groups (author observed 6 together). Maximum length 10 cm.

Delicate Ghostpipefish *Solenostomus leptosomus*

Almost transparent to brown with pale patches. Very similar to Ornate Ghostpipefish (previous species) in shape but lacks the narrow appendages on body and head; instead has leafy bits centrally below snout. A little-known species easily overlooked because of small size and appears to prefer clear deep water. Specimens from Sydney and Bass Point in 25 m depth over sand near reef, feeding on mysids. Maximum length about 75 mm.

Long-tail Ghostpipefish *Solenostomus armatus*

Variable from red to brown, black or green, uniformly coloured with irregular fine white spotting, some radiating from eyes. Protected coastal bays, typically on rubble reef with large rocks or sponges near sand, in depths of 15 m or more. Swims horizontally and hovers at slight angle with head down, rather than vertically like other similar species. Has a distinct caudal peduncle. Maximum length 10 cm.

Sculptured Seamoth

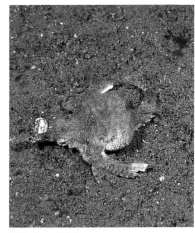

Little Dragonfish

Ornate Ghostpipefish

Delicate Ghostpipefish

Ornate Ghostpipefish

Long-tail Ghostpipefish

71

Robust Ghostpipefish *Solenostomus cyanopterus*

Various seagrass and algae colours from mottled greenish brown to grey and bright green. Best identified by very short or lack of caudal peduncle and smooth dorsal profile. Large females look very deep-bodied when ventral fins form pouch. Coastal protected bays and in deep clear estuaries, usually near weeds or small patches of seagrass. Usually in pairs. Largest ghostpipefish, maximum length 15 cm.

SEAHORSES, SEADRAGONS & PIPEFISHES — SYNGNATHIDAE

Large family with over 50 genera and about 220 species worldwide, about half recorded from Australian waters. Great diversity in shapes. General features: body protected by bony plates, arranged in rings, long tubular snout with toothless small oblique mouth at end. No ventral fins, anal and caudal fins small or lacking, some only present in larval stages. Two main groups: pipefishes with slender straight body and head in line, usually with small to moderate-sized caudal fin; and the seahorses, pipehorses and seadragons which usually have head at angle to body and tail ending in a bony point. Tail prehensile in seahorses, pipehorses and some pipefishes. In all species, males incubate eggs, protecting them with varying degrees of cover, ranging from simply stuck to the outside under body or tail to fully enclosed pouch, which relates to species behaviour. Those in full contact with substrate provide total protection by fully covering eggs with either overlapping or interlocking skinflaps, or pouch with small opening; those free swimming provide least protection with eggs partly exposed to outside. Habitats primarily coastal, most species associate with weeds and seagrasses in estuaries. Few have adapted to fresh water. Sizes range from 25 mm to 65 cm fully grown. Diet comprises primarily small crustaceans, shrimps, crabs and mysids.

White's Seahorse *Hippocampus whitei*

Common New South Wales seahorse, also known as Sydney Seahorse. Juveniles and females usually with several pale saddles over back. Males dark with fine pale spotting and scribbles on face turning to light colour with dark face and chest during courtship. Small but distinct knobby crown on head. Variable from drab greyish brown to yellow, depending on surroundings. Various habitats, from shallow seagrass beds in sheltered bays to depths of about 25 m with sponges. Often under jetties on holdfast of kelp. Nearly always in pairs, but may separate over several metres when feeding. Maximum length 20 cm.

Western Australian Seahorse *Hippocampus angustus*

Highly variable: yellow, orange, brown, grey and almost white, to match colour of sponges. Small tall crown on head and snout typically barred with many dark lines. Protected coastal bays on rocky reefs with mixed short weed and rich invertebrate growth. Often small number of pairs spread over suitable reef section. Maximum length 22 cm.

Short-head Seahorse *Hippocampus breviceps*

Head large, snout short in adults but proportionally longer in young. Variable from brown to yellow, orange and mauve, often with numerous small, black-edged, white ocelli over body and head. Male's pouch large and inflates when courting females. With or without filaments over top of head or back. Sheltered coastal reefs in yellowish to brown sargassum weeds, often in small groups comprising several pairs. Maximum length 12 cm.

Robust Ghostpipefish

White's Seahorse (male giving birth)

White's Seahorse (female)

Western Australian Seahorse

Short-head Seahorse

Big-belly Seahorse *Hippocampus abdominalis*

Without knobby crown, and tail very long. Drab grey or brown to bright yellow or orange. Often has series of dark blotches on head or body. Young pelagic, hanging onto floating seagrass, often reaching large size before settling. Adults mainly in kelp, often where growing on jetty pylons. In deep water with sponges where they match various colours of sponges. Often in loose groups, and pair in summer months. Maximum length 25 cm on mainland, 30 cm in southern Tasmania, and 35 cm reported in New Zealand, probably due to the lower temperatures.

Common Seahorse *Hippocampus kuda*

Small smooth crown on head, snout thick. Often peppered with tiny dark spots all over, more evident on light-coloured individuals. Widespread tropical species living in shallow seagrass beds. Young often in floating weeds, and occasionally adults are found on the surface a long way offshore attached to a piece of weed. On the substrate nearly always in pairs, usually within a few metres of each other. Heavily exploited in the Philippines for Chinese medicine market, to the extent that adults in some areas rarely reach full size. Maximum length 28 cm.

Dwarf Pipehorse *Acentronura tentaculata* (now known as *A. breviperula*)

Tiny drab species with head at slight angle, matching the surroundings perfectly. Although common in some places, only discovered by accident or when specifically searching for them. Shallow sandflats in protected, somewhat silty coastal areas among sparse low plant growth, and in algaes on rock. A similar undescribed species was recently found in Jervis Bay and in Sydney. Maximum length 63 mm.

Double-ended Pipehorse *Syngnathoides biaculeatus*

Green or yellowish, weedy colours. Tail prehensile. Male carries eggs openly under trunk. In seagrass beds, and adults often in large sargassum rafts. Author observed one jumping on top of floating weeds, out of the water, when trying to photograph it. Closely related to deep-water pipehorses sometimes found on our beaches which probably died from trawl catches. Maximum length 30 cm.

Weedy Seadragon *Phyllopteryx taeniolatus*

Readily identified by shape and colour. Juveniles brown and leafy appendages proportionally very large. Some geographical variation in size, number of tail appendages and colour. Shallow-water specimens dark brown or greenish above. Deep-water specimens orange to red above. Blue spotting on snout and bars variable. Body deepens with age, particularly in females. Male incubates about 250 eggs on tail. Young settle where released and feed on small mysids after 2 days' further development. Seadragons are unique Australian endemics. Also known as Common Seadragon. Maximum length 45 cm.

Leafy Seadragon *Phycodurus eques*

Variable from orange-brown or yellowish green to burgundy-red depending on depth. One of the most unusual and spectacular fishes, with incredible camouflage that not only makes it hard to find but also enables it to get close to prey. Floats near substrate like a piece of loose weed in pursuit of mysids, small shrimps or benthic crustaceans. Male incubates about 250 eggs under tail. Hatchlings are about 35 mm long and move to shallow depths to find tiny mysids. Adults usually in depths of about 10 m or more. Coastal bays, protected from large swells typical of southern waters, but cope well in moderate surge. Maximum length 35 cm.

Big-belly Seahorse

Common Seahorse

Dwarf Pipehorse

Double-ended Pipehorse

Weedy Seadragon (female)

Weedy Seadragon (male)

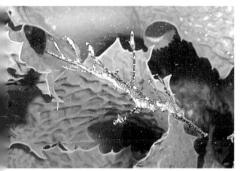

Weedy Seadragon (juvenile)

Leafy Seadragon

Spotted Pipefish *Stigmatopora argus*

Long snout and long, thin prehensile tail. Male very slender, female broad. Bright green to grey, rarely brown, with small blue ocelli over back; male's pouch shows longitudinal black and white lines when swollen with brood. Inhabits seagrass beds in sheltered bays, usually in pairs. Maximum length 27 cm.

Wide-body Pipefish *Stigmatopora nigra*

Similar to Spotted Pipefish (previous species) but lacking small ocelli. Variably brown to green, female with red barring below, which is usually shown during display with laterally extended body. Most habitats with weeds and seagrasses, usually in small groups and often abundant in seagrass beds, but also in deeper water with branching sponges. Tail greatly prehensile, often wrapped several times for hold. Maximum length 16 cm.

Javelin Pipefish *Lissocampus runa*

Body long and smooth, dorsal profile of snout concave. Variable plain light to dark brown or with pale blotches. Secretive in low, delicate weeds on rocks, sliding along underneath in search of prey. Shallow coastal bays on protected reefs and reported from rockpools in some areas. Maximum length 10 cm.

Smooth Pipefish *Lissocampus caudalis*

Dorsal profile of snout straight or slightly convex. Orange-brown, yellow-green and often purplish brown with banded pattern, males with a series of light blotches along the pouch when with brood. Usually in pairs among weeds on isolated rocks on sand or small seagrass patches, matching colour with weed or seagrass roots. Maximum length 10 cm.

Verco's Pipefish *Vanacampus vercoi*

Short snout. Indistinct barred pattern with pale spots; pale over back, dark bar over and between eyes. Southern Australian genus with several similar species. Long-snout Pipefish *V. poecilolaemus* similarly coloured but with long snout. Both rare and restricted to a few seagrass estuaries. *V. vercoi* only common in Pelican Lagoon, Kangaroo Island. Small species, maximum length 11 cm.

Port Phillip Pipefish *Vanacampus phillipi*

Snout moderately long. Adults dark brown with pale barring and blue spot or bars on sides. Common south coast species, found in coastal bays and estuaries. Secretive in seagrass beds and low rock reef on sand with weed cover; often found below jetties under rocks. Maximum length 20 cm.

Spotted Pipefish

Wide-body Pipefish

Javelin Pipefish

Smooth Pipefish

Verco's Pipefish

Port Phillip Pipefish

77

Mother-of-Pearl Pipefish *Vanacampus margaritifer*

Greyish brown to almost black, typically with small pale ocelli all over, often some evenly spaced pale barring along the body. Sheltered coastal bays and rocky estuaries with rubble and weeds, often open substrate along reef edges. Maximum length 20 cm.

Reeftop Pipefish *Corythoichthys haematopterus*

Several very similar tropical species, each with a slightly different pattern of lines or spots on head and body. This one with a series of dark spots along upper ridges and thin lines on cheek and across head between eyes. Commonly found on reef crests on rubble patches and large coral heads. In pairs or small aggregations. Maximum length 17 cm.

Schultz's Pipefish *Corythoichthys schultzi*

Very similar to above but has a longer snout with evenly spaced thin alternating dark and light bars. Variable with habitat, pale without colour on sand and with reddish small spots and fine lines on reef. On sand or rubble patches near or among reef on crests and slopes in protected habitat, singly on reefs and forms small groups on sand. Maximum length 16 cm.

Messmate Pipefish *Corythoichthys intestinalis*

Variable pattern of numerous thin lines, dashes or reticulations along sides, with alternating light and dark colours forming broad bands. Lines longitudinal over head. Sheltered coastal reefs, often silty habitat among algae and on rubble patches; singly, in pairs or forms small groups when out in the open. Maximum length 16 cm.

Red-banded Pipefish *Corythoichthys amplexus*

Broadly banded with dark brown to red. Snout thin and short. Usually in pairs on reefs, sliding over flat corals or sponges in pursuit of tiny crustaceans that live on such invertebrates. Clear coastal to outer reef crests and sometimes deep along walls. Small species, maximum length 95 mm.

Stick Pipefish *Trachyrhamphus bicoarctatus*

Head at slight angle to body. Variable yellow to brown or near black. Typically on substrate with posterior part of body raised. Coastal habitat in current-prone area, usually tidal channels, anchoring with hardened lower caudal fin rays in substrate, facing the current to feed on zooplankton drifting past. Maximum length 40 cm.

Mother-of-Pearl Pipefish

Reeftop Pipefish

Schultz's Pipefish

Messmate Pipefish

Red-banded Pipefish

Stick Pipefish

Long-head Pipefish *Trachyrhamphus longirostris*

Very long and thin, stick-like in appearance, lying almost straight on substrate. Protected bays on sand slopes with sparse seagrass or loose weeds, usually in moderate depths (10+ m). Distinguished from Stick Pipefish (previous species) by longer and straight head, and body not raising at angle from substrate. Maximum length 40 cm.

Brushtail Pipefish *Leptoichthys fistularius*

Very long and slender with large caudal fin, and snout greatly produced. Large adults with iridescent blue on snout. Lives in seagrass beds and is extremely well camouflaged. Southern seaward estuaries and bays with vast areas of seagrass. Australian endemic. One of the largest known pipefish, maximum length 65 cm.

Girdled Pipefish *Festucalex cinctus*

Head thick and snout slender. Often orange patch on gill cover. Usually dark grey or orange-brown with pale cross bars over back: series of small leafy appendages on dorsal ridges. Sheltered coastal bays on open rubble patches with sparse low algal growth, common New South Wales species. Maximum length 16 cm.

Tiger Pipefish *Filicampus tigris*

Solid species with indistinct broad banding. Best identified by the series of evenly spaced white spots along ventral ridges of the trunk. Adults have additional spaced blue bars on back. Sheltered bays, entering shallow depths on sand near seagrass beds or on rubble. Commonly found in Sydney Harbour in coves near heads to depths of 30 m. Maximum length 30 cm.

Sawtooth Pipefish *Maroubra perserrata*

Grey to light brown, usually distinct pale line over top from tip of snout to caudal-fin base and sides with either thin black line or vertical pale barring in relation to age or sex. Common reef species in narrow ledges or in the back of low overhanging rock with sand patches below, usually in pairs or small aggregations. Maximum length 85 mm.

Upside-down Pipefish *Heraldia nocturna*

Free-swimming, and easily identified by fan-like caudal fin. Often observed in pairs at night. The east coast form is mostly dark brown with some white tips on caudal fin; the south coast form is yellow to brown with blotched marking and white caudal-fin margin and tips when adult. Rocky reefs in small caves and ledges swimming upside down against ceiling. Maximum length 10 cm.

.ong-head Pipefish

Brushtail Pipefish

irdled Pipefish

Tiger Pipefish

awtooth Pipefish

Upside-down Pipefish

Cleaner Pipefish *Doryrhamphus janssi*

Distinct species with orange-brown body ending in blue at both ends, and black-and-white marked caudal fin. Secretive in rich coral growth and in the back of ledges. Only recently author discovered these fishes as active cleaners, specialising in *Cheilodipterus* cardinalfishes and *Neopomacentrus* damselfishes. Often shares caves with cleaner shrimps, forming part of working stations where various customers seek treatment for removal of small parasites. Previously known as Jans's Pipefish. Maximum length 13 cm.

Banded Pipefish *Doryrhamphus dactyliophorus*

Easily identified by banded pattern and large flag-like caudal fin. Only similar species in New Caledonia and Indian Ocean, which differ by number of bands. Eggs deep red, attached to trunk on male without additional cover. Protected coastal reefs, in large caves or among boulders with long-spined urchins. Juveniles in small aggregations and adults usually in pairs. Often found in with cleaner shrimps, and probably participate in cleaning. Maximum length 20 cm.

SCORPIONFISHES — SCORPAENIDAE

Large complicated family of spiny fishes, consisting of at least 10 subfamilies, approximately 70 genera and about 350 species globally, of which 33 genera and about 80 species are known from Australian waters. Includes many venomous, potentially dangerous species, such as stonefish and lionfish. Most are capable of inflicting painful stabs and should be handled with care, even when dead. Venom primarily stored in glands at base of each dorsal spine, and stab forces down skin along spine causing venom-injection under pressure. Scorpionfishes have spiny ridges on head, and differences in these are usually diagnostic for genus. Most are extremely well camouflaged and found motionless on substrate to ambush prey. Some are nocturnal. Diet includes a great variety of invertebrates or fishes; some specialise in particular prey. Many species regarded as good food fish and some are of commercial importance. Stings from venomous spines extremely painful and cause numbness. Initial bleeding should be encouraged and heat applied by quickest available means: immersing in hottest bearable water, blowing hot air from hairdryer or heatgun, in front of radiator, or if in remote tropics, hot stone or sand will relieve pain and kill venom. Seek medical advice and try to identify the species, which can be important for treatment.

Fortesque *Centropogon australis*

Variable from bony white to brown, with large dark patches on body and bands over eyes and caudal fin. Small juveniles mottled brown. Sheltered bays and estuaries, sometimes gathering in great numbers. Small juveniles in seagrass beds or in low mixed weed and rock habitat. Adults on rubble slopes along reef edges in deeper parts of estuaries to about 30 m depth. Maximum length 14 cm.

Goblinfish *Glyptauchen panduratus*

Identified best by deep groove dorsally behind head, making head look square with large centrally placed eyes on sides. Colour variable from bony white to black. Protected coastal bays and seaward part of estuaries on mixed rocky-sand and vegetated reefs. Hides under rocks and comes out at night to hunt crustaceans. Rarely swims and moves along substrate in hopping fashion, using fins. Maximum length 20 cm.

Cleaner Pipefish

Banded Pipefish

ortesque

oblinfish

83

Cobbler *Gymnapistes marmoratus*

Similar to Fortesque in colour and shape, but lacks scales and grows much larger. Large black blotch on dorsal fin. Coastal bays and throughout large coastal estuaries, often in silty habitat. Sometimes aggregates in massive numbers, possibly for spawning or migration. Nocturnal, feeding on shrimps and other crustaceans. Juveniles in seagrasses, adults among weeds or partly buried in sand. Also known as Soldierfish. Maximum length 22 cm.

White-face Cobbler *Liocranium* sp.

Undescribed species, similar to Fortesque and possibly overlooked for this reason. White face, otherwise brownish colour with large dark blotches. Well camouflaged, changing colour to suit surroundings. Stab from dorsal fin is extremely painful. Coastal bays and inner reef habitat in current-prone tidal zones. Maximum length 15 cm.

Ruddy Gurnard Perch *Neosebastes scorpaenoides*

Tall dorsal spines, large eyes. Head becomes proportionally larger and front steepens with age. Dark banding on face, body and caudal fin. Common Victorian species where it can be found in shallow bays on sand in mixed rock, sand and weed habitat. Ranges to deep offshore to about 140 m. Usually in sponge reefs when deep. Maximum length 40 cm.

Gulf Gurnard Perch *Neosebastes bougainvillii*

Almost identical in colour to Ruddy Gurnard Perch (previous species) and best identified by almost straight lateral line, lacking the short curve at origin as in other similar species. Differs in other ways, such as the number of pores under the head, but these characteristics are only of use when specimen is available. Offshore species on remote reefs and usually deep. Maximum length 40 cm.

Bighead Gurnard Perch *Neosebastes pandus*

Head particularly large in adults, square-looking. Pectoral fins very large, almost reaching below centre of soft dorsal fin. Rocky reefs, shallow weedy to deep sponge areas, resting in camouflaged positions on substrate to depths of 200+ m. Maximum length 40 cm.

False Stonefish *Scorpaenopsis diabola*

Large unusually shaped head, body somewhat humpbacked. On rubble substrate with head upwards mimicking stones. Shallow lagoons and protected reef-flats. Widespread tropical species, often mistaken for stonefish. Whilst not as dangerous as stonefish, it has a nasty sting. Maximum length 18 cm.

Cobbler

White-face Cobbler

Ruddy Gurnard Perch

Gulf Gurnard Perch

Bighead Gurnard Perch

False Stonefish

85

Raggy Scorpionfish *Scorpaenopsis venosa*

Numerous small tentacles over head and body. Colour in the photograph is typical, with dark triangular area from eye down. Coastal, often silty reefs, especially outcrops on sand or mud slopes, openly on sponges or rock. Solitary, but often several individuals sharing a suitable habitat. Maximum length 18 cm.

Smallscale Scorpionfish *Scorpaenopsis oxycephala*

Dark triangular area below the eye, headed by a white band. Brown to red with pale blotches. Branched skin flaps on fins, head and along lateral line. Coastal to outer reef crests, often found in open substrate at night, probably hunting crustaceans or benthic fishes. Maximum length 30 cm.

Red Rockcod *Scorpaena cardinalis*

Common east coast species, highly variable from light grey to bright red with marbled patterns, and small dark spots on chest. Very well camouflaged, often found next to sponges. Usually with skin flaps on head along lateral line and over body. Several similar species in deep water and elsewhere in New Zealand and Western Australia. Coastal reef to deep offshore and may move into silty upper regions of estuaries. Regularly hooked when fishing close to reefs. Maximum length 40 cm.

Southern Rockcod *Scorpaena papillosa*

Very similar to Red Rockcod (previous species) but lacks spots on chest, has fewer skin flaps, and generally with more mottled pattern and fins spotted. Usually greyish brown or violet-brown, some pale areas behind head or over body, the latter often with dark outlined scales. Coastal, often silty habitat and estuaries, to offshore reefs on kelp reef or sponges. Maximum length 30 cm.

Western Red Rockcod *Scorpaena sumptuosa*

Brown to red mottling all over, and indistinctly in two broad bands over body, extended onto fins with pale creamy interspacing. Deep-bodied, with small skin flaps, eyes elevated on head with distinct groove behind. Shallow protected coastal bays to deep offshore on rocky or coral reefs. Maximum length 40 cm.

Raggy Scorpionfish

Smallscale Scorpionfish

Red Rockcod (juvenile)

Red Rockcod (adult)

Southern Rockcod

Western Red Rockcod

Pygmy Rockcod *Scorpaenodes scaber*

Distinctive small species with orange to red spotting on fins and same colour on nostril flaps. Variable, sometimes showing a large pale area behind the head and caudal peduncle. Several similar species, often confused with *S. littoralis*, restricted to the Northern Hemisphere and this name commonly occurs in Australian checklists. In addition, photographs of Japanese species are often used in Australian identification books. Various habitats, from clear estuarine reefs to deep offshore. Small species, maximum length 12 cm.

Blotchfin Scorpionfish *Scorpaenodes varipinnis*

Red blotches near eye and along dorsal-fin base identifies this species. Secretive on clear coastal reefs, usually out on rock surfaces at night. Widespread tropical species. *S. guamensis* is a similar dark species, but without red markings and large dark spot on lower part of operculum; found in more silty habitat. Maximum length 12 cm.

Coral Scorpionfish *Sebastapistes cyanostigma*

Pink with yellow blotches and fine yellow spotting; white-spotted at night. Secretive in coral heads, often stinging fire corals where few other fish live. Although common on outer reef crests, not often observed except by those checking corals closely. Small species, maximum length 10 cm.

Little Scorpionfish *Maxillicosta scabriceps*

Whitley's Scorpionfish *M. whitleyi* very similar to *M. scabriceps* but occurs in deeper sand channels and generally lighter in colour below, as well as some features on the head are difficult to see underwater. Nocturnal, buried in sand during the day and rarely seen, but surprisingly common in some places at night. Sheltered sandy bays near reefs. Maximum length 12 cm.

Red Gurnard Perch *Helicolenus alporti*

Deep-water genus. Several similar species with global distribution in cool temperate seas. Pale with brown to red bands on head, below each dorsal fin and on caudal fin. Deep on the mainland, but as shallow as 10 m in southern Tasmanian waters. Often hooked when fishing offshore reefs. Seaperch *H. percoides* off New South Wales is usually at depths of 30+ m. Maximum length 40 cm.

Paperfish *Taenianotus triacanthus*

Monotypic genus. Body very compressed. Dorsal fin large, sailfin-like, attached by short membrane to caudal fin. Bearded with numerous small appendages. Variable from almost white, yellow, greenish, brown to pink. Often out in the open, sitting on top of corals or rocks but easily overlooked. Clear coastal to outer reef habitats in shallow as well as deep water to 135 m. Maximum length 10 cm.

Lacy Scorpionfish *Rhinopias aphanes*

Unusual head shape and colour pattern identifies this species. Some variation in basic colour from black to red lines. Easily overlooked even though sits openly on corals, but this is partly due to inhabiting current zones where crinoids are prolific, and it looks just like the feathery invertebrate. Depth range 6–25 m. Several other spectacular species elsewhere, but possibly occur in Australian waters. Maximum length 25 cm.

Pygmy Rockcod

Blotchfin Scorpionfish

Coral Scorpionfish

Little Scorpionfish

Red Gurnard Perch

Paperfish

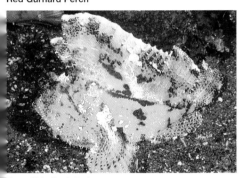

Paperfish (variation)

Lacy Scorpionfish

89

Common Lionfish *Pterois volitans*

Identified by large feathery fins, close banded body pattern, dark spots on fins and white spots along lateral line in adults. Highly variable in some characteristics such as appendages above eye, ranging from large leaf-like to almost non-existent. Commonly encountered in various habitats, ranging from almost brackish estuaries to clear offshore islands. Very widespread in tropical waters. Also known as devilfishes and firefishes. Maximum length 35 cm.

Russell's Lionfish *Pterois russelli*

Very similar to Common Lionfish (previous species), but brownish, dark spot above base of pectoral fin and median fins with only tiny spots, or none at all. Easily overlooked because similar to Common Lionfish and occurs in deeper water, usually a silty environment. Often on isolated outcrops of reef on mud slopes or on shipwrecks. Maximum length 40 cm.

African Lionfish *Pterois mombasae*

Alternating broad and thin red to brown bars on body. Large eye tentacles and no series of dark spots on pectoral fin as in Spotfin Lionfish (next species). Eye very large. Another easily overlooked species, similar to other species and living in moderately deep water — the shallowest seen by the author about 15 m. Sheltered deep coastal slopes in rich invertebrate habitats with soft corals and sponges. Maximum size 20 cm.

Spotfin Lionfish *Pterois antennata*

Distinctive with series of dark spots on pectoral fins, showing best when seen from the back, as usual seen, and long white filaments radiating from pectoral fins. One of the most frequently observed species on clear coastal to outer reefs from shallow to deep water. Feeds on small fishes and crustaceans. Maximum length 20 cm.

Zebra Lionfish *Dendrochirus zebra*

Body with brown to reddish, alternating broad and thin bars. Pectoral fins often with filamentous ray extensions beyond rounded webbing. Median fins with spots on soft rays. Coastal reefs and lagoons, solitary in large coral heads, or congregating on ceilings of large overhangs in shallow to moderately deep water, reported to 80 m depth. Maximum length 20 cm.

Common Lionfish (adult)

Common Lionfish (young adult)

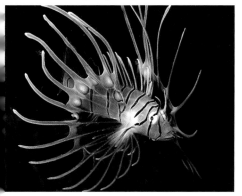

Common Lionfish (juvenile)

Spotfin Lionfish

Russell's Lionfish

African Lionfish

Zebra Lionfish

91

Dwarf Lionfish *Dendrochirus brachypterus*

Distinctly banded pectoral fins and densely spotted soft rays in median fins. Reddish brown to almost black banding, sometimes with strong yellow markings. Coastal reefs and deep clear oceanic estuaries on sponges or short algal reefs, sometimes muddy habitat. Widespread tropical species. Small, maximum length 15 cm.

Longfinned Waspfish *Apistus carinatus*

Very long pectoral fins, white barbels on chin and large black spot centrally on dorsal fin. Nocturnal, buries itself in sand and is rarely seen, except at night crawling on the sand in search of small crustaceans and fish. Coastal protected bays to deep offshore on sandflats, often silty substrate. Maximum length 20 cm.

Reef Stonefish *Synanceia verrucosa*

Various colours matching surroundings, often with bright red and yellow. Easily overlooked but sits openly on reefs and often in very shallow depths. Large bulky body and very large rounded pectoral fins. The most venomous fish known, a sting produces incredible pain and has caused fatalities. Some similar more drab species in muddy coastal habitats. Maximum length 38 cm.

Caledonian Stinger *Inimicus caledonicus*

Best recognised by its unusual head shape, large dorsal fin spines and broad pectoral fins with finger-like rays below, used for crawling. Drab grey-brown, usually darker on sides than dorsally. Often buried in sand and extremely well camouflaged. Coastal sandflats and slopes, usually along seagrass beds or reef margins. Maximum length 25 cm.

PROWFISHES — PATAECIDAE

Small Australian family with 3 monotypic genera, confined to southern waters. Compressed fishes with a long-based single dorsal fin which originates over front of head, and confluent but not attached to caudal fin. Ventral fins absent, and large pectoral fins placed low. Instead of scales a tough skin, outer layer regularly shed to get rid of epibiotic growth, including bryazoa, tubeworms and algae. Excellent camouflage in sponge reefs. Diet comprises primarily crustaceans, especially shrimps.

Warty Prowfish *Aetapcus maculatus*

Variable from almost white, yellow to orange, often a series of black spots along the dorsal-fin base. Pectoral fin almost black in juveniles. Gill opening as a small hole, just below dorsal-fin base, sometimes used for propulsion, combined by pushing from substrate with pectoral fins. Adults with lumpy skin. Coastal rocky estuaries to deep offshore reefs under rocks or among boulders, adults at moderate depths in rocks with sponge growth. Sits on substrate. Maximum length 22 cm.

Red Indianfish *Pataecus fronto*

Dorsal fin very tall above head. Variable from yellow, orange to red, forehead sometimes white. Like the Warty Prowfish (previous species), sometimes uses gill opening for propulsion. Coastal to offshore reefs on substrate, resting against rocks or sponges. Easily overlooked, especially with coloured sponges. The similar Whiskered Prowfish *Neopataecus waterhousii* shows distinctive caudal peduncle, mainly occurs on the south-west coast but one specimen found on a beach in Western Port, Victoria. Maximum length 25 cm.

Dwarf Lionfish

Longfinned Waspfish

Reef Stonefish

Caledonian Stinger

Warty Prowfish

Red Indianfish

93

RED VELVETFISHES — GNATHANACANTHIDAE

Monospecific family, similar and closely related to prowfishes, but have well-developed ventral fins with membrane attached to abdomen, and high dorsal fin with a deep notch. Skin covered with fleshy projections, giving a velvety feel in adults. Reported to have venomous dorsal fin spines.

Red Velvetfish *Gnathanacanthus goetzeei*

Easily identified by its shape. Colour varies from brown to red. Small juveniles ornamented with orange-red spots and lines on fins, body, and radiating 3 ways from eyes. Very secretive in kelp areas, usually only seen at night. Feeds on shrimps. Maximum length 30 cm.

FLYING GURNARDS — DACTYLOPTERIDAE

Small family with 2 genera and 7 species worldwide, one monotypic genus in the Atlantic, others in the Indo-Pacific and 4 known from Australian waters. Tropical deep-water benthic fishes, only one seen occasionally in shallow depths and entering estuaries. Easily recognised by the exceptionally large pectoral fins which reach the caudal fin and when spread out are almost circular in shape. Fins used for display or startling possible predators. Usually partly buried in substrate during the day, and mostly active at night, hunting benthic fishes, crustaceans and cephalopods.

Flying Gurnard *Dactyloptena orientalis*

Pale brownish or greenish grey with banded and spotted pattern on body. Pectorals spotted in juveniles with black and blue blotch near base, adults with smaller spotting and numerous thin blue lines along outer margins of longest rays. Usually on sand slopes adjacent to deep water, but occasionally in large estuaries such as Sydney Harbour on clean sandflats with rubble and some algal growth. Usually crawls slowly on substrate using ventral fins. When disturbed, it spreads its fins out broadly for a while, but often withdraws them to sides and suddenly takes off with a burst of speed, swimming quickly out of sight. Maximum length 30 cm.

GURNARDS — TRIGLIDAE

Large family of benthic fishes with about 13 genera and 120 species worldwide, of which 8 genera and 33 species are known from Australian waters. The head is armoured with bony plates and the body is covered with small ctenoid or more or less embedded cycloid scales. Pectoral fins usually very large, rounded, lower rays free and thickened, used for walking and probing substrate. Inside of fins often ornamented with yellow and iridescent blue markings, patterns diagnostic features. Usually deep-water, mainly seen shallow in southern waters, particularly in Tasmania, where most species included here are seen in depths less than 20 m. On the mainland, some of the same species only trawled in much greater depths. Few enter estuaries when juvenile, feeding over shallow sandflats near the tidal zone, moving to deep water as adults. Often partly buried in sand, nocturnal, hunting fishes, crustaceans and cephalopods. Some larger species are commercially targeted. Most turn red when captured.

Red Gurnard *Chelidonichthys kumu*

Pectoral fins greenish yellow with iridescent blue margin and evenly spaced spots, and small black patch near body. Tiny embedded cycloid scales in over 100 diagonal rows over body. Adults usually very deep (80+ m), juveniles in shallow coastal bays along beaches. Several similar species in the Northern and Southern Hemisphere. The Red Gurnard is thought to be widespread in the Southern Hemisphere. Maximum length 50 cm.

Red Velvetfish (juvenile)

Red Velvetfish (adult)

Flying Gurnard (juveniles)

Flying Gurnard (adult)

Red Gurnard

95

Minor Gurnard *Lepidotrigla modesta*

Pectoral fin dusky with blue outer margin, red near body. Large red or dusky blotch on dorsal fin. Head strongly concave on snout, small and short, rectangular in cross-section. Clear coastal bays, on sand in vicinity of reefs. Mostly deep, reported from 20 to 200 m. Usually seen at night, when mainly reddish in colour. Small species, maximum length 20 cm.

Deepwater Gurnard *Lepidotrigla mulhalli*

Pectoral fins greenish grey with pale blue margin, large black blotch with iridescent blue marking at posterior part. Snout with projecting spines. Dorsal fin reddish but no defined blotch. Offshore on sand, sometimes visiting shallow sandy coves to feed at night. Reported from 20 to 200 m depth. Small species, maximum length 20 cm.

Butterfly Gurnard *Lepidotrigla vanessa*

Large pale-edged dark blotch on spinous dorsal fin. Pectoral fins reddish near body to all yellow with thin blue margin, and small to large black blotch on posterior part. Coastal to offshore, to 100 m depth. Juveniles occasionally in shallow estuaries, including Port Phillip Bay, on sand-rubble along reef edge. Maximum length 25 cm.

Eastern Spiny Gurnard *Lepidotrigla pleuracanthica*

Black spot on spinous dorsal fin with yellow borders. Caudal fin with pale margin and narrow pale band near base. Pectoral fin dusky with iridescent blue margin, sometimes several blue spots anteriorly near margin. Coastal reefs and estuaries, and offshore to about 50 m depth. Rubble and sand near or on low reef. Small species, maximum length 20 cm, usually 16 cm.

Southern Spiny Gurnard *Lepidotrigla papilio*

Black spot in spinous dorsal fin with white or pale yellow borders. Pale band in caudal fin broad. Pectoral fin pale greenish grey with pale blue margin, juveniles with large yellow-edged blue-black ocellus, sometimes still evident in adults. Commonly found in deeper part of large estuaries on scallop beds and near reefs. Small species, maximum length 20 cm.

Minor Gurnard

Deepwater Gurnard

Butterfly Gurnard

Eastern Spiny Gurnard

Southern Spiny Gurnard

97

FLATHEADS — PLATYCEPHALIDAE

Large family, primarily in the Indo-Pacific, with estimated 18 genera and 60 species, of which 12 genera and 44 species are recognised in Australian waters. Heads greatly depressed, bearing bony ridges, frequently armed with large pungent spines. Body less depressed, covered with small cycloid scales. Spines in fins strong and slender, except first in dorsal fin typically tiny, detached and partly embedded. Most species lack a swimbladder and rest on the substrate, sometimes buried with just eyes exposed. Shallow-water species often with elaborate eye lappets, diagnostic for many. Diet includes small fishes and a variety of benthic invertebrates, often cephalopods. Tropical species mostly small, while the southern species are larger and of commercial importance and commonly fished for by anglers in bays and coastal waters.

Midget Flathead *Onigocia spinosa*

Black ventral fins with white edge, more or less distinct banding posteriorly on body. Nocturnal, buried deep in sand during the day and only out at night. Coastal deep sandflats in protected bays, often in silty habitat in depths over 10 m. Abundant in some areas. Very small species, maximum length 10 cm.

Fringe-lip Flathead *Thysanophrys otaitensis*

Several similar species, differing mainly in spiny features on the head and often a specimen is required for positive identification. Snout long. Pectoral and ventral fins black-spotted. Mixed sand and mud habitat in sheltered coastal bays on flats and slopes. Nocturnal, only seen out of sand at night, often in small spread-out groups. Maximum length 25 cm.

Rock Flathead *Thysanophrys cirronasus*

Highly variable, matching surroundings with diffused banding and blotched patterns. Particularly large bony head. Small juveniles often bony white colour, sitting among rubble. Clear coastal reefs among mixed sand rock and weed patches with rock-like appearance. Easily approached, relying on camouflage for protection. Often called Tassel-snouted Flathead. Maximum length 35 cm.

Fine-spotted Flathead *Suggrundus bosschei*

Grey-white with small dark spots all over, forming many narrow bars on caudal fin when rays close together. Corners of caudal fin dusky. Coastal and inner reef sandflats, often buried in fine silty white sand patches near large coral heads. Nocturnal, only out at night. Large for genus, maximum length 45 cm.

Sand Flathead *Platycephalus bassensis*

Several very similar species with sandy colour above and pale below; however, each has diagnostic caudal fin patterns, usually comprising black spots against white area. This species has large black blotches in lower half, others with more and smaller blotches or spots and in some the spots appear stretched into streaks. Most occur in southern waters on sandy substrate in estuaries and coastal bays. Maximum lengths vary between 46 and 90 cm; this species 46 cm.

Midget Flathead

Fringe-lip Flathead

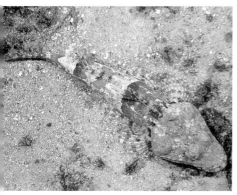

Rock Flathead

Fine-spotted Flathead

Sand Flathead

99

Dusky Flathead *Platycephalus fuscus*

Caudal fin bluish grey in large adult with small to moderate-sized black spot centrally near rear margin. Brown to sandy-pale above, with fine spotting on body and pectoral fins. Offshore along fringes of mixed sand and rock; adults enter coastal estuaries, including silty muddy habitat showing a bronzy colour. Usually buried in sand in the daytime. Sometimes occurs in pairs, with the male following the gravid female closely until ready to spawn. Largest of all flatheads, maximum recorded length 1.2 m and weight 15 kg.

Flagtail Flathead *Platycephalus arenarius*

Distinct caudal fin with long black stripes on white on lower half, gradually changing to brown on top. Body with numerous mixed-sized brown spots over upper body and head. Mainly tropical, ranging into southern New South Wales, where regarded as expatriate. Sandy estuaries and coastal bays. Juveniles form schools over shallow sandbanks in the tropics. Maximum length 45 cm.

Grass Flathead *Platycephalus laevigatus*

Body only slightly compressed and head much less compressed compared to other flatheads. Settling juveniles about 25 mm long are black on top and white below. With growth, the black area breaks up into broad bands and in adults banding is only evident as a series of dark blotches and spots. Inhabits low reef with dominant weed cover, and seagrass beds, often found along edges. Sleeps hiding under weeds, rather than buried in sand. Maximum length 50 cm.

ROCKCODS, GROUPERS & BASSLETS — SERRANIDAE

Complicated family of several difficult to define subfamilies with many shared characteristics between otherwise seemingly different groups. Family limits unclear and defined differently in the literature, including the most recent. Including all doubtful groups, about 50 genera and well over 400 species. Two major and several smaller groups, distinct, presented here as tentative subfamilies as recognised by most recent authors. First includes the rockcods, groupers and coral trouts, constituting about half the family worldwide in tropical seas, and large but yet undetermined proportion in Australian waters. Most have tiny scales, indistinct lateral line, 24 vertebrae and strongly rounded to emarginate caudal fin, except lunate in *Variola*. Reef dwellers, often territorial and usually solitary in the Indo-Pacific, but congregate in selected places at times. Inhabits coastal to outer reefs, some restricted to deep water, and several as juveniles in brackish water. Mostly medium-sized to large fishes, 1–2 m, with Queensland Groper reported to 3 m length. Many of commercial importance. Vulnerable to spearfishing due to home ranging habits on reefs and showing little fear of divers, making it an easy target, and some protected species. Only fair to shoot with a camera rather than a spear. Second-largest group are the basslets, with numerous small colourful planktivores, including here genus *Callanthias*, even though recently placed in its own family. Similar investigation of others will result in more separations, but it seems best to include them in Serranidae for now. The remainder include several confusing groups, especially soapfishes (some authors place them in several separate families), including Grammistinae and Liopropominae. Species included here are arranged according to their appearance, rather than systematically, for easier identification.

Strawberry Cod *Trachypoma macracanthus*

Monotypic genus, orange to red with numerous small white spots all over. Rocky reefs, often among boulders, entering estuaries when young, adults offshore in protected clear-water reefs to about 20 m depth. Nocturnal, semi-exposed during the day, hiding in rocks. Feeds primarily on shrimps, also takes small fish. Maximum length 40 cm.

Dusky Flathead

Flagtail Flathead

Grass Flathead

Strawberry Cod

Eastern Wirrah *Acanthistius ocellatus*

Greenish grey with small blue spots, fins bluish dusky with thin pale blue edges. Juveniles with dusky bands radiating from eye. In caves and crevices, rocky reefs from estuaries to offshore, including tidal pools and depths of 100 m. Southern Hemisphere genus with about 8 species, some banded in deep water. Very similar to Western Wirrah *A. serratus* in south-western waters. Maximum length 45 cm.

Harlequin Fish *Othos dentex*

Highly variable in colour but very distinct in southern waters, with no other similar fish. Basic colour from red or pink to grey, with yellow or green blotches and large blue spots. Monotypic genus, southern coast endemic. Inquisitive and easily approached by divers at close range. Shallow rocky reefs to 30 m, with preference for protected clear coastal waters in caves and crevices. Maximum length 76 cm.

Lyre-tail Cod *Variola louti*

Adults brown to red with numerous blue spots; juveniles with black stripe and white below. Two similar species with lunate caudal fin. Other species *V. albimarginata* are more tropical, as juvenile without black stripe, but pinkish orange all over, whilst adult has distinct pale caudal-fin margin, lacking in *V. louti*. Rocky and coral reefs, juveniles on rubble slopes, adults on outer reef slopes and along drop-offs. Maximum length 80 cm.

White-square Cod *Gracila albomarginata*

Adults easily recognised by large white square on sides, less distinct in very large individuals. Small juveniles purple with strong red margins on caudal, dorsal and anal fins, looking like basslets. Clear outer reef walls and deep bommies in current-prone areas, adults often swimming well away from the wall and juveniles above bommies mixing with various planktivores. Active for cod during the day. Maximum length 45 cm.

Tomato Cod *Cephalopholis sonnerati*

Highly variable from pale brown to deep orange, with numerous brown to red spots; small juveniles bluish grey, sometimes a series of pale blotches or indistinct banding. Adults deep-bodied compared to other members of the genus. Coastal and often silty habitats, most common on isolated outcrops of coral, rocks or with land debris washed in by rivers during floods on mud slopes. Adults commonly seen visiting cleaning stations of Cleaner Shrimp *Lysmata amboinensis* which occurs throughout the tropics and ranges into subtropical zones; on the east coast, south at least to Montague Island. Juveniles in shallow rock or rubble ridges on slopes, often with small shrimps in caves. Large adults usually deep, to 100 m. Maximum length 50 cm.

Eastern Wirrah

Harlequin Fish

Lyre-tail Cod (adult)

Lyre-tail Cod (juvenile)

White-square Cod

Tomato Cod (adult)

Tomato Cod (adult with cleaner shrimps)

Tomato Cod (juvenile)

103

Leopard Rockcod *Cephalopholis leoparda*

Variable from pale brown to orange with darker orange and red spotting. Identified by dark saddle immediately behind dorsal fin and a stripe or series of spots on caudal fin along each corner. Coastal, inner reefs, lagoons, in rich coral growth areas, often reef crests. Solitary, somewhat shy species. Small, maximum length 20 cm.

Flagtail Rockcod *Cephalopholis urodeta*

Usually orange to red with dark tail and obvious white lines in caudal fin; more or less distinctive broad barred pattern on body. Coastal and inner reefs with rich coral habitats, usually common on crests and along upper area of drop-offs, but venturing to about 40 m depth. Maximum length 30 cm.

Peacock Rockcod *Cephalopholis argus*

Best identified by white patch in front of pectoral-fin base and small iridescent blue spots all over. Can change colour quickly, variable from very dark to light greenish and often white bars posteriorly on body. Various coral habitats from coastal to outer reefs, shallow to about 40 m. Maximum length 45 cm.

Coral Rockcod *Cephalopholis miniata*

Orange when small, without spots, gradually changing to red with numerous bright blue spots as adult. Very common species from shallow coastal to outer reefs along drop-offs and in lagoons. Regularly visits Cleaner Shrimp stations. The similar Saddled Rockcod *C. sexmaculata* has a series of dark saddles along upper sides and usually found along steep walls. Maximum length 40 cm.

Bluespotted Rockcod *Cephalopholis cyanostigma*

Juveniles ash-grey with bright yellow to orange fins, and posteriorly on body. Adults pale to dark brown with numerous small blue, black-edged ocelli all over. Juvenile and adult phases until recently regarded as separate species but the change is gradual, and intermediates occasionally sighted. Inner reefs and coastal slopes with rich coral growth to outer reefs, staying close to substrate and rather shy, especially juveniles. Depth range 1–50 m. Reported maximum length 35 cm, probably to 45 cm.

Leopard Rockcod

Flagtail Rockcod

Peacock Rockcod

Coral Rockcod

Bluespotted Rockcod (adult)

Bluespotted Rockcod (juvenile)

105

Footballer Cod *Plectropomus laevis*

Young and sub-adults distinct: body white with dark saddles, and snout and fins yellow, sometimes to very large size. Usually large adults darken to almost black, but broad saddles still evident, with some small blue spots on darker parts. Very small juveniles appear to mimic poisonous Saddled Puffer *Canthigaster valentini*. Large adults sometimes in small groups, hovering near deep reef outcrops or large bommies on open sandy substrates. Clear coastal to outer reefs and deep lagoons in current-prone areas. Large species, maximum length about 1 m.

Bar-cheek Coral Trout *Plectropomus maculatus*

Pale to red-brown with a series of moderate-sized, black-edged, blue spots on head and upper sides, sometimes forming short dashes on head. Coastal and inner reefs, mostly in mixed coral, sponge and weed habitat. Other common Coral Trout *P. leopardus* has smaller spots and prefers clearer conditions, near outer reefs, forming loose aggregations. Both maximum length about 75 cm.

White-lined Rockcod *Anyperodon leucogrammicus*

Juveniles mimic several striped wrasses, *Halichoeres* spp., to get close to prey, mainly juvenile damselfishes. Adults with several white streaks, as in the photograph, becoming less distinct in very large individuals. Coastal slopes to outer reef lagoons in rich coral areas with dominant soft corals and some algal growth. Maximum length 50 cm.

Barramundi Cod *Chromileptes altivelis*

Distinct species. Small juveniles almost white with black spotted pattern, and adults with strongly concave dorsal profile of head, making head look small in proportion to the body. Juveniles in shallow protected reefs, swimming with head towards substrate and waving fins in exaggerated manner like feeding coral polyp. Although common in some areas, adults are not seen much due to their secretive and shy nature. Maximum length 70 cm.

Breaksea Cod *Epinephelides armatus*

Uniformly grey to very dark, but each scale with pale centre. Young with dark face. Clear coastal and offshore reefs in moderate depths to about 100 m. Mainly along steep walls with caves and ledges, usually staying in sheltered parts. Monotypic genus, Australian endemic. Maximum length 56 cm.

Footballer Cod (sub-adult)

Footballer Cod (adult)

Bar-cheek Coral Trout

White-lined Rockcod

Barramundi Cod

Breaksea Cod

107

Foursaddle Grouper *Epinephelus spilotoceps*

Usually with 4 dark saddles, evenly spaced from caudal peduncle to below centre of dorsal fin, but can be absent in small individuals which show distinct, much coarser, honeycomb pattern. Clear coastal to offshore reefs, often on shallow crests sitting in the open but quickly moving for cover unless approached with special care. Maximum length 35 cm.

Brown-spotted Grouper *Epinephelus coioides*

Several very similar species. Brown-orange spots and dusky, patchy, broad banding. Spots large, about pupil-size in young, proportionally much smaller in large adults. Mainly in estuaries and protected silty reef habitats. Adults usually along base of small drop-offs with large caves or in shipwrecks. Maximum length 1 m.

Black Cod *Epinephelus daemelii*

Pale whitish to dark grey with broad dark bands, curving forward ventrally near and on head. Small dark saddle on caudal peduncle usually distinct. Completely black in estuaries. Common New South Wales species but very secretive in caves and ledges, often not seen until diving with a torch at night. Coastal reefs, estuaries and deep offshore. Similar undetermined species in South Australia on the basis of a few specimens, probably tropical west coast expatriates. Maximum length 1.2 m.

Purple Rockcod *Epinephelus cyanopodus*

Pale blue with fine dark spotting. Juveniles with yellow to orange fins, black stripe just inside posterior caudal-fin margin, breaking up with growth and showing as dark patches in corners when adult. Coastal reefs and silty lagoons, often with isolated outcrops of rock and coral or in shipwrecks; large adults usually very deep, to 150 m. Tropical expatriate in Sydney area but occasionally reaches moderate size; seen to about 30 cm. Maximum length 1 m.

Coral Rockcod *Epinephelus corallicola*

Pale whitish grey to dusky with large pale patches, covered by small black spots. Secretive on coastal rocky reefs in silty white sand areas, mostly staying under ledges and protection of large corals. Juveniles in estuaries, tolerating brackish conditions. Usually small, maximum length about 30 cm, reported to 50 cm.

Snout-spot Grouper *Epinephelus polyphekadion*

Several similarly spotted species, this one with 2 distinct dark spots on snout. Body pale with fine spotting all over to dusky blotched pattern, most dense below, and indistinct banded arrangement on upper sides. Usually distinctive black peduncular saddle. Coastal bays and protected inner reefs in ledges and caves. Maximum length to 65 cm.

Foursaddle Grouper

Brown-spotted Grouper

Black Cod

Purple Rockcod

Coral Rockcod

Snout-spot Grouper

Marbled Rockcod *Epinephelus maculatus*

Small juveniles very distinct brown-black with large white blotches, dark areas breaking up into spots as they grow. Adults mostly spotted, with honeycomb pattern over body and head finely spotted. Coastal and inner reefs, mainly rocky boulders and lagoon bommies. Juveniles solitary with small isolated rock-outcrops on sand. Maximum length 50 cm.

Long-finned Cod *Epinephelus quoyanus*

Large pectoral fin, usually held outward when resting on substrate to balance. Similar colour-pattern to several other species, but spots larger on the head. Banded pattern is indistinct and often absent. Coastal, often silty reefs, harbours and in weed or algal reefs, often resting on open substrate near reef. Maximum length 35 cm.

Honeycomb Cod *Epinephelus merra*

Very similar to Long-finned Cod (previous species), several spots joining in diagnostic short bands on sides, and spots on snout small and more numerous. Outer reef lagoons, shallow protected reef crests and rich coral slopes, usually resting openly on substrate near cover. Small species, maximum length 28 cm.

White-speckled Grouper *Epinephelus ongus*

Body dusky with distinct white speckles, extending well over fins, and intermittently mixed with large blotched pattern. Similar to Small-spotted Cod *E. caeruleopunctatus* which has rounded white spots but none on anal and caudal fins. Clear coastal reefs on mixed rock and coral slopes and in caves along drop-offs; other species in more silty habitat. Maximum length 35 cm.

Squaretail Grouper *Epinephelus areolatus*

Best identified by square caudal-fin margin with white posterior margin, and general brownish colour. Body with honeycomb pattern but indistinct blotches on head. Common on muddy deep coastal slopes with outcrops of coral rubble or debris, often in small groups. Shallow to 200 m deep. Maximum length 40 cm.

Red-barred Rockcod *Epinephelus fasciatus*

Easily identified by reddish brown barred pattern and black and white along dorsal fin spine tips. Several geographical variations, some showing less banding than the Australian form. Coastal mixed rock and coral reefs on shallow crests and slopes with sparse growth or sponges. Maximum length 35 cm.

Marbled Rockcod

Long-finned Cod

Honeycomb Cod

White-speckled Grouper

Squaretail Grouper

Red-barred Rockcod

Banded Seaperch *Hypoplectrodes nigroruber*

Highly variable from bony white to bright red over back, but nearly always with 4 black bars over body. Eyes large, bulging on top of head. Shallow coastal end of estuarine reefs to offshore in at least 30 m depth. Rests on substrate perched on ventral and pectoral fins. Juveniles with distinct white stripe mid-dorsally on snout. Maximum length 30 cm.

Half-banded Seaperch *Hypoplectrodes maccullochi*

Pink to brown-red, darker dorsally, forming bands with indistinct narrow pale interspaces. Very common New South Wales fish from shallow estuaries to deep offshore reefs, often numerous individuals on a small reef patch, especially in sponge areas. Maximum length 20 cm, usually 15 cm.

Red Seaperch *Hypoplectrodes cardinalis*

Pink to red. Dark red to dusky streak centrally along sides, its upper edge shaped to dorsal profile and lower edge straight. Very secretive in clear coastal rocky reef, usually only seen when using torch during the day to inspect caves or deep ledges. Smallest in the genus, maximum length 10 cm.

Black-banded Seaperch *Hypoplectrodes annulatus*

Pale creamy to yellowish white with contrasting black angular stripes on head and bars on body. Protected coastal bays and rocky estuaries, usually upside down on ceilings of large caves and overhangs in depths of 10+ m. Stocky and moderately large, maximum length 30 cm.

Spotty Seaperch *Hypoplectrodes wilsoni*

Body stocky and robust, deep anteriorly. Indistinct broad brown banding formed by pale brown scales with thin dark edges, but many similar coloured scales peppered through pale interspaces. Clear coastal to moderately deep offshore reefs secretive under ledges, usually upside down against ceiling. Sometimes hooked. Maximum length 20 cm.

Midget Seaperch *Plectranthias nanus*

Several similar tiny species looking more like hawkfishes than serranids. Easily overlooked because of its size and secretive habits among dense coral growth. This species more exposed than others, often on open patches on vertical parts of coral heads, with additional growth giving some protection. Several other species, some very ornamental, can be found when using a torch in deep water along steep walls. Maximum length 35 mm.

Banded Seaperch

Half-banded Seaperch

ed Seaperch

Black-banded Seaperch

otty Seaperch

Midget Seaperch

113

Orange Basslet *Pseudanthias squamipinnis*

Females bright orange. Large fully coloured males purple with conspicuous purple spot on pectoral fin and long extended third dorsal spine, but many geographical variations in colour and size elsewhere. Possibly several species in the unusually broad range throughout tropical to warm–temperate zones. Clear estuarine reefs to offshore, usually in shallow depth, even turbulent zones just below foaming surface waters, along rock walls near cracks and ledges for cover. Forms small to moderate sized schools in Australia. Tiny juveniles bright orange, often settling in narrow crevices with sea-urchins and commonly called goldfish. Maximum length 12 cm (16 cm in Japan).

Pacific Basslet *Pseudanthias hutchtii*

Juveniles and females plain yellowish; males pinkish grey with thick orange to red stripe from eye to pectoral-fin base, bright pale-blue outer margins of caudal fin, other fins yellowish, and dorsal fin with greatly extended first spine. Some geographical variations, males usually greenish grey in Indonesia. Coastal to outer reef along crests with rich coral growth, close to drop-off edge in small to large aggregations, in which usually males greatly outnumbered by females. Maximum length 9 cm.

Pink Basslet *Pseudanthias hypselosoma*

Juveniles pink, caudal fin clear with pink posterior margin and tips. Adults similar with thin white line below eyes. Male with red blotch on dorsal fin and changing drastically during display, as shown in the photograph. Coastal, often silty habitat, forming large aggregations on rock-piles, isolated coral heads or along upper drop-offs. Maximum length 12 cm.

Lilac-tipped Basslet *Pseudanthias rubrizonatus*

Juveniles and females very similar to Pink Basslet (previous species), but median fin margins lilac, especially on spine tips and thin pink line below eye to pectoral-fin base, as shown in the male in the photograph. Male develops bright red bar centrally on body; during display, posterior area behind turns yellow. Deep coastal slopes with isolated rock formations on sand or deep current channels. Maximum length 10 cm.

Orange Basslet (male)

Orange Basslet (female)

acific Basslet (male)

Pacific Basslet (female)

nk Basslet (male)

Lilac-tipped Basslet (male)

115

Luzon Basslet *Pseudanthias luzonensis*

Female and young very plain with clear fins and just thin yellow stripe from below eye to pectoral-fin base. Male with bright red blotch on dorsal fin (appears black at depth) and longitudinal yellow lines, grouped midlaterally. Usually in 20+ m depth, in clear coastal or protected inner reef waters on slopes with rich invertebrate growth. Swims well above substrate in small spread-out groups. Maximum length 15 cm, usually 12 cm.

Red-stripe Basslet *Pseudanthias fasciatus*

Juveniles and most adults are easily identified by thick red midlateral stripe, but very large males may lose stripe and show broad banding over head instead. Deep offshore reefs, juveniles in 20+ m, and adults usually in 30+ m depth, deepest in tropical zones, throughout the Indo-Pacific. Maximum length in Australia 15 cm (20 cm in Japan).

Red Basslet *Pseudanthias cooperi*

Juveniles pinkish red, greenish along upper half of body, and red dorsal fin. Develops long red tips on caudal fin at an early age and underside of head changes to almost white. Thin vertical dusky bar, centrally on sides when adult, red in males. Males change dramatically during display, turning silvery white over top of body and caudal fin bright red, quickly resuming normal colour afterwards. Coastal and offshore reefs, juveniles in clear coastal bays in rocky ledges. Adults deep, feeding during currents on zooplankton, in schools above bommies or low coral plates where reefs end onto sand. Maximum length 12 cm.

Yellow-back Basslet *Pseudanthias bicolor*

Distinctly coloured with upper half ochre-yellow and lower half pink. Lives deep and colours not as obvious with natural light, its lower part looking blue. Males similar with extended second and third dorsal fin spines. Clear coastal to outer reef drop-offs, usually in small groups close to caves. Maximum length 13 cm.

Mirror Basslet *Pseudanthias pleurotaenia*

Males easily recognised by large pale square on sides, but highly variable and occasionally absent. Juveniles and females orange with yellow fins and 2 reddish parallel lines from eye to pectoral base, continuing over abdomen to caudal peduncle. Small juveniles bright yellow. Various habitats from coastal slopes to deep outer reef walls, often each sex forming large separate aggregations. Usually deep, 30+ m in Australia, but often shallow in equatorial waters. Maximum length 15 cm.

Luzon Basslet (male)

Red-stripe Basslet (male)

Yellow-back Basslet

Red Basslet (adult)

Red Basslet (juvenile)

Mirror Basslet (female)

Mirror Basslet (male)

117

Scribbled Basslet *Pseudanthias smithvanizi*

Knobby pointed snout, deep mauve with numerous small yellow spots forming scribbled patterns midlaterally, looking more blue at depth. Caudal fin lobes extremely elongated in adults. Only along deep drop-offs along outer reefs, usually in small groups in or just in front of large caves to feed on zooplankton. Maximum length 95 mm.

Lori's Basslet *Pseudanthias lori*

Readily identified by series of orange or red saddles along soft dorsal-fin base. Adults develop long caudal fin lobes. Outer reef slopes and drop-offs in large caves with rich invertebrate growth. Usually stays close to reef to feed on zooplankton. Females in small groups, males loosely attached. Maximum length 12 cm.

Fairy Basslet *Pseudanthias dispar*

Females orange; males pink with red dorsal fin, but body colour changing to yellow during display. Outer reefs, schools along upper margin of drop-offs with rich coral growth. Usually numerous females and few males, the latter always busy displaying to each other and occasionally to females. Maximum length 9 cm.

Purple Queen *Pseudanthias tuka*

Snout pointed. Both sexes deep pink to purple; females with yellow back extending to upper caudal-fin tip, mirrored on lower part of fin; males often with dark purple blotch along base of soft dorsal fin. Clear coastal to outer reef zones, usually deep along drop-offs and steep slopes with rich invertebrate growth. Forms colourful groups along upper drop-off margins but deep on southern Great Barrier Reef in 25+ m depth. Maximum length 11 cm.

Sailfin Queen *Pseudanthias pascalus*

Very similar to Purple Queen (previous species), but fins much more pointed and with filamentous tips in adults. Males with dark purple blotch on outer part of soft dorsal fin. Form large schools on outer reef slopes, feeding high above substrate on zooplankton. Usually deep (25+ m) in Australia, but reported much shallower in some oceanic locations. Maximum length 15 cm.

Pygmy Basslet *Luzonichthys waitei*

Small and slender, otherwise very similar to Yellow-back Basslets and often swims with juveniles of this species. Back yellow and the rest looks blue in natural light. Forms large schools along drop-offs on outer reefs in rich coral-growth habitat. Maximum length 7 cm.

Scribbled Basslet

Lori's Basslet

Fairy Basslet (male)

Purple Queen (male above, female below)

Sailfin Queen

Pygmy Basslet

Swallowtail Basslet *Serranocirrhites latus*

Deep-bodied; purplish pink below with yellow bands on top of head and narrow lines on cheeks, small yellow spot on each scale on sides with spots progressively larger above to almost continuous yellow along dorsal-fin base. Singly or small groups in caves along deep drop-offs or upside down on ceiling of large overhangs. Maximum length 8 cm.

Long-finned Perch *Caprodon longimanus*

Females plain pink; males becoming yellow spotted, especially on head and fins, and large black area in dorsal fin. Offshore reefs and islands, mainly seamounts and along rock walls. Feeds midwater, sometimes rising to shallow depths for zooplankton but rarely in depths less than 25 m. Called Pink Maomao in New Zealand. Maximum length 43 cm.

Butterfly Perch *Caesioperca lepidoptera*

Juveniles pink, developing distinct black spot on sides at early age. Adults become spotted and have pale blue fin margins and variably blue streaks on head. Adults form great schools on offshore reefs, sometimes clouding the water column when feeding on zooplankton. Juveniles enter shallow bays on south coast, where adults are sometimes in shallow depths. Most common between 50 and 100 m depth. Maximum length 40 cm, usually 30 cm.

Barber Perch *Caesioperca rasor*

Female plain pink with yellow eyes. Small juveniles black over nape to below eye, fading with age. Males pink to yellow, ornamented with iridescent blue and variable black vertical bar centrally on sides, sometimes absent and occasionally as a very large dusky band or blotch. Coastal, including deep rocky estuaries, to offshore. Adults school, feeding midwater on zooplankton. Juveniles solitary at first, soon forming small groups. Maximum length 25 cm.

Splendid Perch *Callanthias australis*

Lateral line rises sharply from origin, running close along dorsal-fin base. Juveniles pink with mauve fins. Adults variable from orange to red and fins yellow, orange and sometimes white. Offshore, with seamounts and islands; juveniles sometimes on clear coastal reefs. Schools in deep water and only seen relatively shallow, about 25 m, in a few places such as Montague Island, New South Wales, and Wilsons Promontory, Victoria, or Tasmania. Second species Allport's Perch *Callanthias allporti* is only known from trawls in Australia. Maximum length 48 cm, usually to 30 cm.

Swallowtail Basslet

Long-finned Perch

Barber Perch (male)

Butterfly Perch

Barber Perch (female)

Splendid Perch (adult)

Splendid Perch (juvenile)

Yellow Emperor *Diploprion bifasciatum*

Usually pale yellow with broad black band on body and over head, sometimes all black with yellow fins or bluish grey in relation to habitat. Silty coastal reefs and estuaries with rock or algae-rock reefs, often under jetties forming loose aggregations. Kind of soapfish, secretes toxin through skin when under stress. Has large mouth and feeds primarily on other fishes. Not suitable as aquarium fish. Maximum length 25 cm.

Lined Soapfish *Grammistes sexlineatus*

Juveniles with few thick lines, thinning with age and additional lines developing between, eventually changing to series of dashes in large adults. Juveniles in shallow coastal habitats, including estuaries and lagoons. Large individuals on deep mud slopes with isolated outcrops of reef or land debris washed in by rivers. Maximum length 27 cm.

Arrow-head Soapfish *Belonoperca chabanaudi*

Best recognised by unusual shape and deeply notched dorsal fin. Bright yellow saddle spot on caudal peduncle. Solitary in dark caves and ledges along drop-offs in coastal as well as outer reef zones. Easily missed unless torch used to inspect caves. Maximum length 15 cm.

Gold-ribbon Cod *Aulacocephalus temmincki*

Sides brilliant blue. Golden-yellow band from snout over eye, following dorsal profile to upper caudal-fin base, on snout extending into thin line over maxilla. Clear coastal and offshore reefs, in large caves or ledges along steep rock walls, often with islands such as the Solitary Islands. Maximum length 30 cm.

Pinstriped Reef Basslet *Liopropoma susumi*

One of a small group of apogonid-like serranids, closely related to soapfishes, with deeply notched or divided dorsal fin. Usually small and secretive, living in dark part of caves along deep drop-offs. Easily identified by thin longitudinal lines and is the most common and widespread species of the genus. Mainly outer reef habitat, including shallow lagoons. Maximum length 92 mm.

Yellow Reef Basslet *Liopropoma multilineatum*

Unusual colouration, body with bright yellow which posteriorly changes abruptly to red with white stripes. In natural light the red looks like dusky grey streaks. Secretive in the back of large and deep caves with rich invertebrate growth, swimming through narrow channels and holes. Only seen when torch used. Maximum length 8 cm.

Yellow Emperor (normal form)

Yellow Emperor (dark form)

Lined Soapfish

Arrow-head Soapfish

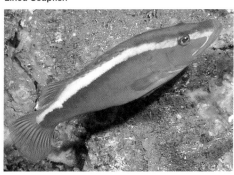

Gold-ribbon Cod

Pinstriped Reef Basslet

Yellow Reef Basslet

BARRAMUNDI — CENTROPOMIDAE

Small Indo-Pacific family with 2 genera and 3 species, both genera with one species each are found in Australian waters. Best known is the Barramundi from northern rivers and coastal waters. Features large scales; lateral-line distinct, smoothly curved; dorsal fin deeply notched; anal fin short-based; head with concave dorsal-profile, and large mouth reaching to below eye.

Sand Bass *Psammoperca waigiensis*

Silvery grey on sides and darker above, faint horizontal dark streaks on head. Similar to the Barramundi, but eye much larger and placed above corner of mouth, versus almost above centre of mouth. Silty coastal slopes and deep muddy substrates, secretive in reef during the daytime. Maximum length 40 cm.

DOTTYBACKS — PSEUDOCHROMIDAE

Large Indo-Pacific family of small, often colourful fishes, with at least 6 genera and 70 species, of which approximately 4 genera and 30 species are known in Australian waters. Family is in need of revision and many species have only recently been discovered. Features: body elongated, head long and eyes large with elongated pupil; colour diagnostic, in a few species it is highly variable and in some it differs between the sexes. Secretive, closely associated with reef, especially where there are lots of holes and narrow ledges. Habitats from silty coastal to pristine outer reef. Territorial and usually aggressive, some species attack their own reflection if seen in lens port, or when shown a mirror. Quick-moving hunters, taking various small invertebrates and fishes. Eggs deposited in clusters and guarded by the male.

Multicolour Dottyback *Ogilbyina novaehollandiae*

Extremely variable in colour, from combined green, red and pink or almost black form. Median fins with thin iridescent blue margin. Dorsal fin tall. Coastal and inner reefs in mixed coral and algae reef, secretive, staying in the shade of ledges when darting between hiding places. Very similar to Queensland Dottyback *O. queenslandiae*, which usually shows a more barred pattern, pink with green or dusky front, and ranges further north. Popular aquarium fish. Maximum length 10 cm.

Long-tail Dottyback *Ogilbyina velifera*

Little variation, usually pale whitish to salmon with grey to yellow over top of head and snout. Tail greatly elongated in centre when adult. Inner reefs and deep lagoons on bommies and along ledges with coarse rubble pieces. Solitary, hunting over open rubble patches within a short distance of cover. Maximum length 12 cm, usually 9 cm.

Lavender Dottyback *Cypho purpurascens*

Deep pink to red, appearing more blue in natural light, especially when deep. Scales with dusky edges forming a series of spots or diagonal lines. With or without ocellus in dorsal fin. Protected reef slopes, rubble slopes and in small caves along drop-offs. Secretive, usually well hidden or when seen in small open pockets surrounded by high reef or in the back of low crevices. Maximum length 75 mm, usually 60 mm.

Two-tone Dottyback *Pseudochromis paccagnellae*

Easily recognised by abrupt colour change between front and back half of body. In natural light, front looks deep blue. Protected coastal to inner reefs, usually along drop-offs with low ledges and small caves with mixed sponge and coral growth. Solitary, but several individuals often share small reef sections. Small species, maximum length 60 mm.

Sand Bass

Multicolour Dottyback

Multicolour Dottyback (variation)

Long-tail Dottyback

Lavender Dottyback

Two-tone Dottyback

125

Dusky Dottyback *Pseudochromis fuscus*

Highly variable from dark brown to bright yellow, usually with dark-centred scales, sometimes dark with pale blue-grey back. Very common species in the west Pacific and eastern Indian Ocean. Coastal reefs to inner reefs, usually in coarse rubble patches with mixed algal and coral growth, in shallow to deep lagoons on flats between bommies or along the base of drop-offs. Maximum length 10 cm.

Blue-barred Dottyback *Pseudochromis cyanotaenia*

Sexually dimorphic: male with mostly yellow head and belly and dark blue sides with light blue barring; female brownish with broadly yellow-margined red caudal fin. Secretive but common on shallow exposed reef-flats and lagoons on inner and outer reefs with numerous holes and crevices, usually in pairs. Maximum length 6 cm.

Orange-tail Dottyback *Pseudochromis flammicauda*

Sexually dimorphic: both sexes mostly grey to black; male has yellow head and red eye, caudal fin bright yellow with red on base; female has dark head (like body) and white eye, caudal fin dull yellow. Inner reef, secretive in gutters with small caves and crevices. Maximum length 55 mm.

Rose Island Dottyback *Pseudoplesiops rosae*

Long and slender. Grey with yellow-pink head. Like other elongate species, it swims by twisting or flicking its tail and posterior body sideways, regularly stopping to inspect substrate for small crustaceans as prey. Semi-exposed reefs, in narrow crevices along rich walls or in the back of large caves. Maximum length 35 mm.

Pink Dottyback *Pseudoplesiops multisquamatus*

Best recognised by evenly coloured pink body and yellow caudal fin, but pink may look bluish grey in natural light. Mainly deep outer reef drop-offs in rich caves and ledges, swimming in the back, darting in and out of small holes in search of small prey. Maximum length 6 cm.

usky Dottyback (normal form)

Dusky Dottyback (yellow form)

lue-barred Dottyback

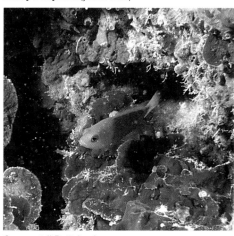

Orange-tail Dottyback

se Island Dottyback

Pink Dottyback

SPINY BASSLETS — ACANTHOCLINIDAE

Small family with 5 genera and 10 species, of which 2 genera and 2 species are found in Australian waters, most confined to New Zealand. Closely related to Pseudochromidae, possessing more dorsal and anal fin spines, but ventral fins with only one or two rays. The tiny (only 26 mm long) black Southern Longfin *Beliops xanthokrossos*, which lives under rocks and is rarely seen, is not included here.

Barred Spiny Basslet *Belonepterygion fasciolatum*

Distinctly coloured species with white mid-dorsal stripe on head, black ear-spot and many narrow dark bars along the entire body. Inhabits thick rubble piles and boulders and lives in lower dead parts of dense coral patches, shallow protected lagoons and inner reef slopes. Maximum length 5 cm.

LONGFINS — PLESIOPIDAE

Small Indo-Pacific family with 7 genera and about 20 species, of which all genera and 17 species are found in Australian waters. Diverse group, including the mouth-breeding scissortails, *Assessor* spp., and the very elongated hulafishes *Trachinops* spp., both of which may perhaps belong in separate families. The large temperate species are known as blue devils, featuring iridescent blue spots or lines and large fins, and are typically curious and often unafraid of divers. Tropical species are small and secretive with the exception of comets *Calloplesiops* spp., which live in the back of caves or large ledge and display to divers before gliding into a crevice. The scissortails and hulafishes are planktivores; others feed on a variety of benthic invertebrates. Despite large mouth, usually take only small prey.

Yellow Scissortail *Assessor flavissimus*

Easily identified by shape and bright yellow colour. Inner and outer reef in sheltered habitats or protected by large caves during heavy seas. Typically in small groups, swimming upside down against ceilings of large overhangs or caves. Brood are produced on a monthly basis, with males incubating the eggs in their mouth. Maximum length 60 mm.

Blue Scissortail *Assessor macneilli*

Like its yellow cousin, easily identified by its shape and dark blue colour. Sheltered coastal to inner reefs, usually in small to large schools in narrow reef channels and in caves. Normally swimming upside down on ceiling of overhangs or with belly towards walls. Breeding behaviour same as the Yellow Scissortail (previous species). Maximum length 60 mm.

Eastern Hulafish *Trachinops taeniatus*

Distinctly coloured with yellow, black and red above and white below, sometimes black absent and shows a bright yellow back. Tail elongates centrally with age. Forms large schools along coastal reefs, feeding well above rocks on zooplankton, also in clearer parts of estuaries in current-prone areas. Male guards and protects egg cluster in small holes by wrapping body around. Maximum length 10 cm.

Southern Hulafish *Trachinops caudimaculatus*

Dull with dark blotch on caudal fin. This fin is round in juveniles, pointed in adults and elongating centrally with age. Particularly common in Tasmania where large schools sometimes cloud the water column. Various habitats from shallow rocky estuaries to deep offshore. Small population found in Investigator groups, South Australia, mixed with local species in deep water. Maximum length 15 cm.

Barred Spiny Basslet

Yellow Scissortail

Blue Scissortail

Eastern Hulafish

Southern Hulafish

129

Braun's Hulafish *Trachinops brauni*

Distinctive with bright blue line on back and long, pointed filamentous tail in large adults. Forms small aggregations on clear rocky outcrop reefs in sheltered coastal bays at shallow depths to deeper offshore reefs to about 35 m depth. Feeds on zooplankton in close vicinity of reef, sometimes mixing with Noarlunga Hulafish (next species), more common throughout range. Maximum length 80 mm.

Noarlunga Hulafish *Trachinops noarlungae*

Pale with yellow on head and tail. Adults develop long pointed yellow tail with trailing filament in centre and bright iridescent blue margin. Form small to large aggregations on rocky reefs or under jetties from sheltered very shallow bays to offshore reefs to about 30 m depth. Common in south-western waters. Maximum length 15 cm.

Red-tipped Longfin *Plesiops caeruleolineatus*

Dusky brown to black, best identified by orange to red dorsal spine tips with iridescent blue line just below, and blue line on anal fin. Secretive on shallow reef-flats and slopes to about 20 m depth, clear coastal to outer reefs. Common but usually seen only at night when it hunts small crustaceans. Maximum length 75 mm.

Alison's Blue Devil *Paraplesiops alisonae*

Sexually dimorphic: female uniform ash-grey to orange-brown with moderately large blue spots over head, blue lines along dorsal and anal fins, and blue margin on caudal fin; males ornamentally coloured with orange head and yellow fins and more blue in fins. Small juveniles with dusky bars along entire body and often white on top of head, found in shallow protected bays, very secretive under rocks or in narrow crevices. Adults often in pairs, in the back of long caves with rich invertebrate growth, mostly along deep walls, and usually seen only at night. Maximum length 15 cm.

Southern Blue Devil *Paraplesiops meleagris*

Small juveniles are pale with large blue spots on head, light blue fins and broad dark band near caudal-fin margin. Darken with age and spots become more numerous. Dorsal and anal fin elongate posteriorly, with ends reaching almost as far as the caudal fin. Appears strong blue in natural light. Coastal to offshore rocky reefs in caves and crevices. Adults often curious and unafraid of divers. Maximum length 33 cm.

Braun's Hulafish

Noarlunga Hulafish

Red-tipped Longfin

Alison's Blue Devil (male)

Alison's Blue Devil (juvenile)

Southern Blue Devil

131

Eastern Blue Devil *Paraplesiops bleekeri*

Similar to southern cousin but broad-banded pattern with 3 white bands and yellow caudal peduncle, and yellow streaked on some fin areas. Usually secretive in the back of far-reaching crevices, shallow in estuaries to deep offshore. Large adults often in front of caves on offshore reefs. Unafraid where used to divers. Maximum length 40 cm.

Comet *Calloplesiops altivelis*

Unique colour pattern with numerous white spots and distinct ocellus above caudal peduncle on dorsal fin. Median fins confluent when raised. Spots on young proportionally larger and less numerous. Coastal to inner reef habitat, secretive in the back of caves and large crevices. Moderately common but not often seen, except when using torch during the day to inspect dark areas. Maximum length 16 cm.

PEARLPERCHES — GLAUCOSOMATIDAE

Small west Pacific family, single genus with about 6 little-known species, all but one found in Australian waters. Deep-bodied, silvery as adults, often with lines as juveniles. Most only in deep water; the western species Threadfin Pearl Perch *Glaucosoma magnificum*, best known from trawls, is occasionally seen by divers in large schools. It has long filaments trailing from corners of median fins. The east coast Pearl Perch, hooked from depths of 100+ m, is plain silvery, truncate caudal fin, and sometimes called Nannygai; however, easily distinguished by lacking colour and typical fork tail of real nannygai. Only the south-western species included here is commonly seen in shallow water by divers.

West Australian Jewfish *Glaucosoma hebraicum*

Juvenile silvery with thick black bar radiating from below and above eye to lower corner of operculum and nape, respectively; several dark stripes above and below lateral line; posterior margin of caudal fin white. Large adults uniformly bluish grey and dark stripe above eye usually still visible. Dorsal fin tips pointed or extended with filaments in young. Sibling species in Japan *G. fauveli* is deeper bodied, rounded soft dorsal fin lacks stripe above eye, and dark spot at end of dorsal-fin base, similar to east coast Pearl Perch. Western species largest, maximum length 1.2 m.

TRUMPETERS & GRUNTERS — TERAPONTIDAE

Moderately large family with 16 genera and about 40 species, of which 13 genera and 30 species found in Australian waters. Typical perch-like fishes, similar to lutjanids. Ability to produce loud noise from swim bladder gave rise to names such as grunters and trumpeters. Most species evolved in fresh water, grunters with about 30 species in the Australian–New Guinea region. Trumpeters are primarily marine, inhabiting coastal and estuarine zones, often entering fresh water. Feature small ctenoid scales extended into sheaths along dorsal and anal-fin bases; prominent spine on opercle, and strong spines in fins. Generally with longitudinal stripes or spots, mostly schooling as adults. Small juveniles often with floating weeds or objects for shelter. Larger freshwater species regarded as good eating; marine species rather small and mainly used as baitfish.

Eastern Striped Trumpeter *Pelates sexlineatus*

Silvery to light brown with 6 dark longitudinal stripes, lower ones less distinct. Tiny juveniles with distinct black spot on caudal-fin base. Juveniles in coastal estuaries in seagrass beds. Adults form schools in protected coastal bays, harbours or large deep estuaries. Maximum length 20 cm.

Eastern Blue Devil

Comet

West Australian Jewfish (adult)

West Australian Jewfish (juvenile)

Eastern Striped Trumpeter (adult)

Eastern Striped Trumpeter (juvenile)

Four-line Trumpeter *Pelates quadrilineatus*

Easily confused with Eastern Striped Trumpeter (previous species), but slightly deeper bodied when adult, and juvenile has half stripe anteriorly between second and third stripes from above eye. Adult usually with dark blotch on dorsal fin and juveniles lack spot on caudal-fin base. Widespread tropical coastal species in bays and estuaries, often schooling under jetties. Maximum length 20 cm.

Western Striped Trumpeter *Pelates octolineatus*

Differs from Eastern Striped Trumpeter (second previous species) by its shorter head and upper lines sometimes in a series of spots. Small juveniles greenish, secretive in seagrasses. Adults along edges of seagrass beds and coastal rocky reefs, often swimming in large dense schools. Northern range uncertain, but reported as far as Papua New Guinea. Maximum length 28 cm.

Flagtail Trumpeter *Terapon theraps*

Juveniles often dark brown with white-silvery spots or indistinct longitudinal stripes. Best identified by tail, which is always distinctive with black and white horizontal stripes. Adults otherwise similar to other species, with a light-coloured body and dark stripes. Mainly pelagic, often forming large schools under floating sargassum rafts. Juveniles with surface debris or floating bits of weed. Surface waters and entering sheltered coastal usually silty bays. Maximum length 30 cm.

Crescent Perch *Terapon jarbua*

Large black blotch on spinous dorsal fin and upward-curving dark stripes from body over nape. The most commonly observed species in tropical waters, it is often seen from shores or jetties over very shallow sand or mudflats, schooling in loose groups. Small juveniles intertidal and often stranded in pools at low tide, entering fresh water. Maximum length 25 cm.

Sea Trumpeter *Pelsartia humeralis*

Identified by the most unusual pattern in the family, with vertical bars, blotches and spots. Restricted distribution, south-western endemic. Juveniles in seagrass beds. Adults form large schools, swimming over reefs in the vicinity of seagrasses in sheltered bays and suitable habitats at offshore islands. Largest marine species, maximum length 38 cm.

Four-line Trumpeter

Western Striped Trumpeter

Flagtail Trumpeter (adult)

Crescent Perch

Flagtail Trumpeter (juveniles)

Sea Trumpeter (adult)

Sea Trumpeter (schooling)

135

BIGEYES — PRIACANTHIDAE

Small distinctive family with 4 genera and about 17 species worldwide, of which 3 genera and 8 species are reported in Australian waters. Very large eyes, giving rise to various common names: red bullseyes, goggle-eyes and glasseyes. Body somewhat elongated and compressed. Ventral fins are connected to the belly by a membrane. Usually reddish brown; blotched or banded patterns can change quickly. Nocturnal fishes, in caves and ledges during the day, feeding midwater on zooplankton at night. Despite very large mouth, only target small prey. Small juveniles often in estuaries hiding in soft corals or kelp. Adults in shallow protected bays, deep lagoons and deep offshore, solitary or small aggregations. May school in some oceanic localities.

Blotched Bigeye *Heteropriacanthus cruentatus*

Body with more-or-less distinct large blotches, reddish brown during the day but pale with dark blotches at night, as shown in the photograph. Fins with dull spotting. The similar **Spotted Bigeye** *Priacanthus macracanthus* has distinct spotting in the fins, is more widepread and ranges to eastern Victoria. The range of Blotched Bigeye is circumtropical and may extend into New South Wales. Clear coastal and rich invertebrate reefs. Maximum length 32 cm.

Glasseye *Priacanthus blochii*

Best recognised from similar species by rounded to truncate caudal fin, lunate in others. Usually a series of small spots along lateral line. Often confused with Blotched Bigeye (previous species) but shows banded rather than blotched pattern at night. Mainly silty coastal waters or deep offshore on muddy substrate with remote bommies and often in shipwrecks along coasts. Maximum length 30 cm.

Crescent-tail Bigeye *Priacanthus hamrur*

Plain reddish brown or banded, sometimes with a series of small blotches along the lateral line. Best recognised by the strongly crescent-shaped caudal fin. Coastal reefs and lagoons, often in small aggregations floating near bommies, to deep offshore, known to 250 m depth. Maximum length 40 cm.

CARDINALFISHES — APOGONIDAE

Very large family of mostly small fishes with at least 26 genera and estimated 250 species globally, of which about 20 genera and more than half the species are reported in Australian waters. Usual features: separate angular dorsal fins; distinctive body shape; large eyes; 2 spines in anal fin compared to 3 with most related families; and often diagnostic patterns. Many occur commonly on coral reefs, forming large schools in branching corals or around bommies during the day, spreading out at night to feed solitary in open water, either floating near or well above substrate in pursuit of prey. A few are temperate and found on the south coast. The majority live shallow, a few deep on continental slopes and some are restricted to fresh water. Diet comprises small invertebrates, some take fishes, mainly from plankton. Large mouth serves as brooding chamber, usually male but for some both sexes, and in at least one species the young are kept in the mouth for a short period after hatching.

Tiger Cardinalfish *Cheilodipterus macrodon* (now known as *C. heptazona*)

Several similar striped species, but this one is the most common and best recognised by yellow colouration on snout when young, usually some traces in eyes of large individuals. Small juveniles 4 lines and black caudal peduncle, number increasing with growth. Coastal to outer reef habitat, usually solitary in ledges or caves at various depths to about 30 m. Maximum length 22 cm.

Blotched Bigeye

Glasseye (adult)

Glasseye (juvenile)

Crescent-tail Bigeye

Tiger Cardinalfish (adult)

Tiger Cardinalfish (large juvenile)

Five-line Cardinalfish *Cheilodipterus quinquelineatus*

Pale with thin black horizontal lines, 4 along sides and one mid-dorsally over head, dividing along each side of the dorsal-fin base. Yellow black-centred spot on caudal peduncle, black part diffused in large adults. Coastal to outer reef lagoons, common in rocky or rich coral habitat, usually in small aggregations. Maximum length 12 cm.

Toothy Cardinalfish *Cheilodipterus isostigma*

Almost identical to Five-line Cardinalfish (previous species), differing mainly in dentition, and midlateral line levels with centre of peduncular spot compared to lower part of spot. More coastal, usually solitary, often under jetties or small groups among staghorn corals, and preferring more silty habitats. Maximum length 14 cm.

Mimic Cardinalfish *Cheilodipterus nigrotaeniatus*

Mimics venomous blenny *Meiacanthus vittatus* which occurs in New Guinea but is not yet recorded from Australian waters. Known to mimic two other *Meiacanthus* blenny species in the Solomon Islands, Malaysia and the Philippines. Apogonids best distinguished from blennies by 2 separate short-based dorsal fins instead of a single long-based fin, and shape of mouth. Openly swims about during the day like blenny, but when approached it dashes for the nearest reef cover, usually not far away. Maximum length 80 mm.

Spiny-eye Cardinalfish *Apogon fraenatus* (now known as *A. melanorhynchus*)

Distinct black lateral stripe in line with centre of caudal-fin spot. Several similar species, with variations in stripe, position of caudal-fin spot, and colour. This species: stripe at level with spot-centre and often with white borders. Coastal and inner reefs under low overhangs of reef over sand. Maximum length 10 cm.

One-line Cardinalfish *Apogon exostigma* (now known as *A. fraenatus*)

Similar to Spiny-eye Cardinalfish (previous species), but midlateral stripe ends below centre of caudal fin spot, adults with black streaks on membranes between first dorsal fin spines. Clear coastal and deep lagoon habitat with large isolated bommies in open mixed low reefs and sand. Maximum length 12 cm.

Spiny-head Cardinalfish *Apogon kallopterus* (now known as *A. urostigma*)

Midlateral stripe distinct in juveniles and young adults, ending below centre of caudal fin spot. Stripe and spot may fade completely in adults, which become brown with yellow first dorsal fin. Common on shallow coastal reef slopes and lagoons with boulders or in ledges. Maximum length 15 cm.

Five-line Cardinalfish

Toothy Cardinalfish

Mimic Cardinalfish

Spiny-eye Cardinalfish

One-line Cardinalfish

Spiny-head Cardinalfish

Cavite Cardinalfish *Apogon cavitensis*

White lines from snout, through upper and lower part of eye, along body and fading near caudal peduncle; thin golden line along back; and small black spot on base of caudal fin. Coastal to inner reefs, usually silty or weedy reef habitat, entering estuaries. Solitary in low crevices on sand. Previously confused with Indonesian *A. hartzfeldi*: and recently described as *A. virgulatus*, now a junior synonym. Maximum length 85 mm.

Southern Orange-lined Cardinalfish *Apogon properuptus*

Complex of several Indo-Pacific species, until recently thought to be a single wide-ranging species *A. cyanosoma* (next species). Width of lines or interspaces varies between species, *A. properuptus* with most of abdomen orange and broad orange stripes. Forms small aggregations on clear coastal reefs and in outer reef lagoons. Maximum length 85 mm.

Orange-lined Cardinalfish *Apogon cyanosoma*

Orange lines narrower than pale interspaces. Clear coastal to outer reef habitat in rich invertebrate reefs, but also in outer reef seagrass beds in large lagoons, forming small to moderate-sized schools. Maximum length 9 cm.

Striped Cardinalfish *Apogon fasciatus*

White leading margin on ventral fins, intermediate stripe from above eye to below gap between dorsal fins. Probably restricted to east coast; reports from elsewhere may be based on similar species. Particularly common in large estuaries, Sydney Harbour and Botany Bay (type locality), but also deep offshore on muddy substrates. Forms small aggregations in ledges or caves. Maximum length 15 cm.

Barred Striped Cardinalfish *Apogon quadrifasciatus*

Dark stripes edged with thin pearly lines, with pearly spots or vertical dashes on abdomen, joining as thin bars in large adults to lowermost pearly line. Leading edge of ventral fins pale blue. Muddy coastal habitat, usually in depths of 20+ m in pairs sheltering below stinging anemones or at entrance of large holes in substrate created by crabs. Maximum length 11 cm.

Rifle Cardinalfish *Apogon kiensis*

Midlateral stripe very thick, adults often with yellow blotch on abdomen, juveniles with black or dusky area on body immediately above anal-fin origin. Although superficially similar to Barred Striped Cardinalfish (previous species), differs with 6 compared to 7 dorsal spines in first fin, and is much smaller. Maximum length 8 cm.

Cavite Cardinalfish

Southern Orange-lined Cardinalfish

Orange-lined Cardinalfish

Striped Cardinalfish

Barred Striped Cardinalfish

Rifle Cardinalfish

Sydney Cardinalfish *Apogon limenus*

Fins of adults pink, broad space between upper 2 lines and midlateral stripes, intermediate stripe from above eye very short. Very common in Sydney Harbour and Botany Bay, but also on offshore reefs. Usually in small aggregations in ledges. Maximum length 14 cm.

Western Striped Cardinalfish *Apogon victoriae*

Similar to Sydney Cardinalfish (previous species), but *A. victoriae* differs with strong intermediate stripe, and similar also to *A. cookii* but readily distinguished by distinct black spot on caudal and pectoral-fin bases. Clear coastal reefs, under jetties to deep offshore, near or in ledges or caves during the day. Maximum length 14 cm.

Four-line Cardinalfish *Apogon doederleini*

Very similar to Sydney Cardinalfish, but lacks half-stripe from top of eye. Four thick black lines along the body. Shallow protected bays to offshore reefs, often mixed with other striped cardinalfish in rocky crevices or own small groups. Maximum length 14 cm.

Cook's Cardinalfish *Apogon cookii*

Similar to other striped species, with half-stripe from top of eye, but lacks caudal fin spot. Very shallow, often subtidal reef-flats or harbours, secretive under rocks or corals, only out at night or in the shade of ledges. Maximum length 10 cm.

Pearly-lined Cardinalfish *Apogon taeniophorus*

Best identified by thick midlateral stripe and narrow interspace with stripe below, often with thickened section in front and behind pectoral-fin base. Shallow coastal reefs and harbours, secretive in ledges, usually seen at night or when disturbing daytime habitat. Maximum length 10 cm.

Blue-eyed Cardinalfish *Apogon compressus*

Intermediate and upper band join below first dorsal fin. Eyes bright blue in natural light. Dark bands reddish brown to black. Coastal to outer reef lagoons with rock piles and in branching corals during the day. Small juveniles with black-centred yellow peduncle spot, mimicking young *Cheilodipterus* apogonids with large teeth. Maximum length 12 cm, usually 10 cm.

Sydney Cardinalfish

Western Striped Cardinalfish

Four-line Cardinalfish

Cook's Cardinalfish

Pearly-lined Cardinalfish

Blue-eyed Cardinalfish

Nine-line Cardinalfish *Apogon novemfasciatus*

Easily identified by rather thick head and body stripes extending onto caudal fin and converging towards centre. Shallow coastal reefs and lagoons, often silty habitat in low ledges or rocks on sand, usually in pairs and often out in the open but close to shelter. Maximum length 10 cm.

Black-striped Cardinalfish *Apogon nigrofasciatus*

Stripes much thicker than interspaces. Possible 2 species, one with narrow yellow interspaces and pinkish fins more tropical, and the other with narrow white interspaces and plain fins ranging further south. Coastal to outer reef habitats, usually solitary or pairs in ledges and caves along steep slopes and drop-offs, often deep, to 50 m. Maximum length 10 cm.

Narrow-striped Cardinalfish *Apogon angustatus*

Very similar to Black-striped Cardinalfish (previous species), but stripes and interspaces about equal width and caudal fin spot at end of midlateral stripe. Fins pinkish. Clear coastal reef crests and slopes to deep outer reefs, usually in mixed low algal and fixed invertebrate-covered boulder areas, often solitary. Maximum length 11 cm.

Ring-tail Cardinalfish *Apogon aureus*

Distinctive broad black peduncular band, as a large spot in small juveniles, expanding with age and widening above and below. Grey-orange with dark snout, and eye with thin iridescent blue lines from tip of snout through eyes with some spots behind. Coastal rocky reefs in small to large groups among boulders or above mixed sponge coral and algal reef. Maximum length 12 cm.

Plain Cardinalfish *Apogon apogonides*

Almost identical to Ring-tail Cardinalfish (previous species), except lacking the black peduncular band or spot. Juveniles almost without markings, just thin double horizontal pale lines on snout to eye. Coastal reef-flats and slopes to moderately deep. Juveniles in small aggregations in front of small caves feeding on zooplankton. Adults in ledges during the day, coming out at night for larger shrimps. Maximum length 10 cm.

Capricorn Cardinalfish *Apogon capricornis*

Similar to previous 2 species, but only a small spot on the caudal-fin base and adults with thin yellow barring on sides. Clear-water habitats, mixed coral and alga reef, coastal to deep offshore along walls under tall overhanging ledges, in number of pairs together, forming small groups. Maximum length 10 cm.

Nine-line Cardinalfish

Black-striped Cardinalfish

Narrow-striped Cardinalfish

Ring-tail Cardinalfish

Plain Cardinalfish

Capricorn Cardinalfish

Long-spine Cardinalfish *Apogon leptacanthus*

Tall and pointed first dorsal fin, elongating with age; iridescent blue bars on head and abdomen. Small to large schools in branching corals during day, out over open sand at night. Coastal to outer reef lagoons with rich coral growth. Small species, maximum length 6 cm.

Sangi Cardinalfish *Apogon sangiensis* (now known as *A. thermalis*)

Pale semitransparent when young; several distinct black spots dorsally at base between dorsal fins and behind second dorsal fin, and centrally at caudal-fin base. Some large individuals with broad dark area midlaterally. Clean sand slopes in protected inner reef and deep lagoon habitat, in small groups with outcrops of coral or rock during the day. Maximum length 8 cm.

Mini Cardinalfish *Apogon neotus*

Pale semitransparent with white abdomen, black stripe along middle and along vertebrae to spot at caudal-fin base. Clear coastal reefs to inner reefs, deep lagoons, usually in small groups near large bommies, black or soft corals, or caves with fans. Probably the smallest apogonid, usually mistaken for juvenile fish. Maximum length 28 mm.

Night Cardinalfish *Apogon doryssa*

At least 3 or 4 very similar species, semitransparent reddish, mainly differing in shapes and sizes. *A. doryssa* deep-bodied with relatively short caudal peduncle, and blue speckles just below dorsal-fin base. The other common species, Long-tail Cardinalfish *A. coccineus*, has a long caudal peduncle, as the name suggests. Although common, it is normally only seen at night along reef walls. Maximum length 5 cm.

Half-band Cardinalfish *Apogon semiornatus*

Semitransparent when small; adult with distinct black stripe from snout to anus and second stripe parallel above, posteriorly on body to caudal-fin base. Common but secretive in shallows under rocks or low plate corals and deep in caves over sand. Clear coastal to offshore reefs. Maximum length 75 mm.

Cave Cardinalfish *Apogon evermanni*

Unusual cardinalfish with black and white spot together posteriorly at base of second dorsal fin and black stripe from eye ending on opercle-edge. Typically in large caves along drop-offs, usually swimming against the ceiling. Common and probably the most widespread species, usually observed at night or when inspecting caves with a torch during the day. Maximum length 8 cm.

Long-spine Cardinalfish

Sangi Cardinalfish

Mini Cardinalfish

Night Cardinalfish

Half-band Cardinalfish

Cave Cardinalfish

147

Ghost Cardinalfish *Apogon bandanensis*

Several very similar species with dusky colour and narrow oblique stripe below eye. Species 1 has thin yellow outer margin on caudal fin and the leading ventral fin edge is blue. Species 2 has additional yellow tips of second dorsal and anal fins, and more-or-less distinct dark saddles on body. *A. fuscus* is plain dusky. Coastal reefs and in rich coral growth in lagoons. Secretive in corals, rising above on dusk, in small to large groups, similar species often mixed. Similar sized, maximum length 10 cm.

Black Cardinalfish *Apogon melas*

Drastic colour differences between day and night (shown in the photograph). Nearly all black during the day, with dusky fins and dorsal and anal fin spots less defined. Coastal reefs and shallow protected bays. Commonly under jetties and in holes or sponges on pylons, secretive during the day, quickly moving behind something at night when exposed in light. Maximum length 11 cm.

Two-bar Cardinalfish *Apogon rhodopterus*

Pale grey, each scale with dusky margin. Two black bars, first from below second and third dorsal spine, and second below end of second dorsal fin; distinct black spot centrally on caudal-fin base. Very similar to Three-spot Cardinalfish (next species). Clear inner to outer reef habitat, secretive in caves and ledges. Maximum length 15 cm.

Three-spot Cardinalfish *Apogon trimaculatus*

Variable with size, juveniles pale with black bars and similar to Two-bar Cardinalfish (previous species), but posterior part of first dorsal fin is white and lacks caudal fin spot. Adults dirty grey or brown, opercle spot and dusky spot on each scale, and banding less obvious. Coastal silty reefs, shy along rocky boulder slopes with lots of small holes for shelter, coming out on dusk. Maximum length 14 cm.

Western Gobbleguts *Apogon rueppelli*

Easily recognised by pale colour and series of dark spots along lateral line. Protected shallow habitats, usually mixed rock and sand reef, along seagrass beds and under jetties. Mainly coastal, but enters estuaries and is also found in suitable habitats at islands offshore. Maximum length 10 cm.

Southern Gobbleguts *Vincentia conspersa*

Variable from pale brown or grey to reddish brown, with more-or-less light specks depending on habitat, depth or place. Reddish when living deep and heavily speckled in South Australia. Very shallow coastal to deep offshore, often well up estuaries in silty conditions. Common among rocks and in caves or ledges. The almost identical *V. novaehollandiae* is found on the east coast. Maximum length 14 cm.

Ghost Cardinalfish

Black Cardinalfish

Two-bar Cardinalfish

Three-spot Cardinalfish

Western Gobbleguts

Southern Gobbleguts

149

Scarlet Cardinalfish *Vincentia badia*

Brown to red, very similar to Southern Gobbleguts (previous species) but with fewer and larger scales, 25 versus 27 lateral-line; 6–7 versus 9 scale rows between lateral-line and ventral-fin base. Shallow protected coastal bays to moderate depths, about 20 m, secretive in rocky ledges and small caves, out at night, floating close to substrate. Maximum length 10 cm.

Pyjama Cardinalfish *Sphaeramia nematoptera*

Easily identified by shape and colour, head yellow and eye red. Spots on posterior body pale brownish to red. Clear inshore reefs to outer lagoons, usually in small to moderate schools among branching corals, often very shallow. Maximum length 85 mm.

Slender Cardinalfish *Rhabdamia gracilis*

Body almost clear; shiny thin green iridescent line from behind eye, midlaterally and thick short angular one over abdomen; black tip on upper lobe (none on lower) of caudal fin. Several similar species, often differentiated by a small black spot in a particular place. Deep coastal to inner reefs, usually schooling above large bommies or coral bommies in 20+ m depth. Maximum length 5 cm.

Schooling Cardinalfish *Rhabdamia cypselura*

Rather featureless species, plain light semitransparent pinkish brown, with just a short dusky dash on snout, and sometimes called Nose-spot Cardinalfish. Forms massive schools during the day, usually along drop-offs or with large bommies in deep lagoons, spreading out individually at night to feed on zooplankton. Maximum length 6 cm.

Urchin Cardinalfish *Siphamia versicolor*

Dark, almost black, with small white spots on back, sometimes showing broad longitudinal bands. Similar to *S. fuscolineata* with evenly spaced black and white longitudinal stripes, found between the venomous spines of Crown of Thorns star. Several other similar species, mostly among urchin spines. Mainly coastal sand or mudflats. All small, maximum length 20 mm.

LONGFIN PIKES — DINOLESTIDAE

Monotypic, confined to southern Australian waters. Body almost cylindrical, head pointed. Originally placed in genus *Esox*, pikes (freshwater), but superficially resembles barracuda or snook, Sphyraenidae. Differs from apogonids with elongate shape, large number of soft rays in dorsal and anal fins, and only one spine instead of 3 in the anal fin.

Longfin Pike *Dinolestes lewini*

Best distinguished from barracudas by long-based second dorsal anal fins and deeper body. Greenish brown in estuaries to silver in clear oceanic waters. Various habitats from shallow seagrass beds to deep offshore near reefs. Small groups to great schools, often near or under jetties. Reputed as good eating. Maximum length 50 cm.

Scarlet Cardinalfish

Pyjama Cardinalfish

Slender Cardinalfish

Schooling Cardinalfish

Urchin Cardinalfish

Longfin Pike

151

BLANQUILLOS & TILEFISHES — MALACANTHIDAE

Small tropical global family with 2 genera and about 10 species, both genera and 4 species known from Australian waters. Slender, flexible body with tiny scales, small head with prominent spine at end of opercle, long-based single dorsal and anal fins. Most species distinctly coloured; some juveniles differ greatly from adults. Typically on sand-rubble patches near reefs, some digging burrows, others building great mounds of rubble for nesting sites. Adults nearly always in pairs. Inhabit protected bays and lagoons, with some species restricted to deep water. The blanquillos *Malacanthus* spp. are often shallow and feed primarily on small benthic invertebrates. Tilefishes *Hoplolatilus* spp. live deep and feed primarily on zooplankton.

Flagtail Blanquillo *Malacanthus brevirostris*

Body pale, tail with 2 black streaks. Juvenile and adult similar. Second species, Blue Blanquillo *M. latovittatus*, as juvenile with long black midlateral stripe; as adult becoming blue and stripe reducing to posterior part, most distinct on caudal fin. Blue Blanquillo usually in pairs on outer reef rubble patches. Flagtail Blanquillo singly or loosely in pairs, usually along reef margins on sand. Maximum length of Blue Blanquillo 35 cm, and Flagtail Blanquillo 30 cm, usually 20 cm.

Blue-head Tilefish *Hoplolatilus starcki*

Small juveniles all blue; adults blue head and yellow tail. Typically in pairs hovering close together near burrow. Deep along sloping base of walls. In Australia, rarely in depths less than 40 m, often much shallower in equatorial waters. Feeds on zooplankton. Maximum length 15 cm.

TAILORS — POMATOMIDAE

Single wide-ranging species. Populations in the Atlantic, the southern Indian Ocean and eastern Australia. Pelagic, schooling, voracious hunter on smaller pelagic species such as pilchards or mullet. Body streamlined, with smooth scales and large tail. Jaws with small compressed sharp teeth in single rows. Inhabit coastal waters and enter estuaries in pursuit of prey, often in large dense schools when migrating, spreading out during the hunt. Excellent game fish, known as Bluefish in America and Elf in South Africa.

Tailor *Pomatomus saltatrix*

Strong-looking silver fish with large tail and big jaws. Swims midwater near reefs, usually schooling in coastal waters, moving fast when sighted by divers. Solitary individuals and juveniles sometimes in coastal lagoons and estuaries. Spawns in open sea. Confirmed maximum length 1.2 m (reported much larger) and weight 14 kg.

Flagtail Blanquillo

Blue-head Tilefish

Tailor

153

REMORAS — ECHENEIDIDAE

Small distinctive family, easily recognised by unusual sucker disc feature on top of head. Four genera and 8 species globally distributed, only one of which is not known from Australian waters. The sucker disc is a modified dorsal fin, comprising transverse movable laminae; used by remoras for attaching themselves to objects, or usually to other fish such as large sharks and rays. Juveniles may attach to smaller fish such as barracudas or batfish. Primarily oceanic, but often brought in by host to coastal waters, including shallow lagoons or estuaries. Food is obtained when host is feeding or whenever opportunity arises, but may take parasitic copepods from host as well.

Slender Suckerfish *Echeneis naucrates*

Usually dark band from mouth to large black area in caudal fin; large adult with faded and more uniform colour, with band reduced to dash over eyes. Most commonly observed species, often seen swimming without host. Young, when still looking for host, form small groups and sometimes try to attach to divers in rather awkward places. Known under various names, but mainly Shark Remora or Striped Suckerfish. Maximum length 1 m.

Short Suckerfish *Remora remora*

Stocky, pinkish grey fish with large disc. Oceanic, occasionally carried inshore by sharks or rays, even into estuaries. Photograph shows 20 cm juvenile in Bermagui River, southern New South Wales. Maximum length 80 cm.

JACKS & TREVALLIES — CARANGIDAE

Large tropical to warm-temperate family, with approximately 25 general and 140 species. Most genera and 62 species are recorded from Australian waters. Primarily pelagic, streamlined fast swimmers, many wide-ranging and migrating. Valued as game and food fish and generally of great commercial value. Body oblong to elongate, compressed, covered with small to tiny, often embedded smooth scales. Usually with enlarged spiny scutes along posterior part of lateral line. Carnivorous, larger species hunting small fishes singly, in pairs or in organised groups. Small species and juveniles take zooplankton. Most species occur in coastal and offshore waters, a few enter estuaries, and usually only as juveniles. Juveniles form small groups and gradually numbers increase, probably so as to find each other. Some smaller species such as *Trachurus* spp. form great and dense schools, appearing from a distance as single entities, while the larger species such as *Seriola* spp. school in great numbers but are more loosely distributed over vast areas. Adults mostly silvery, pale greenish or bluish above, but small juveniles which commonly hide under floating weeds or other object are primarily yellow with dark bars or a series of dark blotches serving as camouflage.

Yellow-tail Kingfish *Seriola lalandi*

Tail yellow with pale, silvery centre part. A broad yellowish band from snout to near the upper caudal peduncle. Small juveniles yellowish, and have numerous narrow dark bands, still evident but fading at about 30 cm length. Usually seen as adults, schooling in small to large numbers. Adults school offshore, occasionally entering estuaries. Commonly fished for. Several similar species: Samson Fish *S. hippos* has a blunt head; Amberjack *S. dumerili* is deeper bodied; and *S. rivoliana* has an oblique stripe over eye from mouth to dorsal-fin origin, and soft dorsal fin anteriorly tall. Maximum length 2 m, weight 60 kg.

Slender Suckerfish

Short Suckerfish

Short Suckerfish (close-up of sucker disc)

Yellow-tail Kingfish

155

Rainbow Runner *Elagatis bipinnulata*

Two pale to bright blue midlateral lines, bluish to olive above and yellow to white below, caudal fin pale to bright yellow. Pelagic, often inshore or in lagoons, moving in small groups over slopes or near drop-offs in surface waters to about 20 m depth. Often comes close to divers. Maximum length 1.2 m, weight 15 kg.

Trevally Scad *Alepes vari*

Best identified by unusual body shape, being deep anteriorly and elongate posteriorly. Forms dense schools in still inner reef waters, usually swimming slowly midwater near large bommies. Another smaller species, *A. kleinii*, has a black spot on operculum and schools in deep water, to 60 m. Maximum length 50 cm.

Northern Yellowtail Scad *Atule mate*

Silvery, greenish above, operculum spot small or indistinct, tail yellow. Dusky barring on body, usually distinct in natural light. Coastal bays near mangrove and over shallow sandflats and slopes, swimming fast when feeding on zooplankton. Often solitary or in small groups, sometimes schooling in sheltered coves. Maximum length 30 cm.

Southern Yellowtail Scad *Trachurus novaezelandiae*

Tail distinctly yellow, operculum spot distinct. Protected coastal bays and estuaries, but also offshore with islands. Forms large schools along reef slopes or walls, commonly under jetties, feeding on zooplankton, often near the surface forming ripple patches. Hunted by the larger pelagics, tuna and kingfish. Maximum length 50 cm, usually 30 cm.

Jack Mackerel *Trachurus declivis*

Lacks yellow tail. Plain greenish silver and distinct operculum spot. Forms great densely-packed schools in coastal and shelf waters at various depths from surface to 500 m, which when seen from the air appear as large dark single entities. Young in shallows. Mainly common in Tasmania. Maximum length 64 cm, usually 50 cm.

Mackerel Scad *Decapterus macarellus*

Shiny silvery with pale blue midlateral line, moderate-sized earspot, very slender body. Forms large schools in deep water, occasionally swimming fast along reef walls in shallow depths or near the surface in pursuit of zooplankton. Oceanic, sometimes inshore. Maximum length 32 cm.

Rainbow Runner

Trevally Scad

Northern Yellowtail Scad

Southern Yellowtail Scad

Jack Mackerel

Mackerel Scad

Russell's Mackerel Scad *Decapterus russelli*

Moderately deep-bodied. Several very similar species, others more slender: *D. macrosoma* has larger earspot; and *D. muroadsi* has yellow stripe along lateral line. Shiny silvery, forming small to massive schools, some species moving inshore, others mainly trawled in deep water. Russell's Mackerel Scad often congregates in coastal bays. Maximum length 35 cm.

Ox-eye Scad *Selar boops*

Best identified from similar species by short curve in lateral line. Yellow stripe usually distinct and operculum spot small. Smooth-tail Trevally *Selaroides leptolepis* has longer lateral line curve and large distinct black operculum spot. Sheltered coastal waters, often congregates in large dense schools near mangroves and jetties; different species form separate schools. Maximum length 30 cm.

Purse-eye Scad *Selar crumenophthalmus*

Long curving lateral line, yellow stripe usually distinct, operculum spot small and often indistinct, caudal fin with dusky posterior margin and tips. Very common tropical species, usually in very large schools in still bays on coast and islands, often near jetties. Maximum length 35 cm.

Big-eye Trevally *Caranx sexfasciatus*

Median fin tips white, small operculum spot, lateral line scutes dark. This is the most commonly observed tropical trevally species, usually in very large schools along clear coastal and inner reefs. Large individuals occasionally solitary or in small aggregations. Juveniles enter estuaries. Similar, more coastal *C. tille* has pale scutes and a more distinct operculum spot. Maximum length 85 cm.

Giant Trevally *Caranx ignobilis*

Uniformly coloured, slightly darker above. Head dorsal profile strongly rounded. Deep-bodied from head to soft dorsal fin. Juveniles have yellowish anal and lower caudal fins and are coastal. Adults adjacent to deep slopes, usually forming schools, but solitary 'giants' often seen swimming along slopes close to substrate. Largest trevally, maximum length 1.7 m and weight 62 kg (catch record).

Black Trevally *Caranx lugubris*

Uniformly grey to black, scutes black, elongated dorsal and anal fin tips, and very deep-bodied. Clear coastal to outer reef slopes and along deep drop-offs, usually solitary or in small numbers. All tropical seas. Maximum length 80 cm.

Russell's Mackerel Scad

Ox-eye Scad

Purse-eye Scad

Big-eye Trevally

Giant Trevally

Black Trevally

Blue-fin Trevally *Caranx melampygus*

Median fins blue, usually with dark speckles, more numerous with age. Head profile almost straight from snout to above eyes. Common coastal reef slopes, usually seen solitary, hunting low on substrate for fishes and benthic invertebrates. Often accompanying large bottom-feeding lethrinids to snap up creatures on the run. Occasionally forms schools. Maximum length 70 cm.

Brassy Trevally *Caranx papuensis*

Dorsal fin and upper half of caudal fin greyish blue, lower half of caudal fin and anal fin pale yellowish with thin white margin. Adults with irregular small dark spot over head or back. Pale spot on lateral-line origin. Coastal, often muddy slopes, hunting prey by swimming low on substrate, singly or in small groups. Maximum length 84 cm.

Thicklip Trevally *Carangoides orthogrammus*

Juveniles yellowish, adults with blue median fins and some scattered yellow pupil-size spots on sides. Snout bluntly rounded. Juveniles in coastal waters, adults deep along drop-offs, usually seen solitary, swimming near bommies or along walls. Maximum length 60 cm.

Banded Trevally *Carangoides ferdau*

Pale grey with 7 dusky bands. Eye large, diameter about equal to snout-length. Small juveniles yellowish with black bands, often with floating objects or swimming with large jellyfish. Adults from coastal to outer reefs. Hunting singly or in small numbers on coastal slopes, swimming low on substrate. Schooling on outer reefs. Maximum length 70 cm.

Blue-spined Trevally *Carangoides caeruleopinnatus*

Deep-bodied, head large and blunt. No black operculum spot. Juveniles broadly banded, dorsal and anal fin tips with filaments which reduce with age. Yellow spots scattered over sides, more numerous in adults. Coastal reef slopes and lagoons, often in silty habitat, solitary near large bommies or short drop-offs. Maximum length 40 cm.

Onion Trevally *Carangoides uii*

Body very short, deeply oblong, and dorsal profile evenly curved from steep snout to dorsal origin. Dorsal and anal fin tips with long filaments, sometimes reaching past caudal fin. Coastal reefs, often silty reef and mud habitat, seen swimming in solitary fashion high above substrate near slopes or large bommies. Small species, maximum length 25 cm.

Blue-fin Trevally

Brassy Trevally

Thicklip Trevally

Banded Trevally

Blue-spined Trevally

Onion Trevally

Bar-cheek Trevally *Carangoides plagiotaenia*

Body elongate, eye level with snout tip. Dusky short vertical bar on cheek. Common species from coastal to outer reef slopes and along walls. Swims high in water column, solitary or in small loose aggregations, often sheltering near large overhangs or shipwrecks. Maximum length 45 cm.

Turrum *Carangoides fulvoguttatus*

Eye above horizontal level of snout tip; head pointed compared with *Caranx* spp. Rather plain, adults with scattered small dark spots on upper sides. Very similar Bludger Trevally *C. gymnostethus* has eye at horizontal level with snout tip, and adults usually with additional golden spots on sides. Both either solitary or in small aggregations in clear-water habitat near deep water. Maximum length Turrum 1 m, and Bludger Trevally 90 cm.

White Trevally *Pseudocaranx dentex*

Moderately large black operculum spot. Juveniles often with yellow stripe midlaterally to caudal-fin base. Distributed in Northern and Southern Hemispheres, possibly different species. Northern Hemisphere populations with yellow tail and yellow along dorsal and anal-fin bases. Coastal waters and estuaries, often in small schools. Second temperate species, silvery Skipjack Trevally *P. wrighti*, forms large schools offshore. Maximum length White Trevally 94 cm, Skipjack Trevally 35 cm.

Golden Trevally *Gnathanodon speciosus*

Juveniles bright yellow with thin black bars which remain visible to almost adult size. Large adults show faint barring over back and usually some scattered eye-size black blotches on upper side. Juveniles often swimming with large fish, near head, 'piloting', but also with jellyfish and even large seasnakes. Adults deep, feeding in small groups on benthic invertebrates, on open sandflats stretched between reefs. Maximum length 1 m.

Giant Leatherskin *Scomberoides commersonianus*

Mouth reaches past below eye. Spots above lateral line large and rounded. Several other species: Small-mouth Queenfish *S. tol* has shorter mouth; Double-spotted Queenfish *S. lysan* has smaller spots or a double series of spots. Mostly solitary, sometimes small groups along coastal slopes to outer reef drop-offs. Usually near the surface, but some species reported to 100 m depth. Giant Leatherskin the largest, maximum length 1.2 m, others about 75 cm.

Bar-cheek Trevally

Turrum

White Trevally (adult)

White Trevally (juvenile)

Golden Trevally

Giant Leatherskin

Northern Dart *Trachinotus bailloni*

Dorsal and anal fin tips long and similar to caudal fin lobes. Silvery with series of pale to black dots along lateral line. Sheltered bays, coastal to outer reef lagoons. Shallow sandflats and along slopes near surface. The Southern Dart *T. coppingeri* more coastal and only known from central Queensland to central New South Wales and Lord Howe Island; it has larger and elongated spots on lateral line. Maximum length 56 cm.

Snub-nose Dart *Trachinotus blochii*

Body deep, solid in adults. Dorsal and anal fin tips similar, but shorter than anal fin lobes. Juveniles near surface along beaches in small groups. Adults deeper in lagoons and reef-flats, sometimes schooling, but very large individuals often seen solitary on rubble zones among reef. Maximum length 65 cm, weight 7.3 kg.

PONYFISHES — LEIOGNATHIDAE

Small Indo-Pacific family with 3 genera and about 20 species. All genera and at least 10 species are found in Australian waters. Usually greatly compressed deep-bodied with slimy skin, producing mucus under stress. Scales tiny and embedded. Mouth very protractile. A series of small spines along the dorsal and anal-fin bases. Sheltered coastal bays or still deep water, muddy and fine sand habitat, many entering estuaries and forming small to very large schools. Shiny silvery sides, usually darker on back with mottled or banded patterns. Diet comprises small benthic invertebrates.

Common Ponyfish *Leiognathus equula* (now known as *L. nuchalis*)

Lacks dorsal filament. Usually dark blotch on forehead and thin indistinct barring on upper sides. Very common in tropical coastal waters, including shallow estuaries, shallow to about 40 m depth. Usually in small groups of similar-sized individuals. Largest ponyfish, maximum length 25 cm.

Threadfin Ponyfish *Leiognathus fasciatus*

Long dorsal spine and numerous narrow bars on upper half of sides. Common in coastal and estuarine habitats. Shallow sandflats, swimming quickly in small schools, occasionally stopping together for a short feed. Maximum length 20 cm.

Slender Ponyfish *Leiognathus elongatus*

Unusually slender in family and best recognised by its shape. Variable from pale with dusky blotches over back to distinctly marked on pearly-shiny back. Coastal bays, often forming great schools swimming well above the substrate feeding on zooplankton. Widespread in the tropical Indo-Pacific; only recorded from north-western Australia, but probably throughout northern parts. Small species, maximum length 12 cm.

Northern Dart

Snub-nose Dart

Common Ponyfish

Threadfin Ponyfish

Slender Ponyfish

SILVER BELLIES — GERREIDAE

Tropical family with 7 genera and estimated 40 species, of which 3 genera and about 10 species are found in Australian waters. Most diverse in American waters. Very similar in looks and behaviour to ponyfishes (previous family), but distinctly scaled. Usually shiny silver on sides, and dorsal fin elevated anteriorly, except in genus *Parequula*. Benthic feeders with excellent eyesight, capturing small prey by suction from the protractile mouth. Silver bellies occur on sand patches near reefs or rubble zones, some preferring still, protected habitats and others surge zones.

Common Silver Belly *Gerres subfasciatus*

Black dorsal fin tip. Often with thin grey barring along lateral line. No yellow in fins. Many similar species, usually only slightly different in body depth and maximum size, and difficult to distinguish without examining a specimen. This species is most common in New South Wales and coastal Queensland waters, but is also found throughout the northern half of Australia. *G. ovatus* is a synonym. Maximum length 20 cm.

Threadfin Silver Belly *Gerres filamentosus*

Easily identified by exceptionally long dorsal fin spine and thin barring over upper sides. Often mixes with the very similar Threadfin Ponyfish in coastal estuaries. Widespread in the tropical Indo-Pacific, shallow to at least 50 m depth, but possibly several similar species. Maximum length 25 cm, usually 15 cm.

Short Silver Belly *Gerres abbreviatus*

Best recognised by its yellow ventral fins. Deep-bodied and dorsal tip moderately tall. Coastal sandflats, entering very shallow depths in front of beaches at high tide. Usually several specimens spread over a small area, with each concentrating on finding prey on substrate. Large species, maximum length 30 cm.

Slender Silver Belly *Gerres oyena*

More slender than other similar species. Dusky edge on dorsal fin tip, and scale-sized pale bluish grey spots on cheek. Juveniles with dusky bars. Very common in coastal waters, shallow sandflats and slopes, singly or in loose aggregations. Reported to 25 cm length, usually to 20 cm.

Melbourne Silver Belly *Parequula melbournensis*

Single south coast species, lacking elevated anterior dorsal fin. Instead, spines shortest anteriorly, progressively increasing in length followed by confluent soft section. Shallow estuaries to deep offshore, at least 100 m depth. Over sand near reef, usually in small aggregations. Monotypic genus, Australian endemic. Maximum length 18 cm.

Common Silver Belly

Threadfin Silver Belly

Short Silver Belly

Slender Silver Belly

Melbourne Silver Belly

WHIPTAILS & SPINECHEEKS — NEMIPTERIDAE

Moderately large tropical family with 5 genera and approximately 64 species, of which all genera and about 30 species are found in Australian waters. Threadfin breams, genus *Nemipterus*, are the most numerous but are restricted to deep water and are not included here; Spinecheeks, *Scolopsis*, and whiptails, *Pentapodus*, each with a number of species, are mostly shallow reef dwellers. Diagnostic features restrictive and identification best by colour; even though juveniles can differ greatly from adults, each has diagnostic patterns or combinations of colours. Spinecheeks are moderately deep-bodied, often referred to as tropical breams, featuring a prominent spine below the eye. Whiptails are more slender and adults often feature long filaments on caudal fin tips. Colourful fishes compared to silver bellies (previous family), but behaviour is similar, feeding on sand and rubble substrates, and swimming in short dashes with sudden stops to study the bottom for movement of potential prey.

Paradise Whiptail *Pentapodus paradiseus*

Juvenile with bright yellow stripe from eye to upper caudal peduncle bordered with black stripe above and midlaterally below. Changing gradually to adult pattern as illustrated. Common Queensland species, in clear coastal habitat, most numerous in mixed rubble and vegetated rocky reef, forming moderate-sized aggregations. Juveniles south to Sydney Harbour. Maximum length 20 cm.

Western Whiptail *Pentapodus vitta*

Black midlateral stripe, adults with blue stripes over snout. Small aggregations in coastal rocky-sand reefs, including under jetties and in seagrass areas. Restricted to the west coast. Also known as Butterfish, Western Butterfish and Striped Whiptail, but the last name is applicable to several species. Maximum size 24 cm, usually 20 cm.

Japanese Whiptail *Pentapodus nagasakiensis*

Bright yellow back and blue midlateral stripe. Adults similar, but colour is less intensive. Intermediate size shown, photographed in Japan. In Australia, mostly known from juveniles. Adults deep, sometimes trawled in northern Australia to 100 m depth. Maximum length 20 cm.

Double Whiptail *Pentapodus emeryii*

Adults with bright blue caudal fin and very long trailing tips. Snout and eye bright yellow, thin yellow line from eye following dorsal profile, and broad yellow midlateral stripe. Juveniles deep blue with bright yellow stripes from snout along body, midlaterally and over eye to end of dorsal-fin base, and thin line mid-dorsally over head. Adults deep on slopes with rich invertebrate growth such as sponges and soft corals on rubble and sand substrate. Usually in small groups swimming well above substrate in depths of 20+ m. Juveniles solitary on sheltered reefs among mixed rock, coral and low algal growth habitat. Maximum length 15 cm (without fin filaments).

Blue Whiptail *Pentapodus* sp.

Undescribed species, confused with *P. emeryii* (previous species), differing as juvenile in the way yellow stripe joins across front of eyes. In *P. emeryii* the stripes continue to tip of snout. Common east coast species in coastal waters, young entering estuaries, adults in small aggregations on deep sandflats and slopes. Maximum length 20 cm.

Paradise Whiptail

Western Whiptail

Japanese Whiptail

Double Whiptail (adult)

Double Whiptail (juvenile)

Blue Whiptail

169

Monocle Bream *Scolopsis bilineata*

Most common spinecheek species, wide-ranging throughout the Indo-Pacific with some colour variations. Juveniles in Australia with distinct black and yellow stripes over upper half of body, changing gradually to up-curving lines from head to centre of dorsal fin. Coastal to outer reef lagoons, usually shallow to about 20 m depth. Maximum length 20 cm.

Striped Spinecheek *Scolopsis lineata*

Juveniles very similar to Monocle Bream (previous species), but paler yellow stripes; adults differ by having horizontal stripes. Shallow coastal lagoons and rubble flats near mangroves, often in large aggregations swimming well above substrate. Maximum length 20 cm, usually 15 cm.

Three-line Spinecheek *Scolopsis trilineata*

More slender than other similar species. Peculiar thin upward-curving white line just below central lateral line. Solitary shy species, inhabiting coastal reef-flats and lagoons, often silty habitat near mangroves, and inner reefs. Maximum length 20 cm, usually 15 cm.

Pearly Spinecheek *Scolopsis margaritifer*

Variable from dusky grey on top with white sides to almost uniform with patch of yellow spots over large area midway along sides. Small juveniles have black midlateral line, with yellow below and white above, and second black stripe high along sides. Reef crests and slopes in coral-rich habitat on rubble patches. Maximum size 18 cm.

Lattice Spinecheek *Scolopsis monogramma*

Juveniles grey with broad black midlateral stripe which changes to yellow-orange posteriorly, and thinner black line from above eye to soft dorsal-fin base. Stripes fade with growth, and adults have long filamented caudal fin tips; intermediate shown in the photograph. Sheltered sandflats near inner reefs, juveniles in harbours. Maximum length 30 cm, usually 24 cm.

Yellow-tail Spinecheek *Scolopsis affinis*

Bright yellow tail, with or without dark stripe. When schooling plain, and solitary with stripe. Similar *S. aurata,* with white tail and yellow stripe, is found in the Indian Ocean; and an unnamed species, deeper bodied with black centred scales above lateral line, is probably in northern Australia. Coastal reefs on slopes. *S. affinis* forms large schools in deep water; seen off Lizard Island, Queensland, in 30 m depth. Maximum length 25 cm.

Monocle Bream

Striped Spinecheek

Three-line Spinecheek

Pearly Spinecheek

Lattice Spinecheek

Yellow-tail Spinecheek

171

Blue-stripe Spinecheek *Scolopsis xenochroa*

Small juveniles with thick blue and black stripes on upper half of body. Adults with unusual mixed pattern on side: blue dash, followed by patch of black spots and then white dash; and blue stripe along dorsal base. Usually on deep coastal sand and rubble slopes with sparse reef to over 50 m depth, juveniles more shallow. Maximum length 20 cm.

Red-spot Spinecheek *Scolopsis taenioptera*

Angular yellow and blue stripe on cheek and red spot on pectoral-fin base. Often dusky midlateral line, but can be put on at will. Common coastal but deep-water species, usually 50+ m depth, rarely shallower to about 30 m. Mud and sand slopes, usually seen solitary but may be strays from schools. Maximum length 20 cm.

White-band Spinecheek *Scolopsis vosmeri*

Easily recognised by dark brown colour and broad white band over end of head. Small juveniles pale below with similar pattern to adult above. Mainly found in the Indian Ocean, but also ranging along the Asian continental margin to Japan and to north-western Australia. Deep coastal slopes, secretive in reefs, small groups. Maximum size 20 cm.

EMPERORS — LETHRINIDAE

Family of medium-sized fishes with 5 genera and 39 species of the Indo-Pacific, of which 4 genera and 24 species are known from Australian waters. Some species reach 1 m in length and are of commercial importance. The largest genus, *Lethrinus*, 28 species, is known as emperors or emperor-snappers. Carnivorous bottom-dwellers, feed on a great variety of small benthic invertebrates, either taken on sight or sifted from sand by simply taking a mouthful and filtering it through gill rakers to extract prey. Feeding opportunists, day or night, usually near reefs on adjacent sand or rubble zones. Distinctly scaled, fins generally large with strong spinous section, and eye also large. Depending on species, habitats range from shallow estuaries to deep offshore; in some, juveniles inshore and adults offshore.

Big-eye Emperor *Monotaxis grandoculis*

Small juvenile with 4 white bars, sometimes 2 dark longitudinal parallel stripes along sides. Adults plain, large rounded head and reddish dorsal fin tips. Juveniles in shallow lagoons or on coastal reefs. Adults along steep walls in clear coastal to outer reef habitats. Maximum length 60 cm.

Yellow-striped Emperor *Lethrinus ornatus*

Distinct species, distinguished from others by yellow to orange stripes along sides below lateral line. Coastal reefs, small juveniles often in freshwater run-offs. Solitary and shy, difficult to approach, swims close to substrate in search of benthic invertebrates as prey. Small species, maximum length 40 cm.

Blue-stripe Spinecheek

Red-spot Spinecheek

White-band Spinecheek

Big-eye Emperor (adult)

Big-eye Emperor (juvenile)

Yellow-striped Emperor

Yellow-lip Emperor *Lethrinus xanthochilus*

Slender species. Adults very plain and best identified by yellow upper lip which is distinct in natural light; juveniles with some dark spotting on upper sides. Adults usually seen on sand slopes adjacent to deep water, solitary and rather shy. Reported to feed on crustaceans and fishes to depths of 150 m. Maximum length 60 cm.

Small-tooth Emperor *Lethrinus microdon*

Very long snout and colour pattern identify this species, but difficult to separate from Long-snout Emperor *L. olivaceus* which is spotted rather than lined on snout. Latter usually in small to large aggregations, and Small-tooth Emperor usually solitary. Coastal reef slopes adjacent to deep water, swimming low on the substrate in pursuit of prey. Maximum length 70 cm.

Spangled Emperor *Lethrinus nebulosus*

Most common Australian Emperor species, juveniles to moderate size in Sydney Harbour. Juveniles pale, with series of pale brownish blotches over entire body. Large adults pale blue, each scale dark at base. Juveniles may form schools, adults solitary or in small aggregations on deep sandflats. Also known as Yellow Sweetlips. Large species, maximum length almost 1 m, weight 10 kg.

Black-blotch Emperor *Lethrinus harak*

Large black blotch on sides, usually bordered with yellow area above and behind. Shallow coastal bays on sandflats and slopes. Solitary, swimming near substrate in search of prey. Often accompanied by goatfish or wrasses, ready to pounce on potential prey disturbed by the feeding emperor. Maximum length 60 cm.

Slender Emperor *Lethrinus variegatus*

Pale below, with a series of large green to grey blotches forming bands or indistinct barring. Shallow coastal bays, usually in vicinity of seagrass beds. Very slender. The almost as slender Lancer *L. genivittatus* is found in a similar habitat with brownish blotched pattern; usually distinct spot just under lateral line below third and fourth dorsal fin spines, and grows slightly larger. *L. variegatus* the smallest emperor, maximum length 20 cm.

Forktail Large-eye Bream *Gymnocranius elongatus*

Several very similar species, usually plain silvery with slightly darkened back, banded pattern turns on quickly with habitat or when feeding. Forktail Large-eye Bream has longer caudal fin lobes than most. Most similar *G. grandoculus* usually with dusky snout and short caudal fin lobes. Sheltered coastal to deep sandflats and slopes, usually solitary in shallows. Maximum length 35 cm.

Yellow-lip Emperor

Small-tooth Emperor

Spangled Emperor

Black-blotch Emperor

Slender Emperor

Forktail Large-eye Bream

175

Collared Large-eye Bream *Gymnocranius audleyi*

Easily identified by dusky half-moon-shaped spot, surrounded by white bars, on nape above end of eye, very distinct in adults but already evident in young in the photograph. Coastal and still inner reef sandflats, often very shallow along reef margins, usually solitary. Maximum length 40 cm.

Gold-spot Emperor *Gnathodentex aurolineatus*

Large yellow blotch below end of soft dorsal fin usually distinct. Body variable, from silvery with thin brown lines to dusky. Clear deep lagoons and outer reef walls, often in large schools. Feed on benthic invertebrates on rubble and sand along reef margins. Maximum length 30 cm.

SNAPPER & BREAMS — SPARIDAE

Global family with 22 genera and 41 species, of which 7 genera and at least 11 species are found in Australian waters. Important commercially and popular with anglers, particularly Snapper *Chrysophrys aurata*, the largest species, reaching 1.2 m in length and 20 kg in weight. Oval-shaped shiny silvery with moderately large slightly ctenoid scales. Mouth low, jaws with conical teeth and anterior canines. Benthic feeders on sand and rubble substrates, many feeding on invertebrates and small fishes at night in shallow depths. Occur deeper during the day. Species school in sheltered bays, but some also in turbulent coastal waters. Juveniles mainly estuarine, either solitary in deep basin or schooling in fresh-water run-offs, depending on species. Some enter fresh water as adults, feeding on shrimps and insects

Snapper *Chrysophrys aurata*

Young with small bright blue spots over back and sides. Variable pale pinkish to silvery, fins often bluish. Small juveniles deep in large estuaries on open substrate with small rocky outcrops. Medium-sized in small groups in coastal bays on sand well away from reefs. Adults usually deep, seen singly on reefs, only moving into shallow depths at night. School seasonally. Sibling species in Japan, differing from Australian one in colour when young, and greatly in shape when adult, not elongating or developing large hump on head. Japanese authors use *Sparus*, Atlantic genus, for their species. Usually spelled *Chrysophrys auratus*, but genus feminine. Maximum length 1.2 m, weight 20 kg.

Tarwhine *Rhabdosargus sarba*

Very similar to bream (next 2 species), but forehead profile more rounded and numerous close-set yellowish spots form lines along scale rows. Coastal bays and sandy estuaries in tidal channels, usually in small aggregations feeding on benthic invertebrates from substrate. Sometimes schooling along coast and occasionally mixes with bream. Maximum length 45 cm, weight about 1.4 kg.

Silver Bream *Acanthopagrus australis*

Small black axil spot, ventral and anal fins usually yellow. Juveniles with dusky bands which show in adults at night. Replaced by Southern Bream *A. butcheri* on the south coast. Both also called Black Bream, but the name should be reserved for the next species. Eastern species also called simply Bream or Yellow-finned Bream. Common in coastal and estuarine rocky habitat, feeding along reef margins on sand. Forms large schools along the coast. Maximum length 65 cm, weight 4 kg.

Collared Large-eye Bream

Gold-spot Emperor

Snapper (adult)

Snapper (juvenile)

Tarwhine

Silver Bream

Black Bream *Acanthopagrus berda*

Dusky brown to very dark, near-black, all over with shiny scale edges. Coastal, usually silty muddy habitat near jetties and river mouths. Known in Queensland as Pikey Bream. Widespread in the tropical Indo-Pacific. Maximum length 56 cm.

SWEETLIPS — HAEMULIDAE

Large family, needing revision, with 18 genera and estimated 120 species. Undetermined number in Australian waters, probably about 40 species. Includes estuarine grunters, subfamily Haemulinae, mainly genus *Pomadasys*, and sweetlips, subfamily Plectorhinchinae, in which *Plectorhinchus* is most speciose. Estuarine species more bream-like, mostly silvery with some spotting, and lack the thickened lips typical of plectorhinchids. Most sweetlips go through elaborate colour changes during growth. Small juveniles usually boldly spotted or striped; and adults often totally different, plain with small spots or numerous thin lines. Grunter-bream are mainly coastal, occurring in shallow estuaries to deeper sandy habitats. Adult sweetlips inhabit reefs, often forming groups during the day, moving onto open substrate at night to hunt benthic invertebrates; juveniles solitary in shallow coastal bays and estuaries, typically swimming in twisting fashion, wagging their large tail.

Spotted Grunter-bream *Pomadasys kaakan*

Spots arranged in bars, most distinct when juvenile. Several other similar species, mainly differing in spotted patterns. Spotted Grunter-bream common in estuaries and near mangrove areas. Adults in deeper coastal bays in pursuit of prawns. Large adults sometimes mistaken for bream (Sparidae) but the truncate versus forked caudal fin readily separates them. Maximum length 66 cm, weight 4.6 kg.

Brown Sweetlips *Plectorhinchus gibbosus*

Plain dusky grey, operculum and preoperculum margins very dark brown to black. Juveniles very similar with proportionally taller dorsal fin, small ones usually on the surface with floating matter, mimicking leaves. Coastal waters, usually silty muddy habitat, often near or below jetties. Maximum length 75 cm.

Giant Sweetlips *Plectorhinchus obscurus*

Large adults grey with numerous small pale spots, snout plain grey and lips very thick, lower fins mostly black, and broad black margin on soft dorsal fin. Small juveniles dirty-yellow with pale longitudinal lines, grey when half-grown, with some evidence of white longitudinal lines. Juveniles coastal; adults deep along inner reef walls, sometimes in small groups. Maximum length 1 m.

Magpie Sweetlips *Plectorhinchus picus*

Change drastically with size. Small juveniles black with white on nose, along belly and as three large spots over back. With growth, black areas decrease and eventually break up into small spots. Large adults with small spots over most of body. The intermediate stage is shown in the photograph. Sheltered inner reef slopes and offshore habitat. Maximum length 90 cm.

Black Bream

Spotted Grunter-bream

Brown Sweetlips

Giant Sweetlips

Magpie Sweetlips

179

Harlequin Sweetlips *Plectorhinchus chaetodonoides*

Drastic changes between juveniles and adults. Small juveniles brown with large white blotches, including snout and fins. Brown areas break up and black spots develop in white areas, spots becoming more numerous with age. Tiny juveniles swim with head down and wave fins frantically when approached. Juveniles in coastal and lagoon habitats; large adults along deep drop-offs, usually solitary, sometimes sharing large caves with other sweetlips during the daytime. Maximum length 60 cm.

Yellow-ribbon Sweetlips *Plectorhinchus polytaenia*

Small juveniles with 3 broad black stripes with narrow creamy interspaces and pale orange on snout and over back. With growth, black stripes split several times, interspaces turn white, and yellow develops centrally in each black stripe. In adults, stripes are yellow with thin black borders, and median fins bright yellow. Juveniles solitary in coastal rocky reef, and adults form small aggregations along deep current-prone slopes. Maximum length 50 cm.

Orange-lined Sweetlips *Plectorhinchus celebicus*

Juveniles with broad brown bands, breaking up with growth to numerous thin orange-yellow lines. All fins bright yellow when adults. Coastal and inner reefs in deep lagoons or protected bays. Usually in small to large schools, hovering in sheltered places during the daytime. Maximum length 40 cm.

Lined Sweetlips *Plectorhinchus lessonii*

Distinct species as adult, with brown to black stripes along body above pectoral fin level. Like many closely related species, there are several colour changes with growth. Post-larvae completely pigmented, including fins, mainly orange-brown with black stripe; several large spots, black and white, over head and body. Larger juveniles mostly black, with 2 creamy white longitudinal lines from head to end of caudal fin, and across head just behind eyes, resulting in a large triangular black cap on head. Inner and outer reef lagoons in caves along steep slopes, juveniles in shallow lagoons. Maximum length 40 cm.

Harlequin Sweetlips (young adult)

Harlequin Sweetlips (juvenile)

Yellow-ribbon Sweetlips (adult)

Yellow-ribbon Sweetlips (juvenile)

Orange-lined Sweetlips

Lined Sweetlips (adult)

Lined Sweetlips (juvenile)

Lined Sweetlips (small juvenile)

181

Oblique-banded Sweetlips *Plectorhinchus lineatus*

Juveniles similar to other striped species, but clean white with 5 thick longitudinal black stripes, snout and fins yellowish. Lines gradually break-up with growth, changing into more numerous lines and spots, and eventually angle. Adult with distinct numerous oblique lines on upper sides. Juveniles solitary on coastal rocky reef, adults along walls with caves for shelter, coastal to outer reefs at moderate depths, sometimes forming large schools. Maximum length 60 cm.

Slate Sweetlips *Diagramma labiosum*

Small juveniles yellow with thick black stripe midlaterally and along dorsal fin. Number of stripes increases with age, series of spots develops between them, but pattern eventually fades to uniformly grey colour. Small juveniles solitary, but form small aggregations with time. Adults usually in groups hovering above deep reef crests during the daytime. The similar Painted Sweetlips *D. pictum* may occur in north-western Australia. Adults distinctly spotted and juveniles with spots on cheek. Maximum length of both about 1 m.

CORAL SNAPPERS — LUTJANIDAE

Large tropical family with 17 genera and 103 species globally, of which 13 genera and an estimated 52 species are reported in Australian waters. Includes subfamily Lutjaninae, benthic snappers; Etelinae, pelagic snappers; Apsilinae, fusilier snappers; and Symphorinae, threadfin snappers. Benthic snappers are the most numerous and are commonly observed by divers. Perch-like, i.e. very similar to the freshwater English perch, called Redfin in Australia, with an elongated scaly body and a single slightly notched dorsal fin with strong spinous section. Many species are commonly called sea perch. Identification is usually easy with diagnostic colour patterns; however, juveniles may differ greatly from adults. Primarily benthic feeders forming small groups, few planktivorous and schooling. Carnivorous, diet varies greatly, but many prey heavily on small fishes at night. Although many considered good eating, care should be taken and local knowledge sought as can be poisonous, depending on species or area in which it occurs. The condition called ciguatera is thought to be caused by predators feeding on small herbivores which consume algae containing the poison. As algae live shallow, those species in deep water are generally not affected.

Red Emperor *Lutjanus sebae*

Deep-bodied with a big head. Large adults red all over. Juveniles with distinctly white body and broad black bands, turning brown or red with age. Small juveniles often among long spines of diadema urchins on coastal mixed sand–rock habitat. Large adults move to deep offshore waters, forming schools. Excellent to eat. Maximum length 1 m, weight 22 kg.

Malabar Snapper *Lutjanus malabaricus*

Juveniles with distinct black bar, bordered with white over caudal peduncle and black band through eye from snout to nape. Dusky when small, changing to bright red as adult, losing the distinct features of the young. Juveniles solitary in muddy coastal habitat with small coral or rock outcrops on slopes. Adults deep offshore. Maximum length 1 m.

Oblique-banded Sweetlips (adult)

Oblique-banded Sweetlips (juvenile)

Slate Sweetlips (adult)

Slate Sweetlips (juvenile)

Red Emperor

Malabar Snapper

Moluccen Snapper *Lutjanus boutton*

Small juveniles greenish yellow with dusky brown head. Large round black blotch develops below soft dorsal fin, just onto lateral line, but often faded in large adults. Small spots develop on each scale, forming lines. Juveniles in shallow coastal waters, often near freshwater run-offs. Adults deep offshore. Maximum length 70 cm, weight 10.5 kg.

One-spot Snapper *Lutjanus monostigma*

Body grey or yellowish brown, fins yellow. Similar to John's Snapper (previous species), but more elongate, and spot mostly below the lateral line. Also similar is Russell's Snapper *L. russelli*, but larger spot with lateral line through middle, and with greyish fins. One-spot Snapper inhabits coastal reefs. Usually seen solitary sheltering along walls, out at night. Maximum length 60 cm.

Black-spot Snapper *Lutjanus fulviflammus*

Small juveniles with distinct black line through eye from snout, changing to yellow past head, with one yellow line above and several below. Large black spot with lateral line through middle. With growth, black spot elongates and black eye-line fades. Juveniles inhabit mangroves and freshwater run-offs in small groups, often mixing with similar species. Adults at moderate depths in shelter of caves on inner reefs. Maximum length 35 cm.

Spanish Flag Snapper *Lutjanus carponotatus*

Juveniles with broad dark stripes, pale interspaces, midlaterally usually white with grey above and below. Stripes turn orange to yellow and divide into numerous ones with growth. Fins yellow. Coastal reefs and lagoons to sheltered parts of outer reefs, often silty habitat, forming loose aggregations on reef tops. Maximum length 40 cm.

Brown-stripe Snapper *Lutjanus vitta*

Juveniles with thick black stripe from snout to caudal fin. Stripe fades with growth to pale yellow, becoming indistinct in large adults which develop additional yellow over back and on caudal fin. Small juveniles in small groups on open sand and mud slopes, sheltering below tentacles of stinging anemones such as *Cerianthus*. Adults solitary or in small groups on rubble flats between reefs. Maximum length 40 cm.

Blue-stripe Snapper *Lutjanus kasmira*

Easily identified by yellow body with 4 iridescent blue stripes and pale ventral area of head to end of anal-fin base. Juveniles form small aggregations in coral rubble and rocky reefs inshore, including estuaries. Adults form small to very large schools, during day usually hovering along reef slopes in protected shallow to very deep habitats. Maximum length 35 cm.

Moluccen Snapper

One-spot Snapper

Black-spot Snapper

Spanish Flag Snapper

Brown-stripe Snapper

Blue-stripe Snapper

185

Five-line Snapper *Lutjanus quinquelineatus*

Very similar to Blue-stripe Snapper (previous species), but additional blue line below eye and over abdomen to end of anal-fin base. Often with dark blotch below soft dorsal fin just above lateral line, particularly in juveniles. Large adults with dark snout and bright yellow ventrally on body. Juveniles in small groups in estuaries along reef margins on rubble. Adults in small aggregations from coastal to inner reefs. Maximum length 35 cm, usually 25 cm.

Sailfin Snapper *Symphorichthys spilurus*

Small juveniles with broad black midlateral stripe and long yellow filaments on soft dorsal and anal fin tips. Stripe reduces to caudal peduncle spot in adults which also become steep-headed and develop numerous blue longitudinal lines. Solitary on mixed sand and rubble flats in large, deep lagoons or broad reef channels. Maximum length 60 cm.

Chinaman Fish *Symphorus nematophorus*

Small juveniles almost white with 4 thick brown-black stripes along upper half of body from tip of snout to upper caudal-fin base, and soft dorsal tip with extended rays. Adults usually greyish brown with numerous pale blue longitudinal lines, and soft dorsal fin tip may have several extended white filaments; stage known as Threadfin Snapper. Large adults in very deep water mainly blotchy red. Juveniles on coastal reefs. Not recommended for eating, commonly affected by ciguatera poison. Maximum length 80 cm.

Midnight Snapper *Macolor macularis*

Eye of adult distinctly yellow. Small juveniles easily identified by colour and very long ventral fins. Second species, Black Snapper *M. niger*, has black eye and short ventral fins; not common in Australian waters. Midnight Snapper gradually changes to bluish grey, scales with pale centres, scribbles on head, turning yellow on head and abdomen. Inner reefs, in caves or near steep walls during the day, sometimes in small loose groups, each maintaining its position in relation to the reef. Maximum length 60 cm.

FUSILIERS — CAESIONIDAE

Small tropical family with 4 genera and about 20 species, of which 3 genera and 7 species are known in Australian waters. Oval-elongated to very elongated, compressed, streamlined, small mouth and large forked tail. Often included with closely related Lutjanidae, but differs in morphological features, most obvious the highly protrusible upper jaw. Planktivores with dominant blue and yellow colouration, usually forming great schools when adults, particularly along outer drop-offs and deep seamounts. Many species rest on substrates at night and often turn bright red. Fusiliers are mostly small but are considered good eating in many areas. The largest, Giant Fusilier *Caesio erythrogaster* from the Indian Ocean, reaches at least 48 cm and may occur in north-western Australia. Until recently, confused with Robust Fusilier (next species).

Robust Fusilier *Caesio cuning*

Large yellow forked tail, colour extending onto body along base of dorsal fin. The closely related Giant Fusilier (see family description above) has caudal fin with yellow streaks and only nape is yellow. Both deeper bodied than other fusiliers, and possibly confused with similar Southern Fusilier *Paracaesio xanthurus*, a planktivorous lutjanid often seen offshore in New South Wales. All schooling species, usually in current-prone channels or along reef walls. Maximum length 30 cm, usually 25 cm, and reported larger sizes probably based on Giant Fusilier.

Five-line Snapper

Sailfin Snapper

Chinaman Fish

Midnight Snapper (young adult)

Midnight Snapper (small juvenile)

Robust Fusilier

Gold-band Fusilier *Caesio caerulaurea*

Pale greenish above to almost white below. Thick blue-bordered golden-yellow stripe from head along top of lateral line, continuing into caudal fin as black streak on upper lobe, and opposite black streak below. Mainly on clear coastal and inner reefs in small to large aggregations feeding spread out high above reef, often mixing with other fusiliers. Maximum length 25 cm.

Black-tipped Fusilier *Pterocaesio digramma*

Caudal fin with large black tips; thin yellow line from eye to caudal peduncle centre and second one high along sides. The similar Yellow-band Fusilier *P. chrysozona* with single thick yellow line from upper eye to caudal peduncle, ending just above centre. Both as adults schooling on clear coastal and inner reef; juveniles sometimes in estuaries; and similar-sized. Maximum length 30 cm.

Three-line Fusilier *Pterocaesio trilineata*

Easily identified by dusky caudal fin tips and 3 thick dark stripes along upper sides. Usually dusky on coastal reefs and less distinct in clear outer reef lagoons over light-coloured substrates. Swims in large schools along coral-rich slopes in shallow depths. Small species, maximum length 16 cm.

Blue-dash Fusilier *Pterocaesio tile*

Reflective broad blue stripe midlaterally, usually showing as a blue dash from eye to halfway along body in natural light. No black caudal fin tips; instead, black streaks along lobes. Usually large dense schools along deep outer reef walls. At night on reefs in ledges, lower half bright red. Maximum length 25 cm.

JEWFISHES — SCIAENIDAE

Large family with almost 50 genera and over 100 species worldwide, of which 8 genera and about 15 species in Australian waters. Moderately elongate, somewhat compressed, scales small and ctenoid. Dorsal fin deeply notched with long-based soft section. Anal-fin base very short, about the size of the pectoral fin. Jewfishes are also known as croakers or drums because of a range of sound produced when pulled from the water or below boats. Mostly deep water, trawled or hooked offshore or very deep estuaries, of which the best known, Teraglin *Atractoscion aequidens*, is usually caught at night off the east coast. Only one species which is occasionally observed by divers included here.

Jewfish *Argyrosomus antarcticus*

Silver to dusky or brown in relation to habitat. Caudal fin pointed when young and upper half slightly concave in large adult. Similar Teraglin (see family description) has strongly concave caudal fin. Offshore silver, darker up estuaries and rivers, series of pearly spots along lateral line. Usually seen offshore on seamounts or in large caves with islands, hovering in schools in shelter or currents. Moving out at night to hunt fishes. Sought-after fish by anglers, good sport and eating. Also commonly called Mulloway. Closely related to the Japanese *A. japonicus*. Maximum length 2 m, usually 1.5 m, heaviest caught 61 kg.

Gold-band Fusilier

Black-tipped Fusilier

Three-line Fusilier

Blue-dash Fusilier

ewfish

GOATFISHES — MULLIDAE

Moderately large family with 6 genera and at least 50 species, of which 4 genera and about 30 species are reported in Australian waters. Elongate, slightly compressed with moderately large, finely-ctenoid scales. Two well-separated dorsal fins and a pair of strong barbels on chin. Caudal fin deeply forked. Most species tropical, only one on the south coast. Within genus almost no morphological differences and only has colour patterns as diagnostic features. Some juveniles very different from adults, and colour often variable — usually changing quickly with mood or between day and night. Most form small aggregations, feeding together on sand and rubble substrates, where probing for invertebrates with barbels.

Black-spot Goatfish *Parupeneus signatus*

Always with distinct black saddle spot on caudal peduncle, usually with bright yellow blotch just in front. Large adults with numerous blue spots and blue median fins. Subtropical waters, common New South Wales species in sandy estuaries to deep offshore reefs. Juveniles in small schools, adults singly to small aggregations. Sibling *P. spilurus* in subtropical Japanese waters and China seas. Also similar *P. ciliatus* widespread in the tropical Indo-Pacific, but lacks black peduncular spot and each scale with dark margin and pale centre. *P. signatus* probably the largest Australian goatfish, maximum length over 50 cm.

Dash-and-Dot Goatfish *Parupeneus barberinus*

Distinct black round spot on caudal peduncle and black stripe from snout through eye to upper caudal peduncle. Body white in young, adults variable, often yellow above black stripe and may turn red below. Sandflats near reefs, usually solitary or in small aggregations. Large adult shown in the photograph. Maximum length 40 cm, usually 30 cm.

Yellow-spot Goatfish *Parupeneus indicus*

Similar to Dash-and-Dot Goatfish (previous species) but black stripe shorter, restricted to head, and large yellow spot centrally on sides on lateral line. Common on coastal and inner reefs on silty sand and rubble flats, usually in small aggregations, feeding or swimming close together. Maximum length 40 cm, usually 30 cm.

Half-and-Half Goatfish *Parupeneus barberinoides*

Distinctly coloured with dark-reddish to black front half, abruptly changing below second dorsal fin to white and yellow. Thick white angular stripe over cheek and usually a distinct small black spot midlaterally below end of dorsal-fin base. Solitary, juveniles coastal entering rocky estuaries, adults deep slopes to inner reefs Small species, maximum length 30 cm, usually 20 cm.

Banded Goatfish *Parupeneus multifasciatus*

Black dash behind eye. Adults mostly grey or brown with pale bars and yellow-edged scales. Young with 2 black bars: first below anterior soft dorsal fin and second over caudal peduncle; interspaced with white, bars shortening with growth to saddles or spots. Young on coastal reefs, adults at moderate depths on inner reef sand and rubble margins. Maximum length 35 cm, usually 25 cm.

Black-spot Goatfish (adult)

Black-spot Goatfish (juveniles)

ash-and-Dot Goatfish

Yellow-spot Goatfish

lf-and-Half Goatfish

Banded Goatfish

191

Double-bar Goatfish *Parupeneus bifasciatus*

Adults with variably-sized dark saddles or blotches touching base of dorsal fins and smaller blotch behind eye, which in young as double black bands, narrowing or fading ventrally. Some geographical variations, possibly several species. Shown in the photograph is the eastern Australian form on the Great Barrier Reef. Juveniles shy, on large rubble pieces in surge channels below the intertidal zone. Adults on clear inner reefs and in deep lagoons, often seen resting on corals. Maximum length 30 cm.

Yellow-saddle Goatfish *Parupeneus cyclostomus*

Adults variable from pale greenish grey to dark brown with yellow saddle on caudal peduncle, occasionally yellow all over. Juveniles bright yellow, and often accompanied by Thalassoma Wrasses; adults usually in pairs or schools. Coastal to outer reef crests and lagoons, shallow to deep offshore. Maximum length 38 cm.

Small-spot Goatfish *Parupeneus heptacanthus*

Plain, grey to deep red with distinct small dark spot below end of first dorsal fin or lateral line. Adults with blue spot on most scales, forming lines along scale rows. Small juveniles in small groups on shallow sand or mudflats. Adults on deep slopes, usually silty sand near reefs or seagrass beds. Maximum length 35 cm.

Southern Goatfish *Upeneichthys vlamingii*

Highly variable between adult and juvenile stages. Adults ornamented with blue spots and lines, and red, yellow or orange areas. Small juveniles almost white, sandy above with black midlateral stripe. Night colour dark with pale area above pectoral and caudal peduncle with 2 pale double bars in-between; pattern indistinct during the day but shown by interruption of lateral stripe in adults. Schooling species from shallow protected sandflats to deep coastal waters. Maximum length 35 cm.

Double-bar Goatfish

Yellow-saddle Goatfish

Yellow-saddle Goatfish

Small-spot Goatfish

Southern Goatfish (adult)

Southern Goatfish (juveniles)

Blue-lined Goatfish *Upeneichthys lineatus*

Adults from brown to red on upper half to red all over; sometimes indistinct broad red stripe midlaterally. Juveniles pale pinkish brown dorsally and lighter below. Night colour red with pale caudal peduncle, pale double bar below dorsal fins interspace, single below end of soft dorsal and sometimes above pectoral base. Usually protected coastal bays, entering clear estuaries when young to moderate depths offshore, usually replaced by Southern Goatfish (previous species) in deep water in southern New South Wales. Similar-shaped west coast species *U. stotti* has horizontal lines on snout. Maximum length 30 cm.

Yellow-stripe Goatfish *Mulloidichthys vanicolensis*

Bright yellow stripe from eye to caudal fin, absorbed by yellow fin. Pectoral fin pale yellow, other fins bright yellow. Second Australian species Square-spot Goatfish *M. flavolineatus* has similar yellow midlateral line but with black spot below first dorsal fin, and lacks yellow fins. *M. flavolineatus* solitary as adult. *M. vanicolensis* usually in large schools, sometimes mixing with schooling Blue-line Snapper *Lutjanus kasmira*. Maximum length 30 cm.

Bar-tail Goatfish *Upeneus tragula*

Mostly pale dorsally, with dusky fine-spotting, brown to black stripe from eye to caudal-fin base, first dorsal fin tip black with small yellow spots, and black and white bars or spots on caudal fin. Several very similar species, differentiated mainly by patterns on caudal fin. Common, yet unnamed one with plain dorsal fin in New South Wales coastal waters. Others more tropical and often school on muddy substrates in deep water. *U. tragula* the largest, most common and widespread in the tropical Indo-Pacific. Coastal reefs and estuaries near reefs on rubble margins, singly or in small groups. Maximum length 30 cm, others 20 cm.

BULLSEYES — PEMPHERIDIDAE

Small family with 2 genera and approximately 20 species globally, both genera and at least 12 species found in Australian waters. Distinct fishes by shape, rounded head, dorsally body profile straight or slightly concave from dorsal-fin origin to caudal fin, lower profile similar but rising upwards from anal-fin origin. Posterior tip of dorsal fin above anterior tip of anal fin. Distinct lateral line, rising slightly from origin, mostly straight to caudal fin, often extended to its posterior margin. Eyes large, positioned above strongly oblique mouth, and very short snout. Nocturnal planktivores, usually floating well above substrate, taking small crustaceans and cephalopods. Usually form schools in caves during the day. Also known as sweepers.

Slender Bullseye *Parapriacanthus elongatus*

Most slender bullseye, easily recognised by shape and pale colour, from silvery grey to light brown. Southern endemic, sometimes forming great schools in shallow sea-grass estuaries, moving seasonally to deep water around rocky reefs to depths of at least 60 m. Often in small groups in ledges during the day. Maximum length 13 cm.

Yellow Sweeper *Parapriacanthus ransonneti*

Moderately slender with bright yellow eyes and head, body translucent pale pinkish posteriorly. Forms great dense schools during the day, usually in large caves along walls or tall bommies in deep water, spreading out at night to feed. Small species, maximum length 10 cm, usually 8 cm.

Blue-lined Goatfish (adult)

Blue-lined Goatfish (night colour)

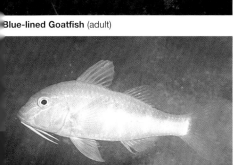

Blue-lined Goatfish (juvenile)

Yellow-stripe Goatfish

Bar-tail Goatfish (night colour)

Bar-tail Goatfish

Slender Bullseye

Yellow Sweeper

195

Bronze Bullseye *Pempheris analis*

Plain shiny brown or yellow on sides, dusky over top of head and body above lateral line. Tips of median fins with more-or-less distinct dusky tips. Common southern Queensland species on coastal and inner reefs, usually in small groups in rocky ledges or under plate corals. Similar *P. adspersus* with dark pectoral base in northern New Zealand, possibly in Australian waters. Maximum length 15 cm, usually 10 cm.

Black-tipped Bullseye *Pempheris affinis*

Usually golden yellow on sides, light grey over head and with shine above lateral line. Adults with distinct black tips on median fins and most of anal-fin margin black, less so in juveniles. Forms small groups in ledges or caves during the day, usually with clean sand below. Mainly coastal, only entering open sea-side of rocky estuaries. Maximum length 15 cm.

Greenback Bullseye *Pempheris vanicolensis*

Identified by yellow iris, long black anal-fin margin and usually shiny green scales over head and back. Pectoral-fin base dusky but not black. Similar *P. oualensis* has black axil spot and lacks black anal-fin margin. *P. vanicolensis* inhabits protected coastal reefs, often very shallow among large boulders forming many small groups distributed throughout areas. *P. oualensis* prefers offshore habitats. Maximum length 15 cm, usually 12 cm.

Silver Bullseye *Pempheris schwenkii*

Usually pale greenish grey or yellowish sides and small shiny scales over back. Only dorsal fin black-tipped and dusky streaks along caudal-fin margins. Very similar *P. adusta* lacks black dorsal fin tip and has anterior lateral line curve, rising well above straight part. Often singly, in small groups or mixed with other species. Coastal, rocky drop-offs in small caves or ledges. Maximum length 15 cm.

Rough Bullseye *Pempheris klunzingeri*

Juveniles pale greyish brown with black markings on dorsal and anal fin. Adults uniformly light to dark brown, often with yellowish or orange bar above pectoral-fin base. South coast endemic, forming schools on rocky reefs, coastal and offshore. Maximum length 20 cm.

Small-scale Bullseye *Pempheris compressa*

Pale shiny brownish, lateral line often yellow and distinct, and broad dusky bar just behind head. Adults form large schools on offshore reefs in caves or along walls, swimming away from wall but closely packed. Small juveniles silvery, somewhat translucent, often swimming in large schools above reefs in protected coastal bays, feeding on zooplankton during the day. Maximum length 20 cm.

Bronze Bullseye

Black-tipped Bullseye

Greenback Bullseye

Silver Bullseye

Rough Bullseye

Small-scale Bullseye

Orange-lined Bullseye *Pempheris ornata.*

Unusually brightly coloured for bullseye, with thick bright yellow to orange lines along sides and bright yellow eye. Although common on coastal reefs and under jetties in South Australia, it escaped discovery until 1978, during the author's honeymoon, when some were collected for the Australian Museum. Smallest Australian species, maximum length 8 cm.

Common Bullseye *Pempheris multiradiata*

Juveniles pale but with distinct black-tipped, yellow ventral fins. Adults with thick light to dark brown longitudinal stripes along scale rows. Various habitats from shallow silty estuaries to deep offshore. Juveniles form small aggregations in ledges, adults often solitary but sharing large ledges and overhangs during the day. Out in the open at night, swimming near substrate. Large species, maximum length 22 cm.

SILVER BATFISHES — MONODACTYLIDAE

Small family with 3 genera and 5 species, of which 2 genera and 3 species are known in Australian waters. Silvery fishes with small deciduous scales. Deep-bodied, compressed, with long-based dorsal and anal fins opposite, their tips slightly elevated. Fin spines reduced, leading soft rays longest. Coastal and estuarine genus *Monodactylus*, silver batfishes, widespread in the tropical Indo-Pacific; swims far up freshwater systems well beyond tidal influences. Genus *Schuettea*, pomfreds, restricted to temperate Australian waters; strictly marine. Diet comprises great variety of plankton and algae.

Eastern Pomfred *Schuettea scalaripinnis*

Easily recognised by silver colour and yellow over back, caudal and anal fins. Readily distinguished from closest similar fishes, the bullseyes (previous family), by long-based dorsal fin. Sheltered rocky reefs along rock walls with kelp on top, from clear coastal to offshore, forming large dense schools during the day. Feed mainly at night. Maximum length 20 cm.

Western Pomfred *Schuettea woodwardi*

Similar to its eastern cousin, but deeper bodied and fins taller. Silvery with yellow in tall sections of dorsal and anal fins, and yellow streaks out along caudal-fin margins. Juveniles in small aggregations on open patches along seagrass beds in protected bays. Adults school in coastal waters. Maximum length 24 cm.

Silver Batfish *Monodactylus argenteus*

Adults shiny silver with dark bar over eyes and yellow dorsal and anal fin tips, latter black in northern waters. Small juveniles usually in brackish or fresh water, almost black with red-tipped dorsal fin. Adults form large schools in coastal bays near freshwater run-offs or breakwaters, and under deep jetties in estuaries. Maximum length 25 cm.

Orange-lined Bullseye

Common Bullseye

Eastern Pomfred

Western Pomfred

Silver Batfish

199

SWEEPS — SCORPIDIDAE

Small family with 2 or 3 genera and undetermined small number of species. Only genus *Scorpis* is found in Australia with 4 species, one of which is rare but common in New Zealand. Deep-bodied fishes, restricted to temperate Australian and New Zealand waters. Highly compressed fishes, some elongating slightly as adult. Shiny silvery blue, some young with dark saddles. Fin spines reduced, dorsal soft rays elevated anteriorly with similarly shaped anal fin opposite. Midwater feeders, taking algae and zooplankton, usually in large schools and some species preferring high-energy zones with large swell. Most sweep are excellent to eat.

Sea Sweep *Scorpis aequipinnis*

Silvery, steel grey with 2 broad dusky, sometimes indistinct, bands fading ventrally. Juveniles very deep-bodied, elongating with age. Mostly in turbulent coastal waters, usually near foaming water where waves breaking on rocks. Small juveniles sometimes in small groups around jetty pylons in surface waters. Maximum length 56 cm, usually 40 cm.

Banded Sweep *Scorpis georgiana*

Very deep-bodied and distinctly banded, even as adults. Bands broad and almost black, most prominent one from dorsal to anal fin tips and other adjacent, fading onto abdomen. Caudal fin dark. Mainly found in caves and ledges in shallow waters, often caught on hook and line. Unlike other sweep, not considered good eating. Maximum length 45 cm.

Silver Sweep *Scorpis lineolata*

Plain silvery, greenish grey dorsally at all stages. Operculum with thin black posterior margin. Very common New South Wales species, juveniles schooling in estuaries under jetties or on shallow reefs, often in tidal pools; adults form very large schools on submerged offshore reefs. Maximum length 36 cm, usually 25 cm.

DRUMMERS — KYPHOSIDAE

Small family with 3 genera and 10 species globally, of which 1 genus and 6 species are found in Australian waters. Closely related to the sweeps but mostly tropical, with heavier, more elongate bodies and incisor-like teeth in a single row in each jaw. Most found in high-energy zones in shallow depths along rocky reefs or in strong tidal current-prone channels between reefs, feeding primarily on algae and associated invertebrates. In cooler southern waters mainly around large boulders or in the vicinity of deep ledges where they go for cover when approached. Juveniles pelagic, sheltering under floating weeds or other objects.

Southern Silver Drummer *Kyphosus sydneyanus*

Silver grey to dark grey above, sometimes with silver streak midlaterally. Median fins broadly dusky to black on caudal fin. Distinct small black spot below pectoral-fin base. Shallow coastal bays and harbours, in vicinity of turbulent seas and tidal channels near or in large rocky reef with ledges and caves. Small juveniles pelagic under floating weeds, orange-brown with short silver streaks over most of head and body. Maximum length 75 cm.

Sea Sweep   Banded Sweep

Silver Sweep

Southern Silver Drummer

201

Northern Silver Drummer *Kyphosus gibsoni*

Very similar to its southern cousin (previous species), but more numerous and smaller scales, and no small distinct spot below pectoral-fin base. Both species were found at Montague Island, New South Wales, forming separate groups. Clear coastal shallow reefs and islands in strong surge zones along rock faces or large boulders. Maximum length 50 cm.

Brassy Drummer *Kyphosus vaigiensis*

Most scales with silver centres, effectively creating grey to brown lines between scale rows, occasionally showing pale grey blotches, as in the photograph, similar to juvenile stage. Similar to Snubnose Drummer (next species), but lacks the elevations in dorsal and anal fins. Shallow coastal reefs and lagoons on current-prone slopes, especially with rock boulder substrate. Maximum length 50 cm.

Snubnose Drummer *Kyphosus cinerascens*

Adults light to very dark grey, scales with small silvery centres, forming lines along rows, more distinct as longitudinal lines below lateral line in young. Soft dorsal and anal fin distinctly elevated, with posterior margins near vertical, in adults. Adults form schools in coastal waters over shallow reefs, feeding midwater on floating algae, usually during outgoing tides. Juveniles often offshore under floating weeds. Maximum length 50 cm.

Western Drummer *Kyphosus cornelii*

Caudal fin forked, and body slender compared to other drummers. Dusky grey to brown, fins often darker and with broad streaks over outer rays of caudal fin. Western endemic. Schools along shallow coastal reefs, sometimes found in ledges. Maximum length 60 cm.

BLACKFISHES — GIRELLIDAE

Small family with single genus and about 10 species, of which 5 are known from Australian waters. Closely related to Kyphosidae, but different in mouth structure; dentition with tricuspid teeth; and long-based spinous dorsal fin which originates more anteriorly. Caudal fin truncate to slightly concave, and body oval-shaped, slightly compressed, and covered with small adherent ctenoid scales. Adults mostly in large estuaries or rocky coastal reefs, depending on species. Estuarine species sometimes congregate in great numbers in coastal bays. Small juveniles of banded species intertidal, in rockpools and seagrass beds, and non-banded ones on shallow rocky reef-flats, in holes and crevices, usually in small groups. Diet comprises primarily algae, either floating or bitten off rocks, and sometimes nibbling on larger floating pieces, feeding in small groups. Some are popular with anglers and excellent to eat.

Blackfish or Luderick *Girella tricuspidata*

Bluish grey in coastal waters to greenish brown in estuaries, darker above with about 12 thin vertical stripes fading ventrally to silvery below. Small juveniles in dense seagrass beds or weeds on rocks, often in large rockpools in New South Wales. Adults sometimes in large schools in coastal waters, moving in and out of large estuaries at specific times of the year. Popular angling fish in New South Wales. Maximum length 62 cm, usually 50 cm.

Northern Silver Drummer

Brassy Drummer (normal pattern)

Brassy Drummer (blotched pattern)

Snubnose Drummer

Western Drummer

Blackfish or Luderick

Zebra Fish *Girella zebra*

Easily identified by white-and-black banded pattern and yellow fins, but juveniles more dusky and sometimes confused with luderick. Various rocky reef habitats from upper reaches of very shallow estuaries to surge reef offshore. Small juveniles commonly under rocks in small rockpools on reef-flats, often in freshwater run-offs. Adults form small groups near reefs with long ledges for shelter, shy in shallow estuaries, more approachable in coastal waters. Maximum length reported to 54 cm, usually 40 cm.

Eastern Rock Blackfish *Girella elevata*

Uniformly dark grey to almost black. Superficially looks like kyphosid (previous family) and sometimes called Black Drummer, but has almost straight posterior caudal-fin margin. Juveniles in coastal rocky reef and clear estuaries. Adults usually in groups, mainly coastal but often around island reefs. Inhabits caves and deep ledges with just enough space to fit, and often some individuals upside down. Largest *Girella*, maximum length 76 cm.

Western Rock Blackfish *Girella tephraeops*

Dark grey to brown, sometimes changing quickly to strongly mottled pattern of mixed bluish grey and light grey, darker dorsally. Large tail with concave posterior margin. Coastal reefs in caves and ledges or swimming through weed areas. Juveniles intertidal, often in rockpools. Maximum length 62 cm.

STRIPEYS & MADO — MICROCANTHIDAE

Small subtropical family with 4 genera and at least 5 species, all found in Australian waters but one, common in New Zealand and Lord Howe Island, is rare on the mainland coast. Population of Stripey *Microcanthus strigatus* in the Northern Hemisphere differs in colour pattern and possibly a separate species. Closely related to butterflyfishes, Chaetodontidae (next family), especially *Tilodon* which cannot be distinguished from that group on external features, except for slightly emarginate caudal fin. Fishes with oblong to deep bodies, and strong spines in dorsal, anal and ventral fins. Teeth close-set, brush-like. Benthic and planktivorous, opportunistic feeders, sometimes forming great schools in coastal bays when currents carry plankton through, taking algae and variety of small invertebrates.

Footballer Sweep *Neatypus obliquus*

Distinctly coloured with yellow and white bands separated with variable brown to black. Inhabits deeper coastal reef in depths over 10 m, adults to 200 m, but sometimes rising to shallow turbulent waters around large boulders feeding on suspended matter. Sometimes forms large schools, but often in small aggregations feeding on substrate among rocks covered with short algae. Maximum length 23 cm.

Stripey *Microcanthus strigatus*

Variable from white to bright yellow with thick black stripes; small juveniles in estuaries often white, and adults variable yellow depending on habitat. Protected coastal waters and rocky estuaries, usually in small groups in ledges or below large overhangs such as large table corals in southern Queensland. Slightly different pattern between eastern and western populations, with the eastern form shown in the photograph. Western form with line below pectoral-fin base, joining above to head-line. Maximum length 16 cm.

Zebra Fish

Eastern Rock Blackfish

Western Rock Blackfish

Footballer Sweep

Stripey

Mado *Atypichthys strigatus*

White with thick black stripes along upper sides, continuing over nape to tip of snout, thinner along lower half, and yellow median fins. Similar New Zealand Mado A. *latus*, with slightly deeper body and upper stripes interrupted on nape by pale vertical line, is occasionally sighted in New South Wales. Mado abundant in southern New South Wales coastal waters and estuaries, but only small numbers in the Bass Strait region. Maximum length 25 cm.

Moonlighter *Tilodon sexfasciatus*

Banded pattern readily identifies this species. Small juveniles with white-edged black ocelli in soft part of dorsal and anal fins. This feature common in butterflyfishes. Also like butterflyfishes, solitary as juvenile on rocky shallow reefs. Adults solitary or in pairs in deeper coastal reef habitat in Victoria, but often shallow under jetties in Western Australia. Largest species, maximum length 40 cm, usually 35 cm.

BUTTERFLYFISHES — CHAETODONTIDAE

Large family with 10 genera and about 120 species globally, of which 8 genera and approximately 50 species are found in Australian waters. Majority inhabit tropical reefs, few adapted to warm–temperate zones. Many closely related species, morphologically almost identical but with distinct colouration; often best diagnostic feature. Other features: very deep compressed body and usually snout pointed to very elongated; scales moderately large with sheaths along spinous dorsal fin section and progressively smaller scales extending over median fin; teeth typically brush-like, slender and close-set with recurving tips; fin spines large and solid, proportionally largest in juveniles. Larval stage called *Tholichthys*, with bony head and often long serrated spines. Most species very colourful, commonly found on coral reefs in shallow water, a few deep-water dwellers to 200 m depth. Because of long pelagic stage many are wide-ranging, extending well beyond breeding grounds. Such expatriates are commonly seen in southern New South Wales and southern Western Australia, carried by currents originating further north. Most are benthic feeders, taking a variety of small invertebrates, but some specialise in capturing particular prey from narrow crevices and a few planktivorous.

Truncate Coralfish *Chelmonops truncatus*

Adults distinctly shaped with angular soft dorsal and anal fins, of which posterior margins almost vertical, and broad dark banding. Small juveniles with more rounded fins and large white-edged black ocellus on soft dorsal fin above last body band. Variable from shiny silvery to brown with black bands. Deep coastal reefs and rocky estuaries, both juveniles and adults. Latter usually in pairs. Maximum length 22 cm.

Square-back Butterflyfish *Chelmonops curiosus*

Replaces Truncate Coralfish (previous species) along the south and south-west coasts. Differs in shape and colour, head profile not as steep, dorsal and anal fins greatly extended and black bands with white margins. Juveniles solitary, adults pairing. Often swims right up to diver without showing any fear. Common in South Australia, but appears to be absent from Victoria. Maximum length 20 cm.

Mado

Moonlighter (adult)

Moonlighter (juvenile)

Truncate Coralfish (adult)

Truncate Coralfish (juvenile)

Square-back Butterflyfish

Lord Howe Butterflyfish *Amphichaetodon howensis*

Slightly variable from pale to bright lemon-yellow with very broad black bands. Juveniles identical to adults, except for proportionally longer fin spines, and lacks prominent ocellus on soft dorsal fin, usually found on similar species. Adults usually offshore with islands or submerged reefs and nearly always in pairs, swimming close together. Primarily deep and usually below 20 m depth, but sometimes in shallow turbulent waters. Juveniles occasionally inshore on clear reef in ledges. Maximum length 18 cm.

Dusky Beaked Coralfish *Chelmon muelleri*

Differs from similar Beaked Coralfish (next species), with darker bands, shorter snout and fins not as tall. Coastal species, including estuaries, on algae–rock reef and common around near-shore islands of southern Queensland. Juveniles mostly seen solitary, secretive in reefs; large adults usually in pairs, swimming in open near substrate. Australian endemic. Maximum length 18 cm.

Beaked Coralfish *Chelmon rostratus*

Distinctly banded with orange. Juveniles similar to adults; fins proportionally taller in adults. Clear coastal and inner reef-flats on rubble and sand margins with mixed soft and hard coral growth. Juveniles solitary and secretive in shallow reefs; adults pair and swim in open near substrate. Maximum length 20 cm.

Margined Coralfish *Chelmon marginalis*

Very similar to Beaked Coralfish (previous species), especially when small, but adults centrally white and dorsal fin spot becomes indistinct or absent in large individuals. Sheltered coastal bays to exposed offshore on coral reefs. Juveniles secretive in corals; adults pair or form small groups. Maximum length 20 cm.

Highfin Coralfish *Coradion altivelis*

Dorsal and anal fins taller than other similar species, especially when juvenile. Juvenile with distinct large ocellus centrally on soft dorsal fin section. Several dark brown bands, second and third behind head and close together, converging and darkening to black below, and extended with black ventral fin. Ocellus fades to dusky spot, or altogether in large adults, which become more yellow with numerous gold-centred scales bordering dark bands and covering space between second and third bands. Coastal to inner reefs with mixed low algae, sponges and various corals, often current-prone areas on large bommies. Maximum length 18 cm, usually 15 cm.

.ord Howe Butterflyfish

Dusky Beaked Coralfish

eaked Coralfish

Margined Coralfish

ghfin Coralfish (adult)

Highfin Coralfish (juvenile)

209

Orange-banded Coralfish *Coradion chrysozonus*

Similar to Highfin Coralfish (previous species), but dorsal and anal fins lower and adult retains dorsal-fin ocellus. Variable brown to orange banding, adults with yellow-centred scales forming lines along scale rows. Usually deep in rich coral growth current-prone channels between reefs in 20+ m depth. Maximum length 15 cm.

Pyramid Butterflyfish *Hemitaurichthys polylepis*

Distinctly marked and easily identified by snow-white body and caudal fin, with orange-yellow anal and dorsal fins, extending from latter partly onto body, and dark brown to almost black head. Typically forms large schools along outer reefs, especially in current channels, feeding on zooplankton. Maximum length 18 cm, usually 15 cm.

Ocellate Coralfish *Parachaetodon ocellatus*

Nearly all-white with vertical brown bands, 5 when juveniles and 4 as adult, with fifth as a short peduncular bar. Large black spot in fourth band, near base on dorsal fin, and dorsal fin tallest and pointed above when fin raised. Coastal sheltered sandy bays; juveniles often in shallow lagoons in open seagrass patches. Maximum length 18 cm.

Three-band Coralfish *Chaetodon tricinctus*

Black-and-white banded pattern, plus bright orange markings, makes identification easy. Mainly common in the Lord Howe Island region with stragglers on the New South Wales coast. Rich coral-growth areas, lagoons and shallow reefs. Often seen nibbling on coral-polyps, probably an important part of the diet. Adults pair or form small groups. Juveniles solitary and lack ocellus found in most similar species. Maximum length 18 cm.

Rainford's Butterflyfish *Chaetodon rainfordi*

Mainly yellow with 2 dusky, orange-bordered bands on body and orange bands on head. Sometimes aberrant forms with stripes interrupted or looping. Sympatric with closely related Gold-banded Butterflyfish (next species), and hybrids are not uncommon. Coastal and inner reefs with rich coral growth. Maximum length 16 cm.

Gold-banded Butterflyfish *Chaetodon aureofasciatus*

Body dusky with bright yellow median and ventral fins, golden bands over eye and just behind head. Hybrids with Rainford's Butterflyfish (previous species) show some additional banding. Coastal and inner reefs, nibbling on corals and mostly found in mixed coral and algal reefs at shallow depths. Maximum length 14 cm.

Orange-banded Coralfish

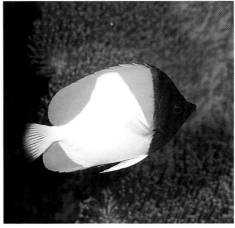

Pyramid Butterflyfish

Ocellate Coralfish

Three-band Coralfish

Rainford's Butterflyfish

Gold-banded Butterflyfish

211

Reticulated Butterflyfish *Chaetodon reticulatus*

Unusual butterflyfish colouration, being mostly black and white, some pale yellow in adults and only ornamental colour restricted to orange margin at end of anal fin. Small juveniles mostly white, with broad black band over head across eye, black markings on snout, black ventral fins and scales with black outlines along lower part of body, forming thin lines along rows. Darkens with age, with adults showing mainly a broad pale band behind head and white over dorsal fin. Outer reefs, often shallow channelled surge reef-flats, swimming in pairs. Juveniles solitary in rich coral growth. Maximum length 16 cm.

Ornate Butterflyfish *Chaetodon ornatus*

Easily distinguished by colour pattern. Pale whitish yellow with oblique orange bands and black stripes across head and snout. Juveniles similar to adults, slightly less colourful and with clear caudal fin. Rich coral reefs, clear outer reef habitat, usually in pairs over crest or along edge of deep slope and drop-offs. Usually one pair territorial over large reef section, actively swimming, occasionally stopping to feed on corals or other invertebrates. Juveniles solitary in rich coral growth. Maximum length 20 cm.

Meyer's Butterflyfish *Chaetodon meyeri*

Distinctly coloured. Grey surrounded by yellow and marked with black stripes at various angles over sides, radiating from behind pectoral-fin base with horizontal below to near vertical, some curved, and vertical through eyes and over snout. Juveniles very similar, but black lines almost straight, angular over body and vertical on head. Clear outer reef, usually on rich coral-flats, feeding on particular hard-coral polyps. Nearly always in pairs, territorial, and usually patrols large reef sections. Juveniles singly sheltering in corals. Maximum length 20 cm.

Eclipse Butterflyfish *Chaetodon bennetti*

Bright yellow, pale to iridescent blue angular lines over head and lower body. Its large blue-edged black ocellus with surrounding dark shading gives rise to its common name. In rich coral-growth areas on coastal slopes and drop-offs, usually in pairs. Maximum length 18 cm.

Oval-spot Butterflyfish *Chaetodon speculum*

Very similar to Eclipse Butterflyfish (previous species), but an overall bright warm-yellow with black eye band and large black oval spot centrally on upper sides. Coastal reef slopes with rich invertebrate growth, often seen feeding on corallimorpharian or disc anemones. Usually in pairs, occasionally in small groups Maximum length 16 cm.

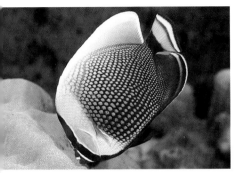

Reticulated Butterflyfish (adult)

Reticulated Butterflyfish (juvenile)

Ornate Butterflyfish (adult)

Ornate Butterflyfish (juvenile)

Meyer's Butterflyfish (adult)

Meyer's Butterflyfish (juvenile)

Eclipse Butterflyfish

Oval-spot Butterflyfish

213

Teardrop Butterflyfish *Chaetodon unimaculatus*

White with yellow over back. Black bar over head, hiding eyes, and over caudal peduncle, and large round black spot just below centre of dorsal fin with shading below in teardrop-like pattern. Various rocky to coral habitats and coastal to outer reefs from intertidal to deep-water drop-offs, in pairs or small aggregations. Maximum length 20 cm.

Latticed Butterflyfish *Chaetodon rafflesi*

Scales with large yellow-golden diamond-shaped centres, resulting in pattern of greenish diagonal criss-cross lines. Black bar hiding eyes and over caudal fin. Small juveniles secretive in small *Acropora* coral heads. Adults in pairs on coastal to clear outer reef habitat with rich mix of soft and hard coral growth. Maximum length 20 cm.

Dotted Butterflyfish *Chaetodon semeion*

Adults warm-yellow with small black spot on each scale, forming thin lines along scale rows, bluish over nape with black patch below eye, and long black bar along base of soft dorsal fin, jumping caudal peduncle, and partly along anal-fin base. Long filament from soft dorsal fin reaching end of caudal fin. Deep water, pairs or small groups occasionally seen along outer reefs. Maximum length 24 cm.

Saddled Butterflyfish *Chaetodon ephippium*

Easily identified by large black area over upper sides below dorsal fin, from spinou. section curving to dorsal end, bordered by broad white band. Adults with long trailing filament from soft dorsal fin, often reaching past caudal fin, and mainly in pairs on clear reef habitat. Juveniles secretive in coastal rocky reefs. Maximum length 24 cm.

Threadfin Butterflyfish *Chaetodon auriga*

White with yellow posteriorly and black patch on and below eye. Thin angular dark lines going upwards anteriorly on body, followed by downward pattern at about fifth line. Black spot in upper posterior corner of soft dorsal fin and long filament in adult, often far beyond caudal fin. All reef habitats from shallow coastal to outer reefs. Adults pair, juveniles solitary and secretive in rocks. Most widespread member of the genus. Maximum length 24 cm.

Vagabond Butterflyfish *Chaetodon vagabundus*

Similar to Threadfin Butterflyfish (previous species) in body pattern, but lacks long dorsal filament and has additional black along soft dorsal-fin base, extending over caudal peduncle to part of anal fin. Only juvenile has black spot on upper posterior corner of soft dorsal fin. Commonly in coastal rocky reefs ranging to deep offshore. Juveniles solitary and secretive in rocks; adults in pairs and openly on reefs. Maximum length 20 cm.

Teardrop Butterflyfish

Latticed Butterflyfish

Dotted Butterflyfish

Saddled Butterflyfish

Threadfin Butterflyfish

Vagabond Butterflyfish

Lined Butterflyfish *Chaetodon lineolatus*

Body white, thin black lines vertically on body over posterior scale margins, and broad black streak, bordered with gold, along dorsal-fin base, over caudal peduncle, and partly onto anal fin. Broad black bar over eye, continuous over nape. Largest butterflyfish, mainly in reef channels on outer reefs, reported to 45 cm, usually to 30 cm.

Pig-face Butterflyfish *Chaetodon oxycephalus*

Very similar and often confused with Lined Butterflyfish (previous species); mainly differs in black band over eye and separated black spot on nape. Uncommon and usually seen on outer reefs in pairs along the base of drop-offs with mixed coral and invertebrate growth feeding on bases of corals, often picking on small anemones. Maximum length 25 cm.

Double-saddle Butterflyfish *Chaetodon ulietensis*

Distinctly coloured with thick black line hiding eye, large deep saddles, and yellow posteriorly to last saddle. Indian Ocean *C. falcula*, sibling species, has short saddles and is broadly yellow over back. Juveniles similar to adults. Coastal reefs; adults usually pair in Australian waters, forming schools in some oceanic locations in the Pacific. Juveniles secretive among rocks or coarse rubble. Maximum length 15 cm.

Black-back Butterflyfish *Chaetodon melannotus*

Easily identified by white body with numerous thin black angular lines extended from black back, and yellow all around over fins and head. Common on coastal and inner reefs. Juveniles secretive among rocks or rubble. Adults in pairs or small aggregations. Maximum length 15 cm.

Tail-spot Butterflyfish *Chaetodon ocellicaudus*

Almost identical and easily confused with Black-back Butterflyfish (previous species), but distinguished by round peduncular spot in broader yellow area over posterior part of body and white versus yellow ventral fins. Mainly clear outer reef slopes with rich coral growth. Only known from the northern Great Barrier Reef in Australia, but common in Indonesian waters. Maximum length 14 cm.

Eye-patch Butterflyfish *Chaetodon adiergastos*

Pale grey with yellow median and ventral fins, large black eye-patch and yellow spot on top of snout. Coastal reefs, rich soft coral and hydroid habitats, shallow flats and along slopes. Usually in pairs, but seems less territorial than most butterflyfish, and often small aggregations comprising several pairs can be seen floating near large bommies. Maximum length 20 cm.

Lined Butterflyfish

Pig-face Butterflyfish

Double-saddle Butterflyfish

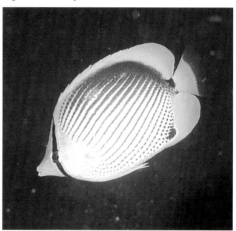

Black-back Butterflyfish

Tail-spot Butterflyfish

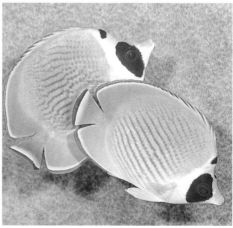

Eye-patch Butterflyfish

Dusky Butterflyfish *Chaetodon flavirostris*

Distinct species with ash-grey sides and yellow to orange median fins. Adults with hump on nape and orange snout with white mouth. Small juveniles with black bar over eyes and round black spot in soft dorsal fin and orange ventral fins. Juveniles solitary in rocks, coastal in sheltered bays and harbours; adults usually in pairs along rock wall, coastal to offshore. Maximum length 20 cm.

Racoon Butterflyfish *Chaetodon lunula*

Mainly yellow. Black eye-patch with white band behind, followed by large angular black band curving to dorsal-fin base. Caudal peduncle black. Juveniles solitary in sheltered coastal bays and estuaries, often silty habitat and very shallow. Adults in lagoons and on deep coastal reefs, usually in pairs. Schools in some Pacific locations. Maximum length 20 cm.

Brown Butterflyfish *Chaetodon kleinii*

Dull species, brownish to yellowish, black bar over head through eye and white area behind black bar. Small juveniles openly on algae reef, often in small groups and swimming with small surgeonfishes or other non-secretive juvenile butterflyfish. Adults usually in small to large groups in lagoons and back reefs with soft coral and hydroid growth. Small species, maximum length 12 cm.

Citron Butterflyfish *Chaetodon citrinellus*

Creamy white to pale yellow, black stripe over head, through eye and to dorsal-fin origin, and thick black anal-fin margin. Juveniles with tiny black spots along scale rows, turning brown or orange in adults. Coastal to outer reefs, often in turbulent areas along rock walls and reef margins. Small juveniles settle in ledges with urchins, forming small groups. Adults in pairs or small aggregations. Small species, maximum length 11 cm.

Gunther's Butterflyfish *Chaetodon guentheri*

Body pale grey to white with small dark spots along scale rows, yellow to orange posteriorly. Black stripe through eye, shaded with white. Several very similar species outside Australian waters. Tropical but cold-water species, only found shallow in New South Wales and Japan in rocky reef and sponge habitats. Open-water species; seen cleaning large pelagic species at Seal Rocks, New South Wales, in small groups mixed with Schooling Bannerfish *Heniochus diphreutes*. Juveniles in shallow coastal bays in small groups. Lives deep in tropical waters, rarely seen in less than 50 m depth. Maximum length 14 cm.

usky Butterflyfish

Racoon Butterflyfish

rown Butterflyfish

Citron Butterflyfish

unther's Butterflyfish (adult)

Gunther's Butterflyfish (juvenile)

219

Western Butterflyfish *Chaetodon assarius*

Creamy white dorsally to white ventrally, with a series of small dark, close-set spots forming at least 4 vertical lines below spinous dorsal fin, reaching abdomen in young, considerably shorter in adults. Brownish dusky anal fin with distinct white margin. Juveniles with black, white-edged ocellus on short dorsal fin, reduced to dark spot in adults. Coastal reefs with soft or hard coral growth. Small settling juveniles with large dorsal fin spine from larval stage, secretive among rocks or small caves; adults swim about openly. Subtropical west coast endemic, common north of Perth. Rare on the south coast, and few specimens are trawled there. Maximum length 13 cm.

Spot-banded Butterflyfish *Chaetodon punctatofasciatus*

Pale yellow above, white below, with a series of small spots densely set into vertical stripes over upper sides. Orange over caudal peduncle, running onto anal fin. Clear outer reef habitat in rich invertebrate growth on slopes and drop-offs. Juveniles very secretive in narrow crevices; adults usually in pairs swimming close to substrate. Closely related to Dot-and-dash Butterflyfish (next species), and in some areas hybrids occur. Maximum length 10 cm, usually 8 cm.

Dot-and-dash Butterflyfish *Chaetodon pelewensis*

Very similar to the Spot-banded Butterflyfish (previous species), but the series of spots and short stripes are at an angle instead of vertical. Patterns often irregular, as shown in the photograph. Juveniles in shallow protected coastal bays, secretive among rocky or rubble pieces on reef-flats. Adults in clear coastal to outer reef habitats with rich invertebrate growth, usually in pairs. Maximum length 10 cm, usually 8 cm.

Merten's Butterflyfish *Chaetodon mertensii*

Adult with orange over posterior half caudal fin, and distinct black stripe with thin white margins over head through eye. Juvenile lacks orange on caudal fin. Adults inhabit outer reefs, usually along base of drop-offs on low-sloping reef with mixed short-algae and invertebrate growth. Juveniles in sheltered coastal bays. Complex of similar Indo-Pacific species with almost identical colour pattern, only one in Australia. Maximum length 12 cm.

Pinstriped Butterflyfish *Chaetodon lunulatus*

Pale yellow to pinkish with thin grey line along each scale row, and black spot at end of dorsal-fin base onto caudal peduncle. Several black stripes: over head through eye; over caudal fin; and along anal-fin base. Sibling Indian Ocean species *C. trifasciatus* has bluish upper sides, and orange caudal peduncle and anal fin. Ranges of species overlap in Bali, Indonesia. Rich coral reefs, feeding primarily on hard-coral polyps. Small juveniles in *Acropora* corals; adults swim about openly in pairs or small groups. Maximum length 12 cm.

Blue-dash Butterflyfish *Chaetodon plebeius*

Distinctly bright yellow with blue dash as if brushed on with paint. Coastal and inner reefs with rich coral growth. Adults swim about in pairs. Juveniles secretive i *Acropora* corals. Feeds almost exclusively on coral polyps; difficult to maintain in aquarium. Sibling Indian Ocean species, without blue dash, appears to be undescribed. Maximum length 12 cm.

Western Butterflyfish (adult)

Western Butterflyfish (juvenile)

Spot-banded Butterflyfish

Dot-and-dash Butterflyfish (adult)

Dot-and-dash Butterflyfish (juvenile)

Merten's Butterflyfish

Pinstriped Butterflyfish

Blue-dash Butterflyfish

Chevroned Butterflyfish *Chaetodon trifascialis*

Body pale yellow above to overall white with light yellow median fins. Black stripe over head through eye, and black posteriorly which changes with growth: juveniles black posteriorly on body, black migrating with growth onto caudal fin until confined to fin with narrow yellow posterior-margin left. Typically found with large *Acropora* plates, adults either above or below, small juveniles between branches. Feeds primarily on the corals. Maximum length 14 cm.

Triangular Butterflyfish *Chaetodon baronessa*

Body very tall with large rounded fins, mostly purplish brown with thin pale chevron lines on body, broad on head. Coastal to outer reef crests and shallow slopes with rich coral growth, often pairs sheltering below *Acropora* plates. Feeds primarily on coral polyps. Almost identical Indian Ocean sibling species *C. triangulum*, broadly black on caudal fin, overlaps in range in Java, Indonesia. Maximum length 15 cm.

Long-nose Butterflyfish *Forcipiger flavissimus*

Black from top of long snout through eye to pectoral-fin base to dorsal-fin origin, abruptly changing to bright yellow body. Clear coastal to outer reefs, from shallow lagoons to deep drop-offs, usually on reef crests or slopes, feeding in pairs on small invertebrates or parts of larger ones such as echinoderms. Similar Very-long-nose Butterflyfish (next species) has longer snout. Maximum length 22 cm.

Very-long-nose Butterflyfish *Forcipiger longirostris*

Snout very long, sometimes almost as long as body depth. Patch of tiny black spots on chest, and eye completely black. Mainly on outer reef walls and at greater depths than other species. Usually in pairs, swimming through long ledges or caves, feeding from narrow crevices. Maximum length 22 cm.

Schooling Bannerfish *Heniochus diphreutes*

Distinct by colour and shape. Anal fin short and ventral fins long. Adults usually in large schools, swimming midwater feeding on zooplankton and cleaning pelagic fishes. Even approaches divers in some places from deep tidal channels in estuaries to outer reefs. Also feeds on substrate invertebrates. Juveniles in coastal bays and harbours, congregating in small groups on isolated outcrops of rock or anything providing shelter, including lost fishing nets, tree branches, etc. Reef Bannerfish (next species) almost identical, with slight morphological differences in shape and especially the length of anal and ventral fins. Maximum length 20 cm.

hevroned Butterflyfish (juvenile and adult)

Triangular Butterflyfish

ng-nose Butterflyfish

Very-long-nose Butterflyfish

hooling Bannerfish (adults)

Schooling Bannerfish (juveniles)

223

Reef Bannerfish *Heniochus acuminatus*

Anal fin long and much more angular compared to Schooling Bannerfish (previous species). Pectoral fins in large adults yellow. Coastal to protected inner reefs along reef walls and slopes, often very common. Adults usually in pairs. Small juveniles may form small groups; shallow in protected coastal bays and estuaries on shallow rocky reefs and occasionally common under jetties, but sometimes deeper or mixed with similar species on isolated rocky outcrops on sand or mud. Maximum length 25 cm.

Singular Bannerfish *Heniochus singularius*

Distinct with white banner and yellow area over dorsal fin, back and onto caudal peduncle, and when adult complete caudal fin. Eye hidden in black band, and when adult snout almost black, separated by narrow white line from eye band. Coastal waters, juveniles secretive and solitary in narrow crevices or small caves along low drop-offs. Adults pair on deep slopes, rather shy if not used to divers. Largest bannerfish, maximum length 30 cm.

Masked Bannerfish *Heniochus monoceros*

Unusually banded with middle black band vertical and other 2 angular from spinous dorsal-fin part to snout, including over eye, and to posterior anal-fin region. Clear coastal to outer reefs, often semi-exposed reef. Juveniles secretive in rocky ledges; adults in pairs on algal reefs, often along drop-offs in large caves or below overhangs. Maximum length 23 cm, usually 15 cm in Australian waters.

Pennant Bannerfish *Heniochus chrysostomus*

Black bands angular, first over head from nape, completely covering eye, onto ventral fins, and second from spinous dorsal fin to end of anal fin. Juveniles with white-edged black ocellus posteriorly on anal fin, near base. Adults extended dorsal spines with very broad membranes. Still, clear coastal waters to outer reefs. Juveniles shallow in lagoons and estuaries; adults mostly on outer reefs in pairs. Maximum length 16 cm.

Horned Bannerfish *Heniochus varius*

Unusual bannerfish in which juveniles have only short elevated dorsal-fin spines and in adults almost non-existent. Mostly black with 2 white stripes. Indian Ocean sibling *H. pleurotaenia* with pale area over abdomen. Juveniles in lagoons; adults in pairs or small groups on reef crest gutters or caves, usually staying in the shelter of the reef. Maximum length 20 cm.

Reef Bannerfish

Singular Bannerfish (adult)

Singular Bannerfish (juvenile)

Masked Bannerfish

Pennant Bannerfish

Horned Bannerfish

ANGELFISHES — POMACANTHIDAE

Large family with 7 genera and at least 80 species, of which 5 genera and about 30 species are found in Australian waters. Closely related to butterflyfishes, but readily distinguished by prominent spine or lower corner of operculum. Slightly more elongate than butterflyfishes, moderately deep and compressed bodies, usually ornamented with bright colours. Regarded as some of the most beautiful coral reef fishes, and sought-after aquarium fish, although larger species are not suitable, except for very large public utilities. Over-exploitation has led to banning of imports in some countries. Fortunately, Australia is blessed with vast resource areas and has strict controls on collecting marine fish for export, and with few but conservation-minded collectors. The members of genus *Pomacanthus* go through dramatic colour changes with growth, juveniles showing no resemblance to adults at all. In nearly all species, juveniles black with vertical white and blue lines which can be straight, curved or form circles, depending on species, or with other slight differences such as colour of pectoral fin. Adults are easily identified by diagnostic colours. Most are secretive on reefs, feeding on algae, sponges or benthic invertebrates; a few are adapted to zooplankton, often feeding high in the water column. Large species can produce loud low-frequency thumping noises which can be startling to divers not familiar with this. Smaller species produce less-impressive noises like the sound of a small drum.

Half-circled Angelfish *Pomacanthus semicirculatus*

Large adults with dusky head, pale yellowish white body, darkening posteriorly, with mixed numerous small dark spots and tiny light spots. Bright electric blue around eye, opercle and preopercle posterior margins and spine, and along entire median- and ventral-fin margins. Dorsal and anal fin pointed and filamentous. Small settling juveniles black with 4 white bars straight over head, strongly curved on body, developing blue fin-margins and thin lines over head and halfway between white bars. Patterns become increasingly complicated with growth, with more lines and spotting. Adults clear coastal to outer reef habitat to about 30 m depth. Juveniles secretive in very shallow rocky habitat, usually between 1 and 5 m depth. Maximum length 35 cm.

Emperor Angelfish *Pomacanthus imperator*

Distinct colour patterns at all stages. Adults with numerous thin yellow lines along body and black mask over eyes. Juveniles with white circles posteriorly on body. In the Pacific, adults with pointed posterior dorsal-fin tip, developing filament when large, which in the Indian Ocean populations is rounded. Two forms overlap in range in Bali, Indonesia, and may be subspecific. Common, but generally deep-water habitats, adults sometimes venturing into shallow depths. Clear coastal slopes to deep outer reef drop-offs. Large adults in cave areas, often with large bommies in deep lagoons. Small juveniles usually deep in 20+ m on rubble or coral outcrops on sand or mud, usually small caves and commonly in cleaning stations with shrimps, taking part in cleaning operations. Maximum length 38 cm.

Six-banded Angelfish *Pomacanthus sexstriatus*

Adults easily recognised by dark head with white stripe and broad vertical black banding on body. Juveniles difficult to identify, with several almost identical species. It has light blue pectoral fin, and body lines are generally white, but the blue in the dorsal and anal fins is somewhat blurred, which is only similar in one other species, *P. annularis*, not recorded in Australian waters. Large adults usually seen in pairs on deep coastal or protected inner reefs. Juveniles in shallow coastal, usually silty habitats, commonly under jetties high on pylons. Large species, maximum length 46 cm.

Half-circled Angelfish (adult)

Half-circled Angelfish (juvenile)

Emperor Angelfish (adult)

Emperor Angelfish (juvenile)

Six-banded Angelfish (adult)

Six-banded Angelfish (juvenile)

227

Blue-face Angelfish *Pomacanthus xanthometopon*

Adults with distinctive blue face and orange mask over eyes and other body and fin colours. Juveniles very similar to several other juveniles, but lines more defined on fin margins and pectoral fin clear. Body line alternating blue and white. Adults pair on inner reefs, usually in channelled reefs or large caves; shy on the Great Barrier Reef. Juveniles solitary and secretive in crevices on shallow reefs. Maximum length 36 cm

Majestic Angelfish *Pomacanthus navarchus*

Adults with distinctive colouration and easily identified. Juveniles similar to other members of genus, but live in outer reef habitat and pectoral fin is purplish blue. Rare in Australia and mainly on northern outer reef drop-offs near caves. Maximum length 25 cm.

Scribbled Angelfish *Chaetodontoplus duboulayi*

Adults with broad yellow band surrounding white patch behind head, yellow continuing over back and connecting with bright yellow caudal fin, and anteriorly onto ventral fins. Small juveniles with yellow headband and tail, yellow over back developing with growth. Variable blue scribbles over dark body, dorsal and anal fin areas, usually in longitudinal fine lines in males. Coastal reefs with mixed algae and sponge growth. Juveniles in narrow ledges or crevices between and under piled-up rocks or large rubble pieces. Adults often in pairs or loose aggregations, easily approached in many areas. Maximum length 25 cm.

Yellow-finned Angelfish *Chaetodontoplus meredithi*

Adults with distinctive blue face and numerous yellow spots, yellow caudal and ventral fins, and yellow outer margin along pectoral fins. Body black with white band behind head. Harbours and coastal to inner reefs, usually in sponge areas and often under deep jetties where sponges are prolific on pylons. Small juveniles in rocky ledges with sea urchins. Replaced on the west coast by sibling *C. personife* which has a yellow-margined black caudal fin as an adult. Juveniles almost identical, and also similar to several more species in the Northern Hemisphere, especially *C. septentrionalis*, but adults have longitudinal blue lines over body and head. Maximum length 30 cm.

Blue-face Angelfish (adult)

Scribbled Angelfish (adult)

Scribbled Angelfish (juvenile)

Blue-face Angelfish (juvenile)

Yellow-finned Angelfish (adult)

Majestic Angelfish

Yellow-finned Angelfish (juvenile)

Three-spot Angelfish *Apolemichthys trimaculatus*

Easily recognised by combination of colours, mainly bright yellow at all stages. Adults with blue lips, black nape-spot and ear-like spot, and broad black anal-fin margin bordered with white to light yellow band on inside. Juveniles lack most of these features and have a distinct black spot at base of soft dorsal fin and thin black line from eye to nape. Rich coastal to outer reef slopes. Adults in small but loose groups at moderate depths. Juveniles secretive in small coral outcrops on sand or mud slopes, usually very deep, 30+ m. Maximum length 26 cm.

Herald's Angelfish *Centropyge heraldi*

Could be mistaken for Lemon Peel (next species), but lacks the blue markings. Female and juvenile uniformly yellow, but male develops dark shading and orange spots near eye. Deep-water species in Australia, only common on rubble slopes on the base of drop-offs on outer barrier reefs in 40+ m depth, where in small aggregations. Maximum length 10 cm.

Lemon Peel *Centropyge flavissima*

Overall bright lemon-yellow with iridescent blue ring around eye, blue on gill margin and spine, and blue median-fin margins. Juveniles have black, blue-edged spot on sides. Patchy distribution, mainly oceanic locations and in Australia mainly along the southern Great Barrier Reef. Indian Ocean sibling has no blue ring around eye, but a black streak posteriorly on opercle. Maximum length 14 cm, usually 11 cm.

Blue and Gold Angelfish *Centropyge bicolor*

Easily identified by colour pattern. Half-gold and half-blue, and large adults with additional orange 'ear' spot. Common on clear-water reef habitats, often shallow in mixed coral and short algae rubble crests and slopes. Adults often in small aggregations with large individual leading, usually moving quickly and close to substrate, stopping for short feeding sessions, grazing on algae. Juveniles secretive and solitary in narrow ledges and crevices. Maximum length 16 cm, usually 12 cm.

Keyhole Angelfish *Centropyge tibicen*

At all sizes black with variable-sized white spot centrally on side, usually vertical oval but can be as large as head and reach almost to anus. Adults develop broad yellow anal-fin margins and yellow ventral fins, and largest individuals, possibly males, with bright blue sheen. Shallow protected reefs in ledges and around rocky boulders, silty coastal to pristine outer reef habitat. Juveniles solitary; adults often in small loose aggregations. Maximum length 15 cm.

Three-spot Angelfish (adult)

Three-spot Angelfish (juvenile)

Herald's Angelfish

Lemon Peel

Blue and Gold Angelfish

Keyhole Angelfish

Damsel Angelfish *Centropyge flavicauda*

Body dark blue with light blue margins on dorsal and anal fins, and leading edge of ventral fins. Looks and behaves like damsel fish. Often in small groups and usually found on rubble zones and in rich corals near reef, sharing habitat of several damsel look-alike species. Small species, maximum length 8 cm.

Pearly-scaled Angelfish *Centropyge vrolikii*

Head white to grey and scales on body with white centres, spots decreasing posteriorly in size and at above anal-fin origin gradually changing over to black. Small juveniles less black, otherwise identical to adult. Shallow coastal rocky reefs with short algae and encrusting sponges in shaded areas to feed. Replaced by Indian Ocean sibling, Eible's Angelfish (next species), along the north-west coast. Their ranges overlap in Indonesia where hybrids are common. Maximum length 12 cm.

Eible's Angelfish *Centropyge eibli*

Closely related to Pearly-scaled Angelfish (previous species), but easily recognised by more even grey colour, thin dusky to orange lines across body and head, and anal fin not black. Similar habitat but with soft coral and hydroid areas, seemingly preferring a slightly different diet. Interestingly, most of the previous *Centropyge* species are mimicked by two surgeonfishes, *Acanthurus pyroferus* (page 366) and *A. tristis*. Maximum length 10 cm.

Coral Beauty *Centropyge bispinosa*

Highly variable, from almost completely blue to red with many thin vertical dark lines. All forms usually with red ventral fins. Blue in shallow depth and pale to red in deep water. Usually deep water but also in rich coral lagoons as shallow as 3 m. Juveniles in coastal but clear-water rocky reefs; adults mostly along sloping base of deep drop-offs in 40–60 m depth. Maximum length 10 cm.

Many-banded Angelfish *Centropyge multifasciata*

Distinctly patterned with numerous bands of equal width, alternating with black and white. Number of bands increases with age. Juveniles with bluish black spot anteriorly in soft dorsal fin. Mainly deep on outer reef drop-offs, occasionally observed in upper reef gutter walls in shallow depths. Typically in caves or large overhangs on ceilings, in small aggregations swimming upside down (photograph inverted), and juveniles in same habitat. Genus used provisionally, probably belongs in other genus. Maximum length 12 cm.

Damsel Angelfish

Pearly-scaled Angelfish

Eible's Angelfish

Coral Beauty

Many-banded Angelfish (adult)

Many-banded Angelfish (juvenile)

233

Regal Angelfish *Pygoplites diacanthus*

Beautifully marked species with orange to yellow, white, black and blue vertical stripes, and bright yellow tail. Juveniles with fewer bands but large blue-edged black ocellus on soft dorsal fin. Grey face and chest which is orange in the Indian Ocean sibling form (possibly other species). Coastal to outer reef lagoons, usually shallow in rich coral-growth areas on reef crests and slopes but known to a depth of 80 m. Maximum length 25 cm.

Black-spot Angelfish *Genicanthus melanospilos*

Interesting genus with several species, but usually inhabit very deep water, and only this species is commonly seen on the Great Barrier Reef. Males look totally different from females, with numerous vertical dark stripes across body and top of head, and large black spot on chest just in front of ventral fins, after which scientifically and commonly named. Female yellow to grey below, with dark streaks along caudal-fin margins. Only outer reef drop-offs, along steep walls with plenty of ledges and caves. Planktivorous, females feeding in small loose aggregations; males more solitary, occasionally mixing with females. Maximum length 18 cm.

Watanabe's Angelfish *Genicanthus watanabei*

As with Black-spot Angelfish (previous species), males and females are very different. Both light bluish grey, males with a series of longitudinal black lines along most of lower body and anal fin, and females with just black blue-edged bar over eye and black median-fin margins. Rare in Australia, but could be contributed to deep-water habitat, usually deeper than 20 m on outer reef walls. Both photographs on a single quick dive at 50 m, and other specimens in sight well down the wall. Maximum length 18 cm.

Lamarck's Angelfish *Genicanthus lamarck*

Easily identified by shape and longitudinal black lines in both sexes. Unlike other members of the genus, colour differences are minor between sexes and juvenile to adult. Males differ mainly in having prolonged caudal-fin lobes and thicker stripes. Outer reefs along deep slopes in Australia, shallow to 3 m in some equatorial areas, usually in loose groups controlled by a large male, and often swimming high above substrate. Small juveniles secretive on deep rubble slopes in 40+ m depth. Maximum length 20 cm, without fin extensions.

Regal Angelfish (adult)

Regal Angelfish (juvenile)

Black-spot Angelfish (male)

Black-spot Angelfish (female)

Watanabe's Angelfish (male)

Watanabe's Angelfish (female)

Lamarck's Angelfish (male)

Lamarck's Angelfish (female)

235

BATFISHES — EPHIPPIDAE

Small family with 5 genera and about 10 species, of which 2 genera and at least 6 species are known in Australian waters. Genus *Platax* commonly encountered and called batfishes. Bodies are disc-shaped. Juveniles have extremely tall fins above and below, which reduce in height progressively with age. Shapes of juveniles are rather unfish-like and often mimic various floating leaves, and one a bad-tasting flatworm avoided by predators. Most small juveniles are pelagic, floating with objects of weed rafts, forming schools when possible. Adults usually form small aggregations, but may school in some areas. Diet comprises benthic invertebrates and zooplankton.

Tall-fin Batfish *Platax teira*

Large adults with head and body almost forming a circle. Median fins large and highest or deepest posteriorly. Variable grey to brown, usually with broad dusky to brown vertical bands and black blotch on abdomen. Small juveniles with exceptionally tall fins, orange-brown with dark brown to black vertical bands, and short dark bar on body at anal-fin origin which remains in adults but less distinct. Shallow coastal protected bays to deep offshore, singly, in pairs or small aggregations. Small juveniles inshore, floating near surface like leaves, and winds or currents may cause long drifts. Larger juveniles often oceanic, forming schools under sargassum weed rafts. Some confusion of batfishes persists in the modern literature, with several species very similar to Tall-fin Batfish as adult, one of which *P. boersi* (only recently recognised as valid) is not yet known from Australian waters and only known from Indonesia to Japan. It may occur in northern Australia. Adult *P. boersi* yellowish with black ventral and lower part of anal fins, and faint broad bar behind head, usually seen in great schools along deep drop-offs. Tall-fin Batfish, maximum length 60 cm, usually 45 cm.

Round Batfish *Platax orbicularis*

Adult very similar to Tall-fin Batfish (previous species), but lacks black abdominal spot and has pale yellow pectoral fins, and usually some small dark spots scattered on sides. Small juveniles brown to orange with angular dorsal and anal fins, variably dark-spotted or blotched, nearly always some white spots or ocelli. Two opposite black spots on caudal peduncle at dorsal- and anal-fin bases diagnostic, often visible to near-adult size. Tiny juveniles commonly float with river run-off along coasts with leaves and other matter. If approached from below, they flatten against surface. Specimen in the photograph was taken down 10 m for the picture: it immediately returned to the surface when released. Settled juveniles often under jetties and form small aggregations, swimming close to substrate and usually over sand. Adults solitary or small groups, forming large dense schools in some areas, but schooling not yet observed in Australian waters. Maximum length 50 cm.

Humped Batfish *Platax batavianus*

Adults with distinct shape: dorsal fin low with anterior part highest and not as rounded as in other adults. Black band over head through eye, black posterior gill margin, and irregular small black blotching on abdomen. Ventral fins and lower tip of anal fin black. Juveniles uniquely striped with zebra pattern and known as Zebra Batfish. In Australia, adults deep on open sandy substrates with large coral heads, usually solitary, occasionally in pairs. Unlike other species, small juveniles deep and rarely seen. Juvenile in photograph at 15 m depth on coastal sand slope adjacent to deep water, staying with crinoid partly visible in the photograph, and seen nibbling on tentacles. Probably the largest batfish; some giants seen at Lizard Island, Queensland, in 25 m depth about 50 cm long, reported to 65 cm from New Guinea where common in shallow coastal waters.

Tall-fin Batfish (adult)   **Tall-fin Batfish** (large juvenile)   **Tall-fin Batfish** (small juvenile)

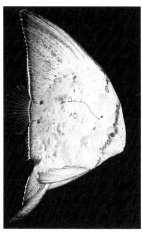

Round Batfish (adult)   **Round Batfish** (large juveniles)   **Round Batfish** (small juvenile)

Humped Batfish (adult)   **Humped Batfish** (juvenile)

Shaded Batfish *Platax pinnatus*

Adults best recognised by protruding mouth, and yellow pectoral and caudal fins in large individuals, black ventral fins and distinct thick black margin posteriorly on median fins. Juveniles easily recognised when small by shape and colour: very tall fins and black all over, except bright orange stripe over front of head, continuing all around over median-fin margins. With age, a broad pale band over the sides develops and widens, and fin heights reduce to more triangular shapes. Tiny juveniles in shallow protected bays swim with undulating motion, mimicking orange-margined black flatworm which has a bad taste and is left alone by predators. Larger juveniles in caves along coastal slopes and drop-offs, often very deep, or under deep jetties. Adults sometimes seen singly on reefs, but usually forming schools, and often seen on the move over open substrates near reefs. Small species, maximum length 35 cm.

BOARFISHES — PENTACEROTIDAE

Small temperate family with 8 genera and 14 species worldwide in both hemispheres. All genera and 10 species are found in Australian waters; most genera monotypic. Large head encased with rough striated bony plates, fin spines strong and large in most. Body deep, elongate to round, very compressed, covered with small ctenoid scales. Vertical fins often tall, particularly in juveniles. Snout length increases proportionally with size and elongates in adults of some species. All species primarily in very deep water, some only known from trawls and few enter estuaries. Only the Long-Snout Boarfish (next species) has an exceptional depth range, from very shallow to 260 m. Shelter on rocky reefs in caves or below large overhangs, often in small groups. Small juveniles differ greatly from later stages but are deep dwellers and rarely seen. Some are white with a few black spots and large feathery vertical fins.

Long-snout Boarfish *Pentaceropsis recurvirostris*

Best-known Australian boarfish, commonly observed on reefs along the south coast. Small juveniles white with black spots and tall vertical fins; only seen once by the author, on a dive without a camera. Similar Giant Boarfish *Paristiopterus labiosus* occurs on the east coast, but grows larger and males become yellow-spotted; occasionally seen on deep reefs, including in estuaries. Similar Yellow-spotted Boarfish *P. gallipavo* occurs on the south-west coast. Long-snout Boarfish found from shallow sandy estuaries to deep offshore. Occurs solitary, in pairs or forms small aggregations, usually in caves or below large overhangs during the day. Maximum length 50 cm.

Short Boarfish *Parazanclistius hutchinsi*

Best identified by sailfin-like dorsal fin, especially when juvenile, large rounded ventral fins, and white-edged black ocellus on soft part of dorsal fin. Only other similar species, *Zanclistius elevatus*, has pointed dorsal fin and ocellus as juvenile only. Latter species rarely seen in eastern Australia because of great depth preference. The Short Boarfish enters shallow estuaries but is mainly known from the south-west coast. Only 2 records from Port Phillip Bay, Victoria: a juvenile near Seaford Pier and the specimen in the photograph off Rye, a young adult, at 15 m depth. Maximum length 33 cm.

Shaded Batfish (adult)

Shaded Batfish (small juvenile)

Shaded Batfish (large juvenile)

Long-snout Boarfish

Short Boarfish

239

OLD WIFES — ENOPLOSIDAE

Single representative, Australian endemic. Relationship with other families unclear: postlarvae similar to terapontids, adults to banjosids and some resemblance to the boarfishes. Tiny juveniles inhabit seagrass beds, lacking tall vertical fins. Adults form great schools in coastal waters and are probably one of the best known fishes by divers in southern waters.

Old Wife *Enoplosus armatus*

Easily identified by shape and colour pattern as adult, as there are no other similar species. Usually observed in schools, but forms pairs, separating from school and choosing a particular spot on a reef. Numerous pairs can be found together in some areas, seemingly in phase with the moon — like most marine creatures when it comes to breeding. Common and often abundant on coastal reefs and rocky estuaries, sometimes forming large schools hovering midwater. The dorsal and probably other fin spines carry a venom; thus specimens should be handled with care. Maximum length 25 cm.

MORWONGS — CHEILODACTYLIDAE

Cool tropical to temperate family with 4 genera and about 20 species, of which 3 genera and 14 species are reported in Australian waters. Species are characterised by thick rubbery lips, long elongated pectoral fin rays, forked caudal fin and usually distinct colours. Reef and soft bottom dwellers, feeding on small invertebrates and worms filtered through the gill rakers from mouthfuls of sand taken. Postlarvae settling on substrate extremely thin and silvery, features carried through from larval stage, and quickly change to juvenile form. Most species solitary or occur in small loose groups. Some seasonally form large schools. Juveniles hide in narrow crevices or under rocks. A few species are commercially trawled in depths to 400 m.

Magpie Morwong *Cheilodactylus gibbosus*

White with black oblique bands, dorsal fin greatly elevated anteriorly. Restricted to the west coast, but very similar sibling Crested Morwong (next species) found on the east coast. Mainly coastal bays and rocky estuaries, singly or in small loose aggregations on a mixed rock and sand habitat. Other similar species in Japanese temperate seas and the east Pacific. Maximum length 30 cm.

Crested Morwong *Cheilodactylus vestitus*

Body white with broad oblique black bands, last extending over lower caudal fin to lower tip. Clear coastal and estuarine reefs with rich invertebrate growth. Feeds on sand patches among reef. Mainly solitary, occasionally in pairs or small aggregations. Maximum length 35 cm.

Magpie Perch *Cheilodactylus nigripes*

Distinct species with white overall colour and broad black bands. Large adults change colour at will and, strangely, second black band turns white, while normally white interspace turns grey. Juveniles solitary and secretive when small, but venturing into open as they grow larger. Adults in deeper parts of estuaries and protected coastal bays to 60 m depth. Often congregates, forming loose groups and displaying to each other, changing colours in a matter of seconds. Small juveniles in shallow protected bays with rocks and weed for shelter, mostly along reef margins to feed from sand. Maximum length 40 cm.

Old Wife

Magpie Morwong

Crested Morwong

Magpie Perch (adult)

Magpie Perch (juvenile)

241

Banded Morwong *Cheilodactylus spectabilis*

Dark grey to brown banding at all benthic stages, but sometimes indistinct in large adults. Only similar species is Red-lip Morwong (next species) on the west coast. Rather stocky for morwong, and extensions of pectoral-fin rays very short. Shallow coastal to deep offshore reefs, juveniles occasionally in shallow rocky estuaries. Usually on sand and rubble, occurs singly or forms loose groups. Large species, recorded maximum length 1 m, usually 60 cm.

Red-lip Morwong *Cheilodactylus rubrolabiatus*

Body with broad bands, variable from solid to spotted and brown to black, with pale interspaces and head more-or-less spotted. Lips, and margins of gills and paired fins, brown to bright red. Similar to eastern Banded Morwong (previous species) and possibly overlap in range in South Australia. Coastal to offshore, inhabits mixed rock and weed reefs in the south and coral reefs in the north. Maximum length 60 cm.

Blue Morwong *Nemadactylus douglasi*

Adults with bright blue fins and silvery blue body, appearing completely blue underwater in natural light, sometimes yellowish over back. Juveniles with black spot on side, as in closely related Queen Snapper (next species). Clear coastal bays to deep offshore, usually on sand slopes near reefs, singly or in small numbers from about 20 m depth to at least 100 m. Maximum length 70 cm.

Queen Snapper *Nemadactylus valenciennesi*

Adults silvery blue, caudal fin yellowish with bright blue margin and thin yellow and blue lines in front and behind eyes. Juveniles with numerous yellow and blue alternating longitudinal lines and black to grey blotch on sides which fades with age but is sometimes still visible in large adults. Inshore rocky reefs and estuaries to deep offshore. Also known as Blue Morwong (Southern). Maximum length 90 cm.

Jackass Morwong *Nemadactylus macropterus*

Adults silvery white to grey with dark broad band from nape to pectoral-fin base, juveniles with faint brown bars on sides. Adults mainly deep offshore, forming large schools, but entering coastal bays and estuaries as shallow as 15 m depth. Juveniles coastal and in deep part of estuaries on rocky or rubble substrate. Maximum length 70 cm.

Banded Morwong

Red-lip Morwong

Blue Morwong

Queen Snapper

Jackass Morwong

243

TRUMPETERS — LATRIDIDAE

Small cold–temperate family with 3 genera and at least 5 species, restricted to Australia, New Zealand and South America. One of each genus is reported in Australian waters. Similar to morwongs but more perch-like in appearance, with deeply notched dorsal fin and small rounded pectoral fins. Fins with large number of elements, and scales on body small and numerous. Mouth protruding and extended in *Mendosoma*, a planktivore restricted to Tasmania. Other trumpeters benthic feeders, taking a variety of invertebrates. Schooling fishes; usually form small local aggregations, but sometimes migrate and travel in great schools, comprising hundreds of individuals. The larger species are regarded as excellent to eat, especially *Latris* which is of great commercial importance in Tasmania and a candidate for fish farming.

Bastard Trumpeter *Latridopsis forsteri*

Shiny silvery grey to bluish, dusky or brownish over back with scribbles or longitudinal stripes above lateral line. Caudal fin in adult with distinct black margin. Solitary or small aggregations in coastal waters near reefs or jetties, forming small to large schools offshore in deep water. Similar but smaller Real-bastard Trumpeter *Mendosoma alporti* restricted to Tasmanian coastal waters, schools midwater. Maximum length 65 cm.

Striped Trumpeter *Latris lineata*

Distinct with long black stripes along upper sides from young to large adults. Deep water species, but young sometimes very shallow in surging coastal areas. Feeds on benthic invertebrates as well as large zooplankton crustaceans. Sought-after fish known also as Tasmanian Trumpeter and Stripey, and in New Zealand as Trumpeter or Kohikohi. Maximum length 1.2 m.

SEACARPS — APLODACTYLIDAE

Small temperate family with 2 genera and 5 species, restricted to the Southern Hemisphere, of which 4 species are known in Australian waters. Robust elongated fishes with small cycloid scales, deeply notched dorsal fin, short-based anal fin, and all fins moderately large. Drab-coloured with large dusky blotched patterns and pale irregular spotting. Typically found in mixed weed and rock habitat in turbulent coastal or current-prone estuarine habitats, feeding primarily on suspended weeds and algae ripped from substrate by surge or currents. Sloppy swimmers, often resting on the bottom until food is sighted. Regarded as poor eating.

Southern Seacarp *Aplodactylus arctidens*

Variable dusky greenish brown to almost black, with pale grey blotching and spotting forming irregular longitudinal banding. Head with smoothly rounded profile. Mainly shallow reefs, often on substrate among short weeds or on sand patches among algae-covered rocks. Becomes active in outgoing tidal currents, often hovering above substrate to feed on weed floating past. Maximum length 65 cm.

Western Seacarp *Aplodactylus westralis*

Dusky greenish brown above to yellowish below, with large pale irregular blotches alternating longitudinally in 4 series. Head profile strongly rounded in front of eyes. Shallow, heavily vegetated reefs in surging coastal waters. Usually in small loose aggregations swimming close to substrate or among weeds. Maximum length 63 cm.

Bastard Trumpeter

Bastard Trumpeter (variation)

Striped Trumpeter

Southern Seacarp

Western Seacarp

Rock Cale *Crinodus lophodon*

Variable bluish grey to black with light spots on fins and a series of larger light blotches along body. Juveniles with distinct ear-spot, black with pale margin. Shallow exposed rocky shores in high-energy zones, often in large aggregations just below foaming surface waters. Very similar to Southern Seacarp (second previous species), but head shape different with concave profile over nape. Maximum length 35 cm.

KELPFISHES — CHIRONEMIDAE

Small temperate family with 2 genera and 3 species, restricted to Australian and New Zealand waters, of which all are found in Australia and one in New Zealand. Distinct head profile with large eyes. Tips of dorsal fin spines with variable number of short filaments, forming distinct tufts in some species. Closely related to the tropical hawkfishes and similarly hug the substrate, but only one species included here seen in the open. Others very similar, secretive in kelp or weeds and occasionally seen at night. Diet comprises small invertebrates taken from weeds and rocks.

Kelpfish *Chironemus marmoratus*

Similar to Rock Cale (previous species), but differs in having a pointed head and dark markings on the body and head with numerous tiny white spots. Common New South Wales species in coastal rocky surge zones, often forming large loose aggregations on rocky outcrops. Wedged against rock surface in surge, but often swims about. Maximum length 40 cm.

HAWKFISHES — CIRRHITIDAE

Moderately large tropical family with 9 genera and 35 species, mostly Indo-Pacific (only 3 species in the Atlantic), of which 7 genera and 12 species are found in Australian waters. Like the kelpfishes (previous family), they rest most of the time on substrate using pectoral fins for balance. Easily recognised by shape and the small tufts on dorsal fin spine tips, which typify this family. Only planktivorous Lyre-tail Hawkfish differs from the norm in more perch-like shape and long, deeply-lunate caudal fin. Others benthic feeders, taking various small invertebrates or fishes. Inhabit shallow depths, usually on reef crests and often in strong surge zones. Some territorial, others in small loose groups.

Blotched Hawkfish *Cirrhitichthys aprinus*

Variable dusky brown blotched pattern with pale interspaces, sometimes forming irregular bands, thin lines radiating from below eye, and distinct eye-sized dark spot on gill at eye level. Caudal fin without spots in contrast to other similar species. Coastal rocky reef and shallow estuaries, mostly in or around sponges at various depths, observed at Montague Island, New South Wales, to 30 m. Throughout the Indo-Pacific, maximum length in New South Wales 12 cm, in equatorial waters only 9 cm.

Spotted Hawkfish *Cirrhitichthys oxycephalus*

Median fins distinctly spotted and body with larger spots, or blotches forming mosaic pattern. Colour variable, pink to white with almost black to bright-red spots or blotches, usually associated with depth. Occurring to 40 m where usually red. Clear shallow coastal to offshore deep reefs. Maximum length 9 cm.

Rock Cale

Kelpfish

Blotched Hawkfish (southern form)

Blotched Hawkfish (northern form)

Spotted Hawkfish

247

Coral Hawkfish *Cirrhitichthys falco*

Caudal and soft dorsal fin distinctly spotted, pale with black to red spots forming saddle-like bands anteriorly over body. Dorsal fin with distinct yellow tufts. Clear coastal reef crests and slopes to about 45 m depth, solitary or in pairs. Maximum length 65 mm.

Lyre-tail Hawkfish *Cyprinocirrhites polyactis*

Light pinkish brown to yellowish, often whitish area over back as shown in the photograph. Distinct from other hawkfishes by its plain colour and long lunate caudal fin. Planktivorous; often swims in small aggregations well above substrate and sometimes mistaken for anthiid or basslet. Deep coastal and offshore reefs in current-prone areas, often resting on sponges when not feeding. Maximum length 10 cm.

Ring-eyed Hawkfish *Paracirrhites arcatus*

Horseshoe-shaped mark with thin orange and blue line behind eye and broad white streak along most of body to caudal-fin base, though the latter is sometimes indistinct. Typically found among branching corals on outer reef crests, usually several present in one coral head. Usually in depths of a few metres. Maximum length 14 cm.

Forster's Hawkfish *Paracirrhites forsteri*

Highly variable, from white with bright red upper half to dusky brown, but always with freckle-like spotted pattern on head in red to black. Rich coastal and inner reef slopes on corals or rubble, singly or in pairs. Also known as Freckled Hawkfish. Maximum length 20 cm.

Longnose Hawkfish *Oxycirrhites typus*

Easily recognised by exceptionally long snout and pale, almost white body with patterns of vertical and horizontal red lines forming squares on sides. Commonly found along deep drop-offs among black corals, on sponges or gorgonian corals. Well camouflaged in natural light. Usually in pairs or small aggregations. Maximum length 10 cm.

Coral Hawkfish

Lyre-tail Hawkfish

Ring-eyed Hawkfish

Forster's Hawkfish

Longnose Hawkfish

249

DAMSELFISHES — POMACENTRIDAE

Very large reef fish family, primarily tropical but some members in temperate zones, with an estimated 30 genera and 300 species globally distributed. The greatest number are in Australian waters, with about 15 genera and 132 species. Diverse group, most of which are placed in 3 subfamilies: Amphiprioninae, comprising anemonefishes; Chrominae pullers and humbugs; and Pomacentrinae damsels or demoiselles. In general, deep rounded and compressed bodies, varying to almost elongate shapes, covered with ctenoid scales which usually extend over fins. Mouth small, jaws with one or a few rows of small conical to compressed teeth. Anal fin with 2 spines, the first very short. Colour often differs between juvenile and adult stages, but not between sexes, except during display and spawning period. Males guarding eggs may show unusual colouration. Most damselfishes are reef-dwellers living close to substrate with good coverage for shelter and nesting. Diet varies from small invertebrates to all kinds of plankton and some graze on algae. Most species are small and have no commercial value except being ornamental on reefs with their bright colours and as aquarium fishes.

Golden Scalyfin *Parma bicolor*

Adults easily recognised by bright golden yellow body and dusky head. Juveniles with bright blue over top of head, colour extending over spinous dorsal fin and solid, unlike blue-lined or spotted pattern of other juveniles in the genus. Restricted distribution on the south-west coast, preferring deep reefs, usually in excess of 15 m depth. Usually solitary and, like other *Parma* spp., territorial. Maximum length 20 cm.

Scalyfin *Parma victoriae*

Highly variable as adult, grey to black or yellow to orange, usually some barring on head. Juveniles similar to several species, being orange with blue lines from head over back and bright blue-edged black ocellus in soft part of dorsal fin, but lacks the 'ear' spot of White Ear (next species). Coastal reefs and rocky estuaries from almost intertidal to depths of 25 m. Large males almost black with thin blue fin margins, aggressively guarding eggs. Maximum length 25 cm.

White Ear *Parma microlepis*

Large adults uniformly brown to black with white 'ear' marking on gill, large in males. Juveniles bright orange with blue lines and blue-edged black ocellus in soft dorsal fin. Blue lines break up into spots with growth. Large juvenile shown in the photograph. Shallow coastal reefs and estuaries to depths of 30 m. Juveniles often in rockpools, very territorial. Maximum length 16 cm.

Girdled Scalyfin *Parma unifasciata*

Easily recognised by single broad white band vertically over centre of body in all but smallest stages. Juveniles orange and adults grey to brownish. The uncommon New South Wales Banded Scalyfin *P. polylepis* has three broad, vertical white bands usually occurs only on offshore reefs. Girdled Scalyfin mainly in surge zones among large boulders in shallow water. Maximum length 20 cm.

McCulloch's Scalyfin *Parma mccullochi*

Large adults mostly black, male with pale yellowish white areas over head and posteriorly on body. Juveniles bright yellow with blue lines and black interspaces over head and upper sides, and small blue spots scattered over yellow sides. Territorial and aggressive, solitary on shallow rocky coastal reefs to at least 35 m depth. Similar Big-scale Scalyfin *P. oligolepis* on the east coast. *P. mccullochi* probably the largest Australian damsel, maximum length 28 cm.

Golden Scalyfin

Scalyfin

White Ear

Girdled Scalyfin

McCulloch's Scalyfin

Immaculate Damsel *Mecaenichthys immaculatus*

Monotypic. Adults silvery, dusky over top, and median fins with blue margin. Juveniles with orange and blue, similar colour pattern to closely related parma. Various habitats from coastal rocky estuaries to deep offshore, both juveniles and adults, and sometimes found together during early summer months. Less aggressive than *Parma* and sometimes in small loose aggregations in boulder areas. Maximum length 15 cm.

Sergeant Major *Abudefduf vaigiensis*

Distinct with 5 black to dark-blue broad vertical bands. Several similar species. *A. vaigiensis* lacks black streaks in caudal fin and black peduncular saddle (features of next 2 species). Very common species in its range, often schooling in great numbers in shallow lagoons, protected bays, around jetties, or on rocky and coral outcrops on sand slopes. Juveniles estuarine and oceanic with floating matter until drifting inshore to settle. Maximum length 15 cm.

Scissor-tail Sergeant *Abudefduf sexfasciatus*

Best identified by black streaks in caudal fin from base to end of pointed lobes. More habitat-specific and not as common as Sergeant Major (previous species), preferring clear coastal reefs, often in small groups on crests with rich soft coral growth. Small juveniles mix with other species, found in estuaries as well as protected coastal reefs. Maximum length 15 cm.

Black-spot Sergeant *Abudefduf sordidus*

Distinct black spot on caudal peduncle. Juveniles indistinctly grey banded, and centre 2 bands joining and black at dorsal-fin base, forming a broad saddle. Coastal reefs and estuaries on shallow rocky reefs; juveniles commonly in small rockpools at low tide. Reported maximum length 17 cm, usually 15 cm.

White-breasted Sergeant *Amblyglyphidodon leucogaster*

Distinct species, mostly grey but white below head. Several geographical variations. Variably white on pectoral fin and sometimes with bright yellow on ventral fins and lower belly. Great Barrier Reef form shown in the photograph. Coastal to outer reef lagoons and on slopes, mainly with rich coral growth. Maximum length 12 cm.

Immaculate Damsel (adult)

Immaculate Damsel (juvenile)

Sergeant Major

Scissor-tail Sergeant

Black-spot Sergeant

White-breasted Sergeant

253

Golden Sergeant *Amblyglyphidodon aureus*

Geographical variations. Adults in Australia mainly bright golden yellow, but often dusky with yellow fins elsewhere. Mainly found on coastal reef slopes in deeper parts where seawhips occur. Lays eggs on whips guarded by very protective male, which won't hesitate to take on a diver who is venturing too close. Maximum length 15 cm.

Black-and-Yellow Damsel *Neoglyphidodon nigroris*

Adults dusky with black bars on face and usually orange to yellow posteriorly. Latter colour highly variable and in some areas lacking yellow altogether. Small juveniles easily identified by bright yellow and black double longitudinal stripe. Indian Ocean form looks very different and, like many other examples, may be sibling species. Clear coastal to outer reefs. Juveniles solitary on reef crests and shallow drop-offs. Adults in current-prone reef channels in rich coral growth. Maximum length 13 cm.

Royal Damsel *Neoglyphidodon melas*

Adults uniformly black. Juveniles distinct with pale colour and bright yellow top, and typically solitary on reef crests with rich coral growth. Usually with soft corals, swimming above corals feeding on zooplankton drifting past. Adults on shallow reefs, mainly in narrow channels, forming small loose aggregations. Maximum length 15 cm.

Honey-breasted Damsel *Dischistodus prosopotaenia*

Adults highly variable and some geographical variations. Great Barrier Reef adult form shown in the photograph. Juveniles brown with broad white band from dorsal to belly and ventral fins, white caudal peduncle, and blue-edged black ocellus in soft dorsal fin. Coastal reefs and lagoons in shallow sandy and soft coral zones. Maximum length 17 cm.

Black-vent Damsel *Dischistodus melanotus*

Adults best identified by large black blotch on belly and dark area over head and body. Small juveniles with large dusky area over head and part of body divided vertically by thin white line, and white-edged black ocellus in soft dorsal fin. Shallow coastal reefs and lagoons, usually solitary. Maximum length 14 cm.

Golden Sergeant

Black-and-Yellow Damsel (adult)

Black-and-Yellow Damsel (juvenile)

Royal Damsel

Honey-breasted Damsel

Black-vent Damsel

255

White Damsel *Dischistodus perspicillatus*

Distinct with pale, almost white, colour and 2 or 3 black spots along dorsal-fin base, anteriormost fading in adults. Clear sandy coastal slopes, flats and lagoons or inner reefs on rubble zones with large coral heads. Maximum length 18 cm.

Spiny-tail Puller *Acanthochromis polyacanthus*

Monotypic but extremely variable with numerous geographical variations, from half-white with half-black to uniformly grey or almost black. Most Australian populations dark with white tail. Pale form shown in the photograph is from Keppel Island, southern Queensland, with typical colouration in that area. Clear coastal to outer reef lagoons, often in current-prone areas along slopes and drop-offs. Juveniles to large size in small aggregations, probably deriving from early stage of schooling behaviour. This species unique among damselfishes in that parents guard their young. Photographs shows adults with small juveniles, and juveniles on their own in a closely associated group. Maximum length 14 cm.

Dick's Damsel *Plectroglyphidodon dickii*

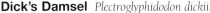

Distinct species with little variation or difference between smallest juveniles and adults. Easily identified by black bar between brownish body and white tail. Clear coastal to outer reef crests, usually in branching coral in loose aggregations. Maximum length 10 cm.

Johnston's Damsel *Plectroglyphidodon johnstonianus*

Variable, similar to Dick's Damsel (previous species) but body pale to bright yellow and tail yellowish. Black bar usually broad but occasionally absent. Great Barrier Reef form shown in the photograph. Mainly outer reef crests and oceanic location with thick branching coral heads. Maximum length 9 cm.

One-spot Puller *Chromis hypsilepis*

Overall bluish or greenish grey, white saddle-like spot on caudal peduncle, and black pectoral-fin base. However, shows great variation when breeding, from very pale grey to almost black, or with bright yellow on head and fins. Gathers in great numbers to spawn, covering large rock-faces with pinkish eggs. Coastal to offshore reefs, usually in deep water where schooling. Maximum length 15 cm.

Black-head Puller *Chromis klunzingeri*

Easily identified by unusual colouration for the genus, with a combination of white body, yellow top and black face. Small juveniles very pale. Limited west coast distribution. Forms small to large groups, rising from reefs to feed on zooplankton. Clear coastal waters to 40 m depth. Maximum length 12 cm.

White Damsel

Spiny-tail Puller (common form)

Spiny-tail Puller (male, guarding babies)

Spiny-tail Puller (juveniles schooling)

ick's Damsel

Johnston's Damsel

ne-spot Puller

Black-head Puller

257

Yellow-back Puller *Chromis nitida*

Easily identified by long white body and black stripe from eye to first soft dorsal ray with greenish to bright yellow above. Juvenile similar to adult. Coastal and inner reefs, including rocky estuaries in current channels, forming small to large schools feeding on zooplankton close to shelter. Maximum length 9 cm.

Half-and-Half Puller *Chromis margaritifer*

Several similar species with black body and white tail, but only one in Australian waters. Small juveniles have proportionally much larger white area than adults. Coastal to outer reefs, including rocky estuaries, very shallow to about 25 m depth, staying close to reef in the vicinity of narrow ledges or small caves. Maximum length 75 mm.

Green Puller *Chromis viridis*

Uniformly pale silvery green, except during spawning period when males may turn golden yellow. Schools, often forming very large aggregations, rising above reef and sometimes filling water column in countless numbers to feed on zooplankton on outgoing tides. Reef crests with large masses of dense branching corals that will accommodate numerous individuals. Maximum length 8 cm.

Blue-green Puller *Chromis atripectoralis*

Very similar and often mistaken for Green Puller (previous species), but has black spot on pectoral-fin base, and adults with blue-centred scales and blue line on snout. Coastal and inner reef crests, forming small to moderately large schools, latter mainly during spawning period, feeding close to substrate on zooplankton. Maximum length 10 cm.

Blue-headed Damsel *Chrysiptera rollandi*

Body creamy white to yellow with black top, shading to pale blue below head and chest. Small juveniles white with blue on top. Clear coastal to outer reef slopes an drop-offs, usually solitary on rubble patches with small dug-out holes under large pieces. Small species, maximum length 75 mm, usually 50 mm.

Talbot's Damsel *Chrysiptera talboti*

Distinct with bright yellow top and ventral fins with grey body, and large black spot in soft dorsal fin. Clear coastal to outer reef crest channels leading to deep slopes or drop-offs, solitary on rubble substrate. Small species, maximum length 60 mm, usually 45 mm.

ellow-back Puller

Half-and-Half Puller

reen Puller

Blue-green Puller

ue-headed Damsel

Talbot's Damsel

259

Pink Damsel *Chrysiptera rex*

Juveniles deep pink with bluish top, adults paler with bluish head and small spots developing on scales, forming a series along scale rows. Solitary, clear coastal to outer reef lagoons, often in surge channels. Maximum length 60 mm.

Surge Damsel *Chrysiptera leucopoma*

Two very different forms as adult: one banded, as in the photograph, and the other yellow to orange fish with iridescent blue stripes from tip of snout to black spot in soft dorsal fin. Usually both forms in the vicinity of each other. Juveniles similar to non-banded form. Typically on shallow rock reef-flats exposed to strong surge, usually numerous individuals spread over large area. Maximum length 70 mm.

Sky-blue Damsel *Chrysiptera cyanea*

Several geographical variations. Generally bright blue with tiny white spots on body scales and over head, and short black stripe from tip of snout over eye. Some populations with orange marking. Photograph shows typical male on the Great Barrier Reef, but females there lack orange. Shallow reef-flats and lagoons, usually in small loose aggregations. Maximum length 85 mm.

Blue Damsel *Pomacentrus coelestis*

Body bright blue and median fins variable yellow, but caudal fin always yellow. In sunlight iridescent blue. Probably most common and widespread blue damsel, often in small groups or in large numbers spread over reef sections. Shallow rubble zones along reef margins on open substrate. Juveniles also known as Neon Damsel. Maximum length 10 cm, usually 85 mm.

Australian Damsel *Pomacentrus australis*

Adults highly variable according to habitat. Drab dusky with blue scale centres in muddy estuaries, to almost white with dusky upper half on clear coastal reefs. Juveniles dark with bright blue spots and scribbles on scales and face. Adult photographed off Keppel Island, Queensland, and juvenile in Sydney Harbour. Singly or small loose aggregations sharing suitable habitat such as a small boulder section in shallow water. Maximum length 10 cm.

ink Damsel

Surge Damsel

ky-blue Damsel

Blue Damsel

stralian Damsel (adult)

Australian Damsel (juvenile)

261

Fire Damsel *Pomacentrus bankanensis*

Small juveniles bright orange-red over back with several thin iridescent blue lines, and blue-edged black ocellus on soft dorsal fin. Caudal fin white at base. Adults lose orange and are dusky over top, but ocellus partially remains. Similar species, White-tail Damsel *P. chrysurus,* lacks blue lines when juveniles and adult dark without ocellus, tail all white. Clear coastal to outer reef crests. Maximum length 85 mm.

Yellow Damsel *Pomacentrus moluccensis*

Bright yellow to almost orange. Small juveniles with white-edged black ocellus in soft dorsal fin. Almost identical to Ambon Damsel *P. amboinensis,* which has similar distribution, usually duller yellow and retains ocellus as adult. Coastal, often silty reefs, usually in small aggregations with mixed coral and algae growth. Maximum length 80 mm.

Half-moon Damsel *Neopomacentrus bankieri*

Genus with several very similar, usually drab, species with yellow or orange posteriorly on body, and variably onto fins. *N. bankieri* with yellow or orange on caudal fin and posterior parts of dorsal and anal fins. Common estuarine and coastal species in sheltered bays. Yellow-tail Damsel *N. azysron* in clearer coastal and inner reef waters. It lacks yellow or orange in anal fin and has a black ear-like spot at origin of lateral line. Both species, maximum length 75 mm.

Short-head Damsel *Amblypomacentrus breviceps*

White with black band over eye and two broad dark saddles over back, sides yellowish or dusky below. Adults develop long caudal fin filaments at tips. Mainly coastal muddy slopes near deep water. Singly or in small loose aggregations. Small juveniles form small schools, often swimming in protection of *Cerianthus* anemones. Maximum length 85 mm (excluding filaments).

Roaming Damsel *Pristotis obtusirostris*

Adults grey with numerous blue spots on scales and head and thin blue lines in fins. Small juveniles pale silvery blue. Unusual among damsels in behaviour, as normally swims openly over sandy substrate without showing any signs of retreating to reefs or coverage as others do. Occurs in small aggregations, but male may be left to guard eggs which are deposited in something hollow such as large shells, half-coconuts or even plastic pipes which also provide shelter for the male if needed. Maximum length 12 cm.

Humbug *Dascyllus aruanus*

White with 3 black bands, no black on caudal fin. Tiny juveniles almost black with little white showing, but soon develop bands with growth. Common species in lagoons and shallow protected bays, forming small to large groups depending on size of coral head for shelter. Rises above coral to feed on zooplankton when currents are running. Maximum length 8 cm.

Fire Damsel

Yellow Damsel

Half-moon Damsel

Short-head Damsel

Roaming Damsel

Humbug

263

Black-tail Humbug *Dascyllus melanurus*

Often overlooked because of close resemblance to Humbug (previous species), but posterior part of caudal fin black and black bands vertical over head versus pale caudal fin and angular headband. Occasionally similar species mix, but usually form own individual groups in protected very shallow depths on clear coastal to outer reef-flats in corals. Maximum length 8 cm.

Headband Humbug *Dascyllus reticulatus*

Variable grey to white, black stripe from dorsal-fin origin, over pectoral-fin base to ventral fins which may fade in large adults, as shown in the photograph. During spawning, complete head may turn black. Mainly coastal reefs in deeper parts of lagoons, forming small to large aggregations, often of mixed sizes. Maximum length 8 cm.

Three-spot Dascyllus *Dascyllus trimaculatus*

Small juveniles jet black, white spot on nape and centrally on side on lateral line. Large individuals may turn grey with white spots greatly reduced or indistinct. Shallow protected coastal bays to deep inner reefs on slopes and in lagoons. Juveniles often with large anemones, forming small to large aggregations, or among spines of long-spined urchins. Adults usually pair. Maximum length 12 cm.

Black Anemonefish *Amphiprion melanopus*

Red face, orange dorsal and yellow caudal fins; in Australia, sometimes lacks white band. Associates with anemone *Entacmaea quadricolor* in Australia, often in large numbers where anemones proliferate. Shallow semi-exposed reef crests. Several very similarly coloured species with single white headband, most outside Australia. *A. mccullochi* mostly black, restricted to Lord Howe and Norfolk Island region; and *A. rubrocinctus*, with orange anal fin, restricted to north-western Australia. Maximum length 11 cm.

Clark's Anemonefish *Amphiprion clarkii*

Extremely variable in body and fin colours, with different combinations in different areas and with different host anemone. Body orange to black, Australian form usually black with orange below, and with yellow to orange caudal fin, with or without white band over base of fin. Associated with various host anemones, usually in pairs. Various habitats from shallow coastal bays to deep offshore along drop-offs where anemones can be found. Maximum length 14 cm.

Orange-fin Anemonefish *Amphiprion chrysopterus*

Yellow or orange dorsal and usually bright orange pectoral fins, and orange snout. Usually in pairs with various host anemones on outer reef crests in more oceanic locations. Small Three-spot Dascyllus in photograph sharing host. Very similar to Clark's Anemonefish (previous species) and much rarer in Australian waters. Maximum length 14 cm.

Black-tail Humbug

Headband Humbug

Three-spot Dascyllus

Black Anemonefish

Clark's Anemonefish

Orange-fin Anemonefish

Barrier Reef Anemonefish *Amphiprion akindynos*

Plain brownish with light snout and 2 white bars. Common Great Barrier Reef species living with various host anemones, ranging from shallow lagoons to deep outer reef areas to about 25 m depth. Adults usually in pairs, and often with juveniles sharing anemone. Maximum length 11 cm.

Eastern Clown Anemonefish *Amphiprion percula*

Usually bright orange with white bands. New Guinea populations often black between first and second white bands. Shallow reef crests and slopes with several host anemones. Almost identical Western Clown Anemonefish (next species) replaces its eastern cousin in northern Australia and eastern New Guinea. Maximum length 8 cm.

Western Clown Anemonefish *Amphiprion ocellaris*

Usually bright orange with white bands. Some geographical variations, including black variety from Darwin area and in Andaman Sea with broader white areas. Aberrant forms with unusual patterns are not uncommon and often on one side only. Variety of habitats and host anemones, from coastal protected shallow bays to moderate depths in outer reef lagoons or inner reef slopes. Usually in small to large aggregations of mixed sizes where anemones proliferate on reef sections. Very common throughout range and often seen in aquarium trade. Maximum length 8 cm.

Skunk Anemonefish *Amphiprion sandaracinos*

Orange-brown with thick white band over top from tip of snout to caudal peduncle. Easily identified; only similar species in the Indian Ocean, outside Australian waters. Coastal protected reefs, usually just below crests or on deeper parts of slope and often at base of short drop. Adults in pairs, but anemone often shared by small individuals. Maximum length 12 cm.

Pink Anemonefish *Amphiprion perideraion*

Similar to Skunk Anemonefish (previous species), but has white headband and the white line over top of head much narrower. Coastal and inner reefs on slopes and in lagoons. Usually numerous pairs in reef sections where host anemones proliferate. Maximum length 10 cm.

Spine-cheek Anemonefish *Premnas biaculeatus*

Monotypic, genus characterised by large spine on cheek, crossing white band if complete, and clearly visible on adults. Variable from bright red to dark brown with 3 narrow white bands, usually encircling body and occasionally short. Nearly always in pairs, and typically large female with small male together. In some areas, particularly Indonesia, the female is dark brown and the male red. On the Great Barrier Reef both usually bright orange to red, as shown in the photographs. Protected coastal bays to inner reef lagoons, associating only with the host anemone *Entacmaea quadricolor*. Maximum length 15 cm.

Barrier Reef Anemonefish

Eastern Clown Anemonefish

Western Clown Anemonefish (normal colour)

Western Clown Anemonefish (Darwin area)

Skunk Anemonefish

Pink Anemonefish

Spine-cheek Anemonefish

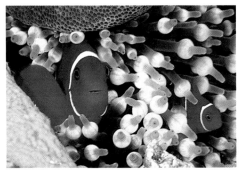

Spine-cheek Anemonefish (pair)

267

WRASSES — LABRIDAE

One of the largest families, more than 60 genera and 400+ species worldwide, many recently discovered and awaiting description, about half of genera and species in Australian waters. Highly diverse and several subfamilies, but species combined in this book as groups of species known to be closely related or similar. Some groups are easily defined by external characteristics, such as lateral line continuous or interrupted into 2 parts, or number of dorsal fin spines. Other characteristics often internal or less obvious, such as number of branchiostegal rays or dentition, and difficult to use without close examination. Most have elongated bodies, a terminal mouth and usually thick lips, protruding canine teeth, and cycloid scales covering body, often extending onto fins and most of head. Colour can vary greatly between juveniles and adults, or between sexes, to such an extent that they can easily be mistaken for different species. Juveniles become usually female first, and males derive from females. Adults which at some stage may be either sex are referred to as initial phase (IP), but males differently coloured, usually very bright, are referred to as terminal phase (TP). Most males territorial and dominate over number of females distributed over section of reef, aggressively guarding from neighbouring males. Males are usually largest, and if male falls victim to predator the next-largest female changes sex and takes over the role of dominant male. Wrasses are carnivorous; diet includes benthic invertebrates, small fishes, zooplankton, and some specialised feeders take parasites from other fishes. Mostly reef-dwellers and all species diurnal, sleeping in crevices or by burying themselves in sandy substrates, depending on group, and normally live shallow but a few known from trawls in depths of 100+ m. Sizes also vary greatly, with the smallest a few centimetres long and the largest over 2 m.

Eastern Blue Groper *Achoerodus viridis*

Males grey to blue, bright blue in sunlight in shallow depths when seen from above. Pattern of radiating blue and orange lines from eyes at stages from larger juveniles to adults. Small juveniles green, changing to brown; large females reddish brown, lighter below and small series of pale blotches along sides. Juveniles up to about 10 cm long in green seagrasses, then moving to vegetated rock-reef, changing colour to suit habitat. Large adults venture over large reef sections, males sometimes entering very shallow depths. Estuaries and offshore to at least 40 m depth. Maximum length 1.2 m.

Western Blue Groper *Achoerodus gouldii*

Large males vary between green and blue. Eyes bright blue and no lines radiating from eyes as in similar eastern cousin (previous species), but females bright green and no series of pale blotches. The 2 species may intermittently overlap in range in Victoria. Juveniles in estuaries and sheltered bays in seagrasses and weeds, moving out with increasing size to coastal and offshore locations to depths of at least 40 m. Maximum length 1.6 m.

Pigfish *Bodianus unimaculatus*

Females pinkish above with thin brown to red lines along scale rows, 2 lines diverting behind eye which continue as a series of brown to red elongated blotches. Male with large pale area below soft dorsal fin and black blotch centrally along base of dorsal fin. Offshore reefs, usually seen in depths of 30 m or more near rocky drop-offs but commonly caught on fishing lines in about 50 m depth. Maximum length 45 cm.

Saddle-back Hogfish *Bodianus bilunulatus*

Adults with large black blotch below soft dorsal fin extending onto caudal peduncle, but overall colour highly variable from almost white to bright red, and with or without dark streaks over head. Small juveniles completely different, with broad black posterior band and bright yellow over top of head to spinous dorsal fin. Mainly on slopes along base of deep drop-offs. Reported maximum length 55 cm, usually 35 cm.

Eastern Blue Groper (male)

Eastern Blue Groper (female)

Eastern Blue Groper (juvenile)

Western Blue Groper (male)

Western Blue Groper (female)

Pigfish

Saddle-back Hogfish (adult)

Saddle-back Hogfish (juvenile)

269

Eclipse Hogfish *Bodianus loxozonus*

Similar to Saddle-back Hogfish (previous species), but black blotch extends from base of soft dorsal fin over body at angle along lower caudal fin to corner. Ventral fins and anterior margin of anal fin also black. Outer reef species, usually seen on deeper part of reef crests swimming well above substrate, sometimes showing curiosity towards divers. Maximum length 40 cm.

Pacific Diana's Hogfish *Bodianus* sp.

Adults pale to brown or red above with a few pale spots along upper sides. Juveniles brown with a series of white spots and dashes, and large black spots in dorsal, anal and ventral fins. Small juveniles form groups when common, under ledges and overhangs along deep drop-offs, usually swimming upside down. Adults usually seen solitary in various reef habitats, but mostly where large soft corals grow and proliferate. In process of being renamed; until recently, confused with Indian Diana's Hogfish *B. diana*, which differs in colour. Maximum length 15 cm.

Coral Hogfish *Bodianus axillaris*

Adults mainly brown to dusky anteriorly and white posteriorly, black spot in soft dorsal fin and in anal fin opposite. Juveniles are easily identified by black overall colour, white snout and normally 8 large white spots distributed evenly from head to caudal-fin base. Similar juvenile Black-belt Hogfish (next species) has yellow spots. Coastal to outer reefs, juveniles in ledges and caves, often observed cleaning other fishes, usually deep in 20+ m, but sometimes in rocky estuaries as juvenile or on outer reef crests as adult. Maximum length 20 cm.

Black-belt Hogfish *Bodianus mesothorax*

Lack black spots in fins, anterior body brown, separated by broad black band from pale posterior part, though the latter feature may become indistinct in large individuals, and fins yellow. Juveniles spotted like Coral Hogfish (previous species), spots yellow. Clear coastal to outer reefs. Only one juvenile known to the author, from Sydney Harbour (Camp Cove). Maximum length 20 cm.

Eclipse Hogfish

Pacific Diana's Hogfish

Coral Hogfish (male)

Coral Hogfish (juvenile)

Black-belt Hogfish (male)

Black-belt Hogfish (juvenile)

Grass Tuskfish *Choerodon cephalotes*

Small juveniles with 2 black spots on side which enlarge with growth into blotches until joining in adults. Large males have enlarged head with blue stripes over snout to above eyes, thickening with age until interspaces reduce to yellow scribbling. Coastal to inner reefs in shallow weed zones, young often in rocky estuaries among weeds. Juvenile photographed at Camp Cove, Sydney Harbour. Adults in small loose aggregations with a large male in charge. Replaced by similar-shaped Baldchin Groper *C. rubescens* on the west coast, readily recognised by startling white below head from mouth to chest, and growing much larger. Maximum length Baldchin Groper 90 cm and Grass Tuskfish 38 cm.

Venus Tuskfish *Choerodon venustus*

Small juveniles light brown with large round dark spot posteriorly on sides which proportionally reduces and fades with age; blue spot develops on each scale and general colour changes gradually to pinkish or reddish until adult. Juveniles sometimes with large red blotch on sides and bright red eyes. Coastal shallow weedy reefs to moderate depths in sponge–algae mixed reef. Small juveniles in rocky kelp habitat (Sydney Harbour); adults in groups distributed broadly over large areas. Maximum length 50 cm.

White-belly Tuskfish *Choerodon anchorago*

Variable, usually white below from chin to caudal peduncle and greenish grey above, white area rising high behind pectoral fin and large white saddle on caudal peduncle. Juveniles white below, greenish brown above, with several thin pale vertical lines across. Coastal, often silty habitat on reef crests and slopes with algae and soft coral growth; small juveniles in seagrass beds near mangrove or freshwater run-offs. Maximum length 35 cm.

Blue Tuskfish *Choerodon cyanodus*

Variable from yellow-green to blue-green, with large white spot high on body just below soft dorsal fin, and large individuals with dusky saddles anteriorly. Shallow, often in groups intertidally, coastal and inner reefs. Shy underwater and usually a single large individual may come in close to investigate an intruder in its territory. Maximum length 60 cm.

Dagger Tuskfish *Choerodon jordani*

Slender species, white below, greyish above, easily identified by distinct white body and black marking posteriorly on upper sides. Juveniles and adults almost identical. Usually in depths of 20+ m on rubble slopes below drop-offs, singly or in small loose aggregations. Smallest tuskfish, maximum length 17 cm.

272

Grass Tuskfish (adult)

Grass Tuskfish (juvenile)

enus Tuskfish

White-belly Tuskfish

ue Tuskfish

Dagger Tuskfish

273

Black-stripe Tuskfish *Choerodon vitta*

Distinctly coloured species with broad black lateral stripe and yellow cheek. Juveniles with black spot on caudal peduncle. Stripe fades in large males, which has blue angular bar over cheek. Inshore in sheltered bays or behind outer reefs over sandflats in small groups. Particularly common on the southern Great Barrier Reef in coastal waters. Maximum length 20 cm.

Harlequin Tuskfish *Choerodon fasciatus*

Adults easily identified by red barring over head and body. Small juveniles with brown banding and several black ocelli in dorsal and anal fins. Coastal in outer reef lagoons. Adults usually in small loose aggregations in large caves, overhangs or on rubble slopes; juveniles solitary along reef channel walls. Maximum length 25 cm.

White-dotted Maori *Cheilinus chlorourus*

Variable, mostly brownish, with several white saddles over back and a series of white dots along scale rows. White dots less distinct in large males, which develop long lobes on caudal fin and small red dots over head, as shown in the photograph. Clear coastal reefs and sand lagoons inside outer reef areas. Maximum length 35cm.

Triple-tail Maori *Cheilinus trilobatus*

Similar and closely related to White-dotted Maori (previous species), but with vertical lines instead of dots on scales, forming patterns of thin vertical lines of various colours depending of size and sex. Juveniles and females with alternating light and dark broad banding, on caudal fin usually darkest. Large males with numerous scribbles and tiny pink spots on greenish head, as shown in the photograph. Coastal reef-flats and slopes, often in silty conditions. Maximum length 40 cm.

Banded Maori *Cheilinus fasciatus*

Distinctly banded pattern at all stages. Adults with broad orange to red area behind greenish head, and thin orange to red lines radiating from eyes. Small juveniles greyish brown with white barring, similar to juvenile *Epibulus* spp. and adult *Wetmorella* spp. Coastal to outer reefs, usually along reef margins to sand or along base of short drop-offs on rubble substrate. Juveniles secretive in corals; adults swim about openly. Maximum length 35 cm.

Black-stripe Tuskfish

Harlequin Tuskfish

White-dotted Maori

Triple-tail Maori

Banded Maori (male)

Banded Maori (juvenile)

275

Little Maori *Cheilinus bimaculatus*

Highly variable according to habitat. Greenish in seagrass beds, and orange to red on shallow to deep reefs respectively. Juveniles with small black spot on side, adults with indistinct broad midlateral dark stripe, male with several filamentous caudal fin rays. Probably the most widespread Maori Wrasse and in almost every habitat, from seagrass beds and rocky estuaries to deep offshore reefs. Smallest species, maximum length 15 cm, extra filaments 1–2 cm long.

Slingjaw Wrasse *Epibulus insidiator*

Colour variable between various stages. Best recognised by shape and unusual mouth which is extremely protractile and when in non-feeding mode extends back to below pectoral-fin base. Juveniles and females either dusky with small yellow spot midway along base of spinous dorsal fin or completely bright yellow. Males with grey head, a black line behind eye, and orange or yellow over back with dark side below. Small juveniles very similar to adult *Wetmorella* spp. Long jaw is used to suck up prey such as crustaceans and small fishes. Coastal to outer reef habitat, usually solitary on invertebrate-rich slopes with ledges. Maximum length 35 cm, usually 25 cm.

Cockerel Wrasse *Pteragogus enneacanthus*

Highly variable, matching habitat: green in algae habitat to reddish brown in hydroids or soft corals. Juveniles usually with eye-sized ocellus on gill cover, but intermittent in adults. Males with first few dorsal fin spines slightly extended and pale lines along scale rows on sides. Genus comprises several similar species with either 9 or 10 dorsal fin spines. Combination of colour and having 9 dorsal spines identifies this species. Various habitats from coastal weedy rocky reefs to reef crests among hydroids in shallows, or soft corals and sponges when deep. Maximum length 15 cm.

Sneaky Wrasse *Pteragogus cryptus*

Brown to bright red, ocellus on gill cover when young and white ventral fin with broad central brown to red band. Differs morphologically from Cockerel Wrasse (previous species) in having 10 dorsal fin spines. Clear coastal to outer reef slopes, secretive among rich coral and algal growth, usually along reef margins with coral head outcrops on rubble sand with soft corals or hydroids on top. Swims close to substrate and occasionally observed when moving between feeding sites. Originally described from the Red Sea, doubtfully the same as the Pacific species. Maximum length 85 mm.

Little Maori

Slingjaw Wrasse (male)

Slingjaw Wrasse (yellow form)

Slingjaw Wrasse (juvenile)

Cockerel Wrasse (male)

Cockerel Wrasse (juvenile)

Sneaky Wrasse (male)

Sneaky Wrasse (juvenile)

277

Six-line Wrasse *Pseudocheilinus hexataenia*

Adults lavender-pink with 6 evenly spaced orange longitudinal stripes, arranged as 3 double stripes with dark-blue interspaces; numerous tiny yellow spots on cheek; and caudal fin light to bright green. Juveniles with blue-edged black ocellus on upper caudal-fin base. Shallow, rich coral habitats, secretive in reefs but often noticed by observant divers. Maximum length 85 mm, usually 65 mm.

Eight-line Wrasse *Pseudocheilinus octotaenia*

Variable pale brown to yellow with thin brown to red longitudinal lines, large individuals with fine yellow spotting on face and median fins and large yellow blotches in series alternating along lines. Clear coastal to outer reefs, usually along drop-offs or slopes in ledges or caves. Maximum length 12 cm.

Pin-striped Wrasse *Pseudocheilinus evanidus*

Pale pinkish brown to orange with numerous thin, light yellow longitudinal lines, dusky snout with red tip and pale streak along cheek. Occasionally with faint broad banding. Clear coastal to outer reef slopes in mixed algae–coral habitat. Maximum length 8 cm.

Yellow-banded Possum-wrasse *Wetmorella nigropinnata*

Pale reddish brown to dusky brown, adults with yellow band over head, just behind eye, and over caudal peduncle between last dorsal and anal fin rays, white tip on snout and large black spots in ventral, soft dorsal and anal fins. Juveniles with additional white banding and yellow-edged black ocelli in soft dorsal and anal fins. Coastal to outer reefs, typically in the back of caves or overhangs along drop-offs in dark areas, slowly moving along in search of tiny invertebrates. Common, but due to small size and secretive nature they are only seen by the most observant divers, especially when using lights in caves as many photographers do. Maximum length 8 cm, usually 65 mm.

White-banded Possum-wrasse *Wetmorella albofasciata*

Similar to juvenile of Yellow-banded Possum-wrasse (previous species), but dorsal and anal fin ocelli white-edged and caudal fin white-tipped and second body band at angle, running from posterior edge of dorsal-fin ocellus to anterior edge of anal-fin ocellus. Juvenile similar to adult. Mainly along outer reef drop-offs and usually in depths of 20+ m. Maximum length 55 mm.

Six-line Wrasse

Eight-line Wrasse

Pin-striped Wrasse

Yellow-banded Possum-wrasse (male)

Yellow-banded Possum-wrasse (juvenile)

White-banded Possum-wrasse

Half-and-Half Wrasse *Hemigymnus melapterus*

Several colour phases between small and large juveniles, and between sexes. Juveniles to about 40 mm greenish with greenish white head, thick white band from dorsal-fin origin to belly, and broad dusky bands over rest of body. Gradually changes to greenish black with yellow tail until nearly adult-size. Adults develop very thick lips, still show half-and-half pattern but paler; scales with iridescent green spots, vertical barring and black edging, and caudal fin dusky with iridescent green spot basally and longitudinal lines posteriorly. Males dusky over head, mixed with green and orange lines. Behaviour changes with different phases. Tiny juveniles settle among long spines of urchins or swim close to substrate among other stinging invertebrates for protection. Next phase more daring on open reef, but wary, quickly seeking cover when approached. Large adults occur openly along reef slopes and drop-offs, often in small aggregations. Also known as Thicklip Wrasse or Black-eyed Thicklip, the latter in reference to black eyes after death. Maximum length reported to 90 cm, usually 50 cm.

Banded Thicklip *Hemigymnus fasciatus*

Several colour phases between small and large juveniles, and differences between sexes. Juveniles slightly elongate, deepening with age; to about 40 mm length greenish above and dusky below with about 5 thin white bars evenly spaced along body; then changing to black with white bars, head pale with orange to pink spotting and lines, and caudal fin yellowish to dusky. Large adults deep-bodied and lips very thick, broad pink bands passing below eye from upper snout to posterior gill margin. Males during display show large black blotch on lower cheek and turn white over back. Small juveniles secretive in narrow ledges in protected coastal waters, often near sea urchins. Adults openly on deep slopes and drop-offs, singly or in loose aggregations. Reported maximum length 75 cm, usually 40 cm.

Crimson-banded Wrasse *Notolabrus gymnogenis*

Various different stages, gradually changing with growth. Juveniles green to brown with irregular white spots, sometimes forming a series and as white streaks from behind eye, continuing along most of body just below lateral line. Adult female greenish grey to brown or red with numerous white spots. The male is completely different, with dusky body, pale cheek, red bar posteriorly on body, red dorsal and anal fins and white tail. Rocky shallow estuaries, coastal to reefs offshore to at least 40 m depth. Juveniles singly and secretively in algae-rich reefs; adults in small loose aggregations with several females and a single male distributed over reef sections. Maximum length 40 cm.

Half-and-Half Wrasse (male)

Banded Thicklip (male)

Half-and-Half Wrasse (intermediate)

Banded Thicklip (intermediate)

Half-and-Half Wrasse (juvenile)

Banded Thicklip (juvenile)

Crimson-banded Wrasse (male)

Crimson-banded Wrasse (female)

Blue-throat Wrasse *Notolabrus tetricus*

Different growth stages. Young similar to Crimson-banded Wrasse (previous species), females with broad black band vertically above belly with pale area behind. Males very different and easily recognised by dusky to reddish brown body with broad white band across middle, and yellow ventral and caudal fins. Juveniles secretive in shallow protected mixed rock–weed reef habitat, commonly under jetties, forming small aggregations when large enough to be venturous. Large adults mainly in deeper parts of bays and known from depths to 160 m offshore. Maximum length 60 cm.

Orange-spotted Wrasse *Notolabrus parilus*

Juveniles and females very similar to Blue-throat Wrasse (previous species) with large individuals showing orange spots along upper sides. Males mainly dusky and white ventrally; broad white streak just below lateral line from above belly to caudal-fin base; head plain but dark parts of body with numerous tiny yellow to orange spots. Juveniles in shallow weed and seagrass areas. Adults on rocky reefs, but mostly seen in densely vegetated areas with kelp and sargassum weeds to depths of about 20 m. Occurrence in Victoria rare and probably intermittent, depending on larval stages drifting in from western waters. Maximum length 32 cm

Red-band Wrasse *Pseudolabrus biserialis*

Variable from grey-brown to red, with white streak passing below eye from snout to caudal-fin base. Juveniles and females with a series of black spots along upper sides. Males usually with wavy red line along white lower body and bright red anal fin. Clear coastal reefs and offshore on algae-covered reefs among boulders, along ledges and sometimes under jetties. Maximum length 21 cm.

Gunther's Wrasse *Pseudolabrus guentheri*

Closely related to Red-band Wrasse (previous species), juveniles and females with similar patterns, including a series of black spots along upper sides. Variable from mainly green or brownish red colour according to habitat and depth. Coastal, often silty habitat to offshore weedy reefs to 20 m depth. Maximum length 18 cm.

Blue-throat Wrasse (male)

Blue-throat Wrasse (female)

Orange-spotted Wrasse (male)

Orange-spotted Wrasse (female)

Red-band Wrasse

Gunther's Wrasse

Luculentus Wrasse *Pseudolabrus luculentus*

Highly variable from almost grey to brown to bright orange and red-brown. Juveniles and females with distinct thin white dashes on lower body, almost forming lines on belly, and several white streaks along cheek below eye. Males with distinct series of alternating white and black spots posteriorly along dorsal-fin base. Clear coastal to offshore reefs at moderate depths, usually along bases of drop-offs or on sloping boulder zones in depths of 10–50 m. Maximum length 20 cm.

Senator Wrasse *Pictilabrus laticlavius*

Distinct green to reddish brown species with purplish longitudinal bands along centre and lower body, juveniles with small blue spots and distinct black spot along base of soft dorsal fin. Rocky estuaries and coastal reefs in weedy habitat. A similar second species in the genus discovered by the author in 1978, False Senator Wrasse *P. viridis*, is green above and broad brown bands below, restricted to the south-west coast in shallow surge zones. Maximum length of Senator Wrasse 25 cm, False Senator Wrasse 14.5 cm.

Black-spotted Wrasse *Austrolabrus maculatus*

Pinkish to yellowish brown above and lighter below, irregular series of pupil-sized black spots or short vertical dashes along upper side of body. Black saddle on caudal peduncle with white in front and behind, which fades or reduces to small black spot in males. Clear coastal to deep offshore reefs in algae or sponge habitat. Maximum length 20 cm.

Pretty Polly *Dotalabrus aurantiacus*

Extremely variable between habitats, from almost black with bluish grey markings to bright yellow-green with or without black markings. Juveniles pale grey with about 4 black bars and white-edged black ocelli posteriorly on base of dorsal and anal fins. Strongly associated with weeds and seagrass beds in coastal bays. Maximum length 14 cm.

Snake-skin Wrasse *Eupetrichthys angustipes*

Variable from grey to brown. Juveniles usually dusky along upper half and pale along lower half of body, with more-or-less distinct broad banding. Males greenish grey along upper half, and banding on body more distinct. Shallow coastal bays to deep offshore, most rocky reef–algae habitats. Maximum length 20 cm (Victoria), usually 15 cm.

Luculentus Wrasse (male)

Luculentus Wrasse (female)

Senator Wrasse

Black-spotted Wrasse

Pretty Polly

Snake-skin Wrasse

Painted Rainbow Wrasse *Suezichthys arquatus*

Slight changes between different stages, but males more colourful and lacking ocelli on upper caudal-fin base and posteriorly on dorsal-fin base which is small in females but very distinct in juveniles. Rocky reefs from shallow estuaries to about 50 m offshore, often in small aggregations. Small juveniles solitary, in small boulder zones or reef margins onto sand. Undescribed sibling in Japan, and similar species in southern Western Australia, *S. cyanolaemus*, with blue on chin. Maximum length 14 cm.

Crimson Cleaner Wrasse *Suezichthys aylingi*

Easily recognised by mostly red body with broad white longitudinal stripe, which in females extends below as lines crossing belly along scale rows, but blue filter effect of water changes red to black or grey according to depth. Mainly in deep coastal to offshore waters along reef margins onto sand, usually in small aggregations. Often observed picking parasites off other fishes, males attending to silvery pelagic species high above substrate. Maximum length 12 cm.

Gracilis Wrasse *Suezichthys devisi*

Juveniles similar to adults. Adults mainly pale, almost white below, with broad brown to red band originating on snout, through eye, continuing along upper side to caudal-fin base. Juveniles with distinct black caudal-fin base spot, males with blue and yellow markings in caudal fin and short angular blue dash crossing dark strip just behind pectoral fin. Rocky estuaries and deep in protected coastal bays on open substrate near reefs. Sibling *S. gracilis* in Japan. Maximum length 14 cm.

Orange-line Wrasse *Halichoeres hartzfeldi*

Bluish grey to green with bright orange band from behind eye to caudal-fin base, ending with black spot when juvenile. Males ornamented with blue and yellow, dusky bar just below lateral line where pectoral fin reaches, and often a series of black spots like buttons lying on top of orange lateral band near caudal peduncle. Open substrate near reefs, often in small aggregations led by colourful male. Maximum length 18 cm.

Zigzag Wrasse *Halichoeres scapularis*

Adults easily recognised by pale body and dark band from behind eye to near end of body with undulating pattern made by pale centres of scales. In juveniles, band has even borders and lighter colour. Coastal mixed sand and reef habitat to outer reef lagoons, singly or in small aggregations. Maximum length 15 cm.

Painted Rainbow Wrasse (male)

Painted Rainbow Wrasse (juvenile)

Crimson Cleaner Wrasse

Gracilis Wrasse

Orange-line Wrasse

Zigzag Wrasse

287

Three-spot Wrasse *Halichoeres trimaculatus*

Overall colour very plain. Juveniles and females light greenish white with just a dark spot on caudal-fin base. Males with additional pink lines and spot on head and anteriorly on body, and yellow caudal fin. Coastal shallow sandy habitats along reef margins or in lagoons, usually forming small aggregations. Maximum length 20 cm.

Checkerboard Wrasse *Halichoeres hortulanus*

Various colour phases with age, but sexes similar. Small juveniles black and white with yellow-edged black ocellus centrally in dorsal fin. Adults pale greenish grey with pink longitudinal stripes over head breaking into spots where extending onto body, black scale outlines over upper sides, and two small yellow saddles immediately below dorsal-fin base on upper sides. The Indian Ocean form has a single yellow saddle and black spot centrally on caudal-fin base. Juveniles secretive on rubble patches below large ledges, venturing out more and more with increasing size; adults occur openly over reef crests and slopes. Maximum length 25 cm.

Hoeven's Wrasse *Halichoeres melanurus*

Males with green body, orange to red lines, thickening over head but breaking up over body with age, blue snout and yellow blotch around pectoral-fin base, often with black blotch or streak immediately behind. One of a group of very similar species of which females are nearly identical, all with alternating thin orange to yellow and green to blue-green longitudinal lines, and several blue-edged black ocelli in dorsal and base of caudal fins. Except for siblings, males with different patterns, especially on head. Commonly occurs in coastal bays and estuaries to sheltered outer reef habitat on reef crests and slopes in small aggregations. Replaced by sibling *H. vrolikii* in the Indian Ocean. Maximum length 10 cm.

Dusky Wrasse *Halichoeres marginatus*

Large males ornamented with metallic green, blue and yellow, spotted fins, and lines over head continuing along scale rows over body. Juveniles and females with dusky brown lines over head and body along scale rows with narrow pale interspaces. Small juveniles with a few small white spots and large white-edged black ocellus centrally on dorsal fin. Shallow rocky and coral reef slopes, mainly inshore. Maximum length 17 cm.

Three-spot Wrasse

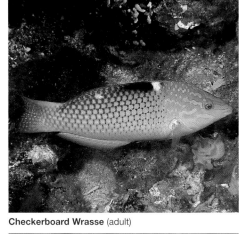

Checkerboard Wrasse (adult)

Checkerboard Wrasse (juvenile)

Hoeven's Wrasse (male)

Hoeven's Wrasse (juvenile)

Dusky Wrasse

289

Cheek-ring Wrasse *Halichoeres miniatus*

One of 3 common and very similar species in the west Pacific. Males with diagnostic cheek patterns: *H. miniatus* with circle; Pearly Wrasse *H. margaritaceus* with horizontal line; and Clouded Wrasse *H. nebulosus* with angling down line. Juveniles all with ocellus centrally in dorsal fin; dark mottling pattern above and light below and often with pink or red on belly. Shallow coastal reef-flats and slopes, usually less than 10 m depth. Maximum length 12 cm in cooler part of range, smaller when more tropical.

Yellow Wrasse *Halichoeres chrysus*

Easily identified by bright yellow colour. Juveniles with several white-edged black ocelli along dorsal fin and upper base of caudal fin. Males with orange lines on head and black anterior dorsal fin spot (small in juveniles) large and obvious. Displaying males typically raise just anterior dorsal-fin section, as shown in the photograph. Usually in small aggregations in clear coastal waters along slopes or on bases of low drop-offs on rubble zones. Maximum length 12 cm.

Brownfields Wrasse *Halichoeres brownfieldi*

Adults bright green above, fading to white below; males develop red midlateral stripe and short red lines along cheek. Juveniles with large blue-centred ocellus at end of dorsal fin, a slightly smaller one at centre, and smallest on caudal-fin base. Clear coastal reef margins and seagrass beds: small juveniles secretive and solitary in protected reefs; large juveniles and adults forming small to moderately large groups, especially over seagrass beds. To depths of about 30 m. Maximum length 15 cm.

Choat's Wrasse *Macropharyngodon choati*

Small juveniles white with large orange blotches and anterior part of dorsal fin coloured as mirror image of ventral fin, with clear membranes following. Orange blotches become more numerous with growth. Colour in males almost solid over top of head, stripes along cheek, and green and yellow mark at short distance behind eye. Coastal to protected inner reef habitat, from shallow algae reef to deep on rubble slopes at bases of deep drop-offs. Common on the southern Great Barrier Reef in coastal waters where forming small aggregations on algal reefs. Maximum length 11 cm.

Western Leopard Wrasse *Macropharyngodon ornatus*

Adults pinkish with green stripes on head and bright green-centred scales. Median fins with series of spots, some connecting, forming wavy lines, and red spot heading dorsal fin over upper half of first 2 membranes. Small juveniles greenish with black spots on body, this one with reddish median fins. Clear coastal reefs, usually along reef margins near sand or on rubble reef patches. Almost identical sibling Eastern Leopard Wrasse (next species) has diagnostic spot above pectoral-fin base. Maximum length 11 cm.

Cheek-ring Wrasse

Yellow Wrasse

Brownfields Wrasse (adults)

Brownfields Wrasse (juvenile)

Choat's Wrasse (male)

Choat's Wrasse (juvenile)

Western Leopard Wrasse (male)

Western Leopard Wrasse (juvenile)

Eastern Leopard Wrasse *Macropharyngodon meleagris*

Adults very similar to Western Leopard Wrasse (previous species), but lacks pectoral-fin base spot. Juveniles differ mainly in having yellow median fins. Common east coast species, inhabiting various habitats from rocky estuaries to deep coastal reefs on rubble and boulder margins near sand, small juveniles in algae-reef zones. Adults in small loose aggregations on reef crests or slopes to depths of about 25 m. Maximum length 14 cm (New South Wales), usually 12 cm.

Diamond Wrasse *Anampses caeruleopunctatus*

Several different stages according to age. Small juveniles from almost white to green, brown or black, swimming over sand along reef margins or among boulders with erect fins, and twisting body like floating leaves. Changing at about 40 mm to dusky with blue spots developing in scale centres, and young adults with a series of black-edged blue spots over body and lines over head. Large males with dusky head, blue lips and blue stripe over head between eyes; yellow vertical bar just past pectoral-fin base, bordering dusky area, and scales with vertical thin blue bar. Various habitats from shallow rocky estuaries and protected shallow coastal bays to semi-exposed reefs and outer reef crests. Maximum length 30 cm.

Speckled Wrasse *Anampses meleagrides*

Three distinct phases of development. Juveniles similar to females but with additional large ocelli at each end of dorsal and anal fins. Female almost black, with numerous small white spots over head and body, and with bright yellow caudal fin. Males dark with blue scribbles in various patterns on body, head and fins; caudal fin appears lunate with dusky orange pattern followed by clear part. Clear coastal to outer reef habitat. Juveniles solitary at moderate depths, about 20 m. Adults on reef crests and slopes, usually females in small aggregations with fast-moving male occasionally coming around for inspection, covering a large territory. Two other white-spotted species in the west Pacific, but not known from Australian waters. Maximum length 22 cm.

Blue-tail Wrasse *Anampses femininus*

Easily identified by colour patterns. Males with black head and several thick blue horizontal stripes. Juveniles and females with yellow body with about 7 iridescent blue longitudinal lines, most converging to eye or breaking up into scribble on head, and bright blue tail. Mainly offshore island habitat, small juveniles sometimes in coastal waters, secretive in isolated kelp plants. Adults in moderate depths, usually just below kelp line in small aggregations, taking cover in kelp when approached. Maximum length 16 cm, reported 24 cm elsewhere in the south Pacific.

Eastern Leopard Wrasse (juvenile)

Diamond Wrasse (male)

Diamond Wrasse (juvenile)

Speckled Wrasse (male)

Speckled Wrasse (female)

Blue-tail Wrasse

Black-backed Wrasse *Anampses neoguinaicus*

Generally greenish white with black over back from juvenile to adult stages. Distinct ocelli at end of both dorsal and anal fins of small juveniles reduces proportionally in size with growth; and small in females which has additional ear-spot. Males differ only slightly in lacking ocelli and ear-spot, but has pinkish band banding behind eye, thin blue spot or bars on light-coloured scales, and pink on caudal fin. Inner to outer reefs in rich coral zones, lagoons and rubble slopes. Juveniles at most southern location, Montague Island, in New South Wales, in shallow bays with prolific hard corals growth. Usually in small aggregations. Maximum length 12 cm.

Blue-ribbon Wrasse *Stethojulis trilineata*

Typically for genus, males are completely different from females. Both pictured together, male above with blue lines and female below with numerous white spots. Other members of genus show same degree of difference between the sexes. Juveniles similar to females. Clear coastal to outer reef habitat, usually in small loose aggregations along upper edge of deep drop-offs or over reef crests. Maximum length 14 cm.

Red-spot Wrasse *Stethojulis bandanensis*

Males distinguished from other similar species with distinct red band over top of pectoral-fin base and different blue-line arrangement. Photograph at subtropical Seal Rocks, New South Wales, where adults are still common. Female shows red band over top of pectoral-fin base also, and has series of tiny ocelli along caudal peduncle and yellow dash on snout. Juveniles similar to females, but lack the brighter colours. Shallow semi-exposed rocky reefs in small aggregations, males swimming high above substrate usually hurrying along using pectoral fins. Maximum length 14 cm.

Cut-ribbon Wrasse *Stethojulis interrupta*

More slender than other members of the genus. Midlateral blue line in males discontinuous over area behind pectoral fin. Juveniles and females mainly yellow with tiny light spots over upper half and pale shiny white with dark spots below, separated by thin striations behind pectoral fins. Clear coastal and protected inner reefs, usually in small aggregations and sometimes in large numbers, but not yet seen in numbers compared with Japanese sibling *S. terina* which congregates in densely packed groups comprising up to thousands of individuals. The scientific name *S. interrupta* is used for several geographical forms that occur in the indo-west Pacific that may prove to be good species in their own right. In northern Borneo the female has a yellow stripe on the head and the mid-lateral blue line on the male is continuous from the tip of the snout to the caudal fin. Some large male in Australia develop a series of dark vertical elongated blotches along their sides that look similar to another Japanese species, *S. maculata*. Maximum length 12 cm

Black-backed Wrasse (male)

Black-backed Wrasse (juvenile)

Blue-ribbon Wrasse (male above, female below)

Red-spot Wrasse

Cut-ribbon Wrasse (male)

Cut-ribbon Wrasse (male and females)

Silver-streaked Wrasse *Stethojulis strigiventer*

Females with silver streaks along face and belly and finely spotted above; juveniles similar, but mainly white below. Males with double thin blue line running laterally from snout to along most of body, and pink to orange band above pectoral-fin base. Coastal and inner reefs on shallow, somewhat silty, habitats with prolific algal growth. Maximum length 12 cm.

Pink Wrasse *Pseudocoris yamashiroi*

Juveniles and females light to dark pink to almost orange. Males totally different, with dusky to greenish grey body, abruptly white below, dark streaks along outer caudal-fin margins and first dorsal spine greatly extended. Usually in small groups along current-prone reef slopes in coastal areas, often feeding high above substrate on zooplankton. Juveniles in rocky estuaries, in Sydney mixing with Hulafish which also feed on zooplankton, as shown in the photograph. Maximum length 16 cm.

Maori Wrasse *Ophthalmolepis lineolata*

Monotypic genus. Mostly light to dark brown over top and white below. Small juveniles with light brown or orange ventrally. Large males with thin blue face scribbles, and midlateral stripe with black below white from pectoral-fin base to caudal-fin base. Various habitats from shallow estuaries to deep offshore. Mainly a reef-dweller and often abundant on submerged coastal reefs where caught on lines, but in southern part of range only deep offshore and rarely seen when diving. Maximum length 47 cm.

Comb Wrasse *Coris picta*

Juveniles and females immaculate white with black longitudinal stripe. Females with yellow caudal fin, and lower margin of black stripe becomes irregular, forming a comb-like pattern in large individuals, as shown in the photograph. Males similar but with pink bars across nape, and changes during display by going mostly grey on body except on head. Small juveniles secretive in rocky reefs, often cleaning other fish; adults forming small to large aggregations. Coastal to deep offshore. Sibling *C. musume* in Japan. Maximum length 24 cm.

Silver-streaked Wrasse

Pink Wrasse (male)

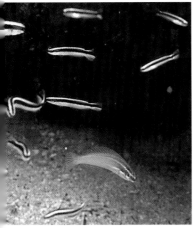

Pink Wrasse (juvenile with Hulafish)

Maori Wrasse (male)

Maori Wrasse (juvenile)

Comb Wrasse

Pixie Wrasse *Coris pictoides*

Juveniles with black over top, separated from lateral stripe by thin white interspace. Elongate black spot centrally on soft dorsal fin. Adults often brown over back. Clear coastal to inner reef habitat, usually deep, 20+ m, along bases of drop-offs. Small species, similar to Comb Wrasse (previous species) but lower margin of the black lateral stripe is even. Maximum length 12 cm.

Western King Wrasse *Coris auricularis*

Three different colour stages. Small juveniles with broad black and white below lateral stripes; large juveniles and females pale pinkish white with red tapering stripe from snout through eye, and following dorsal profile along most of body; males salmon pink with bluish grey over head and banded pattern of white, and broader brown band across deepest part of body. Juveniles secretive in reefs; adults in small aggregations along reef margins on sand in clear coastal to offshore waters to at least 45 m depth. Maximum length 32 cm.

Eastern King Wrasse *Coris sandageri*

Closely related to its western cousin (previous species) with similar patterns, but colour very different. Juveniles with olive-green band and black spot on caudal-fin base, females light purplish grey with large white area and 2 dark blotches over deep part of body, and male strongly banded over deepest part of body with 2 almost black broad bands, interspaced with white and yellow. Offshore habitats, juveniles occasionally coastal, adults mainly around islands on deep rocky slopes in sandy areas. Females in small aggregations, occasionally visited by territorial male, seemingly patrolling large reef sections. Maximum length 45 cm.

Clown Coris *Coris aygula*

Several colour changes with growth. Small juveniles white with 2 large orange saddles, a white-edged black ocellus above each, and black spots on head. Orange saddles and ocelli fade in large juveniles and females, which develop spotted head and dusky body, divided by a white bar. Males similar to females, but head greenish with some pink markings. Clear coastal to outer reefs along rubble reef zones onto sand. Juveniles among small rocks, adults along low drop-offs. Maximum length 60 cm.

Pixie Wrasse

Western King Wrasse (male)

Western King Wrasse (female)

Western King Wrasse (juvenile)

Eastern King Wrasse (male)

Eastern King Wrasse (juvenile)

Clown Coris (male)

Clown Coris (juvenile)

Gaimard Wrasse *Coris gaimard*

Colour patterns between small juveniles, initial phase, and males completely different. Juveniles bright orange-red with large black-edged white blotches over back, eyes and snout. Gradually white blotches reduce in size and caudal fin becomes yellow. Females with bright blue spots over body. Large males green, pinkish over head with green bands, pale central body bar, and with numerous small blue spots posteriorly. Yellow on caudal fin reduces to outer margin with age. Clear coastal to outer reefs along slopes and on crests, rubble and sand patches, often margins bordering onto sand. Juveniles shallow on fine rubble between boulders or reef, often noticed by divers because of bright colours. Adults form small aggregations, using large sections of reef to depths of 50 m. Several closely related species in the Indian Ocean, in which juveniles are near-identical, are not known from Australian waters. Maximum length 35 cm.

Yellow-lined Coris *Coris aurilineata*

Only slight differences between various stages. Mainly green with thin yellow to orange longitudinal lines. Juveniles and females with large white-edged black ocellus about mid-dorsal fin and smaller one on upper caudal-fin base. Males lack ocelli and are slightly more colourful on head. Coastal rock and algal reef habitat, including estuary channels, to sheltered inner reef and usually shallow depths between 3 and 10 m. Maximum length 14 cm.

Bird-nose Wrasse *Gomphosus varius*

Adults easily recognised by the long snout. Different colour patterns between juveniles, adults and sexes. Small juveniles with 2 parallel black stripes along body interspaced with white, and green above; snout short, elongating with age. Female white below head and anterior part of body with small black spots dorsally and mid-body, shading to black over posterior half. Large males bright green with bluish grey head, blue caudal fin and yellow blotch just behind head. Closely related to *Thalassoma* (next genus), swimming mainly with pectoral fins. Lagoons and reef crests in rich coral zones. Juveniles solitary among coral heads on rubble substrate; adults in small loose aggregations distributed over reef sections. Feeds on small benthic invertebrates. Replaced by slightly different Indian Ocean sibling *G. caeruleus*, west from Java, Indonesia. Maximum length 22 cm.

Gaimard Wrasse (male)

Gaimard Wrasse (female)

Gaimard Wrasse (juvenile)

Yellow-lined Coris (male)

ellow-lined Coris (juvenile)

Bird-nose Wrasse (male)

ird-nose Wrasse (female)

Bird-nose Wrasse (juvenile)

301

Two-tone Wrasse *Thalassoma amblycephalum*

Juveniles, females and young males similar, but large males different and variable. Juveniles white with black stripe midlaterally from snout along dorsal-fin base, fading with age. Males with bright green to blue-green head, followed by broad yellow band, and rest of body bluish grey with pink to red vertical bars on scales, forming thin vertical lines which thicken with age until interspaces show as thin pale lines. Small juveniles in ledges with urchins, forming schools at an early age and often moving along close to substrate over large sections of reef. Adults in large schools of mixed sexes, often feeding mid-water on zooplankton. Colourful males often separate from schools. Maximum length 16 cm.

Moon Wrasse *Thalassoma lunare*

Variable from green to blue, juveniles mostly yellowish green with yellow caudal fin. Adults green with yellow caudal fin, often a blue head, and males mostly blue with bright blue-edged pink pectoral fins and elongated pink caudal fin lobes. Very common in various habitats from rocky estuaries to outer reef lagoons, usually forming schools. Adults boldly swim with divers or large fish feeding on substrate to grab invertebrates disturbed by the activities. Maximum length 22 cm.

Yellow Moon Wrasse *Thalassoma lutescens*

Small juveniles pale whitish below with brown to yellow over back, often black midlateral line present; changing at an early age to completely yellow, and orange stripes develop on head. Males greenish yellow, often with large blue area over body behind pectoral fin, which is yellow and blue. Clear coastal to outer reef habitat and oceanic locations on reef slopes and along drop-offs to 30 m depth. Maximum length 25 cm.

Six-bar Wrasse *Thalassoma hardwicke*

Pale greenish above, fading to white below. All stages with 6 short black bars evenly distributed over back, juveniles plain, adults with pink bands over head and one along body. Juveniles solitary in clear coastal waters; adults in small loose groups, mainly on outer reef along upper parts of slopes and deep drop-offs. Maximum length 20 cm.

Two-tone Wrasse (male)

Two-tone Wrasse (juveniles)

Moon Wrasse

Yellow Moon Wrasse

Six-bar Wrasse

Surge Wrasse *Thalassoma purpureum*

Male with green to blue head and red to pink band from eye angling down to gill margin. Several similar species with complicated patterns at all stages. Adults light to bright green with thick longitudinal pink to red stripes and thin cross-barring. Juveniles lack the barring. The most similar male, the Green-barred Wrasse *T. trilobatum* with a similar geographical range, has plain brownish red head, but female almost identical. Shallow clean coastal to outer reef-flats, usually semi-exposed surge zones in a few metres' depth, venturing down to 15 m, depending on conditions. Maximum length 20 cm.

Red-ribbon Wrasse *Thalassoma quinquevittatum*

Juveniles and females bright green with pink-red stripes along upper sides, developing red radiating pattern from eye; soon reversing to purplish red head with green radiating lines from eye. Males extremely colourful and display with bright yellow belly to females. Clear coastal rocky reefs and outer coral reefs along slopes and reef crest margins along deep slopes and drop-offs. Usually seen singly, but males patrol large territories with a number of females distributed in the area. Maximum length 15 cm.

Tube-mouth Wrasse *Labrichthys unilineatus*

Monotypic, and unusual with thick-lipped tubed mouth. Juveniles jet black with thin white midlateral line, changing to a dark greenish colour and white line fading with age. Males with broad white area over body behind head; and ornamented with iridescent blue lines on head, along bases and on margins of fins. Rich coral reef habitat in outer reef zones on shallow crests and slopes, often semi-exposed zones. Maximum length 20 cm.

V-tail Tubelip Wrasse *Labrobsis xanthonota*

Unusually marked species at all stages, with juveniles black below and pale above (opposite to the norm), and thin pale longitudinal lines. Males dark blackish blue with numerous small yellow spots all over body and median fin bases, and strange white area on caudal fin like the inside of a deep 'V'. Clear coastal or outer reef crests along edge of deep drop-offs or slopes with rich coral growth. Maximum length 12 cm.

Surge Wrasse (male)

Surge Wrasse (female)

Red-ribbon Wrasse (male)

Red-ribbon Wrasse (female)

Tube-mouth Wrasse (male)

Tube-mouth Wrasse (female)

V-tail Tubelip Wrasse (male)

V-tail Tubelip Wrasse (female)

305

Yellow-tail Wrasse *Diproctacanthus xanthurus*

Small juveniles with thick alternating black and white stripes, and black caudal fin. Adults lack ventral black stripe and have bright yellow caudal fin. Juveniles form small groups in the shallows in rich coral zones along outer and inner reefs, feeding on *Acropora* coral polyps. Adults occur in small aggregations along upper parts of steep drop-offs, probably dominated by a large male. A small species, maximum length 9 cm.

Blue-streak Cleaner Wrasse *Labroides dimidiatus*

Some changes from juveniles to adults. Small juveniles black with iridescent blue line from tip of snout, along upper sides of body, to upper edge of caudal fin. Adults pale grey or yellow above and white below, separated by black line. Postlarvae, settling about 10 mm long, immediately start cleaning other fishes of parasites. The combination of colour and dance-like movement is recognised by other fishes, including predators which evidently prefer service over an easy meal. Juveniles territorial, working singly along reef walls. Adults in pairs and working from particular caves, in good 'business' position, known as cleaning stations. Fishes from a large section on the reef and also pelagic species learn where to go for the service, and towards the end of the day it can get quite busy with various species queuing patiently. Cleaning includes removal of small parasites, dead tissue from wounds, food scraps from teeth or gills. Many customers change colour so that parasites become easily visible, and open mouth and gills for the wrasse to move through freely. Habitats include rocky estuaries, coastal to inner reefs along slopes and drop-offs, and isolated outcrops of reef on sand. Similar Yellow Cleaner Wrasse *L. pectoralis*, with a yellow head and black spot below pectoral-fin base, prefers outer reef and rich coral growth. Maximum length 10 cm.

Two-colour Cleaner Wrasse *Labroides bicolor*

Small juveniles yellow with black stripe, changing gradually to female colour of grey-blue and large white area posteriorly. Males with blue head. Juveniles solitary in deep ledges and rarely seen cleaning. Adults swim openly over large reef sections to find host fish, rather than working from one place like other cleaners. Coastal reef slopes and deep inner reef lagoons. Maximum length 15 cm.

Yellow-tail Wrasse (adult)

Yellow-tail Wrasse (juveniles)

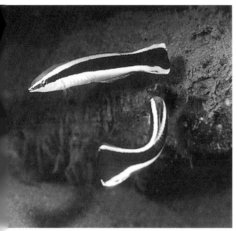

Blue-streak Cleaner Wrasse (pair)

Blue-streak Cleaner Wrasse (cleaning cod)

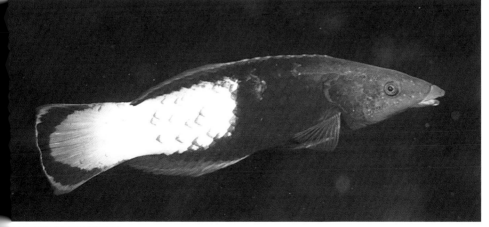

Two-colour Cleaner Wrasse

Fine-spotted Wrasse *Cirrhilabrus punctatus*

Small juveniles chocolate brown with tiny pale spots over body and part of head; and white-tipped snout, like other juveniles in the genus. Adults highly variable and change colour during display; normally greenish grey with tiny blue spots, white ventrally with sub-marginal red band in dorsal and anal fins. Males with extremely long ventral fins, and during display turn pale over top as shown in the photograph. Common Great Barrier Reef species; there are several other *Cirrhilabrus* species but most are small, live deep or in specific areas and are rarely seen. Numerous species throughout the west Pacific. Coastal reefs to offshore along slopes and drop-offs from shallow reef crests to 35 m depth. Maximum length 10 cm.

Blue-stripe Flasher *Cirrhilabrus temmincki*

Closely related to Fine-spotted Wrasse (previous species); juveniles identical except lack fine spotting. Blue lines develop along double lateral line which intensify and thicken during display. Males brown to bright red over top, but change completely during display, flashing thick blue stripes and broad white area ventrally along sides, as shown in the photograph. Originally described from Japan, ranging along mainland Asia to Australia's north-west coast. Clear coastal to outer reef slopes and crests in small aggregations. Maximum length 10 cm.

Exquisite Wrasse *Cirrhilabrus exquisitus*

Juveniles and females mainly green and large black spot on caudal-fin base. Males with red median fins which brighten during display. Outer and inner reef crests in small to large schools, feeding well above substrate on zooplankton. Males often displaying. Indian Ocean populations differently coloured with pink streak over head, and males lacking bright red in dorsal and anal fins. Maximum length 10 cm.

Reindeer Wrasse *Novaculichthys taeniourus*

Juvenile pale brown with white spots and greatly elongated first 2 dorsal fin spines giving rise to common name; also called Dragon Wrasse. Adults drab with pale head and dorsal fin spines not extended. Juveniles solitary; adults usually in pairs on rubble patches of reef crests and slopes. Experts at lifting coral or rock pieces to capture exposed prey, and for this behaviour adults are often called Rockmover Wrasse. Maximum length 30 cm.

Fine-spotted Wrasse (male)

Fine-spotted Wrasse (juvenile)

Blue-stripe Flasher (male)

Blue-stripe Flasher (male, displaying)

Exquisite Wrasse

Reindeer Wrasse (juvenile)

309

Blue Razorfish *Xyrichtys pavo*

Adults pale blue with white area over abdomen and small tear-shaped black spot above lateral line at sixth or seventh scale. Juveniles with first 2 spines of dorsal fin extremely long, connected with broad membrane and separated from rest. Colour pale with broad dusky bands; lower fins dark, sometimes black; 2 white-edged black ocelli in soft dorsal fin. Body highly compressed, head with keel-like ridge over front. Open sand near reef, often small numbers present, spread out along slopes; adults deep, 30+ m. Dives into sand if approached too closely, and usually swims through the sand for some distance; typical behaviour for genus. Maximum length 36 cm.

Leaf Wrasse *Xyrichtys dea*

Juveniles variable from brown to black, sometimes green. Often mistaken for Blue Razorfish (previous species) but, although first 2 dorsal fin spines are separate, a low membrane connects to the next spine and rest of fin. Juveniles often shallow on sand near reefs, but adults very deep and rarely seen. Pinkish with blue speckling along back, iridescent blue line over frontal ridge of head, and blue-edged round black spot above lateral line. Maximum length 25 cm.

White-blotch Razorfish *Xyrichtys aneitensis*

Small juveniles with only slightly elongated first dorsal spines, and connected by obvious membrane; 2 distinct white-edged black ocelli in soft dorsal fin. Adults pale sandy coloured with large rounded white blotch on abdomen. Clean coastal sand slopes well away from reefs, often forming loose aggregations, each individual with a particular spot to dive into for cover. Maximum length 20 cm.

Razor Wrasse *Cymolutes torquatus*

Small juveniles bright green with pale mottling, females pale with thin barring as in the photograph, and males with dusky bar behind head and pinkish median fins. Very similar Knifefish *C. praetextatus* lacks bar behind head and has curious small white-edged black line on membrane between first 2 dorsal fin spines. Small juveniles in seagrass beds; adults on slopes in vicinity of seagrasses. Maximum length 20 cm.

Cigar Wrasse *Cheilio inermis*

Best recognised by extremely elongate shape and long snout. Colour variable: juveniles green to brown with dusky longitudinal stripe; adults variable, brown to greenish grey and bright yellow phase. Seagrass beds or weedy reefs, and yellow form usually in soft coral gardens. Resembles odacids (next family) from temperate zones. Maximum length 48 cm.

Blue Razorfish (adult)

Blue Razorfish (juvenile)

Leaf Wrasse (juvenile)

White-blotch Razorfish

Razor Wrasse

Cigar Wrasse

311

CALES & WEED WHITINGS — ODACIDAE

Small wrasse-like temperate family restricted to Australian and New Zealand waters with 4 genera and 12 species, of which 10 Australian and 2 New Zealand species are endemic. Diverse group with mostly elongate to very elongate species, differing mainly from labrids in dentition and having only 4 rays in ventral fins, or no ventral fin. Like most weed-dwelling fishes, colour relates to habitat which is between the greens and reds of various algae and plants, usually providing good camouflage with shape and colour patterns aligning with general flow of seagrass or weeds. Males display with colourful fins which are raised only for this purpose, remaining camouflaged when fins down. Food comprises small invertebrates picked from weeds or substrate, or swimming mysids common in southern waters. Juveniles usually secretive and extremely well camouflaged. A few species engage in cleaning other fishes from parasites, but only part time.

Rainbow Cale *Odax acroptilus*

Adults deep-bodied compared to other species, variable from yellow-green through olive green to reddish brown, usually with a double series of large black blotches along centre and lower side. Males with iridescent blue lines along face and submarginally in dorsal, anal and ventral fins. Small juveniles green to red with clear parts in dorsal and anal fins and shiny silvery blotches along lower half of head and body. Adults on rocky kelp reef, coastal to offshore. Juveniles often among broad-leaf seagrasses or short but thick algal growth. Maximum length 30 cm.

Herring Cale *Odax cyanomelas*

Variable green or brown to bluish black. Small juveniles usually bright green with large section of dorsal and anal fins clear, and small sections pigmented like separate short fins. Females with spotted and blotched patterns. Males change to almost completely black with iridescent blue streaks in caudal fin, and bright yellow eye becomes very obvious. Weedy surge areas along foreshores, usually in large loose groups with numerous females and a few males from intertidal to about 30 m depth in kelp. Maximum length 40 cm.

Blue Weed Whiting *Haletta semifasciata*

Greenish grey to bright pale blue, darker over top and shading to light below. Eye yellow to orange, and obvious in blue males. Common southern species, schooling in large numbers in coastal bays, swimming just above seagrass beds and often caught by anglers around jetties. Juveniles solitary and secretive in weeds or seagrass beds. Maximum length 35 cm.

Rainbow Cale (male)

Rainbow Cale (male, variation)

Rainbow Cale (juvenile)

Herring Cale (male)

Herring Cale (female)

Blue Weed Whiting

313

Long-ray Weed Whiting *Siphonognathus radiatus*

Bright green or brown depending on habitat. Green in seagrass beds and brown on rocky weedy reefs. Juveniles with white streak along cheek continuing along lower sides, males with thin blue lines on head and thin bright orange and blue lines in dorsal fin near base, used for display. Shallow protected bays, particularly common in South Australia. Maximum length 20 cm.

Short-nose Weed Whiting *Siphonognathus attenuatus*

Extremely slender with short snout. Distinct white-edged black ocellus or false eye on caudal fin, which combined with shape of fin effectively reverses image of fish. Disguise fools predators which usually attack head first. Ocellus proportionally larger in juveniles and no differences between sexes. Along weedy reefs and seagrass bed margins over sand patches, usually in small groups in depth range from 10 to 25 m. Maximum length 13 cm.

Long-nose Weed Whiting *Siphonognathus beddomei*

Slender species with unusually long snout. Green or brown, females with distinct black spot in top of caudal fin. Males with iridescent blue lines on snout and body, a large blue-edged red blotch along outer margin of last 2 rays of ventral fins. Juveniles identical to females. Young and females often in small aggregations swimming together over weed-covered reefs in sheltered bays, as well as offshore on reefs exposed to surge. Males usually solitary, in vicinity of females. Adults often seen cleaning fishes, particularly cowfishes (Aracanidae). Maximum length 14 cm.

PARROTFISHES — SCARIDAE

Large tropical family with representatives in all oceans, 9 genera and about 80 species worldwide, of which 6 genera and about 30 species are known in Australian waters. Two subfamilies based on differences in dentition. Scarinae, included here, has teeth fused into strong beak-like plates, giving rise to their common name. In many ways parrotfishes are similar to closely related wrasses, showing various colour phases with growth and between sexes, but adapted to feeding on algae and coral by scraping their surfaces or simply biting and crushing hunks, and often digesting the lot. Their waste products have become an important factor in the reef-building process, as most species are large and occur in great schools, thus depositing vast quantities of sand over time. The streaks of white discharge are commonly seen during displays and when along reef crests. Colour is often the only way to identify species. Male and female phases are usually linked by observation. Many small juveniles have broad brown longitudinal bands and are very difficult to identify underwater. In some tropical zones, parrotfishes are of commercial importance.

Humphead Parrotfish *Bolbometopon muricatum*

Drab but impressive species as large adult. The largest parrotfish, forming great schools like herds of bison or buffalo. Greenish grey, and only adults develop large hump on head. Juveniles otherwise similar with several vertical series of white spots over upper sides. Coastal to outer reef slopes, grazing corals during the day, sleeping in crevices at night. Maximum length 1.2 m.

ng-ray Weed Whiting

Short-nose Weed Whiting

ng-nose Weed Whiting (male)

ng-nose Weed Whiting (female)

Humphead Parrotfish

315

Two-colour Parrotfish *Cetoscarus bicolor*

Three distinctly different stages. Small juveniles pure white with orange headband and yellow-edged black spot in dorsal fin. Larger juveniles when changing to female gradually darken with plain dusky head; body with numerous black spots below lateral line and almost white above. Males become multicoloured with dominant green colours. Juveniles solitary in rich coral zones in shallow lagoons or along protected reef slopes. Females in small aggregations, often with several large males nearby. Mostly juveniles are noticed by divers. Maximum length 90 cm

Surf Parrotfish *Scarus rivulatus*

Males best identified by yellow pectoral fins and orange cheeks. Females plain grey to light brown with some pale longitudinal lines along lower sides. Forms schools in very shallow depths, feeding on algae at high tide over reef-flats. Coastal, often silty areas, to outer reef lagoons. Maximum length 40 cm.

Bridled Parrotfish *Scarus frenatus*

Colour pattern on head of males diagnostic, but underwater the pale tail with moon-shaped band in caudal fin are best features for identification. Females pale brown with pinkish brown fins, body scales below lateral line with grey to almost black centres, forming patterns, often in horizontal bands over posterior part of body. As for many other parrotfishes, the female and male phases can be linked by observation when they interact. Females usually in small groups with males nearby. Mainly in outer reef zones, feeding on shallow flats. Maximum length 47 cm, usually 35 cm.

Shabby Parrotfish *Scarus sordidus*

Highly variable species, males changing colour markedly during display. Juveniles striped, females brown with pale head, and males multicoloured from dusky to green, often very pale caudal peduncle, and bright yellow sides during display. Common species on inner and outer reef crests. Maximum length 40 cm, usually 30 cm.

Two-colour Parrotfish (male)

Two-colour Parrotfish (juvenile)

Surf Parrotfish

Bridled Parrotfish (male)

Bridled Parrotfish (female)

Shabby Parrotfish

Bleeker's Parrotfish *Scarus bleekeri*

Males with distinctly coloured white cheek; females pale with dark brown to almost black barring. Females often in large schools or mixing with other species to feed on shallow reef-flats; males usually solitary along slopes nearby. Coastal and inner reefs. Maximum length 40 cm.

King Parrotfish *Scarus flavipectoralis*

Females plain yellowish; males usually showing half green posteriorly and half purplish grey anteriorly, with thick green stripe from tip of snout to above pectoral-fin base. Clear coastal and inner reefs, usually along slopes or low drop-offs in about 10 m, males solitary, females in small aggregations. Maximum length 35 cm.

Forsten's Parrotfish *Scarus forsteni*

Females distinct with curious iridescent blue and gold blotch centrally on sides. Males similar to several other species, best identified by large dusky area over head and lack of stripe behind eye, and long pink stripes submarginally along caudal fin onto extended lobes. Almost identical *S. tricolor* has green stripe over and behind eye; northern west Pacific, not known from Australia, but often its photograph is used for *S. forsteni*. Juveniles dark brown with small white spot centrally on sides. Clear coastal to inner reefs in lagoons and on slopes with rich coral growth. Maximum length 45 cm.

Blue-bridle Parrotfish *Scarus dimidiatus*

Males blue-green with purplish blue over snout, scales over posterior half of body outlined with dusky purple, and purplish blue streak from behind eye to pectoral-fin base. Females yellow with dusky blotches along upper sides. Protected coastal bays, inner reefs and lagoons on coral slopes and crests, feeding in small loose groups in gutters or between large coral heads on rubble patches or coral bases. Rather shy species. Maximum length 35 cm.

Schlegel's Parrotfish *Scarus schlegeli*

Females dark grey-brown with 5 pale forward-curving bars evenly spaced from behind pectoral-fin base to caudal peduncle. Males dark with light shades of blue, light above head continuing over body to broad band vertically over middle of body, with a bright yellow spot in upper corner. Usually with large schools of mixed parrotfish species, moving over reef-flats grazing algal patches. Maximum length 40 cm.

Yellow-head Parrotfish *Scarus spinus*

Males easily identified with deep blue body and bright yellow-green head; even at a distance the head looks bright yellow in natural light. Females dark brown, white teeth and a few white speckles over sides, usually occurring in small groups with a male nearby. Shallow coastal to inner reef crests, males solitary. Small species, maximum length 30 cm.

Bleeker's Parrotfish

King Parrotfish

Forsten's Parrotfish (male)

Forsten's Parrotfish (female)

Blue-bridle Parrotfish (male)

Blue-bridle Parrotfish (female)

Schlegel's Parrotfish

Yellow-head Parrotfish

319

GRUBFISHES — PINGUIPEDIDAE

Moderately large family with 4 genera and probably over 60 species worldwide; only genus *Parapercis* Indo-Pacific and about 20 species are reported in Australian waters. Several undescribed species and genus badly in need of revision. Distribution of many species unknown because of many similar species and confusion of names, including common ones. Small slender fishes, featuring long-based dorsal fin with short spinous section of 4 or 5 spines and anal fin headed by feeble spine; large bulging eyes placed high on head. Mostly mixed reef, rubble and sand-dwellers, often among corals and seagrasses on open patches. Usually resting on substrate, perched on ventral fins, and often on high points giving good view of surrounding substrate. Colour variable with habitat and although many species are similar, patterns are diagnostic and usually the only means for identification underwater. Differences between growth stages and sexes are only slight. Diet comprises primarily small crustaceans, fish larvae and occasionally zooplankton. Curious fishes, often coming to investigate diver disturbing substrate, and easily approached.

False-eye Grubfish *Parapercis clathrata*

Males with false eye spot at snout-length distance behind eye. Apart from blotched pattern on head, a patch of tiny black spots on cheek in juveniles as well as adults is a diagnostic feature. Usually thin line along lower body with black dashes superimposed on grey blotches. Caudal fin with distinct streak over posterior half of central rays; important feature when comparing similar species. Coastal to outer reef crests on rubble patches, and common in algal zones or rocky-weed reef habitat. Shallow to about 20 m depth. Large tropical species, maximum length 24 cm, usually 18 cm.

Thousand-spot Grubfish *Parapercis millepunctata*

Both sexes with distinct white blotch centrally near end of caudal fin. Body pattern variable from juveniles with smaller blotching to adults where interspaces of blotches form net-like pattern. Often identified as *P. cephalopunctata* from northern west Pacific which has black tail, similar to Black-tail Grubfish (next species). Clear coastal reefs in boulder zones. Maximum length 18 cm, usually 14 cm.

Black-tail Grubfish *Parapercis hexophthalma*

Caudal fin black with white margin in juveniles, black reducing proportionally with age into long streak with white tip. Body and head with thin black scribbles and spots, forming small elongate circles on lower cheek in males. Clear coastal to outer reef crests and slopes, common in outer reef lagoons on rubble zones. Maximum length 25 cm.

White-streaked Grubfish *Parapercis stricticeps*

Distinct in having dusky upper third with saddle patches of black scribbles on body and head. Lower part with a series of dark blotches joined by lines, but this pattern common with several species. Restricted to the east coast. Commonly identified as Peppered Grubfish (next species). Coastal reefs and rocky estuaries to about 20 m depth. Maximum length 18 cm.

False-eye Grubfish (adult)

False-eye Grubfish (juvenile)

Thousand-spot Grubfish

Black-tail Grubfish

White-streaked Grubfish

321

Peppered Grubfish *Parapercis xanthozona*

Distinctly barred with reddish brown along lower half of body and head. Single bar below eye, end of mouth and end of gill cover, and about 10 bars on body, those posteriorly with black centres. Upper body plain with dusky speckling. Shallow coastal reef slopes on rock and rubble patches. Photograph taken in Bali, Indonesia, and Australian confirmation needed. Included here as the name is widely used in our literature for several species, and usually showing photographs of White-streaked Grubfish (previous species). Maximum length 15 cm.

Double-stitch Grubfish *Parapercis multiplicata*

Easily identified by a series of double or triple white dashes over grey to reddish brown back. Paler, almost white lower half crossed by brownish bars below each series of white dashes, and distinct black to brown spot below pectoral-fin base. Mainly outer reefs, usually at moderate depths on rubble zones away from drop-offs. Maximum length 15 cm.

Lyre-tail Grubfish *Parapercis schauinslandi*

Some differences between juveniles and adults. Juveniles pale with 2 series of red blotches along body, red stripe from tip of snout through eye to above pectoral-fin base in line with upper series of spots, and caudal fin rounded to truncate. Adults with large blotches, forming bands anteriorly, head yellowish and caudal fin becomes strongly lunate. Changes related to habits: juveniles feed on substrate and adults on zooplankton, feeding well above substrate at times. Maximum length 18 cm.

Pink-banded Grubfish *Parapercis nebulosa*

Pink above to white below with darker pink to brown blotchy bands, adults with thin pale lines between eyes and across snout. Coastal waters and estuaries in weed, soft coral or mud habitats. Mainly open sandy substrate and hiding under small dug-out pieces of solid matter. Maximum length 25 cm.

Spotted Grubfish *Parapercis ramsayi*

Series of large black spots along ventral sides of body. Juveniles with distinct white-edged black ocellus on upper caudal-fin base. Various habitats and depths depending on area, only shallow in a few selected areas along coasts, most commonly in depths of 50 m. Maximum length 20 cm.

Sharp-nose Grubfish *Parapercis cylindrica*

Dusky bars along lower half of body and stripes pattern along upper part, separated by broad whitish area. Several similar species; dusky band separates it from Three-line Grubfish (next species), others not known from Australian waters. Common species on clear coastal reef crests and rubble zones, including clear estuaries. Maximum length 15 cm.

Peppered Grubfish

Double-stitch Grubfish

Lyre-tail Grubfish

Pink-banded Grubfish

Spotted Grubfish

Sharp-nose Grubfish

323

Three-line Grubfish *Parapercis* sp.

Similar to Sharp-nose Grubfish (previous species), but cheek pale and 3 thin black lines run behind eye along upper sides of body. Although rather common on still rubble-sandflats, and widespread in the Indo-Pacific, it appears to be undescribed. Maximum length 10 cm.

Wavy Grubfish *Parapercis haackei*

Only sharp-nosed species in southern range. Dusky band from behind eye to caudal-fin base reduced in large adults to dark wavy line. Sheltered coastal bays and large estuaries, commonly found under jetties. Juveniles solitary, secretive under solid objects. Adults usually pair but do not stay close together. Maximum length 10 cm.

STARGAZERS — URANOSCOPIDAE

Moderately large family with 8 genera and 30 species, of which 5 genera and about 11 species in Australian waters. Generally deep-water dwellers, known primarily from trawls; however, few live in remarkably shallow depths, just beyond intertidal zones. Features: large bulky head with dorsally placed eyes; protrusible mouth; large backward-pointing spine dorsally above pectoral-fin base, which can be highly venomous. Some have bait in mouth which is wriggled to attract prey. Buries in substrate with just eyes exposed, latter often raised to just above the surface. Diet includes fish and cephalopods, and prey sucked in whole. Only a few species commonly observed underwater.

Eastern Stargazer *Kathetostoma laeve*

Pale sandy colours with large dark diffused blotches, more distinct in small individuals and almost banded in juveniles. Common in Port Phillip Bay and often under or near jetties buried close to pylons or rocks. Usually discovered when accidentally disturbed and fish moves away quickly to bury itself elsewhere. Large specimens can be aggressive and may bite. Observed shallow in wading depths between beach and sandbanks, and reported to 60 m depth where sometimes hooked on fishing line. Maximum length 75 cm.

THORNFISHES — BOVICHTIDAE

Small Southern Hemisphere family with 4 genera and 7 species, of which 2 genera and 3 species are reported in Australian waters, showing close affinities with Antarctic fishes. Slender fishes with large, close-set, dorsally placed eyes and 2 dorsal fins. The first is spinous and short-based, the second soft-rayed and long-based. Two common southern species, and a third known from a few specimens collected in Bass Strait surveys. One species mainly estuarine, entering fresh water and often living far inland up rivers; features small scales and flathead (Platycephalidae) appearance. Other species only marine, coastal; features spine pointing outwards and backwards from upper corner of gill cover, and lacks scales on body and head. Only latter species included here.

Thornfish *Bovichtus angustifrons*

Large head with tapering body, head spines obvious in large adults. Colour variable, usually matching surroundings with marbled patterns from grey to red. Large pectoral fins and superficially similar to dragonets (Callionymidae); often referred to as such by common name. Coastal rocky reef from shallow still waters to fully exposed surge reef, usually on vertical rock faces, jetty pylons or in caves, and usually in spread-out groups. Maximum length 28 cm.

Three-line Grubfish

Wavy Grubfish

Eastern Stargazer

Hornfish

325

BLENNIES — BLENNIIDAE

Very large family with more than 50 genera and well over 300 species, of which about 20 genera and probably over 100 species are found in Australian waters. Several very distinct groups presently recognised as subfamilies, some of which are divided into tribes. Further studies will probably reclassify some groups to families status. Most species small and tropical; diversity reduces rapidly into subtropical to temperate regions. Generally slender, some eel-like, with slimy skin replacing scales; teeth in comb-like arrangements in each jaw and often with greatly enlarged canines, venomous in some; long-based single dorsal fin with flexible spines and soft rays. Benthic fishes, usually scraping algae off rocks and corals; a few feed midwater on zooplankton or small benthic invertebrates. Some specialise in feeding on external parts of other fishes, including scales, fin bits or mucus, approaching prey by trickery such as mimicking harmless fishes or cleaners. Many use holes left by tubeworms or empty shells for cover or nesting sites in which males guard eggs.

Tasmanian Blenny *Parablennius tasmanianus*

Large frilly tentacle above each eye, greatly extended by long filament on top. Pale brownish to bluish grey with a series of small dark blotches and a few white scribbles, breaking up into fine vermiculated patterns in large individuals. Small juveniles in rockpools may be black or dark-spotted. Shallow rocky reef habitat in bays and estuaries, commonly under jetties on pylons in holes or sponges. Maximum length 13 cm.

Horned Blenny *Parablennius intermedius*

Similar to Tasmanian blenny but face spotted instead of banded and adults retain large spots compared to very fine pattern; also tentacle above eye much shorter in males. Coastal shallow reefs and estuaries, commonly on jetty pylons with mussels and sponges in small loose groups dominated by a large male. Maximum length 12 cm.

Banded Blenny *Salarias fasciatus*

Frilled tentacles above eyes and on ridges behind. Dorsal fins very tall. Pattern variable with lines and blotches, usually striations on anterior half and banding on rest of body. Algae-rich reefs, intertidal to a few metres in depth, sheltered to exposed areas among rocks or branching corals, feeding on algae settling on lower dead parts. Maximum length 14 cm.

Rippled Rockskipper *Istiblennius edentulus*

Simple filament above eye, distinctly banded, dorsal fin busily spotted. All intertidal, often seen hanging on rocks out of water as level drops from wave action. Often in pools under rocks at low tide and when disturbed jump to other pools or channels. Several other similar species, each with diagnostic patterns on body and fins. Maximum length 17 cm, usually 14 cm.

Red-streaked Blenny *Cirripectes stigmaticus*

Small genus with transverse band of cirri across nape, with a few species in Australian waters. Mostly dark with small spots, bands or thin irregular lines. Red-streaked Blenny often noticed when large and displays red scribbles on face and side of body. Like other *Cirripectes* members, in rich coral growth, shy and quickly hides. Shallow reef-flats with algae patches among coral heads. Maximum length 10 cm.

Tasmanian Blenny (close-up)

Tasmanian Blenny

Horned Blenny

Banded Blenny

Rippled Rockskipper

Red-streaked Blenny

Crested Sabretooth Blenny *Petroscirtes mitratus*

First part of dorsal fin elevated. Pale whitish with pale brown to greenish series of dark blotches, sometimes forming band along upper sides with pale spots mixed in. Colour to suit surroundings. Small juveniles in floating or sargassum weeds, adults on coastal reefs with good algal growth, often on jetty pylons. Maximum length 65 mm.

Xestus Sabretooth Blenny *Petroscirtes xestus*

Very similar to Crested Sabretooth Blenny (previous species), but dorsal fin rather tall over long anterior section. Best diagnostic feature is bearded chin with numerous close-set cirri, as clearly visible in the close-up photograph. Usually very common, but easily missed because of excellent camouflage and often secretive habits. Young often under mantle of upside-down jellies *Cassiopea* spp. when on sand, or with small outcrops of pale algae growing on shells or other objects on clean sand. Adults use empty mollusc shells and tubes for nesting or shelter. Maximum length 65 mm.

Short-head Sabretooth Blenny *Petroscirtes breviceps*

Highly variable and mimics many *Meiacanthus* blennies which possess venomous teeth. Can have black lines on white or yellow, depending on model. Non-mimic shown, but variable according to habitat from brown to green blotched. Coastal to outer reef-flats and lagoons, in seagrasses and rubble zones. Very common and widespread, young with floating sargassum weeds. Maximum length 12 cm.

Variable Sabretooth Blenny *Petroscirtes variablis*

As the name suggests, highly variable and changes colour with habitat. Usually in green or brown weeds, showing same general colour, mainly darkest in a broad band along upper sides and light below. Head rather pointed and a few small cirri below chin and above eyes. Coastal lagoons, mangrove areas with sargassum zone in front, and seagrass beds. In small aggregations, feeding by scraping algae off plant leaves such as broad seagrasses. Maximum length 10 cm.

Yellow Sabretooth Blenny *Petroscirtes fallax*

Best recognised by black and yellow or white stripes, males more yellow. Juveniles paler but dorsal fin yellow, the latter orange in adults. Although not a specific mimic, the yellow and black lines may serve as a deterrent to predators, since some venomous *Meiacanthus* spp. have similar colours. Mainly rocky estuaries and coastal reefs. Swims close to substrate, often in pairs. Maximum length 10 cm.

Crested Sabretooth Blenny

Xestus Sabretooth Blenny

Xestus Sabretooth Blenny (close-up)

Short-head Sabretooth Blenny

Variable Sabretooth Blenny

Yellow Sabretooth Blenny

Yellow-lined Harptail Blenny *Meiacanthus lineatus*

Body with black and yellow stripes along upper two-thirds, and white ventrally. Yellow line originating at upper edge of eye often changes to white over body. Adults with extended corners on caudal fin, typical for members of the genus and the reason for its common name. Clear coastal bays to sheltered inner reef habitat on rubble zones along base of slopes and short drop-offs. Maximum length 12 cm.

Gold-stripe Harptail Blenny *Meiacanthus luteus*

Thick golden-yellow stripe directly above black midlateral stripe. Adults develop very long filaments on caudal-fin tips. Coastal and inner reefs on rocky, algae-rich reefs, often silty habitat. Common in southern Queensland inshore from Keppel Island. Maximum length 10 cm.

Eye-lash Harptail Blenny *Meiacanthus atrodorsalis*

Head and part of body bluish grey, gradually changing to white or bright yellow, a blue-edged angular black line through eye, and thin black line along base of dorsal fin. Clear coastal to outer reefs along drop-offs and deep slopes, often close to rock faces on rubble substrate. Maximum length 10 cm.

Two-colour Combtooth Blenny *Ecsenius bicolor*

Several colour forms. The half-black, half-orange variety is most commonly observed in Australian waters. The other common variety, all dark with a yellowish head, is rarely noticed, but the much rarer lined variety with obvious colours is often photographed. Such variations sometimes relate to age but apparently not sex. Clear coastal to outer reef crests and slopes in rubble zones or gutters down from rich coral areas. Large genus with many small and similar species. Maximum length 85 mm.

Tube-worm Blenny *Plagiotremus rhinorynchos*

Variable from nearly black to orange with pale blue longitudinal lines and fins yellow to pale mauve. Upper line bright blue in dark phase. Typically uses empty tubeworm shells for home and nesting site. Males entice females to deposit eggs by displaying and dancing in front of entrance. Coastal and rocky estuarine reefs. Maximum length 12 cm.

Yellow-lined Harptail Blenny

Gold-stripe Harptail Blenny

Eye-lash Harptail Blenny

Two-colour Combtooth Blenny

Two-colour Combtooth Blenny (variation)

Tube-worm Blenny

Mimic Blenny *Plagiotremus tapeinosoma*

Best recognised by very elongate body and a series of vertically elongate close-set black spots forming band over upper sides from tip of snout to caudal-fin base. Most common species and often in small groups. Mixes with similar sized and shaped schooling fishes, mimicking poorly in colour, which seems enough to get close to prey to take bites out of fins. Clear coastal reefs, sometimes in small aggregations. Maximum length 12 cm.

Lance Blenny *Aspidontus dussumieri*

Slender with straight black stripe from eye to caudal-fin base; pale yellow to brow above and white below; dorsal and anal fins with thin black margin. Adults may develop filaments centrally or at tips of caudal fin. Coastal, rocky estuaries to inne reefs in algae habitat. Swims close to substrate, reverses into empty tubeworm holes when approached. Maximum length 12 cm.

False Cleanerfish *Aspidontus taeniatus*

Almost perfect copy of Cleaner Wrasse *Labroides dimidiatus* in colour and shape. Mouth different, almost vertical, and situated below overhanging snout. Uses disguise to get close to prey, taking bites from fins, but experienced fish recognise it as an imposter and often chase it. Sometimes form small aggregations which move over reef crest and feed on substrate as well as on zooplankton. Maximum length 10 cm.

Hairtail Blenny *Xiphasia setifer*

Body eel-like with a series of broad dark blotches and bands. Dorsal fin tall anteriorly with blue-edged black ocellus and blue lines. Shallow to deep sandflats using vertical burrows of eels or other fishes for cover. Usually seen with just head out of hole, but occasionally out in the open moving between holes; reverses into next hole. Specimen 20 cm long was taken from the gut of a flathead caught off Bermagui, New South Wales. Maximum length 40 cm.

THREEFINS — TRIPTERYGIIDAE

Very large family of mostly tiny fishes with probably more than 20 genera and 200 species worldwide many of which appear to be undescribed. About 9 genera and an unknown number of species are found in Australian waters. Mostly tropical, a few centimetres long and difficult to identify, and many species undescribed. In Australia, temperate species along the south coast recently revised and named Blenny-like fishes with scales; dorsal fin in 3 parts, sections separated by a gap or joined at base by membrane; and long-based anal fin, its base longer than any dorsal fin section. Colour can vary between sexes, with some males showing bright colours during display. Highly camouflaged fishes and many species secretive in reefs. Usually only males noticed during display when colours are bright. Often mistaken for gobies, but snout pointed and ventral fins divided into 2 simple fins, each with 2 or 3 long rays.

Jumping Blenny *Lepidoblennius marmoratus*

Large smooth head with eyes high and body gradually tapering to caudal fin. Gre to greenish above with mottled pattern. Very similar Jumping Joey *L. haplodactylu* from the east coast has a more blotched or banded pattern and has cycloid versus ctenoid scales. Shallow inshore reefs and rock platforms with deep pools, includi exposed areas. Occasionally seen out of the water along the edges of pools. Maximum length 12 cm.

Mimic Blenny

Lance Blenny

alse Cleanerfish

Hairtail Blenny

mping Blenny

Yellowback Threefin *Helcogramma decurrens*

Males turn bright yellow over back and black under head and abdomen when defending territory or displaying. Females camouflaged, pale with diffused banded pattern. Shallow rocky reef in crevices or on rock faces, commonly on jetty pylons. Usually only brightly coloured males noted, but females found nearby. Maximum length 65 mm.

Striped Threefin *Helcogramma striata*

Greyish brown to dark brown with thin white to bluish lines and speckles on snout, often showing bright red stripes along upper sides when photographed with a flash. Coastal reefs, mainly in sponge- and ascidian-rich reefs, often forming small aggregations on large sponges, usually in depths over 10 m, range 6–30 m depth. Maximum length 40 mm.

Black-cheek Threefin *Enneapterygius rufopileus*

Displaying males bright orange-red with black cheeks and dorsal fins, and 2 white saddles over back. Clear coastal reefs and deep rockpools to offshore islands, mostly very shallow to about 10 m depth, and usually in pairs. Similar Ring-scale Blenny *E. annulatus* has less colourful male, orange-brown with white first dorsal fin, found in still coastal and rocky estuarine habitat. Maximum length 50 mm.

Tasselled Threefin *Apopterygion alta*

Dorsal fin clearly separate and first fin with tasselled tips on each spine, unusual in family. Variable from pink to red with pale banding, large individuals ornamented with yellow and blue spot dorsally on head. Occurs deeper than any other known threefin to 80 m depth in sponge reef, but also shallow under piers in Port Phillip Bay. Maximum length 65 mm.

Common Threefin *Norfolkia clarkei*

Geographical variations and colour changes according to habitat. Dark strongly banded to pale grey or orange, but usually a distinct band curving slightly backwards from below eye and followed by second more vertical one nearby inside preopercle margin. Shallow rocky estuaries to deep offshore. In shallows, patterns usually distinct as in the photograph, deep-water forms usually plain matching colour of sponges, depth range to 30 m. Maximum length 80 mm, growing largest in the south.

Crested Threefin *Norfolkia cristata*

Very similar to Common Threefin (previous species) and best distinguished by tall versus low first dorsal fin. Replaces this species in most of South Australia's offshore rocky reefs and islands. Inhabits rock faces and caves, usually shallow to about 15 m depth. Maximum length 73 mm.

Yellowback Threefin

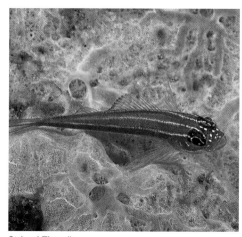

Striped Threefin

Black-cheek Threefin

Tasselled Threefin

Common Threefin

Crested Threefin

WEEDFISHES & SNAKE-BLENNIES — CLINIDAE

Large family with at least 20 genera and 100 species, most of which are found in the Southern Hemisphere, and particularly well represented in Australia and South Africa with about 40 species each. Australian snake-blennies were revised by scientists in the United States, who recognised 4 genera and 13 species, several of which described as new. Many of our 28 weedfishes remain undescribed, but are well known and have been awaiting naming in the Australian Museum for many years. Presently all tentatively placed in 2 genera until the group is revised. Majority of species of entire family live in the southern region among richly vegetated reefs and in seagrasses. Well-camouflaged and highly variable to suit habitat, from yellow to brown or green, but most have diagnostic patterns or morphological features. Many inhabit sheltered coastal bays and estuaries, but some prefer surge and cling to weed with strong recurving ventral fins. Diet consists of various small invertebrates and fishes living on or among weeds. Unusually for small fishes, they have internal fertilisation and give birth to live young.

Sharp-nose Weedfish *Heteroclinus tristis*

Snout more pointed than others and first dorsal fin tall. Colour pattern highly variable, often a series of figure-8 dark blotches along upper sides, and fins with numerous round transparent parts. Juveniles secretive in weeds; large adults often along reef margins with weed on sand to hunt shrimps. Large species, maximum length 30 cm.

Johnston's Weedfish *Heteroclinus johnstoni*

Best identified by long nasal tentacles with star-like arrangement of long lobes and bushy eye tentacles, juveniles strongly banded and adults with a series of ocellated black spots along upper sides, one in each dark vertical band. Common in shallow coastal bays on low reefs covered with weed and algae, and often under jetties, but also offshore and recorded to 50 m depth. Juveniles secretive under rocks or in ledges. Large adults often seen, being more exposed and also due to size. Our largest species, maximum length 40 cm.

Common Weedfish *Heteroclinus perspicillatus*

Pale grey to green, white or almost black, with dark lines radiating in eye. Pale forms usually with distinct large spot just below first dorsal-fin base. Dark forms usually with white band from first dorsal fin to belly, and black spot just below first dorsal-fin base less distinct but still visible. Probably most variable and most common species which is least weed-associated, often found in sandstone reef under slabs showing very pale colouration and changing colour when moving into darker surrounding weeds. Maximum length 20 cm, usually 15 cm.

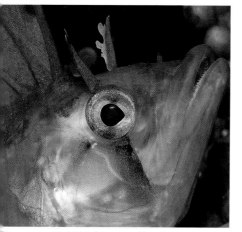

Sharp-nose Weedfish (close-up of head)

Sharp-nose Weedfish

Johnston's Weedfish (adult)

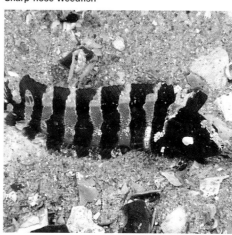

Johnston's Weedfish (juvenile)

Common Weedfish (general form)

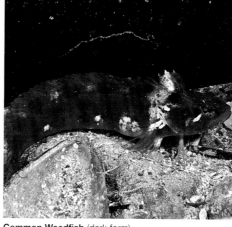

Common Weedfish (dark form)

Emerald Weedfish *Heteroclinus* sp.

One of 9 undescribed species along the south coast. Thin black line below eye and several distinct black spots along preopercle margin. Body pale brown or mostly covered with tiny iridescent green spots, and a series of small black spots along dorsal-fin base. Rocky reef with algal cover, subtidally to 15 m depth. Maximum length 65 mm.

Golden Weedfish *Cristiceps aurantiacus*

First dorsal fin separate, large and distinctly taller than second, originating in front of above eyes. The very similar Crested Weedfish *C. australis* has lower fin and it originates above eye; a common south coast species. Third in genus, Silver-sided Weedfish *C. argyropleura* has triangular-shaped first fin which is attached to the second by a low membrane; least observed and often deep to 60 m. Golden Weedfish mostly in kelp when adult, light brown to golden yellow; juveniles pale with faint barring. Maximum length 18 cm.

Spotted Snake-blenny *Ophiclinops pardalis*

Pale grey to dark brown, silvery white streak behind eye, continuing as a more-or-less distinct series of white spots along lower side of body and similar series above along dorsal-fin base. Similar Earspot Snake-blenny *O. hutchinsi* only known from the mainland coast above Recherche Archipelago, Western Australia. Mixed rock, seagrass or weed habitat, under seagrass mats or rocks. Maximum length 7 cm.

Adelaide Snake-blenny *Ophiclinus antarcticus*

Variable yellow to dark brown; a series of white spots along dorsal-fin base and sometimes a second series midlaterally. The similar brown to black Frosted Snake-blenny *O. gabrieli*, with silvery white over top of head and along dorsal-fin base, is restricted to the Bass Strait region. Under rocks or logs, commonly near jetties with accumulating decaying seagrass leaves, probably feeding on amphipods among it. Maximum length 17.5 cm.

Variable Snake-blenny *Ophiclinus ningulus*

Different colour forms with depth, from almost plain yellowish brown with alternating dark and light spotting along dorsal-fin base in deep water, to almost black with pure white stripe over snout to along part of dorsal-fin base in shallows. Particularly common in Port Phillip Bay under rocks with weed or in sponge habitat to at least 20 m depth. Maximum length 75 mm.

Emerald Weedfish

Golden Weedfish (juvenile)

Golden Weedfish (female)

Spotted Snake-blenny

Adelaide Snake-blenny

Variable Snake-blenny

Black-back Snake-blenny *Ophiclinus gracilis*

Black over top with pale line over snout extending to dorsal-fin base and pale white to pink below, sometimes all dark with a few pale spots midlaterally along entire body. Most widespread species, common in the Melbourne region in bays under rocks in decaying vegetation, often silty environment. Maximum length 10 cm.

Eel Blenny *Peronedys anguillaris*

Very elongate with black over top from above eyes and below from anus to caudal-fin tip, sides pale pinkish with indistinct lines along, most evident on head. Only known from still South Australian bays with prolific seagrasses forming mats over decaying ones; found in small numbers among the latter. Pollution is a threat to this species. Doubtfully reported from Moreton Bay, Queensland. Maximum length 13 cm.

DRAGONETS — CALLIONYMIDAE

Large family with at least 9 genera and 125 species; however, some authors divide genera further, and many tiny species remain undescribed because of size (one species, 12 mm as adult male). Recent studies suggest as many as 19 genera, of which 12 are found in Australia; however, other experts disagree. About 35 species in Australian waters. Fishes with tough skin instead of scales and thick mucus which gives it a bad taste and has a strong odour, giving species caught on line the common name of stinkfish. Eyes placed high on head, mouth small but greatly protrusible out and downwards, gill opening reduced to pore, and large preopercle spine armed with antrorse spines. Dorsal fin in 2 parts, short spinous and long soft-rayed sections; pectoral and ventral fins rather large and meeting each other. Mostly sand-dwellers near reefs, often buried when resting, but a few found on reefs and some tropical species living in rich coral zones only. Species associated with sand or mixed sand and reef highly variable, matching substrate in colour. Tropical reef species more distinct and some gaudily coloured. Diet comprises tiny invertebrates picked from substrate.

Painted Stinkfish *Eocallionymus papilio*

Some geographical variations in colour and size, and differences between the sexes. Males usually spotted above, with vertical striations along lower half of body, and female similar above but blotched on lower sides. Dorsal fins in males much taller and more colourful than in females. Head often shaded dusky to bright orange from snout to behind eyes and to opercle's lower corner. Small juveniles sometimes bony white on top. Displaying males intensify red colours, especially in dorsal fins. Very common in southern waters and most observed species in shallow reef and seagrass habitats. Maximum length 13 cm.

Common Stinkfish *Foetorepus calauropomus*

Colour highly variable with depth, pale greenish grey in shallows, to bright red when deep. Some variation between the east and south coast populations. Female in shallow upper regions of Sydney Harbour with fine blue scribbles, not seen in southern populations. Males with greatly rounded snout in New South Wales. In Victoria mainly deep: shallowest 15 m, to 100 m depth; in New South Wales often in shallow seagrass beds subtidally. Reported to 35 cm, maximum length usually 30 cm.

Black-back Snake-blenny

Eel Blenny

Painted Stinkfish (male)

Painted Stinkfish (female)

Common Stinkfish (New South Wales)

Common Stinkfish (Victoria)

Fingered Dragonet *Dactylopus dactylopus*

Spine and first ventral fin ray separate from rest, spinous section of dorsal fin greatly elongated with broad membranes, connected by membrane to soft-rayed part. Body pale with brownish saddles, latter with numerous small blue ocelli. Fins dark, anal fin with iridescent blue spots. Juveniles with proportionally taller fins and obvious yellow-edged black ocellus low in first dorsal fin. Common on shallow mud and sandflats in coastal waters, often in a few metres' depth, but may bury during most of the day and usually only observed when disturbed. Juveniles solitary, but adults usually in small loose groups. Maximum length 18 cm.

Mandarin Fish *Synchiropus splendidus*

Unique colour pattern with green and orange. Juveniles and females with rounded first dorsal fins, elongated in males. Locally common but difficult to find, living as adult in specific drab-looking corals in still coastal zones. Such corals live in algae-rich habitat and appear to be covered with greyish brown or purplish algae, which are actually polyps. This densely branching coral can be home to an entire mandarin fish family, with a colourful male dominating. Maximum length 6 cm.

GOBIES — GOBIIDAE

Largest family of marine fishes with estimated 200 genera and 1500 species worldwide. However, as studies progress, division into separate families can be expected. In Australia, there are about 80 genera and about 350 species. Tropical species often very small (a few centimetres long) and secretive, and many undescribed. No doubt more will be discovered in future surveys on tropical reefs. Species diversity is greatest in equatorial waters and rapidly decreases towards temperate zones. Most gobies have ventral fins united into a single large cup-shaped fin, and only clearly separate in sleeper gobies. Dorsal fins in 2 parts: the first with flexible spines and the second soft-rayed, usually headed by a single spine. Anal fin similar and opposite second dorsal fin. Primarily benthic fishes resting on substrate (a few hover close above), living on sand, rock, corals, weeds, in burrows and among corals. Some bury themselves in substrate to sleep or escape predators. Many tropical species live in association with particular corals or specific crustaceans, especially the alpheid shrimp. Eggs are usually guarded by a male; hatchlings have a pelagic stage. Most gobies take small prey; diet comprises invertebrates and fishes, depending on species. Some temperate species take larger prey, but many filter microscopic organisms from sand.

Crab-eyed Goby *Signigobius biocellatus*

Distinct ocelli in dorsal fins, black ventral and anal fins with blue spots. Adults nearly always in pairs, moving close together when feeding from sand. Raises dorsal fins when alarmed, waving ventral fin and moving in rocking motion, simulating a sideways-moving crab. Protected inner reefs on fine often silty sand and rubble along reefs, making burrow under partly buried large solid objects. Maximum length 10 cm.

Broad-barred Sleeper Goby *Valenciennea wardi*

Large white-edged black spot in first dorsal fin and body broadly banded. Typically for genus, hovering close to substrate and regularly scooping up sand with large mouth, feeding on organisms sifted out with gill rakers. Coastal mud slopes, adults usually in pairs but shy compared to other species and quickly retreating to burrow even when approached from a long distance. Maximum length 12 cm.

Fingered Dragonet (adult)　　　　　　　　**Fingered Dragonet** (juvenile)

Mandarin Fish

Crab-eyed Goby　　　　　　　　　　　**Broad-barred Sleeper Goby**

343

Black-lined Sleeper Goby *Valenciennea helsdingeni*

Black parallel longitudinal stripes along body and white-edged elongate black streak in dorsal fin easily identifies species. Some geographical variations: lower line dark orange-brown in northern Australia and both lines orange in the Indian Ocean. Adults mainly on deep slopes, but also shallow in quiet part of large coastal bays. Juveniles occasionally in clear estuaries on rubble near rocks. Adults ranging to temperate zones, where reach 25 cm in length. Usual maximum length 18 cm.

Orange-spotted Sleeper Goby *Valenciennea puellaris*

Pale, bone colour with numerous moderately large orange spots over upper sides, and with shiny pale blue markings on face. Adults form pairs, staying close together. Juveniles in small groups where common. Coastal to sheltered inner reefs on white sand and rubble slopes. Large tropical species, maximum length 20 cm.

Teardrop Sleeper Goby *Valenciennea longipinnis*

Body pale with several dark reddish longitudinal stripes and a series of spots or dashes, intermittently connecting. Lower line with a series of dark spots, each shaped like the lower part of a teardrop. Shallow coastal sand and rubble flats, often just away from mangrove zones, usually in pairs. Maximum length 15 cm.

Golden-head Sleeper Goby *Valenciennea strigata*

Bright yellow to orange or golden head easily identifies this species, especially when juvenile. In adults this colour reduced to area in front of eyes. Some equatorial populations occasionally lack this colour on white coral sand. Juveniles solitary in holes on rocky reefs in clear coastal to inner reef habitats. Adults usually in pairs. Maximum length 18 cm, usually 14 cm.

Byno Goby *Amblygobius bynoensis*

Body pale, with dark stripe edged with pale blue from snout through eye to just past pectoral fin, meeting some indistinct barring anteriorly on upper sides. Protected bays and harbours, often silty habitat or fine white sand just below intertidal zone. Make burrows under solid objects, adults usually in pairs, hovering close to substrate. Maximum length 10 cm.

Dusky Barred Goby *Amblygobius phalaena*

Caudal fin pale with one or more black spots, body barred, offset by pale blue borders in males. Often confused with closely related Indian Ocean species with distinct white bars in males. Coastal and rocky estuaries, often silty algal habitat along reef margins bordering onto sand. Maximum length 12 cm, usually 10 cm.

Black-lined Sleeper Goby

Orange-spotted Sleeper Goby

Teardrop Sleeper Goby

Golden-head Sleeper Goby

yno Goby

Dusky Barred Goby

Sphynx Goby *Amblygobius sphynx*

Pale, greyish brown to bright green, matching habitat colour, with 4 evenly spaced broad dusky bars, each with black line in centre and numerous tiny pale spots. Some adults with black spot in upper half of caudal-fin base. Very shallow seagrass beds to moderate depths with algae-covered rocks, hovering close above substrate. Maximum length 10 cm.

Red-lined Goby *Amblygobius rainfordi*

Head yellowish, graduating to dusky body with longitudinal black-edged red lines, thickest ones with additional pale blue outer edges, and a series of white spots over body along dorsal-fin base. Clear coastal and inner reefs on shallow slopes with rich coral growth, usually hovering along base of large corals. Maximum length 85 mm.

Large-mouth Goby *Redigobius macrostoma*

Pale yellow to brown with dense mottling above and indistinct barring below, first dorsal fin with distinct round black spot, reflecting blue at angle. Several similar tropical species, mostly in mangroves. This one the most southern, in sheltered bays and estuaries, entering lower reaches of freshwater streams. Among rocks and often on pylons of jetties or bridges across lake entrances. Maximum length 50 mm

Banded Reef Goby *Priolepis cincta*

Dusky brown to yellow with narrow white bands over head and body, caudal-fin posterior margin white and conspicuous in large individuals. Several similar species, secretive in ledges, this one the most widespread and often observed when inspecting reefs with a torch. Coastal to outer reefs in shallow to very deep reefs. Maximum length 50 mm in coral region, to 70 mm in the Sydney area due to lower temperatures.

Broad-banded Shrimp Goby *Amblyeleotris periophthalma*

Body with broad dark bands and often a series of spots over interspaces and orange spots on head. First dorsal fin filamentous. Great number of similar species with dark reddish bands of various widths. Protected coastal sand and mud slopes in burrows with alpheid shrimps. Maximum length 11 cm.

Diagonal Shrimp Goby *Amblyeleotris diagonalis*

Dark bands narrower than light interspaces and at a slight angle, more angular on head and first narrow, as line from tip of snout to eye. Protected sand slopes from coastal to inner reefs. Photograph taken at Camp Cove, Sydney Harbour, probably the most southern record. Several shrimp gobies seen there, but all extremely shy compared to those in the tropical zone, possibly due to predatory pressures. Maximum length 10 cm.

Sphynx Goby

Red-lined Goby

Large-mouth Goby

Banded Reef Goby

Broad-banded Shrimp Goby

Diagonal Shrimp Goby

Giant Shrimp Goby *Amblyeleotris fontanesi*

Dark banding subequal to pale interspacing, fins purplish blue, large adults with tiny orange spots on head. Coastal deep mudslopes, often in large numbers spread over suitable habitat, current-prone tidal areas. Largest shrimp goby, living with probably the largest alpheid shrimp of edible size, maximum length 25 cm (as observed in Papua New Guinea).

Burgundy Shrimp Goby *Amblyeleotris wheeleri*

Dark bands wine-red, some blue speckles along outside borders, and fins bluish. Colour according to habitat: when coastal, often muddy habitat, colours dark; and when outer reef, usually lagoons on white sand, colours light. Lives with grey or yellow alpheid shrimps. Maximum length 10 cm.

Black-chest Shrimp Goby *Amblyeleotris guttata*

Distinct species with black ventrally under head and belly, and black ventral fins. Body with numerous orange spots in adults. Clear coastal to outer reef lagoons, usually on coarse white sand slopes. Maximum length 11 cm.

Yellow Shrimp Goby *Cryptocentrus cinctus*

Several colour forms, most obvious the xanthic bright yellow with small blue spots over head and dorsally over part of body. Variations of mostly white to almost black in banded forms, black snout or black over head behind eye, but always showing small blue spots over head area. Usually in spread-out pairs along sand slopes, and locally common with yellow forms often outnumbering others. Pairs of mixed forms are not known at this stage, but different paired forms are often neighbours. Maximum length 10 cm.

Smiling Goby *Mahidolia mystacina*

Highly variable, yellow or dusky grey to brown-banded. Small males with tall dorsal fin and white or yellow-edged black spots on last membranes of first dorsal fin. Large individuals, probably females, with a series of bands in first dorsal fin. Coastal fine sand and mud habitats on flats and slopes, common in most areas. Maximum length 10 cm.

Giant Shrimp Goby

Burgundy Shrimp Goby

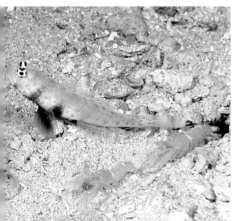

Black-chest Shrimp Goby

Yellow Shrimp Goby (yellow form)

Yellow Shrimp Goby (general form)

Smiling Goby

Twin-spotted Shrimp Goby *Vanderhorstia ambanoro*

Pale, almost white below and bluish grey above with a double series of black spots along upper sides. Spots larger or more numerous when found on dark substrate than on white sand. Ventral fin conspicuously banded with pink and blue in males used only for display. Muddy coastal slopes to deep outer reef lagoons and inner reef-flats on white sand with rubble. Maximum length 12 cm.

Slender Shrimp Goby *Vanderhorstia* sp.

Young and female with a black spot over fourth and fifth membranes in first dorsal fin, the latter moderately tall. Body, fins and cheek peppered with orange spots, most obvious when adult and living on dark substrate. First dorsal fin of male without black spot. Mud to sand slopes and flats, mainly deep large open sandflats between reefs. Usually in pairs hovering high above burrow during currents to feed on zooplankton. Common Great Barrier Reef species, but usually confused with Merten's Shrimp Goby *V. mertensi* which probably occurs in northern Australia (photograph taken in Indonesia). Males are metallic blue with orange midlateral stripe and juveniles have a large black spot on white first dorsal fin. Maximum length both species 11 cm.

Rayed Shrimp Goby *Tomiyamichthys(?)* sp.

Distinct with large dorsal fin and 4 anterior spines greatly extended with filaments, body below fin and head almost black, and rest of body pale with indistinct banding. Typically rests on substrate with dorsal fin fully erected, first ray almost horizontal and close above head, reaching past snout. Undescribed species from northern Australia and Indonesia, moderately common near Lizard Island, Queensland, on sandflats between inner reefs and large lagoons, usually in pairs. Maximum length 75 mm.

Pretty Lagoon Goby *Oplopomus oplopomus*

Pale sandy colour, small blue spots over body and short lines or dashes on head. Variable according to habitat. On dark sand a series of additional dark spots and adults become ornamented with small orange spots on body, some orange or yellow in fins and blue-edged black streak posteriorly in first dorsal fin. Common in protected shallow lagoons, often creating crater-like burrows. Maximum length 10 cm.

Mud Reef Goby *Exyrias bellissimus*

Body very robust, all median fins large, first dorsal slightly higher than second fin with short filaments at spine tips. Eyes elevated on top of head. Body mostly dark, head pale. Silty habitats along reef margins, often below large branching corals growing on mud and rubble substrate. Maximum length 15 cm.

Twin-spotted Shrimp Goby

Slender Shrimp Goby (adult)

Slender Shrimp Goby (juvenile)

Rayed Shrimp Goby

Jetty Lagoon Goby

Mud Reef Goby

Puntang Goby *Exyrias puntang*

Dorsal fins with distinct black and pale yellow alternating along spines, black on anterior spines extending onto membranes. Body and head pale grey with small dark spots above and a few white spots over sides. Shallow coastal rocky lagoons, often near freshwater run-offs. Sits out in open on rocks or coral rubble. Maximum length 14 cm.

Ornate Sand Goby *Istigobius ornatus*

Adults with yellow margin over dorsal fins and busy pattern of spots and dashes in median fins and dark bars on cheek, juveniles with yellow tip on first dorsal fin. Shallow coastal rocky reefs, subtidally to a few metres' depth. Several very similar species with a series of black or brown spots and dashes along sides. Juveniles particularly difficult to identify. Maximum length 12 cm.

Sloth Goby *Istigobius hoesei*

Pale grey with a series of light brown spots, pale blue spots and long dashes from behind pectoral-fin base to lower caudal-fin base with double pale spots on interspaces. Sheltered coastal bays and harbours, particularly common in the Sydney area, often in small loose aggregations on sand or mud along reef margins. Maximum length 10 cm.

Long-finned Goby *Favonigobius lateralis*

Thin white, slightly chevroned, bars along side. Inhabits clear coastal sandy habitat near beaches and under jetties. Several similar coastal and estuarine species. The most similar Tamar River Goby *F. tamarensis* mainly inhabits upper reaches of estuaries and fresh water. Maximum length 9 cm.

Orange-spotted Sand Goby *Coryphopterus* sp. (now known as *Fusigobius* sp.)

Pale white with bright orange blotches all over and, depending on the surroundings, with dark shading or blotches matching colour of sand. Found on sand patches close to reef or below large overhangs. Several similar species but less colourful, usually very camouflaged on course sand or rubble patches on reefs. This species is the most commonly observed in Australian waters. Maximum length 50 mm.

Poisonous Goby *Yongeichthys nebulosus*

Stocky species, pale grey with dusky brown mottling and a series of large dark blotches along sides. Skin contains poison that deters predators, and fish often on sand or mud in open surroundings, easily approached at close range. Coastal mud and sandflats, singly or in loose groups. Maximum length 15 cm.

Puntang Goby

Ornate Sand Goby

Sloth Goby

Long-finned Goby

Orange-spotted Sand Goby

Poisonous Goby

353

Yellow-finned Goby *Acanthogobius flavimanus*

Adults have a large head and elongate body. Pale brownish with a series of dark saddles and spots. Juveniles with pale yellow ventral and anal fins. Introduced Japanese species now established in major shipping harbours in the southern states. Aggressive, feeds on small fishes, including other gobies and juvenile tupong. Adults marine; the 26 cm adult was photographed near Mornington Pier, Port Phillip Bay. Juveniles move into rivers. Maximum length 30 cm.

Sculptured Goby *Callogobius mucosus*

Body and especially the head depressed. Large round pectoral and caudal fins. Variable from grey to dark brown with blotched pattern. Similar Flathead Goby *C. depressus* is more common on the east coast. Sheltered bays in mud and sand habitat under rocks or in narrow ledges. Commonly seen under jetties when turning over objects. Maximum length 11 cm.

Sailfin Goby *Nesogobius pulchellus*

Body sandy-coloured with a series of blue dashes midlaterally. Male with large sailfin-like first dorsal fin, usually ornamented with red stripes or a series of spots. Very common southern species in seagrass beds and low weed-covered reefs, often in pairs or small groups. Harbours and estuaries. Maximum length 7 cm, usually 5 cm.

Threadfin Sand Goby *Nesogobius* sp.

One of at least 9 new species along the south coast deposited in the Australian Museum more than 10 years ago for description. Most are sandy coloured but males display with brightly coloured fins. Several species with iridescent blue dashes, almost forming a line midlaterally. This species has long filament on last dorsal fin ray. Common on sand patches along seagrasses in Port Phillip Bay. Maximum length 6 cm.

Tortuosum Goby *Pleurosicya annandalei*

Several very similar, often semitransparent, small gobies, usually associating with invertebrate hosts such as corals or sponges. Some live on single species host, but others less choosy and a few found on plant leaves. Rarely leave host and feed primarily on zooplankton drifting into close range, but a few species nibble on host. Eggs are mostly deposited on host in small patches of rather large eggs with male closely guarding. This species is not often observed but, like others once the host is known, close examination of Pink Fan-coral *Solenocaulon tortuosum* usually reveals it. Often in small groups living on the hollow sides of the branches. These fans occur on sand slopes in moderate current channels, usually in depths over 20 m. Maximum length of goby 36 mm.

Yellow-finned Goby

Sculptured Goby

Sailfin Goby

Threadfin Sand Goby

Tortuosum Goby

355

Many Host Goby *Pleurosicya mossambica*

Pale pinkish, yellowish or greenish, depending on host, often semitransparent with whitish colour behind eyes and a series of white dashes internally over vertebral column; iris red, and usually red line from eye to tip of snout. Lives with many hosts, including various coloured sponges, ascidians, molluscs, sea-cucumbers and soft corals. Eggs are usually deposited on the least active, or passive, part of the host. Specimen on blue ascidian was photographed in Bali, Indonesia. Sheltered reefs from protected shallow bays to deep along inner reefs in current-prone areas. Similar Cling Goby *P. micheli*, semitransparent with white line internally over vertebral column, lives on hard corals. Maximum length 26 mm.

Soft Coral Goby *Pleurosicya boldinghi*

Stocky fish usually light pinkish colour but appearing white in natural light, and thin reddish line in front of each eye. Lives on large soft corals, *Demdronephthya* spp., on deep sand or mud slopes in current-prone areas, usually in depths over 20 m, and usually in small groups in relation to the size of the host. Eggs are deposited on the host near base. Maximum length 45 mm.

Slender Sponge Goby *Pleurosicya elongata*

Body very slender, snout long and pointed. Semitransparent with a series of small reddish dots mid-dorsally over back, a series of long dashes internally over vertebral column inside, and reddish line in front of each eye. Lives on fan sponges, usually drab-coloured on top and pinkish or purple underneath. Turning over these flexible, floppy sponges usually reveals the small goby, often several per sponge. Maximum length 40 mm.

Flathead Sponge Goby *Phyllogobius platycephalops*

Flattened species, especially head and snout. Iris yellow with red rings, and body colour similar to sponge with tiny white speckles variously distributed. Lives underneath various flexible fan sponges along coastal reefs in shallow depths. Usually solitary, and no other similar species present. Maximum length 50 mm.

Long-snout Sponge Goby *Luposicya lupus*

Body elongate, snout long and pointed. A series of small white spots along lower sides. Iris pale yellow, some thin reddish lines in front and behind eye with some white spotting between. Found on various large sponges, usually underneath or in shade, and often in small groups or mixed with other similar species. Maximum length 35 mm.

Many Host Goby

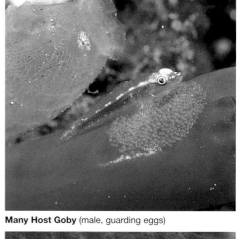

Many Host Goby (male, guarding eggs)

oft Coral Goby

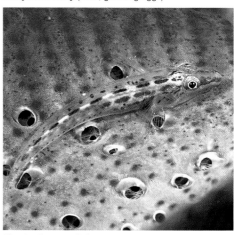

Slender Sponge Goby

athead Sponge Goby

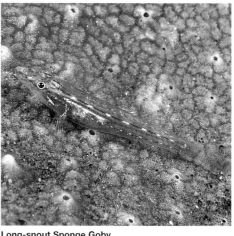

Long-snout Sponge Goby

357

Seawhip Goby *Bryaninops yongei*

Semitransparent, a series of white dashes internally with reddish spots over top mid-dorsally, and usually 2 pale short bars over abdomen. Lives on seawhip *Cirrhipathes anguina*, usually in pairs, sometimes juveniles also present. Eggs are laid on cleared section along whip. Common where host occurs, usually along slopes in channels prone to moderate currents. The similar but more elongate Black Coral Goby *B. tigris* lives on black corals growing on deep slopes. Maximum length 40 mm.

White-line Seawhip Goby *Bryaninops amplus*

Very transparent with silvery white line along top of vertebral column and some white speckling along lower sides. Lives on *Junceella fragilis* or closely related whips which are common in more silty inner reefs, where proliferate in certain current-prone areas. Maximum length about 40 mm in Australia (reported to 60 mm in the Philippines).

Purple-eyed Goby *Bryaninops natans*

Semitransparent with bright pink to purple eyes and abdomen yellow inside. Despite small size, often noticed and photographed by divers. Swims or floats in current in small groups above *Acropora* coral heads. Protected inner reefs along drop-offs and in current channels. Maximum length 20 mm.

Neon Pygmy Goby *Eviota pellucida*

Bright orange with thin yellow lines on top of head, most distinct between tip of snout, running through eye, to above conspicuous white line on dark abdomen. Shallow protected habitats with mixed rich coral and algae growth, often in lagoons. Maximum length 30 mm.

Striped Pygmy Goby *Eviota bifasciatus*

Pale whitish with longitudinal reddish black stripes, one mid-dorsally inside semitransparent back and one below white midlateral stripe along sides, bluish on eye and snout. Forms small groups, occasionally in large numbers over *Acropora* thickets, hovering just above to feed on zooplankton during currents. Maximum length 45 mm.

Hairfin Pygmy Goby *Eviota prasites*

Pale purplish brown with a series of white spots along lower body and cheek, shor series midlaterally behind eye and along mid-upper sides. First dorsal fin with thin dark hair-like filaments. One of many similar species often with many fewer feature than this species. All small and secretive in reefs. Maximum length 25 mm.

Seawhip Goby

White-line Seawhip Goby

Purple-eyed Goby

Neon Pygmy Goby

Striped Pygmy Goby

Hairfin Pygmy Goby

Red-lined Pygmy Goby *Trimma striatum*

Pale grey on head graduating to pinkish body with about 6 thin bright red lines along head, extending onto body but ending abruptly. Usually upside down on ceilings of caves or in ledges with rich invertebrate and algal growth. Coastal to inner reefs in shallow depths. Maximum length 35 mm.

Ring-eye Pygmy Goby *Trimma* sp.

Bright orange or red with just thin white ring around eye and yellow ring around pupil. One of many undescribed species on coral reefs. This species nearly always found resting on sponges along shallow drop-offs or slopes with rich invertebrate growth. Maximum length 40 mm.

DART GOBIES & WORM GOBIES — MICRODESMIDAE

Moderately large family of gobioid fishes with 12 genera and about 45 species. Two distinct groups presently regarded as subfamilies: Microdesminae, worm gobies and Ptereleotrinae, dart fishes. Possibly warrant family status, but until only recently were all included into the Gobidae. Worm gobies are long and slender with almost a tubular body and small head. Timid fishes, usually seen hovering above burrows of other gobies or jawfishes, ready to dive for cover at any sign of danger. Usually seen solitary over sandflats or slopes near reef outcrops or sparse seagrass habitat. Probably all 5 species are present in Australian waters. Dart gobies make their own burrows or share with others, and often occur in large schools above reefs when feeding on zooplankton. Some species pair and hover near their burrow.

Orange-line Worm Goby *Gunnellichthys viridescens*

Orange line from tip of snout to caudal fin, almost reaching posterior margin, outlined with pale blue on head and fin. Dorsal and anal fins with thin blue margins. Solitary hovering close to substrate on slopes and sandflats in current-prone areas. Common on sandflats north side of Lizard Island, Queensland, in 15–20 m depth. Maximum length 12 cm.

Black-lined Worm Goby *Gunnellichthys pleurotaenia*

Easily recognised by black line from tip of snout through eye to tip of caudal fin. Shallow coastal waters in vicinity of seagrass beds and mangroves, swimming along edges over sand in 1–10 m depth. Maximum length 12 cm.

Black-spot Worm Goby *Gunnellichthys monostigma*

Very pale with small but distinct black spot on opercle. Adults with pale blue centrally over head and dusky stripe along peduncle to end of fin. Occurs solitary, usually above burrows of other sand gobies which make burrows. Sand slopes and flats in coastal areas, or still inner reef sandflats but deep there, range 6–30 m depth. Largest species, maximum length 15 cm.

Red-lined Pygmy Goby

Ring-eye Pygmy Goby

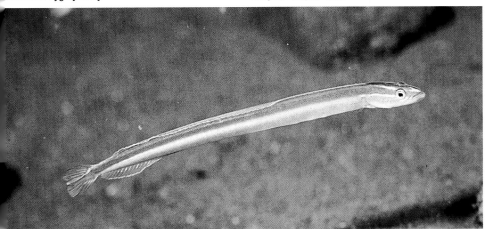

Orange-line Worm Goby

Black-lined Worm Goby

Black-spot Worm Goby

361

Red Fire Goby *Nemateleotris magnifica*

Easily recognised by white body and head shading into bright orange-red tail, and tall white spiky first dorsal fin. In Australia usually in pairs, flicking their tall dorsal fin in signalling fashion, and mainly in outer reef areas along base of drop-offs in depths of 20 m or more. Maximum length 75 mm.

Purple Fire Goby *Nemateleotris decora*

Very similar to Red Fire Goby (previous species), but tail blue and red, and tall first dorsal fin purplish red, appearing bright blue or purple underwater, depending on depth and light. Mainly on deep slopes at the base of outer reef drop-offs. Lives especially deep in Australia, where rarely in less than 50 m depth. Maximum length 75 mm.

Lyre-tail Dart Goby *Ptereleotris monoptera*

Pale greenish or bright blue above, light below, with dusky shading below eye and caudal fin distinctly lunate in adults, developing filaments at tips with age. Clear coastal rocky reefs to deep along drop-offs, often forming large schools in tidal current-prone places, sometimes mixing with other similar species. Maximum length 12 cm.

Tail-spot Dart Goby *Ptereleotris heteroptera*

Variable blue to green-blue, rarely brown. Obvious feature is black blotch centrally on caudal fin with rest of fin pale blue to bright yellow. Small juveniles iridescent blue. Often in pairs, sometimes forming small groups, especially when juveniles. Clear coastal reefs and deep lagoons or slopes. Maximum length 10 cm.

Arrow Goby *Ptereleotris evides*

Adults usually pale blue or greenish blue anteriorly, changing abruptly to dark posteriorly at vertical between origins of second dorsal and anal fin. The latter fins are dusky and usually held erect when swimming. Dusky streaks along outer caudal fin rays, for which sometimes called Scissortail Dart Goby. Small juveniles yellowish above, pale below and dark spot on upper caudal-fin base. Juveniles in small schools along sheltered low drop-offs; adults forming pairs in clear inner reef slopes and on rubble zones in deep lagoons on outer reefs. Maximum length 10 cm.

Red Fire Goby

Purple Fire Goby

yre-tail Dart Goby

Tail-spot Dart Goby

rrow Goby

SURGEONFISHES — ACANTHURIDAE

Large circumtropical family, 3 subfamilies: Acanthurinae, the surgeons, largest with 4 genera and 50 species; Nasinae, the unicorns, with single genus and 15 species; and Prionurinae, the sawtails, with a few species. All with representatives in Australian waters and about 35 species. Surgeonfishes feature a movable spine on caudal peduncle, venomous in a few species, used for defence or fighting and can inflict painful wounds. The unicorns have several fixed, often recurving spines, used for defence. Sawtails have a series of bony plates with a fixed short spine. Family of generally medium-sized fishes, ovate to oblong and usually with highly compressed bodies. Mouth rather small and usually adapted for grazing algae, with small numerous teeth in jaws, but some feed on plankton. Planktivores usually in large schools and benthic feeders either school or pair, but often depending on geographical area. Colour can vary drastically between juveniles and adults. Spines are often surrounded by bright warning colours.

Orange-blotch Surgeonfish *Acanthurus olivaceus*

Adults often dusky over posterior half with abrupt change from greyish yellow front to yellow, and large dark-edged orange streak just behind eye, occasionally all dark but brighter orange streak. Small juveniles lemon yellow with lunate tail, usually solitary but form groups when find each other. Adults often in moderately large but loose aggregations, depending on area and if common. Sheltered rocky and algal reefs, often in deep outer lagoons where algae may build up after storm damage. Maximum length 35 cm.

Pencilled Surgeonfish *Acanthurus dussumieri*

Adults with yellow band over nape between and slightly beyond eyes. Juveniles dark with yellowish dorsal fin and half-white caudal fin from base, turning yellow with age. Caudal-peduncle spine white and surrounding groove black. Juveniles inshore, often entering rocky estuaries, adults moving offshore to deeper water. Maximum length 50 cm.

Pale Surgeonfish *Acanthurus mata*

Brown to pale bluish grey, with double yellow horizontal band over snout between eyes and extending solid behind eyes to gill opening and thin blue longitudinal lines on head continuing onto body, becoming less distinct posteriorly. Juveniles uniformly pale blue. Caudal-peduncle spine black. Juveniles in shallow coastal waters, feeding on benthic algae. Adults schooling offshore and often feeding midwater on zooplankton. Maximum length 45 cm.

Yellowfin Surgeonfish *Acanthurus xanthopterus*

Adults dusky yellow anteriorly, gradually changing to very dark posteriorly. White band over caudal-fin base, extending slightly along outer rays, but variable to almost completely pale blue without white caudal band. Usually bright blue line along dorsal-fin base and with small yellow area in front and below eye, and outer two-thirds of pectoral fins yellow. Juveniles deep-bodied and strongly striped along body and fins, stripes breaking up into scribbles in subadults. Juveniles solitary in shallow coastal waters, including freshwater run-offs, forming small groups at larger sizes and moving to silty inner reef habitat. Large adults in small aggregations along deep slopes or the base of drop-offs. Juveniles and subadults often confused with *A. grammoptilus*, the white-spined species from north-western Australia. Maximum length 56 cm.

Orange-blotch Surgeonfish (adult)

Orange-blotch Surgeonfish (juvenile)

Pencilled Surgeonfish

Pale Surgeonfish

Yellowfin Surgeonfish (adult)

Yellowfin Surgeonfish (juvenile)

365

Orange-socket Surgeonfish *Acanthurus auranticavus*

Dark brown to almost black body with extremely fine scribble patterns, white band over caudal-fin base, dark elongate mark like 2 joining spots at short distance behind eye. Area around spine orange, usually brightening during display but barely visible when fish feeding on substrate. Shallow coastal to outer reef-flats, in small groups and often joining other similar species. Similar Dark Surgeon *A. blochii* has small yellow dash behind eye. Maximum length 45 cm.

Eye-line Surgeonfish *Acanthurus nigricauda*

Variable from pale greyish or yellowish brown to almost black, often changing colour quickly, with white line on caudal-fin base. Long black line behind each eye and along caudal-peduncle spine, the latter extending forward and tapering nearly to above anal-fin origin. Caudal fin all white in juveniles and extremely lunate with filamented tips in large adults. Shallow reef-flats, grazing benthic algae, often with other species. Maximum length 40 cm.

Eye-spot Surgeonfish *Acanthurus bariene*

Distinct blue-edged black spot just behind eye, body pale dusky to orange-brown, with extremely fine scribble lines all over and finely spotted over cheek. Caudal fin with light orange to white bands along outer margins and long tips, and light orange vertical streak from behind eye-spot to pectoral-fin base, spine white. Deep coastal to outer reef slopes, usually singly when grazing on substrate. Maximum length 40 cm.

Mimic Surgeonfish *Acanthurus pyroferus*

Adults yellowish to dark brown with dusky fins. Head often pale and eyes dark. Usually broad black band over posterior gill margin to pectoral-fin base with orange area immediately behind. Caudal fin strongly lunate with broad yellow posterior margin. Small juveniles completely different and several colour forms that mimic small angelfishes *Centropyge* spp. In Australia, usually *C. heraldi*, *C. vrolikii* and rarely *C. bicolor*. All have the typical round caudal fin of angelfishes and colours are exact. Only shape of mouth is different and mimic can only be distinguished at close range. A yellow form with orange scribbles appears to have no specific model. Once outgrowing model, mimic changes to adult colouration. These juveniles gain protection from predators during vulnerable early stages by mimicking clever small angelfishes, which are experienced in avoiding predators. Usually predators make no attempt to strike, having probably tried unsuccessfully before, and concentrate on easier prey. Maximum length 20 cm.

Orange-socket Surgeonfish

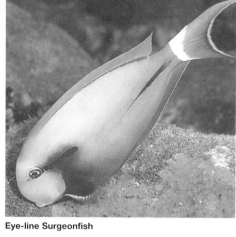

Eye-line Surgeonfish

Eye-spot Surgeonfish

Mimic Surgeonfish (adult)

Mimic Surgeonfish (*Centropyge heraldi* mimic)

Mimic Surgeonfish (*Centropyge vrolikii* mimic)

367

Lined Surgeonfish *Acanthurus lineatus*

Young and adults easily identified by numerous yellow to orange, blue and white longitudinal lines. Caudal fin strongly lunate in adults. Common in small to large aggregations on coastal to outer reef-flats. Usually subtidal to a few metres deep in narrow reef channels in current-prone areas. Maximum length 35 cm.

Convict Surgeonfish *Acanthurus triostegus*

Pale greenish white, sometimes yellowish above with thin black bars. Juveniles almost identical to adults. Coastal bays and harbours, shallow reef-flats and often boulder areas, feeding on benthic algae, sometimes forming great schools. Maximum length 26 cm, usually 20 cm.

Blue Tang *Paracanthurus hepatus*

Easily identified by bright blue and black on head and body, and yellow caudal fin. Juveniles similar to adults, but latter with more elongate body shape. Small juveniles usually in *Acropora* thickets, swimming just above to feed on zooplankton, quickly diving between coral branches if approached. Adults swim about more freely, but also have numerous narrow crevices to retreat to. Juveniles feeding primarily on zooplankton and adults additionally grazing benthic algae. Popular fish with divers and aquarists, also called Wedge-tail Blue Tang, Flagtail Blue Surgeonfish and Palette Surgeonfish. Maximum length 30 cm.

Sailfin Surgeonfish *Zebrasoma veliferum*

Caudal fin yellow in Australian populations, and truncate. Dorsal and anal fins broadly rounded but greatly elevated in small juveniles in which total height is greater than total length. Variably with alternating banding of light yellow and black to dark brown. Usually band over eye solid black, and other dark bands with narrow alternating narrow light and dark brown bands within. Small juveniles with grey to bright yellow fins and head with 2 black vertical stripes, first over eye. Coastal reefs and deep lagoons on low reefs, small juveniles shy, among high, dense coral growth with algae on substrate. Mostly solitary, adults sometimes in pairs. Maximum length 40 cm.

Lined Surgeonfish

Convict Surgeonfish

Blue Tang

Sailfin Surgeonfish (adult)

Sailfin Surgeonfish (juvenile)

Big-nose Unicornfish *Naso vlamingii*

Adults grey to yellowish brown with numerous small blue spots. Females with thin vertical lines behind head over central area of body, becoming more lined with age. Males usually fully lined to ventral parts and spotted only over back. They develop a large nose reaching over mouth, with thick blue line from tip to below eye, blue lips, and long filaments on caudal-fin tips. Displaying males show large pale blue area over body behind head, and blue markings intensify to electric blue. General colour often changes with mood, habitat or purpose, especially when visiting cleaning stations, turning exceptionally pale to assist the cleaner fish in finding parasites. Juveniles similar to adults but lack the enlarged snout and are finely spotted. Clear coastal to outer reef slopes and drop-offs, adults forming schools swimming openly to feed on plankton. Maximum length 55 cm.

Orange-spine Unicornfish *Naso lituratus*

Easily identified by colour. Two bright orange forward hooked spines on caudal peduncle, orange lips and black face mask. Adults develop long trailing filaments on caudal-fin tips. Shallow clear coastal to outer reef crests and slopes, usually grazing algae among coral heads or in reef gutters. Maximum length 45 cm.

Blue-spine Unicornfish *Naso unicornis*

Juvenile to adult, usually uniformly grey to yellowish grey, but caudal-peduncle spines bright pale blue, including in small juveniles. In large males it occasionally changes, with a broad white speckled band just behind head, or with a whitish back at night. Juveniles on clear coastal rocky reefs with algae growth, adults along shallow parts of slopes adjacent to deep water. Maximum length 70 cm.

Spotted Unicornfish *Naso brevirostris*

Adults very pale grey to greenish grey, with small dark spots all over head and body which changes to thin vertical lines with age and particularly distinct in males. Caudal fin white and dusky blotch on base. Juveniles lack horny protrusion on snout, which is particularly long in males. Young on shallow reefs feeding on benthic algae. Adults schooling along deep slopes and drop-offs, feeding on plankton in currents. Maximum length 50 cm.

Big-nose Unicornfish (male, displaying)

Big-nose Unicornfish (male with cleaner wrasse)

Big-nose Unicornfish (female)

Orange-spine Unicornfish

Blue-spine Unicornfish

Spotted Unicornfish

371

Humpback Unicornfish *Naso brachycentron*

Males with long protruding horn in front of eyes, absent in females, both with peculiar hump below spinous dorsal fin, forming highest part of body. Hump forms when about 20 cm long. Outer reef slopes and drop-offs, usually in small aggregations on reef crest along edge to deep parts. Maximum length 70 cm.

Sleek Unicornfish *Naso hexacanthus*

Body dusky to greenish grey, sometimes yellow over chest area, with dark margin along opercle and preopercle margins. Caudal fin blue, especially obvious when viewed underwater with other features less distinct. Usually in schools along deep outer reef drop-offs, feeding on plankton in currents. Reported maximum length 75 cm, usually 50 cm.

Slender Unicornfish *Naso lopezi*

Slender body readily identifies this species. Pale grey, almost white below with small dusky spots over upper half of body and head, and sometimes white ring around caudal peduncle. Usually only seen along very deep drop-offs in schools, rising to shallow depths during current runs to feed on plankton. Maximum length 60 cm.

Sawtail *Prionurus microlepidotus*

Mostly dark grey with a series of 5–7 black bony plates with a short spine along caudal peduncle. Small juveniles deep-bodied with white or yellowish caudal fin. Adults more elongate, especially males which may show white mottling pattern over body at times, and caudal-fin colour as body. Coastal reefs and rocky estuaries, sometimes forming schools in turbulent coastal areas to feed on plankton matter. Maximum length 50 cm.

Spotted Sawtail *Prionurus maculatus*

Similar to Sawtail (previous species), but usually with 3 plates on caudal peduncle and is yellow spotted or with yellow bars on lower sides. Coastal to offshore reefs, mixing with other species in coastal waters and forming own schools offshore. Juveniles in weedy reefs. Maximum length 40 cm.

Humpback Unicornfish

Sleek Unicornfish

Slender Unicornfish

awtail

Spotted Sawtail

MOORISH IDOLS — ZANCLIDAE

Single widespread Indo-Pacific species. Shares many characteristics with closely related surgeonfishes, such as strongly compressed bodies, but body almost circular, which in surgeonfishes is elongated. Snout produced, small mouth at tip, and jaws with long slender bristle-like teeth covered by fleshy lips. Adults develop sturdy spine in front of eyes but lack spines or plates on caudal peduncle, which are characteristic of surgeonfishes. Long white wimple-like dorsal fin filament typifies this fish.

Moorish Idol *Zanclus cornutus*

Easily recognised by shape and colour. Commonly observed throughout its range from coastal to offshore reefs, juveniles often on rocky reefs in estuaries. Expatriates found well beyond breeding range, travelling as larvae in currents. Various depths from shallow algal flats to deep sponge areas, feeding on great variety of algae and invertebrates. Juveniles solitary; adults usually in pairs, but may form great schools apparently to move over large areas to feed or migrate. Maximum length 22 cm.

RABBITFISHES — SIGANIDAE

Primarily tropical family with 2 subgenera and about 30 species distributed in the Indo-Pacific, of which 16 are found in Australian waters. Rather unusual group, with every species having identical fin counts, except slight variations in pectoral fins, and featuring numerous venomous spines. Unique in having a spine at each end of ventral fins with 3 rays between, and 7 spines in anal fin. Mouth small, well in front of eyes, jaws with single row of small close-set incisiform teeth. Long-snouted species in subgenus *Lo*. Mostly weed, algae or seagrass-dwellers, some venturing onto coral reefs as well, and a few on coral reefs only. Live colours are distinct but on death quickly fade and many species virtually impossible to identify, especially from seagrass beds. Small juveniles sometimes enter fresh water.

Happy Moments *Siganus nebulosus*

Adults pale greenish grey with numerous pale blue spots all over. Juveniles whitish grey with broad grey to almost black midlateral band, and with white spots all over. Usually dark spot at eye diameter distance behind eye. Adults may occasionally show this dark spot. Nostrils with distinct elongate flap. Small juveniles secretive in seagrasses or dense algal growth on rocks in estuaries. Adults form moderately large schools in coastal algae-rich habitats and harbours. One of several similar species variously distributed over the Indo-Pacific, often confused with the Japanese *S. fuscescens* which differs considerably in colour and even in Japan a second similar new species is recognised. At least 3 similar species in tropical Australian waters. Happy Moments subtropical. Maximum length 30 cm.

Pearly-spotted Rabbitfish *Siganus margaritiferus*

Very similar to Happy Moments (previous species), but less spotted as adult, slightly more slender and lacks elongated flaps on nostrils. Adults pale, greenish grey with pearly whitish spotting over back and ventral areas, spots not elongating anywhere. Juveniles green in seagrasses with numerous white spots and a few dark spots mixed in. Coastal reefs with rich algae growth, swimming in small groups. Rather shy and if approached quickly moves from feeding session to other area. Juveniles in seagrass beds, often feeding in great numbers by grazing algae on the leaves. Maximum length 25 cm.

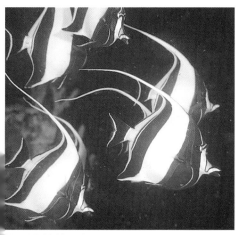

Moorish Idol (adult)

Moorish Idol (juvenile)

Happy Moments (adult)

Happy Moments (juvenile)

Pearly-spotted Rabbitfish (adult)

Pearly-spotted Rabbitfish (juvenile)

White-spotted Rabbitfish *Siganus canaliculatus*

Very similar to Pearly-spotted Rabbitfish (previous species), but adults greyish brown with numerous small white spots, many elongating horizontally, and caudal fin more pointed. Juveniles pale grey with numerous small round white spots, deeper-bodied compared to Pearly-spotted Rabbitfish, and dorsal profile of head evenly rounded. Coastal to inner reef slopes in coral and algae areas, juveniles very shallow in small aggregations in silty algae reef or rubble habitat, adults on deeper slopes in reefs with algae, sponge and hydroid growth, solitary or in small groups. Maximum length 30 cm.

Scribbled Rabbitfish *Siganus spinus*

Mosaic pattern of lines and scribbles over head, body and caudal peduncle. Caudal fin truncate. Coastal rocky and mixed algae coral reefs, usually in small groups swimming over reef sections and shallow flats with regular feeding stops. Often joined by juveniles of Pearly-spotted Rabbitfish. Similar Maze Rabbitfish *Siganus vermiculatus*, deeper bodied and growing much larger, common throughout Indonesia and probably occurs in northern Australia. Scribbled Rabbitfish small, maximum length 20 cm.

Schooling Rabbitfish *Siganus argenteus*

Grey to pale blue with yellow spots in dense patch on top of head, over sides and often forming irregular longitudinal lines along lower half. Dark stripe or patch above pectoral-fin base. Caudal fin forked. Another very similar species known from the west Pacific, apparently undescribed, with lunate and taller caudal fin, and probably occurs in Australian waters. Forms large dense schools in coastal and inner reef algae zones. Maximum length 37 cm, usually 30 cm.

Java Rabbitfish *Siganus javus*

Distinct species with numerous white spots above and fine longitudinal lines below. Large black blotch in caudal fin, and head and fins often yellow. Mainly estuarine and silty coastal reefs, juveniles entering lower reaches of rivers, feeding on benthic algae, but adults sometimes in schools feeding midwater on plankton. Maximum length 40 cm in Australian waters (reported to 53 cm from Oman).

Lined Rabbitfish *Siganus lineatus*

Large golden blotch below end of dorsal fin, body bluish grey with numerous irregular yellow longitudinal lines and spots. Sibling Gold-saddle Rabbitfish *S. guttatus* is spotted instead of lined, and replaces this species north of Australia and west of New Guinea. Sheltered reefs, often in groups near caves or below overhangs after feeding sessions on benthic algae. Maximum length 40 cm.

White-spotted Rabbitfish (adult)

White-spotted Rabbitfish (juvenile)

Scribbled Rabbitfish

Schooling Rabbitfish

Java Rabbitfish

Lined Rabbitfish

Blue-lined Rabbitfish *Siganus doliatus*

Pale yellow upper half, including dorsal and caudal fins, and whitish below with numerous blue lines across head. One or two lines along dorsal-fin base, partly scribbling into vertical lines below, covering nearly all of body. Two angular bands, first from chin to eye and second parallel just behind head. Juveniles more yellow with less lines, but thicker ones. Clear sheltered inner reef zones, usually in small groups over shallow reefs with some algae and good coral growth. Maximum length 25 cm.

Double-barred Rabbitfish *Siganus virgatus*

Almost identical to sibling Blue-lined Rabbitfish (previous species), mainly lacking blue lines over most of body, but apparently hybridising where ranges overlap. Some variation between coastal and offshore fish. Usually coastal, often silty reefs in shallow depths but occasionally on outer reefs where more colourful and show some vertical lines on sides as in Blue-lined Rabbitfish. Small juveniles enter rivers and often live in pure fresh water, at some stage moving in small groups onto dense coral slopes with good algal growth in between. Adults usually in pairs feeding on benthic algae. Shy species, swimming away quickly when disturbed feeding. Reported from Western Australia as *S. doliatus* based on offshore specimens showing vertical blue lines through second dark bar and part of body. Coastal specimens in silty water have reflective white abdomen. Maximum length 30 cm.

Masked Rabbitfish *Siganus puellus*

Bright lemon yellow with black band from chin to eye, continuing above into close-set patch of black spots, and thin lines or scribbles from almost white to pale blue. Slender compared to other similar species. Clear coastal to inner and outer reef lagoons, usually in rich coral and algal zones on slopes. Juveniles among *Acropora* branches and adults in large branching corals. Often swim in pairs or small aggregations. Maximum length 30 cm.

Coral Rabbitfish *Siganus corallinus* (now known as *S. tetrazonus*)

Adults usually with black patch over eye. Highly variable, bright yellow to orange-yellow with numerous blue spots or lines, partly or all over head and body, but not dorsal and caudal fins. Head nearly always spotted but body often with spotless areas, which can be anywhere, or occasionally no spots at all. Sometimes with thin vertical lines along lower part of body. Juveniles with numerous thin straight vertical lines over body and top of head, dusky band from eye to tip of snout. Clear coastal to outer reef lagoons and slopes, usually in tall coral growth areas, swimming in pairs along bases of bommies or short drop-offs, feeding on substrate below. Small juveniles solitary, secretive among boulders or in crevices of large coral heads. Maximum length 30 cm.

Gold-spotted Rabbitfish *Siganus punctatus*

Pale, greenish grey with close-set brown to orange spots, and sometimes large round dark spot at short distance behind eye. Juveniles similar to adult, but spots fewer and proportionally much larger. Adults pairing on deep coastal slopes. Juveniles in shallow coastal waters, often among mangroves in freshwater run-offs. Maximum length 35 cm.

Blue-lined Rabbitfish

Double-barred Rabbitfish (adult)

Double-barred Rabbitfish (juvenile)

Double-barred Rabbitfish (juvenile, freshwater)

Masked Rabbitfish

Coral Rabbitfish (adult)

Coral Rabbitfish (juvenile)

Gold-spotted Rabbitfish

379

Foxface *Siganus vulpinus*

Subgenus *Lo* with longer snout, and easily recognised by colour, black and white striped head, and bright yellow body. Western population with black blotch near centre of body thought to be identical to Japanese *S. unimaculatus*. Small juveniles dusky upper half and white lower half with yellow median fins. Clear coastal to outer reef crests and slopes, usually seen in pairs swimming close above reefs over corals, feeding on lower substrate in-between. Small juveniles secretive in dense corals, forming small groups but pairing at an early age, as soon as adult pattern shows. Maximum length 25 cm.

LEFT-EYED FLOUNDERS — BOTHIDAE

Very large family with 15 genera and 90 species in the Indo-Pacific alone, and over double that number of genera and species worldwide. Probably 6 genera and about 50 species are found in Australian waters. Mostly tropical with a few representatives in southern waters, and only larger and commonly observed species included here. Generally deep-bodied and extremely compressed with eye on left side of head. Left or ocular side pigmented to match surroundings, right or blind side unpigmented, used as underside or side to lie on substrate. Lateral line poorly developed or absent on blind side, pectoral fins present, and caudal fin free from dorsal and anal fins. Larval stage swims upright, initially bilaterally symmetrical with eye on each side. Changing at various stages depending on genus with eye travelling to left side when settling on substrate. After settling mostly buried with only eyes exposed, and usually active on dusk or only nocturnal, but a few active diurnally. Diet comprises benthic invertebrates and small fishes. Large species regarded as excellent table fish.

Leopard Flounder *Bothus pantherinus*

General colour matching substrates with combined pale and brown spotting, often with a series of pale spots surrounding dark spots like a small flower, and such flower spots evenly distributed all over. Floral Flounder would perhaps be a more appropriate name. Left pectoral fin with greatly extended filamentous rays, reaching caudal fin in males. Shallow sandflats and slopes, commonly seen along coastal reef margins. Maximum length 30 cm.

Peacock Flounder *Bothus mancus*

Eyes wide apart. Pale, sandy colour with bright blue spots evenly distributed over ocular side, forming ringed patterns in large males and usually 2 dark blotches along midline. Left pectoral fin black in males with filaments and held upright like a flag. Unlike most flounders, often leaves sand and visits rocky or coral reefs, gliding over reef and rubble. Seaward reefs. Maximum length 45 cm.

Foxface (adult)

Foxface (juvenile)

Leopard Flounder (close-up of eyes)

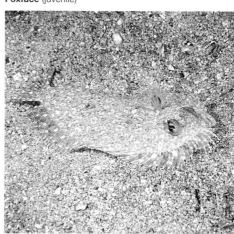

Leopard Flounder (male)

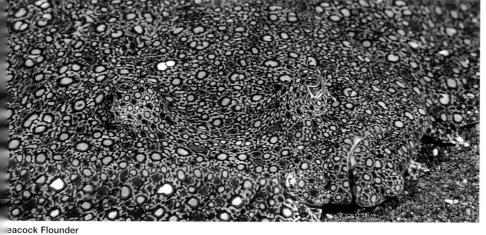

Peacock Flounder

LARGE-TOOTH FLOUNDERS — PARALICHTHYIDAE

Small family with 5 genera and about 28 species in the Indo-Pacific, and only 2 species commonly encountered in Australian waters. Until recently placed in Bothidae (previously family). Best separated by fully developed lateral line on blind side. Ventral fins short-based, their length much greater than the base width, and clearly separate. Caudal fin bluntly pointed over middle rays. Both eyes on left pigmented side and blind underside usually unpigmented. Mouth moderately large with uniserial teeth in each jaw and often with enlarged canines. Buries in substrate along reef margins to ambush prey. Diurnally active and fast swimmers, getting quickly out of sight when disturbed. Larger species excellent to eat.

Small-tooth Flounder *Pseudorhombus jenynsii*

Matches sand colours. Tips of median fins white and often showing as distinct white margin. Variously spotted. Usually 4 larger spots, standing out from other pattern, centrally placed as in corners of square box, each whitish with black centres and surrounds, and fifth similar spot behind, midlaterally and halfway to caudal fin. Only common member of the genus in the southern half of Australia. In sandy or muddy estuaries and sheltered coastal bays. Maximum length 35 cm.

Large-tooth Flounder *Pseudorhombus arsius*

Very similar to Small-tooth Flounder (previous species), but with smaller spotted pattern, larger mouth and centre of caudal fin more pointed. Small but distinct white spot at end of pectoral-fin base (also present in Small-tooth Flounder, but more anterior and less distinct). Coastal and estuarine, but mainly on clean white sand. Maximum length 40 cm.

RIGHT-EYED FLOUNDERS — PLEURONECTIDAE

Large family of small to medium fishes with 45 genera and about 100 species, many of which are commercially important, especially in Japan where represented with approximately 40 species. About 5 genera and 12 Australian species, many of which occur in southern temperate waters. Elongate to very deep-bodied with both eyes on right side (except one Japanese species and occasional mutant) Left side unpigmented and used to lie on substrate. Lateral line distinct, running almost straight from upper gill opening. Eyes small and close together, directly above each other. Fins entirely soft-rayed with large number of elements, sometimes anterior ones greatly extended. Southern *Ammotretis* larvae placed in aquarium quickly settle on substrate and pigment almost immediately. Left eye migrates through head to right side; in some other genera the eye travels over nape. Benthic fishes usually remain buried during the day with just the eyes exposed; a few are diurnally active. Diet consists primarily of crustaceans.

Greenback Flounder *Rhombosolea tapirina*

Almost diamond-shaped and snout pointed. Sandy coloured with dusky blotches. Various habitats from muddy shallow bays to deep offshore. Small juveniles often in lower reaches of rivers. Active species during the day, young commonly along the edge of sandy beaches in sheltered bays. Rests on sand with blind-side pectoral fin, which has supportive fleshy tips, and extremes of dorsal and anal fins. Maximum length 45 cm, usually 40 cm.

Long-snout Flounder *Ammotretis rostratus*

Dorsal fin extending over snout, and snout extending over front of mouth. Shape, including fins, broadly rounded when seen from above with large rounded caudal fin. Grey to brown in relation to habitat. Common bay species. Similar Spotted Flounder *A. lituratus* more offshore and has 9–10 right ventral fin rays versus 7, which can be counted underwater. Maximum length 25 cm.

Small-tooth Flounder

Large-tooth Flounder

Greenback Flounder

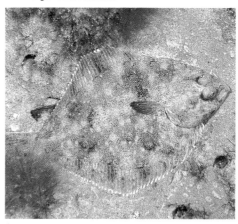

Greenback Flounder (variation)

Long-snout Flounder

383

SOLES — SOLEIDAE

Large family, mostly small fishes, with 30 genera and over 100 species, but at present poorly defined. About 15 genera and unknown number of species are found in Australian waters. Usually elongate, but a few deep-bodied. Both eyes on right side, left side unpigmented and used as underside. Pigmented side often with distinct banded or spotted patterns. Head small, preopercle concealed, eyes small, snout elongated over mouth, teeth in both jaws on blind side only. Often with numerous papillae on blind side of head. Fins all soft-rayed and usually almost surround body, except head ventrally. Some possess toxin glands on bases of median-fin rays. Benthic fishes, usually buried in substrate in fine sand or mud, feeding on small invertebrates or fishes. Some congregate in large numbers along reef edges.

Peacock Sole *Pardachirus pavoninus*

Pigmented side covered with various-shaped dark-edged white blotches, some with black spots in centre and yellow spots smaller than white blotches distributed in-between. Usually buried and when disturbed tries to bury itself immediately. If held or distressed, a milky toxic substance is secreted from almost entire outline of body, serving to stun predators. Coastal sand or mudflats and slopes, sometime in small loose groups. Maximum length 22 cm.

Southern Peacock Sole *Pardachirus hedleyi*

Highly variable pattern of different sized or shaped dark-edged white spots or blotches all over, mixed with some darker spots, according to habitat. Can change quickly to match different surroundings. Series of toxic glands along dorsal and anal-fin bases. Coastal to offshore, usually on clean sand with fine rubble accumulating at particular reef edges. Maximum length 15 cm.

Peppered Sole *Aseraggodes* sp.

Sandy, from light to dark brown with pattern of white scribbles or spots and indistinct but particular pattern of dark blotches spread over body and head, and fins with white speckling randomly over rays. Very common in New South Wales but as yet undescribed. Coastal bays and harbours in mud or sand along reef margins, usually in small aggregations. Maximum length 10 cm.

Black Sole *Synaptura nigra*

Best recognised by shape. Very deep-bodied and tapering to caudal fin with dorsal and anal fins confluent with caudal fin. Ocular side pale brown to blackish, and blind side white. Estuaries and sheltered coastal bays, usually in very fine sand or mud, buried during the day. Very slimy, but excellent to eat. Largest species, maximum length 35 cm.

Small-headed Sole *Aesopia microcephala*

Variable pale to dark brown with dark-edged pale bands, narrow over head, broader over body. Median fins with alternating blue and black outward streaks over outer halves, especially bright in juveniles which curl their body when disturbed, simulating the bad-tasting flatworm as a defence. Estuaries and harbours in muddy substrates. Maximum length 22 cm.

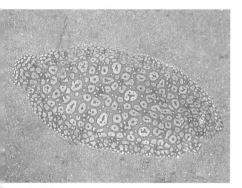

Peacock Sole

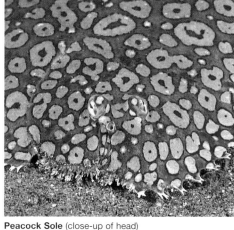

Peacock Sole (close-up of head)

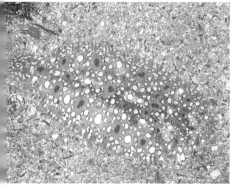

Southern Peacock Sole

Peppered Sole

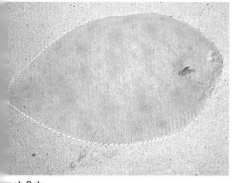

Black Sole

Small-headed Sole

TRIGGERFISHES — BALISTIDAE

Moderately large tropical family with 12 genera and over 40 species, primarily Indo-Pacific, about 30 o which are in Australian waters. Ovate, compressed bodies, covered by tiny to moderate-sized hard plate-like scales, often enlarged near gill opening. Dorsal fin in 2 parts: first fin with 3 spines of which first stout and lockable into upright position by second, and third small; second fin soft-rayed. Pectora fins small and paddle-like, and ventral fins rudimentary encased with small scales. Mouth small but with large and very strong teeth in jaws. Most species distinctly coloured and easily identified. Juveniles often differ from adults, but little differences between sexes. Diet comprises a mixture of algae and invertebrates. Most feeding on benthic matter and a few species taking plankton. Benthic species aggressive, territorial and usually seen solitary. Planktivores usually form large schools.

Black Triggerfish *Melichthys niger*

Looks black underwater with just white lines along bases of soft dorsal and anal fins. Almost identical Indian Triggerfish *M. indicus* has white margin posteriorly on caudal fin. Close examination with good light shows a fine pattern of zigzag lines along scale rows and males with thin iridescent blue lines radiating from eyes Clear outer reef crests near deep slopes, usually retreating to deeper parts when approached. Males seem to dominate several females in their territory. Maximum length 30 cm.

Paddlefin Triggerfish *Melichthys vidua*

Large adults green below and dusky above, and yellow pectoral fin. Smaller individuals brownish grey and whitish caudal fin with thin lines radiating from eyes. Clear coastal to outer reef drop-offs, staying close to substrates in ledges or small caves. Maximum length 35 cm.

Gilded Triggerfish *Xanthichthys auromarginatus*

Unlike most species, males and females quite different. Males with purple from lower cheek to mouth, and broadly yellow-margined median fins, both markings lacking in females. Clear outer reef drop-offs along walls in or in front of ledges an caves. Females outnumber males and a male usually in close vicinity of females. Maximum length 22 cm.

Hawaiian Triggerfish *Rhinecanthus aculeatus*

Easily recognised by colour pattern. Typically for genus, mouth small and at distance from eye. Shallow coastal but clear reefs, often surge-prone flats or lagoon on outer reefs, in depths just subtidally, and rarely deeper than a few metres. Maximum length 25 cm.

Wedge-tail Triggerfish *Rhinecanthus rectangulus*

Black stripes between eyes, below broadening to almost black ventral zone,with V-shaped lines and shapes on its side over caudal peduncle. Shy species on surge reefs in shallow depths, just below intertidal zones. Maximum length 25 cm.

Black Triggerfish

Paddlefin Triggerfish

Gilded Triggerfish

Hawaiian Triggerfish

Wedge-tail Triggerfish

Boomerang Triggerfish *Sufflamen bursa*

Best recognised by double vertical stripe over end of head, converging at lower pectoral-fin base. Little change from juvenile to adult. Clear coastal to outer reef slopes, solitary in rich coral zones. Maximum length 30 cm.

Half-moon Triggerfish *Sufflamen chrysopterus*

Great differences between adults and juveniles. Juveniles black midlaterally with yellow above and white below, latter covering more than lower half. Adults mostly dark on sides, paler above, with blue from lower anterior part of mouth to lowest ventral part of body. Shallow semi-protected ocean reef margins among boulders on sand, juveniles often in spread-out groups. Maximum length 30 cm.

Bridled Triggerfish *Sufflamen fraenatus*

Juveniles dusky over top half at eye level with dusky lines. Lower half almost white with thin pencil lines. Adults rather featureless without lines or spots, plain pale with yellowish grey, just dusky in front of eyes and pectoral-fin base. Coastal, often silty reefs near mangroves; juveniles among low boulder reefs on sand, digging small burrows to hide below rocks. Maximum length 35 cm.

Striped Triggerfish *Balistapus undulatus*

Distinct striped pattern at all stages. Green or bluish grey with yellow to orange stripes curving from nape backwards along body. Male lacks stripes over snout, and adults with large black blotch surrounding peduncular spines. Clear coastal to outer reef slopes and drop-offs, usually in rich invertebrate habitat, often at moderate depths in sponge areas. Maximum length 30 cm.

Blue Triggerfish *Odonus niger*

Adults dark blue with light blue head, and often bright blue caudal fin. Two blue lines from eye over snout, lower joining short lines behind mouth, giving impression of larger mouth. Indian Ocean form has long stripe from mouth to pectoral-fin base. Teeth red in adults. Small juveniles completely different, usually pale green with thin brown longitudinal lines, usually in small groups in coastal waters with small isolated outcrops of rock or coral on sand or mud slopes. Adult congregate in great numbers in current channels feeding high above substrate on zooplankton. When hiding in reefs, they curiously leave brightly coloured caudal fins exposed with lobes crossed, and often numerous tails can be seen in relatively small reef sections. Maximum length 40 cm with fin lobes.

Boomerang Triggerfish

Half-moon Triggerfish (adult)

Half-moon Triggerfish (juvenile)

Bridled Triggerfish (adult)

Bridled Triggerfish (juvenile)

Striped Triggerfish

Blue Triggerfish (adult)

Blue Triggerfish (juvenile)

389

Giant Triggerfish *Balistoides viridescens*

Mostly dusky grey with pale caudal peduncle, pale yellow fins and distinct face pattern with black streak along top of mouth, yellowish green area over snout below eye to pectoral-fin base. Dark triangular band with numerous orange or yellow dots from top of head, over eye to pectoral-fin base. Coastal reef slopes adjacent to deep water, usually seen solitary. Can be very aggressive when guarding nesting sites, but may attack divers for no obvious reason. Also known as Titan Triggerfish. Largest triggerfish, maximum length 75 cm.

Clown Triggerfish *Balistoides conspicillum*

Best-known triggerfish, easily recognised by large round white spots over ventral half in adults and most of body in small juveniles. Eye well hidden in black band over head. Usually seen solitary, swimming openly along outer reef walls, taking cover in caves or ledges if cornered. Small juveniles secretive in caves with rich invertebrate growth and usually deep. Maximum length 35 cm.

Yellow-spotted Triggerfish *Pseudobalistes fuscus*

Adults pale blue with numerous yellow spots all over, fins darker blue. Small juveniles yellow with alternating black and white saddles over back. Black over interorbital, below each dorsal fin and over caudal peduncle, and small blue spots form at an early age. Similar to young Yellow-margin Triggerfish (next species), but blue instead of black spots and saddle markings more distinct. Blue pattern develops into network of blue lines with yellow interspaces which in turn break up into regular pattern of small yellow spots when about half adult size. Adults usually over sandflats near reefs, feeding from sand, usually blowing sand away to expose prey. Juveniles secretive on low reef on sand. Maximum length 55 cm.

Giant Triggerfish

Clown Triggerfish (adult)

Clown Triggerfish (juvenile)

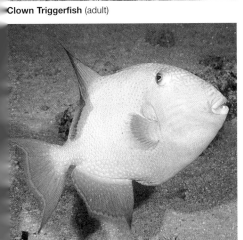

Yellow-spotted Triggerfish (adult)

Yellow-spotted Triggerfish (juvenile)

391

Yellow-margin Triggerfish *Pseudobalistes flavimarginatus*

Large adults best identified by plain pinkish or grey colouration on head in front of eyes, and short horizontal dusky streaks below eye. Median fins with bright yellow to orange margins. Body with irregular but some distinct small spotting in semi-adults and juveniles. Small juveniles white above, yellow below with distinct black spots and several dark saddle-like blotches over back. Juveniles often in small groups on coastal reef slopes. Adults usually solitary, but nest in spread-out groups over sandflats. Males dig nesting sites and compete for gravid females. She chooses partner and after spawning guards the nest as well. Maximum length 60 cm.

Starry Triggerfish *Abalistes stellatus*

Adults very pale, bluish grey to yellowish above and white below, usually with three long white spots over back. Pectoral fin pale yellow at base. Small juveniles black above with 4 white saddles evenly distributed over back. Sides and ventrally white with dark spots or scribbles. Coastal, often silty habitat on sand or mud slopes, staying loosely in touch with reefs and often swimming high above substrate. Usually makes no attempt to hide in reefs, but rather swims away when approached. Juveniles with small outcrops of rock or solid objects on open sand areas, in narrow crevices or digs out sand for a safe spot. Maximum length 25 cm.

LEATHERJACKETS & FILEFISHES — MONACANTHIDAE

Large family with 30 genera and estimated 100 species, of which 27 genera and almost 60 species are found in Australian waters. Small to medium-sized fishes ranging from about 25 mm to 1 m. Prominent, separate first dorsal-fin spine (distinct feature in most), often armed with a series of downward-directed barbs on its edges, usually followed by second much smaller embedded spine, and both usually folding into groove. Body covered with tiny prickly scales, forming a tough leathery or velvet-like skin. Head moderately large, eyes set high and just below dorsal-fin spine. Mouth small, terminal with large prominent teeth in jaws. Gill opening as vertical slit just anterior and above pectoral-fin base. Species about equally distributed between tropical and temperate zones. Southern species usually growing large and males brightly coloured. Often abundant in coastal areas and are some of the best-known reef fishes. Small tropical species are usually referred to as filefishes.

Mosaic Leatherjacket *Eubalichthys mosaicus*

Variable from yellow to orange or brown with dusky areas and some dark spotting, adults with white streak from gill opening to halfway along side. Juveniles almost circular with irregular pale blue lines, series of dashes, or mosaic pattern over body converging onto head and caudal peduncle. Adults become more elongate with age, and found mainly on coastal reefs along margins with boulders and sponges to deep offshore, often swimming openly over reefs. Small juveniles settling in sponges on reefs, and in bays commonly found against sponges on jetty pylons. Maximum length 60 cm.

Yellow-margin Triggerfish (adult)

Yellow-margin Triggerfish (juvenile)

Starry Triggerfish (adult)

Starry Triggerfish (juvenile)

Mosaic Leatherjacket (adult)

Mosaic Leatherjacket (juvenile)

393

Gunn's Leatherjacket *Eubalichthys gunnii*

Juveniles similar to Mosaic Leatherjacket (previous species) with mosaic pattern, but grey to brown with light interspacing. Adults more elongate, greenish or yellowish brown, and often with dusky head. Deep offshore reefs, juveniles in estuaries to near adult size and commonly found under jetties. Maximum length 60 cm.

Black Reef Leatherjacket *Eubalichthys bucephalus*

Adults dark brown to almost totally black, eye with contrasting pale white and yellow. Small juveniles brown or green with spots compressed into longitudinal bands. Clear coastal to offshore reefs, usually in depths where kelp growth ends, on rocky reefs in ledges or among boulders. Shy species, usually staying close to cover, often in pairs. Maximum length 40 cm.

Yellow-stripe Leatherjacket *Meuschenia flavolineata*

General colour variable from pale brown to ash-grey and caudal fin mostly black. Males with bright orange patch surrounding peduncular spine patch. Females with yellow blotch basally on caudal fin and usually a thick yellow stripe on caudal peduncle, extending and tapering towards eye reaching just past second dorsal fin. Small juveniles greenish or brownish with irregular spotting. Adults on kelp reef, juveniles in weeds. Maximum length 30 cm.

Stars-and-Stripes Leatherjacket *Meuschenia venusta*

Juveniles and adults similar. Broadly banded pattern along sides. Juveniles brownish above and white below, with dark brown stripes, near black over front of head. Bands break up into numerous close-set spots in adults and head develops numerous longitudinal lines converging on long snout. Deep coastal and offshore reefs, usually in depths over 20 m. Maximum length 21 cm.

Horseshoe Leatherjacket *Meuschenia hippocrepis*

Adults multi-coloured with blue, green, black and yellow. Centrally on side with large yellow area, containing light blue elongate spot in middle, and with thin dark blue lines above and below yellow area, often joining anteriorly into horseshoe shape. Small juveniles show signs of mark as small bluish grey spot surrounded by thick yellow circle. Common on coastal reefs and deep rocky estuary reefs in kelp areas, often in large groups. Juveniles in bays, commonly under jetties. Maximum length 60 cm, usually 45 cm.

Gunn's Leatherjacket

Black Reef Leatherjacket

Yellow-stripe Leatherjacket

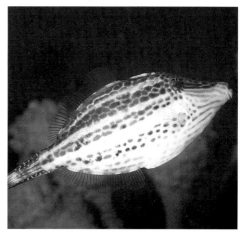

Stars-and-Stripes Leatherjacket

Horseshoe Leatherjacket

Six-spine Leatherjacket *Meuschenia freycineti*

Considerable geographical differences, especially between the east and south coasts. Southern females very pale with 4 dark brown stripes along body. Eastern females brown with dark and less distinct stripes. Southern males, as shown, with numerous blue lines and scribbles over head and over large area behind eye, dorsally and ventrally along body and around spiny peduncular patch. Eastern males more yellow over head and usually a large yellow blotch on sides, and also different caudal fin pattern. Coastal to deep offshore, and rocky estuarine reefs in large bays in ledges and sponge areas. Maximum length 50 cm.

Southern Leatherjacket *Meuschenia australis*

Large males become brightly coloured with yellow, blue eyes, and blue in dorsal and caudal fins. Females pale yellowish with dusky bands similar to female Six-spine Leatherjacket (previous species), but middle stripe has peculiar bend over pectoral-fin base in this species. Coastal bays on algae and sponge reefs in ledges and caves, often in shallow caves obscured by kelp above, to depths of at least 30 m. Mainly Tasmanian – Bass Strait species, occasionally entering Port Phillip Bay. Also called Brown-striped Leatherjacket. Maximum length 32 cm.

Yellow-finned Leatherjacket *Meuschenia trachylepis*

Adults with pale yellow fins, except caudal fin thick yellow to orange with white posterior margin, blue lines and scribbles along back and base of anal fin. Patch of fine but distinct scribbles on side diagnostic for this species. Juveniles pale brown to bright green with a series of dusky blotches along body, secretive in weeds. Adults on rocky reef with sparse algae growth. Maximum length 40 cm.

Blue-lined Leatherjacket *Meuschenia galii*

Greenish brown or yellow to orange with longitudinal white to light blue lines and spots, blue strong in large individuals. Male has orange caudal fin with blue margin, and blue dashes form corners inwards. Shallow weed reefs in protected bays to deeper offshore in algae and sponge zones, occasionally along kelp reefs. Maximum length 40 cm.

Six-spine Leatherjacket (male)

Six-spine Leatherjacket (female)

Southern Leatherjacket (male)

Southern Leatherjacket (female)

Yellow-finned Leatherjacket

Blue-lined Leatherjacket

Large-scale Leatherjacket *Cantheschenia grandisquamis*

Distinct species. Patch of blue spots on chin, dusky spot surrounding anus, bright yellow to orange caudal fin with electric blue outer rays, and thin electric blue lines along dorsal and anal-fin bases. Protected coastal waters and seaward parts of large rocky estuaries on algae reef or with kelp patches. Maximum length 36 cm.

Spiny-tail Leatherjacket *Acanthaluteres brownii*

Males differ from females, with brighter colours. Blue is brighter and yellow over posterior body, shaded dusky over caudal peduncle but bright yellow around spiny peduncular patch. Schools over seagrass beds in large open bays or estuaries, females greatly outnumbering males. Maximum length 46 cm.

Toothbrush Leatherjacket *Acanthaluteres vittiger*

Large males with complicated patterns. Usually a long white streak from eye to patch of bristles, posteriorly on body. Head black with thin blue lines and scribbles over snout. Females green to brown with pale blotched pattern, thin dark lines over and along head. Small juveniles usually bright green with broad silver-white streak midlaterally from behind eye tapering over caudal peduncle. Adults on mixed algae and invertebrate-rich reefs. Juveniles primarily in seagrass beds, forming schools at intermediate sizes and moving to deeper reefs. Maximum length 32 cm.

Bridled Leatherjacket *Acanthaluteres spilomelanurus*

Males distinct with white or blue line bordered with black, from below chin curving upwards to lower eye margin, and many small blue spots along lower sides and posterior part of body. Females greenish brown, whitish below, with pale irregular spots over back and dark spots midlaterally. Shallow coastal bays and large open estuaries over seagrass beds, usually in schools, comprising mixed sexes. Maximum length 14 cm.

Barred Filefish *Cantherhines dumerilii*

Adults with dusky bars posteriorly in middle of sides and yellow median fins, males more orange on peduncular spines and caudal fin. Juveniles with scattered white spots over head and body. Usually in pairs on shallow clear reef-flats with rich coral and hydroid growth, feeding on various invertebrates including coral polyps. Maximum length 35 cm.

rge-scale Leatherjacket

Spiny-tail Leatherjacket

othbrush Leatherjacket (male)

Toothbrush Leatherjacket (female)

dled Leatherjacket (male)

Barred Filefish

Strapweed Filefish *Pseudomonacanthus macrurus*

Highly variable, usually pale, greenish grey with broad green to yellow bands at angle from chin to eye, and horizontally along body. Often a white streak immediately below central band in males. Additional small black spots in both light and dark areas; in heavily spotted individuals, bands less distinct or absent. Adults in pairs near or among seagrasses with broad leaves, or in thick algae reef. Maximum length 18 cm.

Peron's Leatherjacket *Pseudomonacanthus peroni*

Almost identical to Strapweed Filefish (previous species), but has spotting rather than crossbands in caudal fin and more soft rays in dorsal and anal fins (dorsal 32–33 versus 29–31). Greenish in seagrass beds and brownish on algae reef, usually well camouflaged. Sheltered coastal bays and inner reefs among weeds. Maximum length 40 cm.

Fan-belly Leatherjacket *Monacanthus chinensis*

Pale greenish grey to dark brown with darker blotched pattern, arranged in broad angular bands. Dorsal profile of snout distinctly concave above. Large, greatly expandable ventral flap. Coastal bays and estuaries in kelp and algae reef, often silty habitats. Rare south of New South Wales, and one record of Western Port, Victoria. Maximum length 40 cm.

Unicorn Filefish *Aluterus monoceros*

Large adults pale bluish grey. Juveniles with pale scribbles and small dark spots. Pelagic, adults forming large schools and often swim below large sargassum rafts. Juveniles with floating matter and ride large swimming jellies which sometimes bring them close to shore. Large adults occasionally seen on deep sandflats when nesting. Maximum length 75 cm.

Scribbled Leatherjacket *Aluterus scriptus*

Yellow to brownish with numerous short blue scribbles and spots, forming lines with age, especially over head, and additional black spots over head and body, usually slightly larger over caudal peduncle. Caudal fin very long in adults. Juveniles with floating weeds and may be pelagic for a long time, sometimes reaching a large size before settling on reefs. In sandy habitat floats vertically close to substrate with head down, mimicking a floating leaf and settles with weed or rocks for shelter. Adults on coastal reefs, usually in 20+ m depth. Longest leatherjacket when long tail included, maximum length 1 m.

Strapweed Filefish

Peron's Leatherjacket

an-belly Leatherjacket

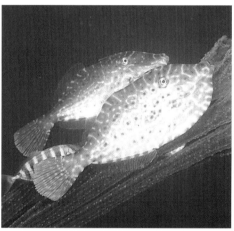

Unicorn Filefish

cribbled Leatherjacket (adult)

Scribbled Leatherjacket (juvenile)

Blue-finned Leatherjacket *Thamnaconus degeni*

Juveniles and females similar and often swim with Toothbrush Leatherjackets, but readily separated by the bluish caudal fin. Males ornamented with bright blue spots on head and lines along upper and lower body. Juveniles shallow over seagrass beds; adults in deep parts of estuaries and offshore, forming schools of mixed sexes. Maximum length 29 cm.

Long-nose Filefish *Oxymonacanthus longirostris*

Easily recognised by colour and shape. Green with a longitudinal series of orange spots and long tapering snout with small terminal mouth. Ornamental ventral flap, black and bright orange area with white spots, used for display. Coastal to outer reefs with large patches of *Acropora* corals. Juveniles form small groups; adults usually in pairs, feeding on coral polyps. Maximum length 10 cm.

Mimic Filefish *Paraluteres prionurus*

Whitish with a series of black saddles and fine spotting. Males with yellow and blue on caudal fin and a series of yellow spines on caudal peduncle. Changes colour during display: face pattern and general colour intensifies. Mimics Saddled Puffer *Canthigaster valentini*, a small, poisonous species common in the tropical region. Best recognised by the long dorsal and anal fins, compared to the short-based fins of pufferfish. Sheltered coastal to outer reefs in mixed algae and soft coral habitats, and often in small groups. Maximum length 10 cm.

Diamond Filefish *Rudarius excelsius*

Bright green to nearly black with pale dorsal outline and numerous pale skin flaps protruding from sides, distinct with almost diamond-shaped outline. Coastal slope and flats with weeds and algae. Rarely noticed because of small size. One of the smallest filefish species, with maximum length just 25 mm.

Pygmy Leatherjacket *Brachaluteres jacksonianus*

Usually greenish with some blotched and indistinct banded patterns and spotting. Juveniles often with small ocelli all over, but some geographical and habitat variations. Southern populations often orange-yellow when adult, with pearly spots and lines. Unusual member of family. Can inflate abdomen like pufferfish for protection, or expand it forwards to an almost circular shape when displaying in territorial disputes with other males (as shown in the photograph). Often found at night anchoring itself by biting onto weed, a common habit with many other members of the family. Small temperate species, maximum length 9 cm.

Blue-finned Leatherjacket

Long-nose Filefish

Diamond Filefish

Mimic Filefish (male, displaying)

Mimic Filefish (female)

Pygmy Leatherjacket (male, displaying)

Pygmy Leatherjacket (juvenile, sleeping)

TEMPERATE BOXFISHES — ARACANIDAE

Small family of primarily temperate Indo-Pacific fishes with 6 genera and 11 species, most of which are found in Australian waters. Only one other species in South African waters and deep-water species off New South Wales also found in Japanese waters. Closely related to tropical boxfishes (next family), each having hard-shelled carapace protecting body, with holes for fins and slits for gills. In Aracanidae the gills are not rigid, and all median fins, including tail, protrude together from carapace, whilst in the tropical Ostraciidae the gills are rigid, and the dorsal and anal fins protrude through separate holes. Carapace in Aracanidae comprises rows of triangular plates, forming large hexagonal and square patterns over sides. Sexually dimorphic fishes, with males often ornamented with bright blue and yellow, and females often more spinous with horn-like protrusions above eyes or as a series along bony ridges. Differences still confuse some scientists, who fail to recognise some forms as a single species, especially those trawled. Most live deep, but in southern waters several enter very shallow depths and are commonly observed. Benthic feeders, often seen blowing the sand away to expose prey.

Shaw's Cowfish *Aracana aurita*

Males easily distinguished from Ornate Cowfish (next species) by spots instead of lines along lower ventral ridge or keel. Females have almost horizontal lines over snout, compared to more angular in other species. Postlarvae black, juveniles light brown with irregular longitudinal-lined pattern. Females with distinct white and brown areas. Males become marked with blue spots and lines, most obvious in caudal fin, being contrasting yellow, with large blue submarginal loop and lines over rays connecting from base. Coastal reefs and deeper parts of large estuaries, along the south coast from 10 to 160 m, but in New South Wales usually restricted to deep water. Maximum length 20 cm.

Ornate Cowfish *Aracana ornata*

Males with alternating black and white lines ventrally and black-edged blue lines over snout and caudal peduncle. Body further covered with numerous blue-centred, squarish-shaped black spots, and bright orange caudal fin with blue loops. Females with close-set dark lines, angular over snout and often forming circles or semi-circles on top of body. Shallow coastal bays, mainly in seagrass areas. Often in a few metres' depth, in some areas very common with sexes mixed in about equal numbers. Maximum length 15 cm.

Humpback Boxfish *Anoplocapros lenticularis*

Best recognised by unusual shape. Female with tubed lips and long straight dorsal profile from head to highest part of body, and yellow to orange with whitish bands and black scribbles. Males more rounded over high back, orange-brown with 2 broad white bands angling away from the top. Clear coastal rocky reefs with algae or low vegetated reefs. Juveniles below overhanging ledges with sponges. Adults, especially large males, swimming about more openly in similar habitat and often found deep in large caves. Maximum length 20 cm.

Eastern Smooth Boxfish *Anoplocapros inermis*

Distinct but smoothly rounded ridge over back. Females pale yellowish brown with dark blotch in each triangle over upper half of head and sides. Males pale yellow and blue, and general shape more elongate. Small juveniles smooth, showing no elevated ridges, yellow to brown with dusky spots. Coastal to offshore reefs, adults in moderately deep waters, juveniles and sub-adults often in rocky estuaries. Similar Western Smooth Boxfish (next species) geographically isolated, but has more pointed back and males with black scribbles over back. Maximum length 35 cm.

Shaw's Cowfish (male)

Shaw's Cowfish (female)

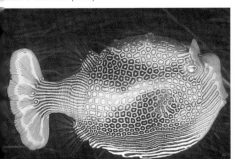

Ornate Cowfish (male)

Ornate Cowfish (female)

Humpback Boxfish (male)

Humpback Boxfish (female)

Eastern Smooth Boxfish (male)

Eastern Smooth Boxfish (female)

405

Western Smooth Boxfish *Anoplocapros amygdaloides*

Very similar to eastern sibling (previous species), but juveniles and females pale whitish brown with fewer dark brown blotches and dorsal profile over head almost straight compared to more rounded. Coastal reefs to offshore, juveniles and sub-adults in estuaries, often silty conditions, commonly under piers. Large adults mainly deep offshore. Maximum length 30 cm.

TROPICAL BOXFISHES — OSTRACIIDAE

Tropical family with 6 genera and 20 species, about half of each known in Australian waters. Comprises some unusual species commonly referred to as boxfishes, trunkfishes or cowfishes. Like their temperate cousins (previous family), the body is encased in a bony carapace, but to a greater extent and with a separate hole for each moving part, including the various fins, gills, eyes and mouth. Various genera are distinguished by the presence or absence of lateral, dorsal or ventral ridges. Some have long spiny horn-like protrusions in front of eyes, giving rise to the name cowfishes, and others are square-shaped for which called boxfishes. Apart from the differences already mentioned between the temperate and tropical families, the mouth is set low, lips more tubed, and spines are usually on extremities of ridges, pointing either forwards or backwards. No strong sexual dimorphism compared to the temperate species, except for some smaller species which show colour differences between sexes.

Longhorn Cowfish *Lactoria cornuta*

Bright yellow to greenish grey. Juveniles at an early age developing long horns in front of eyes, projecting forwards, and at end of ventral ridges, pointing backwards. Large adults have very long caudal fins, reaching almost body length. Shallow lagoons near seagrass beds, feeding on benthic invertebrates, exposing prey by blowing sand away. Maximum length 50 cm, including caudal fin.

Round-belly Cowfish *Lactoria diaphana*

Adults similar to Longhorn Cowfish (previous species), but all spines short and additional spine centrally on back, and caudal fin not exceptionally long. Juveniles with inflated-like rounded belly. Yellowish to brown with dusky spots and blotching. Juveniles pelagic, often settling well beyond breeding range and may get quite large before settling on substrate. Smallest juvenile found on substrate in New South Wales about 15 mm long. Shallow rocky reefs onto sand with rich algae growth to deep offshore. Well camouflaged and swimming low on substrate. Maximum length 30 cm.

Thorny-back Cowfish *Lactoria fornasini*

Best identified by colour. Adults yellow to brown with bright blue spots and scribbles all over, forming lines over back in large individuals. Juveniles with dark blotches and small blue spots. Still coastal bays and estuaries on sand and mud or rubble reefs with some short algal growth, and often with sponges. Shallow to about 30 m depth. Maximum length 20 cm.

Western Smooth Boxfish

Longhorn Cowfish (adult)

Longhorn Cowfish (juvenile)

Round-belly Cowfish

Thorny-back Cowfish

407

Turretfish *Tetrosomus concatenatus*

Cross-section of carapace triangular, with a series of small spines on top of dorsal ridge. Variable from bone white to greenish grey, hexagonal plates often outlined with brown or black and some large individuals, possibly the males, with blue spot in centre of each plate, and other spots over head and tail. Rocky estuaries and harbours to deep offshore, in seagrass habitat and sponge reefs. Maximum length 30 cm.

Humpback Turretfish *Tetrosomus gibbosus*

Variable from yellow to dark brown, sometimes with pale blue spots. Very similar to Turretfish (previous species), but easily distinguished by dorsal ridge highly raised centrally into large flat thorny spine. Coastal sand and rubble flats, often near seagrass beds or deep offshore on soft bottom habitat. Maximum length 25 cm.

Yellow Boxfish *Ostracion cubicus*

Small juveniles easily identified by cube shape and bright yellow colouration and numerous small black spots, elongating and darkening with age. Some spots may change into black-edged white ocelli. Large adults dusky yellow, often with irregular yellow lines on head below eye and on body behind pectoral fin, and fins greyish blue with numerous small black spots. Coastal species, most common and widespread boxfish. In New South Wales, juveniles settle during the summer months on rocky reefs in narrow ledges with urchins, sometimes in small aggregations. Adults along deep coastal slopes, deep lagoons and protected inner reefs on mixed reef rubble and sand habitat to depths of about 40 m, feeding on benthic growth and invertebrates. Maximum length 45 cm.

Black Boxfish *Ostracion meleagris*

Juvenile to female stages jet black to dark brown with numerous small white spots on body and head, and in adults also over caudal-fin rays. Males derive from females and change colour, except dorsally above eye level. Sides changing to brown and blue with dark-edged yellow to orange spots, and broad stripe over interorbital. Blue brightening with age. Most common seaward reef boxfish. Juveniles solitary in clear coastal rocky reefs, secretive among boulders with urchins. Adults usually in pairs on reef crest with shelter from large corals or rocks, and usually males are noticed because of brighter colours and swimming about more openly over rubble patches. Maximum length 20 cm, usually 15 cm.

Solor Boxfish *Ostracion solorensis*

Small juveniles yellowish white with thick black longitudinal stripes on sides, with spots ventrally and fine reticulations dorsally. Pattern on sides changes to coarse reticulations in females. Males become mostly dark blue with light blue-centred black spots. Thin light blue lines with black edging in front and behind eyes, centrally on cheek, and vertically from posterior edge of eye to front of pectoral-fin base. Juveniles along upper part of drop-offs in ledges; adults usually in pairs in rich coral-growth areas on slopes and crests of sheltered seaward reefs. Maximum length 12 cm.

Turretfish

Humpback Turretfish

Yellow Boxfish (adult)

Yellow Boxfish (juvenile)

Black Boxfish (male)

Black Boxfish (female)

Solor Boxfish (male)

Solor Boxfish (juvenile)

409

PUFFERFISHES — TETRAODONTIDAE

Large family with about 20 genera and at least 100 species, of which 16 genera and about 50 species are found in Australian waters. Two subfamilies: Tetraodontinae, short-snouted species; and Canthigasterinae, long-snouted species. Common name derives from capability to inflate themselves to almost balloon-like proportions to deter predators. In addition, many species have small spines or prickles on skin which are erected during inflation. All species are poisonous, with toxins in skin and often concentrated in internal organs. Powerful toxin may not have much effect on many fish predators, but can be fatal to humans or other land-based creatures if consumed; even old dried skins can kill a cat if left on the beach or jetty. Some species brightly coloured as if to advertise their unpleasant properties and often mimicked by harmless species. All have small beak-like mouth with fused teeth, only divided in front. Fins entirely soft-rayed, small paddle-like similar-sized dorsal, anal and pectoral fins. Usually large short-nosed species are semi-reef-dwellers, often on sand along reef edges, usually coastal or estuarine but some enter fresh water. Long-snouted species are primarily reef-dwellers, often in caves and ledges. Diet includes a great variety of algae and invertebrates; some are scavengers and only a few small species specialise in particular invertebrates. Also called toadfish, or toados, and blow fishes.

Starry Toadfish *Arothron stellatus*

Variable, and several different growth stages. Very small juveniles with numerous thin alternating yellow and black vertical lines, and with growth lines breaking up into a series of spots, first dorsally and last over belly. Spotted areas brown to grey and large adults become light grey and almost white below, with numerous small dark spots over most of body and fins; just the ventral part is plain. Large juveniles sometimes bright yellow or orange with black stripes ventrally over abdomen. Juveniles coastal in muddy habitat with debris on shallow slopes. Adults mainly along deep coastal slopes. Maximum length 1.2 m, usually less than 1 m.

Stars-and-Stripes Toadfish *Arothron hispidus*

Adults variable dark brown to light grey, with numerous white spots all over and white ring around eye. Juveniles with longitudinal white stripes ventrally and large white-edged black spot over pectoral-fin base. Coastal bays, lagoons and deep sand stretches with sparse growth between inner reefs. Maximum length 50 cm.

Reticulated Toadfish *Arothron reticularis*

Adults best identified by numerous small white spots, particularly close-set on caudal fin and white lines ventrally under head to mouth and surrounding eyes and pectoral-fin bases. Small juveniles dark brown with dusky interorbital and many thin dusky longitudinal lines, best distinguished from similar juvenile Narrow-lined Pufferfish (next species) by many small white spots on caudal fin showing at a very early age. Coastal bays on sand and mud along reef edges; juveniles enter fresh water. Maximum length 45 cm.

Narrow-lined Pufferfish *Arothron manilensis*

Adults almost white to light brown with thin black to yellow longitudinal lines over body, curving around front of large black spot encircling pectoral-fin base. Caudal fin and snout often yellow. Small juveniles brown with a few thick lines, shown with juvenile *Siganus virgatus* (page 379). Sheltered coastal bays and lagoons along reef edges or seagrass beds on sand or mud, often in pairs lying in small depressions on substrate. Juveniles enter fresh water. Maximum length 30 cm.

Starry Toadfish (small juvenile)   **Starry Toadfish** (adult)

Starry Toadfish (intermediate size)   **Stars-and-Stripes Toadfish**

Reticulated Toadfish   **Narrow-lined Pufferfish**

Yellow-eye Pufferfish *Arothron immaculatus*

Closely related to Narrow-lined Pufferfish (previous species) and sometimes in mixed pairs. Similar in colour but no lines, usually brownish and yellow eye. Coastal sand and mudflats adjacent to slopes, sleeping in low depressions in substrate or against solid object most of the day. Sometimes in small aggregations. Maximum length 30 cm.

Scribbled Pufferfish *Arothron mappa*

Highly variable pattern, changing with growth from coarse reticulating black lines to circular and lined patterns, some radiating from eyes as juveniles to very fine scribbles all over, occasionally forming thin longitudinal lines. Large individuals with light brown sides and tiny light blue spots all over. Along deep slopes and drop-offs, juveniles in ledges with rich invertebrate growth. Maximum length 60 cm.

Guinea-fowl Pufferfish *Arothron meleagris*

Adults usually completely black, including fins, with tiny white spots all over. Occasionally a bright yellow form, with or without some black spots; if present, larger black spots often show the white spots as in the normal black form. The latter form nearly always identified as the Black-spotted Pufferfish (next species). Tiny juveniles with proportionally larger and fewer spots from white to yellow. Juveniles coastal in muddy habitat; adults in deeper offshore habitat but occasionally in shallow protected inner reefs, sometimes in pairs of black and yellow forms. Maximum length 45 cm.

Black-spotted Pufferfish *Arothron nigropunctatus*

Juveniles brown to blue-grey with sparse, randomly placed black spots over body. Mouth black and pale band over snout followed by dark eyes and often dark interorbital. Adults sometimes retain juvenile pattern, but usually showing great variations with combinations of grey, yellow-orange and white, with few or many dark spots. Sometimes completely yellow with a few marks, but usually mouth remains dark and separates it from the larger xanthic White-spotted Pufferfish (previous species). Coastal to outer reef slopes and crests in rich invertebrate growth, occasionally in pairs. Maximum length 30 cm.

Yellow-eye Pufferfish

Scribbled Pufferfish

Guinea-fowl Pufferfish (adult)

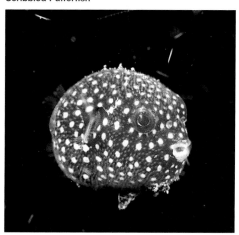

Guinea-fowl Pufferfish (tiny juvenile)

Black-spotted Pufferfish (male)

Black-spotted Pufferfish (female)

413

Ferocious Pufferfish *Feroxodon multistriatus*

Juveniles with numerous thick stripes over sides and dorsally, almost vertical on head, strongly bending up and back below dorsal fin, with spots below and on caudal peduncle, pattern breaking up with growth into striations and finer spots. Unprovoked attacks recorded in Queensland, in one of which a girl lost 3 toes, almost certainly by this species. Coastal bays on sandy substrates. Reported maximum length 40 cm; however, it grows to at least double this length. Specimen in the photograph is 90 cm long, and several of these 'giants' were seen off Lizard Island, Queensland.

Ringed Toadfish *Omegophora armilla*

Best identified by black circle or near-circle around pectoral-fin base. Almost white below and dusky over back with large blotched pattern over sides, a broad dusky band from eye to chin. Large individuals with some blue spotting. Similar Blue-spotted Toadfish *O. cyanopunctatus* lacks black ring and is heavily blue-spotted as adult; restricted to south-west Australia. Deep coastal and offshore reefs, entering shallows of large open estuaries. Maximum length 25 cm.

Barred Toadfish *Contusus richei*

Juveniles irregularly barred across back, changing to more spotted pattern when adult. Head rather bulky, and dark pattern with larger and fewer spots or bands compared to similar Prickly Toadfish *C. brevicaudus*, which has close-set blotches over back and shorter caudal peduncle. Both common in large coastal estuaries, forming schools over seagrass beds, also under jetties and entering deep water. Maximum length 22 cm.

Smooth Toadfish *Tetractenos glaber*

Distinguished from similar species by yellowish to reddish caudal and dorsal fin. Upper half of body with close-set grey to black spots, sometimes fusing into bands over interorbital and centrally across back. Very common coastal bay species, usually forming large schools along reefs over sand. Buries in sand to sleep. Maximum length 15 cm.

Common Toadfish *Tetractenos hamiltoni*

Very similar to Smooth Toadfish (previous species) but fins clear, body lighter coloured and spotting over back usually finer. Primarily schools in shallow estuaries in sandy and muddy habitat and protected coastal bays. Often buries itself in sand with just eyes exposed. Maximum length 14 cm.

Halstead's Toadfish *Reicheltia halsteadi*

Sides and ventrally shiny white, and dorsally with light brown scribblings rather than round spots as in other similar species. Eyes large and colourful, pupil shiny green and iris yellow to orange. Solitary species along beaches and reefs, just beyond turbulent zones. Maximum length 16 cm.

erocious Pufferfish

Ringed Toadfish

arred Toadfish

Smooth Toadfish

ommon Toadfish

Halstead's Toadfish

415

Orange-barred Pufferfish *Polyspina piosae*

Creamish above and white below with dusky stripe with orange blotches or bars from chin and below eye to caudal-fin base. Skin with numerous tiny spines, sometimes coloured yellow in places, showing up as spotted patterns. Singly or in small groups on sand near reefs, protected shallow coastal bays to about 40 m depth. Maximum length 10 cm.

Weeping Toado *Torquigener pleurogramma*

White below and grey to brownish above with numerous, variously sized small white spots. Several similar species in genus, this one the most common; best recognised by several thin dusky vertical lines along sides of head, and dusky stripe from above gill opening to centre of caudal-fin base. Sometimes forms great schools in coastal bays. Maximum length 20 cm.

Milk-spotted Puffer *Chelonodon patoca*

White below and grey above with large round white close-set spots. Dusky areas on snout, above pectoral fin, below dorsal fin and on posterior two-thirds of caudal fin. Often yellow ventral area under head and pectoral fin. Coastal and estuarine, over shallow sand or mudflats, often in schools, and entering fresh water. Maximum length reported 38 cm, usually 25 cm.

Silver Pufferfish *Lagocephalus sceleratus*

Long elongated body typical of the genus. Several similar pelagic species; but Silver Pufferfish the most common. Juveniles often in coastal bays over sand. Adults sometimes school near islands of the west coast and are feared by divers and swimmers. May attack unprovoked. Powerful jaws can bite through hooks and with ease through bone. Might appear edible, but, like all pufferfishes, it is poisonous and should not be eaten. Maximum length 80 cm.

Clown Toby *Canthigaster callisterna*

Distinct sharp-nosed species with double midlateral black stripe interspaced with white. Dorsally greenish grey with fine dark blue speckles and lines. Juveniles similar to adults, males with brighter blue lines on head. Clear coastal to deep offshore reefs, often in pairs, swimming openly over reefs, sometimes well above substrate. Juveniles in caves or along walls. Maximum length 25 cm.

Bennett's Puffer *Canthigaster bennetti*

Upper half dusky, greenish grey and lower half pale. Both parts with light blue spots, usually mixed with pale orange or pink. Distinct blue-edged black spot at dorsal-fin base and adults with thin iridescent blue lines radiating from eyes. Shallow protected bays on algae reef or in sargassum weed zones near mangroves. Adults normally in pairs. Maximum length 9 cm.

Orange-barred Pufferfish

Weeping Toado

Milk-spotted Puffer

Silver Pufferfish

Clown Toby

Bennett's Puffer

Netted Toby *Canthigaster solandri*

Adults with bluish green spots and lines, becoming white below and black spots below dorsal-fin base. Juveniles with numerous and close-set white spots over lower half of body. Eastern population with netted pattern over lower sides and caudal fin with fine-lined pattern instead of spotted elsewhere, similar to *C. compressa* from Indonesia and New Guinea. Several other similar dark species with numerous small round spots and lines radiating from eyes. Netted Toby juveniles rare in central New South Wales, but known south to at least Bass Point (small specimen in the photograph). Sheltered clear coastal bays and inner reefs. Maximum length 9 cm.

False-eye Puffer *Canthigaster papua*

Orange-brown with fine black-edged iridescent blue spots and thin lines, some forming a circle around dorsal-fin base. Juveniles with proportionally larger and fewer spots and only lines over head. Most lines break up into spots with growth and often elongate dorsally over body and below snout. Some geographical variations which need taxonomic investigation. Juveniles secretive on clear coastal reefs, adults on outer reefs, usually in pairs along drop-offs in caves with rich invertebrate and short-algae growth. Maximum length 10 cm.

Ambon Puffer *Canthigaster amboinensis*

Spots white when small and light blue when adult. Best distinguished by lined pattern on head around eye at all stages. Adults with large patch of dark blue spots on cheek, close-set in a vertical series and joining ventrally into thin lines. Shallow rocky surge zones, adults very flighty, juveniles secretive among rocks. Maximum length 12 cm.

White-spotted Puffer *Canthigaster janthinoptera*

Best distinguished from similar species by larger white spots, and eye-lines greenish in adults. Usually occurs in deeper water. Clear protected reef habitat along steep slopes and drop-offs, and usually secretive in the shelter of reefs. Juveniles off Sydney in sponges, usually in 20+ m depth. Maximum length 8 cm.

Netted Toby (adult, Queensland)

Netted Toby (juvenile, New South Wales)

False-eye Puffer (adult)

False-eye Puffer (juvenile)

Ambon Puffer

White-spotted Puffer

Circle-barred Puffer *Canthigaster ocellicauda*

Easily distinguished from similar Saddled Puffer (next species) by circular dark spot with yellow margin around dorsal-fin base. Common on outer reef drop-offs in dark areas of large caves, often feeding upside down on ceilings but usually only observed when using a torch. Also found deep, with plate corals on flat substrates between reefs, where it forms small aggregations. Maximum length 75 mm.

Saddled Puffer *Canthigaster valentini*

Easily identified by 4 distinct black saddles evenly distributed over back between eyes and caudal peduncle. Middle 2 tapering to stripe on belly, first curving over front of pectoral-fin base. Adults become heavily spotted and develop numerous thin lines over snout and chin. Males with iridescent green lines radiating from behind eyes. Mostly observed species on shallow to moderately deep reefs, swimming openly about and is easily approached. Commonly in pairs and males territorial, often contesting borders, fighting with mouth. Obviously marked, as if advertising its poisonous skin properties. Mimicked by other fishes; best example is Mimic Filefish *Paraluteres prionurus*. Maximum length 10 cm.

Crowned Puffer *Canthigaster coronata*

Very similar to Saddled Puffer (previous species), but saddles with orange spots or margins and light area orange-spotted in adults. Male with additional blue spotting on snout. Also common, but less observed due to preference for deep water. Adult usually in pairs on deep coastal sand or mud slopes with invertebrate-rich rubble ridges. Juveniles in ledges or boulder areas, usually in 10+ m depth. Maximum length 14 cm.

PORCUPINEFISHES — DIODONTIDAE

Small family with 6 or 7 genera and about 20 species, of which all genera and about 16 species are found in Australian waters. Closely related to pufferfishes, but teeth totally fused into beak-like jaws and have large spines over most of body and head which point outwards when the body is inflated. Spines, modified scales, are rigid, movable or both, depending on genus. Other features include prominent eyes, large soft-rayed paddle-like rounded fins, and small slit-like gill opening just anterior to pectoral-fin base. Juveniles pelagic (one species fully pelagic), and benthic as adults, occurring shallow to deep offshore. Mostly active at night, sheltering in caves during the day, feeding on a variety of invertebrates, often hard-shelled species. Reputed to be poisonous; however, some are eaten by Pacific Islanders with no ill effects. Also known as burrfishes and globe fishes.

Globe Fish *Diodon nichthemerus*

Spines on sides nearly always yellow, especially in black areas when juvenile, or when in clear deep coastal waters. Large adults in silty habitat mostly grey with little colour. Very common south coast species, often in schools under jetties or hiding in tyres or holes in pylons during the day. Schools hover together above the substrate and spread out at night to feed on benthic invertebrates. Maximum length 28 cm.

Circle-barred Puffer

Saddled Puffer (female)

Saddled Puffer (males, fighting)

Crowned Puffer

Globe Fish

421

Fine-spotted Porcupinefish *Diodon holocanthus*

Pale creamy or light grey colour with fine dark brown to black spots over body and head, sometimes with irregular blotched pattern. Usually several large plain dusky to light brown blotches dorsally, above eye, centrally and dorsal-fin base. Sheltered bays and deep estuaries, usually silty habitat with outcrops of debris in open areas. Maximum length 30 cm.

Blotched Porcupinefish *Diodon liturosus*

Similar to Fine-spotted Porcupinefish (previous species), but lacks fine spotting, large blotches usually black with white margins, and an additional blotch below eye and near gill slit. Juveniles often in shallow lagoons. Adults deep in coastal reefs, sheltering in ledges or under coral overhangs during the day. Maximum length 45 cm.

Three-bar Porcupinefish *Dicotylichthys punctulatus*

Spines shorter than in other similar species. Greenish grey above, lighter below, with 3 dark bars on sides. First below eye and others in front and behind pectoral-fin base at similar distances. Small black spots over body and head, except snout. Most spines pale, some surrounded at bases with black spots. Common east coast species, sometimes in schools. Sheltered coastal waters, entering shallow estuaries. Maximum length 43 cm.

Rounded Porcupinefish *Cyclichthys orbicularis*

Short-bodied, variable pale greenish grey to pink-brown with indistinct blotched pattern. Most spines short and partly erected without body being inflated. Clear deep coastal slopes in algae and sponge-rich reefs. Often in large sponges during the day, commonly seen on night dives near reefs. Smallest species, maximum length 20 cm.

Fine-spotted Porcupinefish

Blotched Porcupinefish

Three-bar Porcupinefish

Rounded Porcupinefish

GLOSSARY

Abdomen. Belly, contains digestive and reproductive organs.
Acute. Sharp or pointed.
Adipose. Fatty.
Allopatric. Living in separate geographical areas.
Anal. Behind the anus.
Anterior. Towards front or head.
Antrorse. Turned forwards.
Axil. Angular region on the body at the base of the pectoral fin.

Barbel. Fleshy tentacle-like extension, usually near the mouth.
Benthic. Living close to or on the bottom.
Bucklers. Bony plates along fin bases or belly.

Canine. Long conical tooth.
Carapace. Hard outer shell covering the body.
Carnivore. Consumer of animal matter.
Caudal. Of or pertaining to the tail.
Cirri. Tiny barbels or spines.
Claspers. Male organs to transmit sperm (sharks and rays).
Compressed. Flattened laterally, from sides.
Ctenoid. Term used for scales with spiny edges or surface.
Cycloid. Term used for scales with generally smooth edges or surface.

Depressed. Flattened dorsally, from above.
Dimorphic. Colour and body shape different between sexes.
Diurnal. Active during the day.
Dorsal. Pertaining to the back.

Emarginate. Margin slightly hollowed (fins).
Epibiotic. Organisms attaching to surface of skin.
Esca. Bait-like portion of a luring apparatus (anglerfishes).

Gill opening. Exhaust for water flow through gills.
Gills. Lung function or respiration chambers.
Gravid. Pregnant female carrying unborn young.

Herbivore. Consumer of vegetable matter.

Illicium. Rod-like portion of a luring apparatus (anglerfishes).
Interorbital. Area between eyes on top of head.

Intertidal. Zone that covers the area between high and low tide marks.

Keel. Reinforced ridge on body, often on caudal peduncle or head.

Lanceolate. Spear-shaped or broadly pointed, often refers to caudal fin.
Larva. Immature stage, usually differing greatly from adult.
Lateral. Pertaining to the sides.
Lateral line. Sensory canal system, ranging from simple tubes to complicated pressure cells in a series along the sides, often penetrating through scales in tubes or cut-outs (notched).
Lunate. Shaped like a crescent moon (usually referring to shape of caudal fin).

Median. On the midline of the body.
Median fins. Fins along median extremes, usually dorsal, caudal and anal fins.
Meristics. Countable features.
Mimicry. The act of an organism purposely resembling another.
Monospecific. Containing a single species in a family.
Monotypic. Containing a single species in a genus.

Nape. Upper part of the head over and behind the eyes.
Nasal. Relating to the nose or nostril.
Nocturnal. Active at night.

Ocellus. Marking that simulates an eye.
Omnivore. Consumer of both animal and vegetable matter.
Opercle. Upper bony edge of the gill cover.
Operculum. Gill cover, containing opercle and preopercle bones.
Origin. The starting point or beginning of longitudinal part at head end.
Oviparous. Producing eggs that develop and hatch outside the body of the female.
Ovoviviparous. Producing eggs that hatch inside the female or at birth.

Paired fins. Pectoral and ventral fins, usually opposite and mirroring each other.
Pectoral fins. Uppermost of the paired fins, usually on the sides, immediately behind the gill openings.
Peduncle. Body part from the end of the anal fin to the caudal-fin base.

Pelagic. Oceanic, belonging to the open sea.
Phytoplankton. The plant component of plankton.
Planktivore. Consumer of plankton.
Plankton. Organisms drifting freely in the water column.
Posterior. Towards the rear or tail.
Postlarva. Larva after absorption of yolk.
Prehensile. Adapted for holding by wrapping around object (fish use the body or tail).
Preopercle. Front part of the operculum, an angled bone below and behind the eye.
Protrusible. Usually applied to jaws; greatly expandable.

Retrorse. Pointed or curved backwards.
Rostrum. Bony projecting snout.
Rudimentary. Reduced part without obvious function.

Scute. Bony scale with keel-like ridge or spine.
Segmented ray. Fin ray showing cross-striations; soft ray.
Spiracle. Opening behind the eye, leading to gill and mouth cavity, that occurs in most sharks and rays.
Subterminal. Situated near but not at the end of something.
Sympatric. Living in the same area.
Synonym. Another name given to the same species.

Terminal. Situated at the end of something.
Thoracic. Pertaining to the chest area of lower body region near the head.
Thorax. Chest area.
Tricuspid. Having three cusps or points (teeth).
Truncate. Used to describe a mainly straight vertical posterior edge of the caudal fin.

Ventral. Of or pertaining to the underside.
Ventral fins. The lower-most paired fins along the underside.
Viviparous. Giving birth to live, usually free-swimming, young.

Zooplankton. Small animals (usually microscopic) drifting freely in the water column.

INDEX — COMMON NAMES

429

INDEX — SCIENTIFIC NAMES